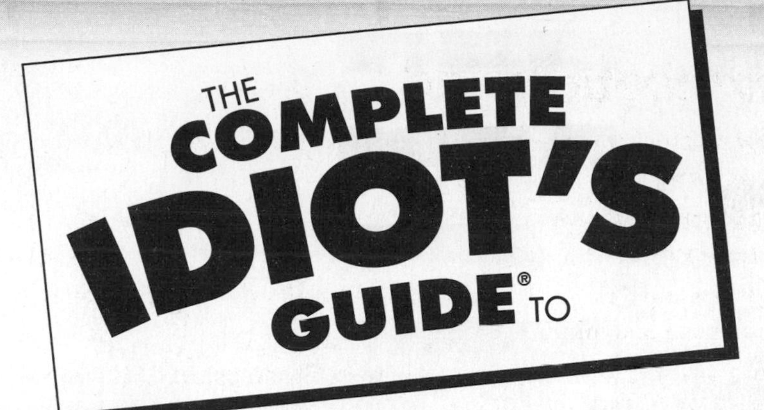

Hawaii

by Corey Sandler and Michael Roney

A member of Penguin Group (USA) Inc.

To Maureen, who is always there for me. M.R.

To Janice, my constant traveler. C.S.

ALPHA BOOKS

Published by the Penguin Group

Penguin Group (USA) Inc., 375 Hudson Street, New York, New York 10014, USA

Penguin Group (Canada), 90 Eglinton Avenue East, Suite 700, Toronto, Ontario M4P 2Y3, Canada (a division of Pearson Penguin Canada Inc.)

Penguin Books Ltd., 80 Strand, London WC2R 0RL, England

Penguin Ireland, 25 St. Stephen's Green, Dublin 2, Ireland (a division of Penguin Books Ltd.)

Penguin Group (Australia), 250 Camberwell Road, Camberwell, Victoria 3124, Australia (a division of Pearson Australia Group Pty. Ltd.)

Penguin Books India Pvt. Ltd., 11 Community Centre, Panchsheel Park, New Delhi—110 017, India

Penguin Group (NZ), 67 Apollo Drive, Rosedale, North Shore, Auckland 1311, New Zealand (a division of Pearson New Zealand Ltd.)

Penguin Books (South Africa) (Pty.) Ltd, 24 Sturdee Avenue, Rosebank, Johannesburg 2196, South Africa

Penguin Books Ltd., Registered Offices: 80 Strand, London WC2R 0RL, England

International Standard Book Number: 978-1-59257-595-4
Library of Congress Catalog Card Number: 2007926845

12 11 10 09 8 7 6 5 4 3 2

Interpretation of the printing code: The rightmost number of the first series of numbers is the year of the book's printing; the rightmost number of the second series of numbers is the number of the book's printing. For example, a printing code of 07-1 shows that the first printing occurred in 2007.

Printed in the United States of America

Publisher: *Marie Butler-Knight*
Editorial Director: *Mike Sanders*
Managing Editor: *Billy Fields*
Executive Editor: *Randy Ladenheim-Gil*
Development Editor: *Ginny Bess Munroe*
Senior Production Editor: *Janette Lynn*
Copy Editor: *Jennifer Connolly*
Book & Cover Designer: *Kurt Owens*
Indexer: *Angie Bess*
Layout: *Becky Harmon*
Proofreader: *John Etchison*

Contents at a Glance

Appendixes

Contents

Part 6: Moloka'i and Lana'i 303

Appendixes

Introduction

If you're looking for a book that will make it incredibly easy for you to plan and enjoy the best possible Hawaiian vacation, then look no further!

This is the no-fuss Hawaii guide, right down to the scores of ready-made Ultimate Itineraries we provide throughout. We've distilled and filtered all the great stuff we know about from our travels around the Hawaiian islands, queried our many Hawaiian friends for even more "insider's secrets," put everything into these pages, and made sure that all of this essential information and advice is super-easy for you to follow.

Sure, this is called a *Complete Idiot's Guide*, but that doesn't mean we've "dumbed down" anything, or that you're anything less than a discriminating traveler. What it means is that you're a smart person who knows what you don't know. It means you're smart enough to look for the easiest way to learn all you need to know about Hawaii. So that's what we're giving you here.

Packed with ready-made itineraries, useful maps, selective suggestions for the very best places to visit, and insider's tips on finding memorable experiences while avoiding many of the typical tourist traps, this book is designed to be friendly, fun, and eminently useful.

Hawaii is probably one of the most popular tropical destinations in the world, and it is *the* most popular among Americans. During our own sojourns to the Islands of Aloha, we've run into countless visitors who have said it's their fourteenth trip, or even twentieth trip. Pretty wild stuff!

There's certainly a lot to love about Hawaii—it's exotic and yet familiar. In fact, it's the furthest and most exotic place an American tourist can travel these days without a passport, since beginning in early 2007 U.S. citizens need one to return from Canada and Mexico.

So what would you rather do? Secure a passport in order to watch someone shovel snow in Toronto (not that there's anything wrong with that), or travel unencumbered by such documentation to a Polynesian paradise where you can sit under a swaying palm, mai tai in hand?

For us, it's no contest.

What's in This Book

We've organized this book in a way that makes the most sense for planning and enjoying a trip to Hawaii. Part 1 provides historical and cultural information on the islands, as well as expert guidance for booking your trip. The rest of the parts focus on Honolulu and the specific islands, and are divided into "Relaxing" and "Enjoying" chapters.

- **The "Relaxing" Chapters:** These are packed with essential information on each destination, including geography, the primary attractions, getting around, and places to stay. These are designed to help you plan and book your trip, and are intended to be read mainly before you go.
- **The "Enjoying" Chapters:** These get into the nitty-gritty of visiting each destination, including ready-made "Ultimate Itineraries" for each island, depending on your style of travel, detailed information on all of the sites and activities, recommendations for great places to eat and drink, and more. These chapters will be valuable for your planning, but will also come in very handy while you're actually in Hawaii.

Ultimate Itineraries

The Complete Idiot's Guide to Hawaii has one particularly special feature that is unique to this series: **Ultimate Itineraries** in which we've already made the day's planning decisions for you. We're created these for an assortment of travel styles:

- Young Families
- Older Families
- Single Traveler
- Romantic Getaway
- Easy-Going; Nonstrenuous
- Culture in Paradise
- Adventure in the Great Outdoors

Each of these itineraries provides plans for one or two days of traveling, including what to see and where to eat. Sets of itineraries appear at the beginning of each "Enjoying" chapter and are cross-referenced to detailed information elsewhere.

We've also provided suggested itineraries for covering several islands at once. These follow the front matter of the book.

Bonus Features and Tips

Our guidebook is also seasoned with a number of bonus features and tips to provide interesting background on a topic, or to alert you to something special about a place. Repeating bonus features include:

Money Matters

Here we list all the bargains, best deals, and smart strategies you should use during your visit to Hawaii.

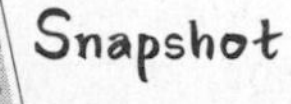

Snapshot

Look for these notes to quickly find all the information about a locale.

IN ADDITION TO THESE...

the book also includes numerous unique boxed features throughout. Like this one here.

Useful tips occur throughout the book, marked by icons. These include:

- Beautiful spots that the masses haven't yet discovered
- How to have a top-shelf experience at a bargain price
- How to do it better than the rest
- Lesser-known restaurants and locations that are quintessential Hawaii
- Unforgettable, scenic drives around the islands

What Things Cost

Throughout the book, you'll see dollar signs next to each accommodation and restaurant listing. The more dollar signs, the more stress you'll put on your credit card. Here's how those symbols translate to real money.

For Hotels:

$ = under $100

$$ = $101 to $150

$$$ = $151 to $200

$$$$ = $201 to $250

$$$$$ = over $250

For Restaurants:

Price ranges are for dinner, per person, including appetizer, entrée, one drink, dessert, and tax (reduce by about 40 percent for lunch):

$ = under $15

$$ = $16 to $25

$$$ = $26 to $35

$$$$ = $36 to $45

$$$$$ = over $45

Keep in mind that you can get the best deals during Hawaii's "low" season (summer) and through special timeshare and Internet promotions. To grab these special deals, and for leads on additional properties, including uncensored guest reviews, follow our Internet shopping tips in Chapter 5.

Bon Voyage

Is there anything else we can do for you? We'd also offer to pick you up at your house and drive you to the airport, but our wives need the minivans that day. Enjoy your trip!

Acknowledgments

When it comes to writing a book, no man (or to be politically correct, *no person*) is a (tropical) island, and we certainly had some much-appreciated assistance with this venture.

First and foremost, we'd like to thank our families, who have offered patience and support through the days it has taken us to create this tome. Of course we'd like to give a big shout out to Ed Claflin, our esteemed agent, as well as to Randy Ladenheim-Gil, Mike Sanders, Ginny Bess, and Gary Antonetti for being our able partners in publishing.

Thanks also to all who contributed their invaluable perspectives on enjoying Hawaii to the max, including Leslie Rapparlie and Heather Bowlan, as well as Beverly Asaro, Shelby "Kahuna" Asch, Jay "Kai" Berman, Pam Brasher, Sarah Clarehart, Foster Ducker, "Honolulu" Ted Padova, Maya Roney, and Paul Ziobro.

Finally, we want to acknowledge the good folks at the Hawaii Visitors & Convention Bureau, who supplied the professional color photos we've used in the book.

Trademarks

All terms mentioned in this book that are known to be or are suspected of being trademarks or service marks have been appropriately capitalized. Alpha Books and Penguin Group (USA) Inc. cannot attest to the accuracy of this information. Use of a term in this book should not be regarded as affecting the validity of any trademark or service mark.

Ultimate Hawaiian Island Itineraries

Here are five tried-and-tested itineraries for visiting multiple Hawaiian islands over the course of a week or so, designed according to the makeup of your traveling party and your traveling style. These combine the itineraries featured in the "Enjoying" chapters throughout the book, with specific suggestions for families, singles, those seeking a romantic vacation, folks looking for something easy-going and nonstrenuous, and you high-energy types looking for some outdoor adventure.

In this section, we've kept the descriptions of each stop brief; you'll find more thorough write-ups of each place mentioned in the island-focused chapters elsewhere in the book. It's usually worthwhile to make advance reservations for recommended restaurants and tours.

Itinerary #1: For Families, *O'ahu-Maui*

DAY 1

Have breakfast at **Zippy's,** followed by some shopping at the **Chinatown** markets, lunch at the **Liliu'okalani Gardens,** and afternoon at the **Honolulu Zoo.** Have dinner at **Auntie Pasto's.** (See the itineraries in Chapter 5.)

DAY 2

Head out early to **Pearl Harbor** and the USS *Arizona* memorial. Spend the afternoon at **Waikiki Beach,** followed by an early dinner at **Kyo-ya** right in Waikiki.

DAY 3

Explore the rest of O'ahu by heading for **Sea Life Park** in Southeastern O'ahu, then into **Kailua** for lunch, followed by an afternoon on beautiful **Kailua Beach,** one of the best in Hawaii. Enjoy dinner at **Buzz's Original Steak House** in Lanikai. (See the itineraries in Chapter 7.)

DAY 4

Take a morning flight to beautiful Maui. After checking into your hotel, head to the stunning **'Iao Valley** just outside of Wailuku, then down to the historic whaling village of Lahaina and the **Aloha Mixed Plate** restaurant for lunch. Follow that with a cruise on **Whale Watch Maui** from Lahaina's main dock. Cap off the day with sunset and dinner at the fun **Bubba Gump Shrimp Company** in Lahaina. (See the itineraries in Chapter 9.)

DAY 5

This is a chill day. Mosey around your place of lodging and spend the afternoon on the beach.

DAY 6

Spend the morning driving up Maui's huge mountain, 10,023-foot **Haleakala.** Have lunch at the scenic **Kula Lodge,** set at 3,000 feet on the mountain. Then head down to the funky North Shore town of **Pa'ia** for some shopping and lazy time at **Baldwin Beach.** Enjoy dinner at the **Hula Grill** in Lahaina.

DAY 7

After breakfast at your place, head for the Whaler's Village shopping center in Ka'anapali to visit the **Whale Center of the Pacific.** Grab a real Hawaiian lunch while enjoying the view at the **Aloha Mixed Plate** restaurant in downtown Lahaina. Then head north on Route 30 for a drive clockwise all the way around **West Maui.** Have dinner back at **Mala** in Lahaina.

Itinerary #2: For Singles, *Big Island-Maui-Kaua'i-O'ahu*

DAY 1 Fly into Kona on The Big Island. On your first full day there, head down the Kona coast to **Honaunau Bay** for snorkeling, then over to the **Bayview Coffee Farm,** followed by lunch at **Manago** in Captain Cook. After lunch drive up the scenic Kohala Coast and enjoy a light dinner and live music at the **Beach Tree Bar.** (See the itineraries in Chapter 11.)

DAY 2 Grab a quick breakfast at **Buns in the Sun** and head east to **Hawaii Volcanoes National Park.** Check in at the Visitors' Center and make your way down Chain of Craters Road. Enjoy dinner at the **Kilauea Lodge,** only a few minutes from the park. Stay in Volcano or Hilo that night.

DAY 3 Fly early from Hilo to Maui. Take a half-day snorkel cruise from Ma'alaea to the island of **Molokini.** Later, head back down to Ka'anapali and enjoy the song, dance, food, and open bar of the evening-long **Drums of the Pacific lu'au** at the Maui Hyatt. (See the itineraries in Chapter 9.)

DAY 4 Get up before dawn to view the sunrise from **Haleakala,** Maui's massive 10,023-foot mountain. Afterward, stop for breakfast at the **Kula Lodge,** then drive to the cool and funky town of **Pa'ia.** Pick up lunches at the **Moana Bakery & Café** and head straight to the North Shore's stunning **Ho'okipa Beach Park.** Afterward, enjoy dinner with the windsurfing crowd at the **Café des Amis.**

DAY 5 Take a morning flight to beautiful Kaua'i, "The Garden Isle." Head to the hip little town of **Kapa'a,** where you can browse the shops and galleries. Have lunch in town, then drive about 20 minutes further up the highway to beautiful and scenic **Kilauea Point,** then a few miles further up Route 56 to the Princeville Airport, where you can catch a helicopter for an exciting air tour of the fabulous **Na Pali Coast.** Cap off a near-perfect day at **The Living Room Lounge** in the Princeville Resort. (See the itineraries in Chapter 13.)

DAY 6 Get up early, have breakfast and drive west from Lihu'e on Route 50, 45 minutes to the town of Waimea. Turn up Route 550 and drive the 12 miles to spectacular **Waimea Canyon.** Spend a few hours there, then head for the atmospheric town of **Hanapepe,** where there's interesting shopping. Have dinner at **The Beach House** in Po'ipu. (See the itineraries in Chapter 13.)

DAY 7 Fly to Honolulu. Tour **Pearl Harbor** in the morning, then head downtown to the **Honolulu Academy of the Arts.** Later, enjoy live music, good food, and pink beer (that's right!) at the **Mai Tai Bar,** followed by some dancing at the clubs in the **Ala Moana** area. (See the itineraries in Chapter 7.)

Itinerary #3: A Romantic Getaway, *The Big Island-Kauai-O'ahu*

DAY 1

Fly into Kailua-Kona. Spend your first morning lounging around at **Kahalu'u Beach Park,** just a few minutes south of town. In the afternoon, admire the tropical beauty at **Hawaii Tropical Botanical Gardens.** Then head east out to The Big Island's easternmost point at **Puna,** where you can enjoy another scenic drive (with hardly any people) along Route 137 between Kapoho and Puna. Finish up your day with an intimate dinner for two at **Paolo's Bistro** in Pahoa Village. Spend the night around Hilo. (See the itineraries in Chapter 11.)

DAY 2

Drive up to **Hawaii Volcanoes National Park.** Check in at the Visitors' Center and make your way down Chain of Craters Road. Enjoy dinner at the **Kilauea Lodge,** only a few minutes from the park. Stay in Volcano or Hilo that night.

DAY 3

Enjoy brunch at **Café Pesto** in Hilo, then head back to the west side of the island via the Saddle Road. Enjoy the spectacular **Rainbow Falls** and **Boiling Pots** waterfalls. Later, head to **Huggo's** to enjoy friendly, but not obtrusive, service and a gorgeous view of Kailua Bay.

DAY 4

Take a morning flight to Kaua'i. Head up Route 56 and to the town of Wailua and the **Wailua River,** Kaua'i's only navigable waterway. Catch a flat-bottom boat to the atmospheric **Fern Grotto.** Drive north past Kapa'a to scenic **Kilauea Point,** followed by drinks and pupus at **The Living Room Lounge** in the Princeville Resort. Then head straight into lovely Hanalei and take a memorable 3-hour sunset catamaran cruise down the **Na Pali Coast.** Later, hang at the cool and casual **Hanalei Gourmet** restaurant in downtown Hanalei. (See the itineraries in Chapter 13.)

DAY 5

Visit the ultra-picturesque **Wai'oli Hui'ia Church and Mission** in Hanalei, followed by a bite to eat at **Tropical Taco** in downtown Hanalei. Later, spend a couple of hours at the stunning **Limahuli Gardens** in Kalaheo, then drive back to Kapa'a for some unusual world fusion cuisine and great music at **Blossoming Lotus** in Kapa'a.

DAY 6

Pick up a picnic lunch and spend the entire day relaxing on the beach. On the North Shore, we recommend **Lumahai Beach,** a white crescent immortalized in the movie *South Pacific.* Near Lihu'e check out **Kalapaki Beach** fronting the Marriott beach resort. Have dinner at **Duke's Canoe Club** right on the premises.

DAY 7

Fly to Honolulu. Tour **Pearl Harbor** in the morning, then spend the afternoon on world-famous **Waikiki Beach.** Later, enjoy a decadent French dinner at **La Mer.** (See the itineraries in Chapter 5.)

Itinerary #4: Easy-Going; Nonstrenuous, *O'ahu-Maui-Kaua'i*

DAY 1 Fly to Honolulu and ensconce yourself in a comfortable hotel. On your first full day after arriving, take the pink Waikiki Trolley line over to the **Ala Moana Beach Park.** There's plenty of room to stretch out and enjoy the sun and surf on this idyllic beach. Have lunch at the **Kiawe Grill.** Spend the afternoon at the world-class **Bishop Museum,** and enjoy a dinner of first-rate Tuscan food at **Assaggio's** in the Ala Moana Center. (See the itineraries in Chapter 5.)

DAY 2 After breakfast at **Keo's in Waikiki,** spend the morning at **'Iolani Palace** and the afternoon at **the Mission Houses Museum.** Go all out for dinner and enjoy the innovative (and delicious!) island fusion cuisine at **Alan Wong's.**

DAY 3 Get out of town today. Leave your hotel early on a round-island tour with **Polynesian Adventure Tours** in one of their 25-passenger mini-coaches. You'll visit **Diamond Head,** the **Polynesian Cultural Center** (including an "Adventure Canoe Tour," and all-you-can eat luncheon buffet, and a canoe pageant), as well as a visit to the **Mormon Temple** near La'ie, views of rainforests, mountains, waterfalls, and of course, crashing surf. Enjoy evening cocktails and a good meal **at La Mer** back in Honolulu. (See the itineraries in Chapters 5 and 7.)

DAY 4 Fly early to Maui. Enjoy a lunch at the award-winning **Gerard's Restaurant** in the same building as Lahaina's Victorian **Plantation Inn.** After lunch, take a whale-watching cruise on the Island Marine Institute's **Whale Watch Maui** from Lahaina's main dock. For your evening's dinner and entertainment, make your way to Lahaina's far south side and attend the **Feast at Lele Lu'au,** notable for its intimate atmosphere, fine food, and table service. (See the itineraries in Chapter 9.)

DAY 5 Leave your hotel or condo at 7 A.M. to ride a van run by **Temptation Tours** to the top of **Haleakala** for stupendous views of Maui. On your way down the mountain, your tour company will stop at a scenic upcountry restaurant for lunch. Spend the afternoon at the **Bailey House Museum** in Wailuku. Then enjoy evening cocktails and a good meal with live music at the **Hula Café** at Whaler's Village in Ka'anapali.

DAY 6 Fly to Lihu'e on the gorgeous "Garden Isle" of Kaua'i. Head up Route 56 and to the town of Wailua and the **Wailua River** for a flat-bottom boat to the atmospheric **Fern Grotto.** Then return to the Lihu'e area and proceed to **Kilohana Plantation** for a delightful lunch at **Gaylord's.** Spend the afternoon shopping in the galleries and take a carriage tour of the grounds. In late afternoon, refresh yourself with **High Tea** at Kilohana. Repair to **Duke's Canoe Club** at the Kaua'i Marriott Resort & Beach Club in Lihu'e for dinner. (See the itineraries in Chapter 13.)

DAY 7 Take a scenic **Hollywood Movie Tour,** including lunch, along Kauai's east and north coasts. After the tour, spend an hour browsing around Kapa'a's many shops and galleries, then enjoy some eclectic and delectable dinner cuisine amid the palms at **Café Coco.**

Itinerary #5: Adventure in the Great Outdoors, *Kaua'i-Maui-Moloka'i-The Big Island*

DAY 1

Fly into Lihu'e on the "Garden Isle" of Kaua'i. On your first full day, get up early and cruise up Route 56 for some awesome water sports at the **Anini Beach Windsurfing School.** For lunch, enjoy a fresh fish taco and homemade lemonade at **Tropical Taco** in downtown Hanalei, then get into some of the best snorkeling in Hawaii at **Tunnels Beach.** Enjoy dinner and live entertainment at **Hanalei Gourmet** in downtown Hanalei. (See the itineraries in Chapter 13.)

DAY 2

If you're on the north coast, grab some sturdy shoes, a pack, and something for lunch, then go directly to **Ke'e Beach** and walk the first two scenic miles of the Na Pali coast's famous **Kalalau Trail.** Relax back at Ke'e Beach in the afternoon, then reward yourself with a fun dinner at **Zelo's Beach House** back in Hanalei.

DAY 3

Fly to Maui in the morning. Head to the north side of West Maui and hike up the **Waihee Ridge Trail** for spectacular views. In the afternoon, drive back to Pa'ia and beautiful **Baldwin Beach,** where you can relax for the afternoon. Enjoy dinner and entertainment at the **Moana Bakery & Café** in Pa'ia. (See the itineraries in Chapter 9.)

DAY 4

Get up early, get to the Ma'alea dock by 6:30 A.M., and take a half-day snorkel cruise to the island of **Molokini.** Or, tackle one of the trails in the crater of massive **Haleakala** (10,023 feet). Later, enjoy dinner at **Mala** in Lahaina.

DAY 5

Take an early boat or plane to the nearby island of Moloka'i and head out for the **Halawa Falls Hike,** a 4.2-mile return trail through Halawa Valley to Moaula Falls. For lunch, head back to Kaunakakai and **Oviedo's Lunch Counter.** Then proceed to the north side of the island and **Wailoku Lookout,** for a great view of Moloka'i's impressive sea cliffs. Head back to Maui for dinner.

DAY 6

Fly out early to Kailua-Kona on The Big Island. Head straight over on Highway 19 for a trip into Waipi'o Valley with **Waipi'o Na'alapa Trail Rides.** Grab a late lunch at one of the several restaurants in Waimea's **Parker Square** on your way back to Kona. Later, treat yourself to one of the best dinners on the island at **Pahu i'a** in Kohala. (See the itineraries in Chapter 11.)

DAY 7

Drive up Route 190 to the Saddle Road (Route 200) between Mauna Loa and Mauna Kea, which with all of its climbs, dips, and turns could be classified as an adventure in and of itself. Get to **Hawaii Volcanoes National Park** by early afternoon. Start with the Kilauea Iki Crater hike (great for a picnic lunch), then check in at the Visitors' Center and make your way down Chain of Craters Road. Get an atmospheric and delicious dinner at the **Kilauea Lodge.**

Part 1: Pre-Trip Planning

Before you set off for paradise, you've got to know a little about it. This part fills you in on Hawaii's geography, history, culture, and food, and then gives you the information and resources you need to book your trip.

The Big Picture

In This Chapter

- Hawaii's geography and climate
- Hawaii's people
- When you should go to Hawaii
- A little history

Hawaii is one of the world's loveliest places. Its beauty is unquestionable, with rugged volcanic mountains, towering sea cliffs, spectacular waterfalls, alpine tundra, tropical rainforest, white- and black-sand beaches, turquoise waters, plentiful rainbows, and a year-round tropical climate.

But, as you learn in this chapter, there's more to Hawaii's mystique than just its good looks.

Hawaii's Splendid Isolation

The volcanic Hawaiian island chain is more than 2,500 miles from the nearest continental landmass, making it one of the most remote places in the world. This splendid isolation has allowed thousands of animal and plant species to thrive, 90 percent of which exist nowhere else.

Its location and remoteness also give it a climate—or perhaps more accurately a *collection of microclimates*—quite unlike anywhere else on Earth. There are places in Hawaii where it's possible to drive from a tropical rainforest at sea level to an alpine desert at nearly 14,000 feet; the trip from sun and surf to high mountain takes less than two hours.

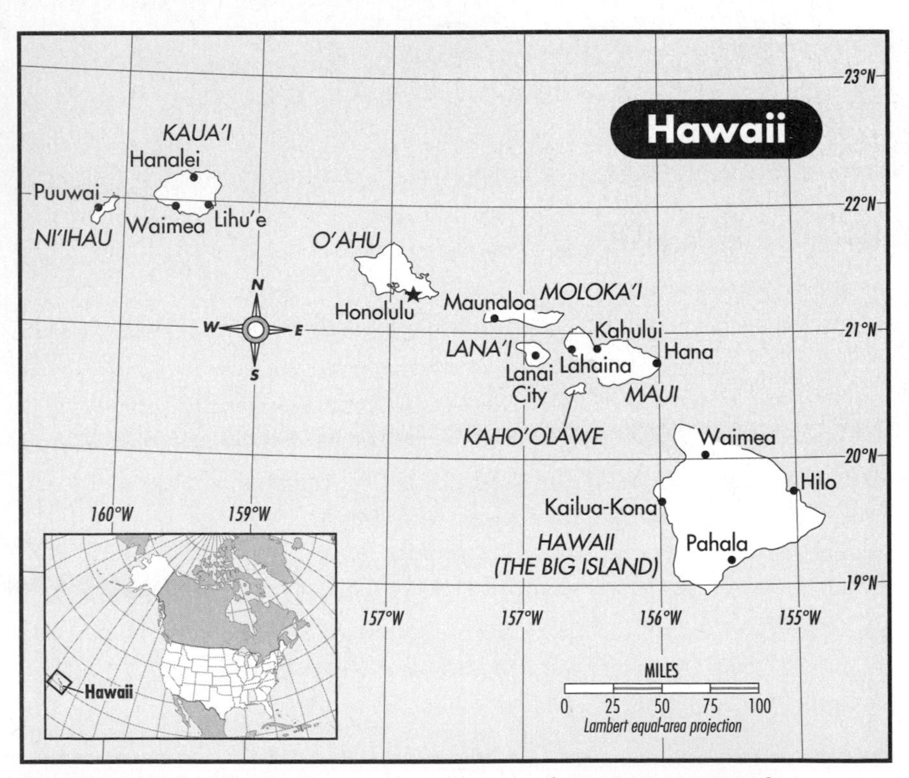

The Hawaiian Islands combine some marvelous attributes: unique geography, exceptional beauty, relative isolation … and easy flight connections from all over the world.

The Hawaiian Islands were originally settled by Polynesian peoples from the southwestern Pacific, followed by Europeans and Asian immigrants from all over the Pacific Rim, and then later by others from around the world. Those successive generations of settlers have created a cultural mélange that delights and charms. Yet today Hawaii is also unmistakably American, allowing visitors to enjoy the exotica along with all of the comforts of home.

The result of all this is a place that's rich in history, overflowing with beauty, packed with culture, and loaded with activity options; delightfully different, yet comfortably familiar. Amidst all of its various unusual cultures, economies, and landscapes, you can shop and eat at familiar establishments and easily make a phone call to back home—if you really must.

Hawaii's Unique Geography

What we know as the Hawaiian islands are actually the peaks of a volcanic mountain range in the middle of the Pacific, just below the Tropic of Cancer from about 19 degrees to 22 degrees north of the equator. Rising up to 30,000 feet above the sea floor, these peaks form eight major islands and 124 low atolls, forming a 1,500-mile crescent over an area of 6,459 square miles.

The eight major Hawaiian Islands from west to east are **Ni'ihau, Kaua'i, O'ahu, Moloka'i, Maui, Lana'i, Kaho'olawe,** and The Big Island of **Hawaii.** These volcanic peaks sit on the Pacific plate, which has over the eons spewed lava from deep beneath the Earth's crust. The plate has steadily and slowly moved from east to west, causing all of that lava bubbling up to build the string of islands. The oldest islands are Ni'ihau and Kaua'i in the western part of the chain, and The Big Island, in the east, is the youngest.

Today, The Big Island sits over the current location of the vent, giving it the only active volcanoes in the islands. Deep down on the ocean floor, that vent is now building a new Hawaiian island a bit east of The Big Island. It should break the surface in another 20,000 years or so, so you don't need to make your reservations for that one quite yet.

Hawaii: Which Island Is for You?

Island	*Climate*	*Beaches*	*Mountains*	*Nightlife*	*Peace and Quiet*
Kaua'i	-	+	+	-	+
O'ahu	-	+	+	-	+

continues

continued

Hawaii: Which Island Is for You?

Island	*Climate*	*Beaches*	*Mountains*	*Nightlife*	*Peace and Quiet*
Maui	+	+	+	+	+
Lanai	+	-	-	-	+
Molokai	-	-	+	-	+
Big Island	+	+	+	-	+

Hawaii's tropical climate and trade winds make it enjoyable any time of the year.

(Photo courtesy of HVCB/Kirk Lee Aeder)

Hawaii's Climate

Hawaii has a tropical climate, but one that is delightfully tempered by the trade winds that blow across the broad Pacific, northeast to southwest during most of the year.

As those trade winds blow in from the ocean, they tend to condense to form clouds, dropping moisture in the form of rain as they hit the mountains of the islands' windward coasts. Therefore, the northern and eastern coasts of the islands, as well as the higher elevations, tend to be rainier and much more lush than the leeward coasts. By contrast, the southern and western coasts are generally sunny and arid.

While Kau'i's Mount Wai'ale'ale gets more than 400 inches (at least 33 feet) of rain annually, **Puako** on the western side of The Big Island gathers a measly 9 inches each year. At Honolulu on O'ahu the average yearly rainfall is 23 inches, while at Hilo, on the eastern side of The Big Island, the annual total is 129 inches.

TYPICAL TEMPERATURES THROUGHOUT HAWAII

Hawaii is mild and tropical, but temperature does differ according to season and elevation. The average temperature in Hawaii is 72°F (22°C), although mountainous regions can be much cooler. (Figure a decrease of 10 degrees for every 3,000 feet in elevation.)

The average temperature in downtown Honolulu on O'ahu is 72°F (22°C) in January and 78°F (26°C) in August, with extremes from 57°F to 88°F on record. You'll find very similar temperature ranges along the coasts of all the Hawaiian islands, with Kaua'i reporting in at about five degrees cooler in the winter, and The Big Island's Kona Coast about five degrees warmer.

The average water temperatures off **Waikiki Beach,** near Honolulu, range from 75°F (24°C) in late February to 79°F (26°C) in late September. Mountainous regions are considerably cooler, and you'll even see winter snows atop Maui's Haleakala. A bone-chilling temperature of 1.4°F (–17°C) has been recorded on the summit of The Big Island's Mauna Kea, and winter snows frequently blanket the crests of Mauna Kea and Mauna Loa.

Even though it has a tropical climate, Hawaii does have seasons. Summers tend to average about 10°F warmer than winters. There are also significantly more clouds and rain in the winter months, especially on the windward sides of the islands.

What Time Is It in Hawaii?

Hawaii is on (surprise) Hawaii–Aleutian Standard time, which it maintains throughout the year. That means that from November through March the hour of day anywhere in the islands is about two hours earlier than on the U.S. West Coast, and five hours earlier than on the U.S. East Coast. Add an hour of difference (three to the West Coast; six to the East) when most of the United States goes on daylight saving time from April through October. Hawaii is east of the international date line, which means it's earlier in the same day as the mainland United States.

Hawaii's Flora and Fauna

Hawaii's indigenous plant species came to the islands thousands of years ago via seeds carried by birds, winds, or currents and tides. However, humankind has over the years introduced a tremendous variety of animal and plant life from many other parts of the world.

Hawaiian Animals

Because Hawaii is so isolated, many species on the islands have evolved on their own and are unique. In fact, as we've noted, scientists estimate that 90 percent of the indigenous Hawaiian species exist nowhere else. These include Hawaii's state bird, the nene (Hawaiian goose), which is similar to the Canadian goose, but with feet adapted to walking on lava; a very large variety of small forest birds; and the Hawaiian stilt. When it comes to native (non-human) Hawaiian mammals, there are but two: the Hawaiian monk seal and the hoary bat.

Polynesian settlers, followed later by Captain James Cook and other Europeans, introduced non-native plants such as melons and pumpkins, and alien animals such as chickens, mongooses, rats, frogs, toads, deer, sheep, pigs, goats, and even horses. Today chickens run wild over many of the Hawaiian islands—especially on Kaua'i, where there are no mongooses to eat the eggs.

Because the native Hawaiian species had evolved for thousands of years in relative isolation and without natural predators, many did not fare well against the intruders. Consequently, today a number of them are endangered. Only about a thousand Hawaiian monk seals remain, and of the more than 70 native bird species that lived in the islands at the time of European contact, 24 are now extinct.

Hawaii's state bird, the nene, is unique to the islands.

(Photo courtesy of HVCB/Ron Dahlquist)

Migratory animals play a big part in Hawaii wildlife. Every fall flocks of small golden plover make a nonstop 3,000-mile flight from Alaska to Hawaii, where they spend the winter, together with ducks from Alaska, Canada, and the northwestern United States. Meanwhile, thousands of Pacific humpback whales swim south from Alaska to Hawaii every winter to mate, birth, and nurse their young. Dolphins are also common in Hawaiian waters, as are the giant Pacific sea turtle and such prized game fish as ahi (yellowfin) tuna, marlin, ono, opakapaka, and mahimahi.

Hawaiian Plants

The incredibly wide range of microclimates in Hawaii—from humid tropical rainforest, to dry, hot desert, to alpine tundra—provides the islands with a wide variety of vegetation.

Of course, there is the ubiquitous coconut palm, in many ways a symbol of Hawaii. These tall, graceful trees grow along the coast and each generally produces about 75 coconuts per year. Another tree you can expect to see along the coastlines is the hala, also called the screw pine, which looks like a spindly cross between a palm and a yucca, growing to about 20 feet in height.

The most common native forest tree is the ohia lehua, recognizable by its large red flowers. There's also the hibiscus, which grows all over the island in more than 5,000 varieties. (One species even grows into a 60-foot-high tree in some upland forests.)

And then there's the koa tree, a species that exists naturally nowhere else in the world, which grows at higher elevations as much as an inch in diameter per year, reaching 100 feet in height, and attaining a trunk diameter of five feet or more. Koa historically provided the material of choice for carved oceangoing canoes, and today its wood is the most prized cabinet and furniture wood in Hawaii.

The Real Story of Hawaii: A Little History

Hawaii's history dates back almost 2,000 years. However, the Hawaiians were a people without writing who preserved their history in chants and legends, so exact dates tend to be a little fuzzy.

Modern Hawaiian history began on January 20, 1778, when English explorer Captain James Cook landed on the island of Kaua'i; but even Cook knew that the original Polynesian discoverers had come from the South Pacific hundreds of years before his time.

Before the Outsiders Came

Hawaii was settled by two distinct waves of Polynesian migration. Ancient statues and shrines tell us that as early as 600 or 700 C.E. people sailed thousands of miles to Hawaii from the Marquesas Islands (part of French Polynesia in the South Pacific), navigating in wooden boats using the sun, stars, the flight of birds, and other natural guideposts. Then, around 1000 to 1100 C.E., a second wave of Polynesian settlers arrived from Tahiti and subjugated the original Hawaiians, who became known as *Menehune*, which loosely translates in Tahitian to "outcast."

Around the twelfth century, a powerful Tahitian priest named Paao arrived and installed a strict naturalistic religion with multiple deities. It also included human sacrifice and a rigid system of social castes, called *kapu*. The caste system included (in descending order of power) the king, the chief minister and a high priest; the *ali'i* or chiefs; the *kahuna*, or priest craftsmen (specialists in professions such as canoe-building, medicine, the casting and lifting of spells); the *makaainana* (commoners) who did most of the hard work; and the *kauwa*, or outcasts, who were believed to be slaves of the lowest order.

Paao also imported a Tahitian king named Pili, and that started the Hawaiian royal lineage. This dynasty lasted another 700 years, although for most of that time there was no single king ruling all of Hawaii. Instead, there were a number of small kingdoms that reigned over individual islands and occasionally waged war on one another.

Hawaiians lived this way in relative isolation until the arrival of Captain Cook. After that fateful event, Hawaii would never be the same.

GETTING TO KNOW THE ANCIENT HAWAIIAN GODS

The ancient Hawaiians built numerous temples (*heiau*), which contained images symbolizing the gods, and you can see the ruins of these today on most of the islands.

The four major ancient Hawaiian gods represented universal forces, and were known as **Ku,** the ancestor god for all generations of humankind; **Lono,** the god in charge of the elements, as well as fertility and harvest; **Kane,** the god who created the first man from dust, and from whom all chiefs were said to have descended; and **Kanaloa,** the ruler of the dead who was often pitted against the other gods. There were also 40 lesser gods, the most famous of which was **Pele,** the goddess of volcanoes.

Captain Cook's Arrival ... and Departure

On January 19, 1778, Captain James Cook landed on the island of Kaua'i, and became the first European to "discover" Hawaii. Cook and his crew left Plymouth, England, on July 12, 1776, in HMS *Resolution* and HMS *Discovery*. The goal of their voyage was to determine whether or not there was a northwest passage above the North American continent.

He stopped to replenish and repair his ships, and named this group of islands "The Sandwich Isles" after a friend and supporter, John Montague, the Earl of Sandwich. He then took off again in search of the passage, sailing all around the North Pacific without success.

Cook returned again to Hawaii almost exactly a year later, on January 17, 1779, mooring in Kealakekua Bay on the Kona coast of The Big Island. There he was greeted as some sort of eighteenth-century rock star, the Hawaiians lavishing him with gifts and holding ceremonies in his honor. It so happens that Cook's arrival on both occasions coincided with the Hawaiians' annual Makahiki celebration, a period when all wars ceased and games were held to honor the god Lono. Due to the circumstance of his arrival, the Hawaiians apparently regarded Cook as Lono's representative.

Cook and his crew took full advantage, partying with the islanders for several days before departing again. However, just after leaving, a storm on the northwest coast of The Big Island damaged the *Resolution*, breaking its mast and forcing a return to Kealakekua. The islanders could not understand how a god could have allowed this to happen, and relations between the Hawaiians and the foreigners immediately grew tense. A misunderstanding soon followed, which led to a fierce battle on the beach during which Cook was killed by a mob of villagers. Present at Cook's slaying was a warrior known as King Kamehameha or Kamehameha the Great—the royal who ultimately established his rule of the entire Hawaiian island chain.

Whalers and Missionaries

After Captain Cook's "discovery," more ships from Europe and North America came calling in Hawaii, bringing domestic animals, trees, fruits, and plants never before seen in Hawaii, as well as diseases, alcohol, and firearms. With little immunity to new diseases, thousands of Hawaiians became ill and died, while their traditional way of life declined.

In the 1820s, Yankee whaling ships from places like Nantucket and New Bedford began visiting Hawaiian ports, and for the next 50 years, Hawaii became a major remote base and port of call for whalers. The grizzled and sea-weary New England whalers enjoyed the local women and grog to excess in places like Lahaina, on Maui, and Kailua Kona on The Big Island.

However, before long, all of the good times and general debauchery attracted the attention of Christian missionaries, who arrived on the islands in the 1820s. They befriended the Hawaiian royalty and went to work curtailing all of that sin. They built upright wooden churches throughout Hawaii that closely resembled the ones they had left at home. They focused on bringing the whalers into line, as well as on converting the local islanders.

At that point the somewhat decimated Hawaiian people had already dismantled their *heiaus*, rejecting their pagan religious beliefs, and between 1837 and 1840 approximately 20,000 Hawaiians entered the Christian fold.

Those same missionaries took it upon themselves to create a written version of the Hawaiian language, and established schools throughout the islands. They also introduced Western medicine and undertook the Kingdom of Hawaii's first modern census.

Hawaii's Royalty

Hawaii's monarchy is a fascinating story, filled with both strong and weak leaders, powerful warriors and reluctant royals, dictators, reformists, and visionaries.

- **Kamehameha I, a.k.a Kamehameha the Great** (1795–1819): Was present at Kealakekua when Captain Cook's ships anchored there. He unified the Hawaiian Islands in battle and formally established the Kingdom of Hawaii in 1810, and defended traditional Hawaiian values and the ancient *kapu* caste system.
- **Queen Kaahumanu** (1772–1832): Kamehameha the Great's favorite wife, who soon shared power with Kamehameha II and was a regent for Kamehameha III. She played a leading role in the overthrow of kapu.
- **Kamehameha II** (1819–1824): Became king at 22 years old, and in 1823 sailed with Queen Kamamalu and a few chiefs to England, and were entertained by the aristocracy. However, while there, he and the queen contracted measles and died.
- **Kamehameha III** (1825–1854): The last son of Kamehameha the Great was only 10 years old when he ascended the throne upon the death of his older brother. He reigned for 29 years, the longest of any Hawaiian monarch, during a challenging period when a large numbers of foreign residents brought new trade and land problems to the islands.
- **King Kamehameha IV** (1855–1863): Although he was powerless against the epidemics that were wiping out native Hawaiian islanders, he tried to curtail the influence of the missionaries. In 1862 his only child died, as did he the next year. His reign is often characterized as a "golden age," because he was fun-loving and a lenient ruler.
- **King Kamehameha V** (1863–1872): A stern and strong-willed man of 375 pounds, his reign fostered a new era of Hawaiian identity and restored some of the power of the local chiefs, although the influence of European planters and businessmen continued to increase.
- **Lunalilo** (1873–1874): William Lunalilo was confirmed as King of Hawaii by the Hawaiian legislature after an informal popular vote. He spent his reign trying to make the Hawaiian government more democratic, and endorsed the American cession of Pearl Harbor, which led to public outrage and was dropped.

- **Kalakaua** (1874–1891): Known as the "merry monarch," David La'amea Kamanakapu'u Mahinulani Nalaiaehuokalani Lumialani Kalakaua loved parties, balls, and entertaining global figures in the arts and politics. He revived the hula, which had been banned by missionaries in the 1820s as immoral. Toward the end of his reign, his cabinet was overthrown, a new constitution deprived him of almost all his power, and an ill-fated insurrection took place resulting in his replacement by Princess Lili'uokalani.
- **Lili'uokalani** (1891–1893): This Hawaiian queen was originally named Lydia Kamaka'eha before she chose her royal moniker. She tried to create a new constitution to restore the power of the monarchy, but powerful American businessmen, mostly sugar farmers, took it upon themselves to create a provisional government and a militia. Ultimately, the monarchy was completely overthrown and on January 31, 1893, the U.S. flag was raised over Honolulu. Hawaii was officially annexed on July 7, 1898, and became a territory in 1900. Lili'uokalani was an accomplished author and songwriter, and wrote the book *Hawaii's Story by Hawaii's Queen*, which is still available in bookstores.

Sugar and Politics

In 1840, Britain, France, and the United States recognized Hawaii as an independent kingdom under the rule of King Kamehameha III. However, Britain and France wanted to control the islands, and Kamehameha III placed Hawaii under U.S. protection in 1875. By 1887, the United States was granted permission to establish a naval base in Hawaii at Pearl Harbor, which opened in 1908.

Meanwhile, descendants of the missionaries had established Hawaii's sugar industry. Many islanders were dying of measles, the common cold, the flu, and other such common European ailments, so the plantation bosses began recruiting labor from overseas, starting with China, and eventually over the years from Japan, Portugal, Puerto Rico, Korea, and the Philippines.

As Hawaii's sugar industry grew, the United States became increasingly involved in its affairs, and soon the plantation owners announced a provisional government. That eventually led to the overthrow of the monarchy under Queen Lili'uokalani in 1893 and the establishment of Hawaii as a territory in 1900.

Under increasing U.S. influence, the population of Hawaii grew and its economy grew as well, as the islands increased sugar and pineapple production to satisfy the U.S. mainland. Hawaii's importance as a military outpost became critical when Japan attacked Pearl Harbor on December 7, 1941. This brought the United States as well as Hawaii into World War II.

Hawaii became the fiftieth state on August 21, 1959, and has since become increasingly Americanized, as well as globalized through the influences of its many immigrants from all over the Pacific and the world.

However, the islands and their people never lost the essence of their unique culture, which to this day is an integral part of the fabric of Hawaiian life. And that, along from all of the phenomenal weather and scenery, is part of what makes Hawaii such a special place.

Chapter 2 The Good Life

In This Chapter

- Food and drink
- Music and entertainment
- Sports
- Using Hawaiian lingo and expressions

Here's the good news: there's a whole lot more to Hawaiian culture than the late, great Don Ho, tiny bubbles, and hula dancing. Spiced with the influence of Asian and European immigrants, anchored by Polynesian tradition, and mellowed by American sensibility—Hawaii's unique customs are to many visitors an absolute delight for anyone who is lucky enough to experience them.

Food: Good Eats from Everywhere

The cultural kaleidoscope of Hawaii is perhaps expressed no better than through the distinctive cuisine that features flavors representing nearly every corner of the globe—from China and Korea, to Portugal, Puerto Rico, and around the Pacific Rim. If you like good food, you're definitely going to be one happy diner in Hawaii.

SPAM, SPAM, SPAM, SPAM

One of the staples of the Monty Python comedy troupe was a routine that featured a restaurant serving nothing but Spam, which in case you've managed to avoid it, is a highly processed chopped and reconstituted pork product in a can. And among gourmands, it generates automatic derision in almost every corner of the world.

But for reasons that have to do with the old history of the Hawaiian Islands as a place where a great deal of the local food once had to be imported by ship from far away, Hawaiians seem to love this stuff. In fact, more of it is sold in Hawaii than anywhere else on Earth, some six million cans a year.

Spam was introduced here during World War II, when fresh meat was scarce and "C Rations" were in plentiful supply, thanks to American GIs based in the islands. The taste seems to have stuck, and today you can still find dishes based on Spam in restaurants high and low. You'll find Spam on the breakfast menu at McDonald's in Hawaii. It's also available at gourmet restaurants, at roadside stands, and in convenience stores from Honolulu to the farthest reaches of the state. **O'ahu** even hosts an annual **Waikiki Spam Jam,** featuring live music, food, crafts, and a Mr. or Ms. Spam pageant.

Traditional Hawaiian Cuisine

Spam aside, of course, Hawaii has an abundance of indigenous and tasty flora and fauna. Hawaiians of many generations past cultivated yams and taro tops, hunted pigs, fished for crabs, and gathered coconuts. (As far as we can tell, they did *not* invent ham and pineapple pizza, which some call Hawaiian pizza, although you certainly can find that delicacy in the islands these days.)

Today, many of these ancient staples still show up on the Hawaiian dinner table. However, there are some differences. Most people can now afford pork, which was once a luxury consumed by royalty only.

THE TRADITIONAL HAWAIIAN KITCHEN, TRANSLATED

Haupia: A traditional Hawaiian coconut-flavored dessert that has the consistency of gelatin and is often described as a "stiff pudding."

Kalua Pig: A traditional favorite that is standard fare at lu'aus, a kalua pig consists of the whole animal slow-roasted for several hours in an underground oven called an *imu.*

Lu'au: A spinachlike, edible leaf that is wrapped around chicken, pork, or butterfish and then steamed.

Poi: A purple, Polynesian staple food made by mashing the root of the taro (or *kalo*, in Hawaiian) plant. Ancient Hawaiians believed that the taro plant represented the original ancestor of the Hawaiian people, called *Haloa.* Whenever poi was on the table, all arguments were required to cease in reverence for the great ancestor.

Poke: Raw fish salad mixed with seaweed and spices. Hawaiian celebrity chef Sam Choy is famous in the islands for an annual poke recipe contest that offers more than $15,000 in cash and prizes.

Pupu: This is really just another name for Hawaiian-style hors d'oeuvres. Any type of savory appetizer can be called a pupu, but the variety you usually find in these parts often involves Asian-style treatment with barbecue or Teriyaki chicken, shrimp, or vegetables.

Taro: A traditional Hawaiian plant grown in flooded fields, the leaves of which are usually wrapped around fish and meats, or eaten by themselves as a vegetable. The taro root is cooked and pounded into poi.

Pacific Rim Cuisine

"Pacific Rim," also called "Hawaiian Regional" on some menus, is a thoroughly modern cuisine genre in Hawaii (and now elsewhere around the world), made up of flavorful Asian and classic European influences combined with fresh local fish and produce. This style of cooking is usually found in the better (and more expensive) restaurants on the islands, though you can also find quite reasonably priced dishes that also fit in this category.

If you're ordering Pacific Rim, your plate is likely to be decorated with presentations such as macadamia nut crab cakes with papaya black bean salsa and ginger beurre blanc, or perhaps fire-roasted ahi with furikake mashed potatoes and black bean sauce. Get the mixed message?

Other Food in Hawaii

Because of its history as a melting pot of cultures, Hawaiian cuisine borrows the best of many world cuisines, from Japanese, Chinese, Korean, native Hawaiian, and even Portuguese, to a fusion of them all.

The Hawaiian "plate lunch" or "mixed plate" is one such fusion, and is a popular standard dish throughout the islands. The product of the lunches cooked and shared by Japanese, Filipino, Korean, and Hawaiian plantation laborers during the heyday of the plantation economy, it features marinated and grilled meats, two scoops of rice, and a macaroni salad. The mixed plate is available at mom and pop restaurants throughout Hawaii, and is something you should check out at least once during your visit.

Mmmm—That Coffee

Of course, no trip to Hawaii would be complete without savoring a mug of that famously aromatic beverage, Kona coffee.

Hawaii is the only place in the United States that grows coffee beans; in fact, roughly seven million pounds of coffee beans per year. The archipelago's volcanic soil, warm winds, and plentiful rainfall make it an ideal environment for coffee growing.

Kona, the most well-known Hawaiian coffee, has grown on the nutrient-rich volcanic lava rock slopes of The Big Island's West Coast since the early nineteenth century. Its flavor is often described as delicate yet complex. A fine coffee on its own, it also is used often in blends to mellow harsher, more acidic coffees. If you're buying Kona coffee in a grocery store, look carefully at the labeling to determine whether it's 100% Kona or a blend.

Don't stop with Kona, though. Other coffees are grown on every Hawaiian island. Like fine wine, each type is meticulously cultivated and each carries a distinctive flavor. Try them all and bring home a bag of your favorite to summon memories of your vacation when you brew a morning cup at home.

Hawaiian Java

Name	*Price*	*Characteristics*
Kona	High (over $15/pound)	Delicate, spicy, aromatic
Waialua	High	Full, complex, fruity

Name	Price	Characteristics
Kaua'i	Moderate ($10–$15/ pound)	Light, mildly acidic, subtle
Maui	Moderate	Smooth, medium-bodied
Moloka'i	Moderate	Rich-bodied, chocolaty, herbal

Hawaiian Music and Entertainment

Hawaii's history as a crossroads of culture has provided it with some delightfully unique (and justly famous) musical genres, as well as some traditions borrowed from elsewhere and seasoned with a distinctive Hawaiian twist.

Groovin' to Those Hawaiian Tunes

Like Hawaiian cuisine, Hawaiian music borrows from the many varied traditions of the state's mosaic of settlers. In turn, music from this relatively small state has had a profound influence on greater American music over the years.

You've probably heard Hawaii's signature slack-key guitar—a loose, laid-back style that can be heard on many Hollywood movie soundtracks. This genre originated from Mexican cowboys who came to Hawaii in the late nineteenth century. Mexican immigrants also brought their high-pitched falsetto singing style to the Hawaiian Islands.

The horizontally held steel guitar, a major element in American country music, was also a Hawaiian invention. The first steel guitars were created by taking traditional Spanish guitars, brought over by the Portuguese, and modifying the instruments' shapes.

The Portuguese also are credited with bringing over the precursor to Hawaii's most illustrious string instrument, the ukulele.

You'll also hear reggae everywhere throughout Hawaii, but it ain't the Jamaican variety. "Jawaiian" blends that distinctive beat, instrumentation, and vocal styling with indigenous Hawaiian elements, and is performed by such local artists as Bruddah Norm, Justin, Ka'ala Boys, Butch Helemano, and Kawika Regidor.

Dancing the Hula

Traditional Hawaiian folk music is deeply religious in nature. It tells stories and carries out rituals with chanting, called *mele*, and mimetic dance, called *hula*.

Hula came to the Hawaiian Islands with the area's first settlers, the Polynesians. The old style of hula is called *kahiko*. This was a solemn, spiritual performance in which female dancers wore wrapped cloth skirts and left their breasts bare, and male dancers wore loincloths. Both men and women wore many leis and pieces of handmade *tapa* accoutrements, made from the inner bark of the paper mulberry or breadfruit tree, which were considered too sacred to continue wearing after the dance. When the performance ended, they were left as offerings to the gods.

It should come as no surprise that Christian missionaries of the mid-1800s considered this rather sensual dance immoral and outlawed it, but it's obviously made a comeback. Today, though, hula dancers are more modestly dressed. The new style of hula, called *'auana*, is accompanied by song and Western instrumentation.

It's easy to catch a hula show anywhere in Hawaii, from Vegas-style presentations designed especially for tourists, to authentic, down-home presentations you can observe on street corners and in neighborhood clubs and restaurants.

"Pigging Out" at a Lu'au

The ultimate fusion of Hawaiian food, music, and dance takes place at the lu'au, a traditional feast for celebrating accomplishments, people, and events.

You will see plenty of modern hula dancing and cheesy performances at today's lu'aus, but the ancient feast was a very different affair. Women and men were not allowed to eat together, and women were denied certain foods such as bananas, coconuts, pork, and turtle.

These days, everyone can enjoy the savory lu'au pork and side dishes that cook for four hours wrapped in banana leaves in a pit lined with stones. You might even want to tell the cook it's *ono*, the Hawaiian word for "delicious." This dish is offered at most lu'aus, as well as at the restaurants listed as offering Hawaiian food in the "Enjoying" chapters.

THE BEST LU'AU EVER

King Kamehameha III (1825–1854) knew how to throw a party. In 1847, he invited his 10,000 closest acquaintances to a lu'au where they were served 271 hogs, 482 large calabashes of poi, 602 chickens, three whole oxen, two barrels of salt pork, two barrels of biscuits, 12 barrels of laulau, cabbages, 4 barrels of onions, 80 bunches of bananas, 55 pineapples, 2,245 coconuts, 4,000 heads of taro, and 180 squid.

Hawaiian Sports

Though it lacks any professional sports teams, Hawaii has no shortage of athletic events. The National Football League plays its annual all-star game, the Pro Bowl, in Honolulu's Aloha Stadium, a tradition dating back to 1980. The Professional Golf Association (PGA) holds several tournaments annually at Hawaii's world-renowned golf courses. And one of the world's most grueling events, the Ironman Triathlon, is held annually on The Big Island.

But any discussion of sports in Hawaii starts and ends with its most famous pastime: surfing.

Surfing

Surfing's origins are hazy, though many believe that it started some 4,000 years ago in the Polynesian islands. But it was Captain Cook's expeditions to Hawaii in the late 1770s that brought to the outside world the first documented sightings of the sport, which involves riding a breaking wave on a surfboard while standing upright.

Surfing roots extended deep into Hawaii's early culture. Under the ancient *kapu* caste system, the chieftains used the sport to show their courage and skill in Hawaii's fierce waves. It also kept the classes separate, as the ruling class and the commoners had their separate beaches and board-types.

But as the ancient traditions collapsed, so did surfing's significance as a means of keeping the sides separate. The rise of Christianity in the 1800s also spelled the demise of surfing.

The sport rebounded, however, in the twentieth century, as European and American tourists visited the island and spotted locals riding boards standing up. Authors like Mark Twain and Jack London made note of the activity during their visits to the islands, and in the first half of the twentieth century, Duke Paoa Kahanamoku, arguably Hawaii's most famous athlete and the father of modern surfing, showcased surfing around the world as part of his exhibition swimming matches. Surfer movies in the 1950s further led to the resurgence.

Today, Hawaii is home to some of the most well-known surfing spots, and surfers, on the planet. **The Banzai Pipeline,** on the North Shore of O'ahu, poses some of the most challenging surf out there. You also can find tons of surfers daily at **Waikiki Beach,** another notable spot, as well as on all of the other major islands.

THE BIG KAHUNA: THE FATHER OF MODERN SURFING

One of the biggest contributors to the resurgence that the sport of surfing enjoyed in the first half of the twentieth century was Duke Paoa Kahanamoku. "The Big Kahuna" helped bring the sport to such surfing hotspots as Australia and California. But that was largely due to the remarkable success he had as a swimmer.

Kahanamoku set his first world record in 1911, when he swam the 100-yard freestyle event in 55.4 seconds. He went on to become a five-time Olympic medalist, including three gold and two silver medals.

Following his Olympic success, Kahanamoku staged swimming exhibitions in places like Australia and the United States, and on the side, showed off some of his surfing skills. His accomplishments made him the first person inducted into both the Swimming Hall of Fame and the Surfing Hall of Fame.

Though he died in 1968, his contribution to the sport lives on with every surfer trolling the ocean for waves, from the East and West coasts of the United States to beyond. *Sports Illustrated* named him the number-one athlete in all of Hawaii's history.

Windsurfing

Hawaii's nearly constant trade winds, which blow from the northeast at 15 to 20 miles per hour throughout most of the year, makes this island chain one of the very best spots in the world for skipping and flying over the water with a surfboard and a sail. The real pros, of which there are many here, routinely do flips over the waves in places like Ho'okipa Beach Park on Maui. It takes some practice, but lessons are readily available on all of the islands.

Snorkeling

Surrounded by hundreds of square miles of coral reefs that host over 400 species of tropical fish, and often go right up to the shoreline, Hawaii is a snorkeler's paradise. All you need is a mask, a snorkeling tube, and some fins (you can rent equipment at any resort pool shop and at hundreds of stores) and you're in business. However, snorkel only on guided tours or close to shore in protected bays.

Outrigger Canoeing

Another popular sport practiced on the Hawaiian Islands is outrigger canoe racing. Outrigger canoes are canoes with a balance alongside called an outrigger. Each canoe has between six and nine crew members and races range from 500 meters to about 42 kilometers in length. During the longer races, crew members actually switch in the middle of the race by jumping out of the canoe and are replaced by paddlers who have been trailing in a motorboat. There are some 60 clubs and 10,000 active paddlers in Hawaii.

Sportfishing

We're not talking about sitting in a rickety rowboat and catching a couple guppies for the day. Hawaii is home to some of the premiere sportfishing waters in the world, where anglers come to hook 1,000-pound marlins, yellowfin tuna, and mahimahi. Many International Game Fish Association records have been set in waters off the coast of Hawaii, with the Kona Coast on The Big Island particularly noteworthy for its trove of sport fish due to deep waters and volcanoes that block the wind.

Golf

Hawaii's beautiful weather will want to keep you outside, and if it's not the beaches, rivers, or mountains, some take in the weather on the tropical golf courses. The PGA has found the **Po'ipu Bay Golf Course** in **Koloa,** on Kaua'i, to be so picturesque that it has chosen it for its annual Grand Slam of Golf tournament, which pits the winners of all four major championships against each other. The tour usually holds additional tournaments in Hawaii annually, and Hawaii is also home to the celebrated young female golfer Michelle Wie, who turned pro in 2005 at the age of just 15.

Football

American football has been a fixture in Hawaii since U.S. servicemen began introducing the game to the islands in the 1920s. Today, it is popular at the high school and college levels, with the top college team being the University of Hawaii Rainbow Warriors.

Hawaii also has been home to the National Football League (NFL) Pro Bowl since 1980. The Pro Bowl is usually played the week after the Super Bowl and features the top players from each league squaring off against each other. Since the game has no bearing on standings, players tend to play a less intense defensive game, which usually leads to high-scoring and entertaining affairs.

Triathlon

Hawaii's Ironman Triathlon is a race that starts off with a 2.4-mile swim, followed immediately by a 112-mile bike ride, and capped off with 26.2-mile run. If just reading that doesn't make you exhausted, it should! First held in 1978 by a group of 15, the race, held in **Kailua-Kona,** is the premiere event of its kind in the world and attracts some 1,500 competitors.

Using Hawaiian Lingo and Expressions

Though English is the main language, many locals intersperse elements of the traditional Hawaiian language in their daily conversation, and these days it's making a comeback in the islands as Hawaiians strive to nurture their traditional culture. Beyond *aloha* (hello and goodbye) and *mahalo* (thank you) here are some other words and phrases you may come across.

a'ole	no
ae	yes
a hui ho'u	until we meet again
aloha kakahiaka	Good morning
aloha 'auinala	Good afternoon
aloha ahiahi	Good evening
Aloha au ia oe	I love you.
hale	house
kai	sea
kane	man
kahuna	Hawaiian priest
keiki	child or children
Kipa hou mai	Come visit again
kona	leeward side
makai and mauka	sea and mountain
manini	newcomer
ohana	family or extended family
Okole maluna!	Cheers!
O wai kou inoa?	What is your name?
ono	delicious
pupu	snack or hors d'oeuvres
wahine	female
wikiwiki	hurry

PRONOUNCING HAWAIIAN WORDS

The apostrophe-like mark you see in Hawaiian words is called an Okina. It shows a glottal stop, or a very brief break in the way you pronounce the word—kind of like the English "oh oh."

The consonants **h**, **k**, **l**, **m**, **n,** and **p** are pronounced just like they are in English. However, the letter **w** is pronounced a little differently:

After **i** and **e** it is pronounced as a **v.**
After **u** and **o** it is pronounced like a **w.**
At the start of a word or after the letter **a** it is pronounced like a **w** or **v.**

Vowels are pronounced like this:

A is pronounced as in *bar.*

E is pronounced as in *lend.*

I is pronounced like the **y** in *pity.*

O is pronounced as in *dope.*

U is pronounced as in *you.*

If You Want It, Hawaii's Got It

For a group of islands in the middle of the Pacific Ocean, Hawaii certainly has much to offer its visitors, not to mention the world at large. From the traditional to the thoroughly modern, the food, shopping, and entertainment here are colored with an amalgam of cultural sensibilities from all points of the compass. It's ready for you now, so enjoy a little mahi mahi, then wax up the old surfboard (or pull out the credit card) and prepare to dive in!

Chapter 3

Preparing for Your Trip

In This Chapter

- Researching your trip on the Internet
- Booking accommodations
- Getting to Hawaii
- Getting around once you're there
- Planning your trip on any budget

Hawaii is the land of crystal blue water, rugged mountains, lush vegetation, beautiful sandy beaches, and water sports galore—a picture-perfect paradise by most people's standards. It almost can be too much … but you can handle it! How do you decide between surfing lessons or a whale-watching excursion? How do you choose between a walk to the rim of an active volcano, or a long, luxurious waterside massage? And how can you afford not to go?

Planning the perfect Hawaiian vacation means deciding what you want out of your time there and what you're willing to spend to get it. In this chapter we point you toward the best resources for planning and booking your trip, with some perspective on various accommodations and modes of transportation to fit your vacationing style. We also give you some budgeting tips, including a worksheet, at the end of the chapter.

Planning Your Trip Online

We're going to go out on a limb and predict that you'll have a darn good time in the Aloha State. But let's not get ahead of ourselves.

You've started out exactly right, by buying this book, which is intended to help you set your goals and plan the outline of your trip. But before you set foot on the airplane to Hawaii, spend a bit of time on the wings of the Internet to acquaint yourself with the up-to-the-second details and offerings.

General Information Sites on Hawaii

General information sites provide you with background on Hawaiian culture and happenings. You can learn about anything from the state's economy to how to find the best golf courses. The sites listed here have a lot of information all in one place.

- **www.hawaii.com:** This site, partly owned by Gannett Co., the publishers of *USA Today* and the *Honolulu Advertiser*, is a good hub for Hawaii planning, providing information on the climate, accommodations, highlights, and travel specific to each island, including links to booking resources.
- **www.gohawaii.com:** Here the Hawaii Visitors and Convention Bureau offers links to Hawaiian arts and culture, golf, outdoor adventures, wedding and honeymoon planning, and family activities on all the islands.
- **www.hawaii.gov:** The official government website for the State of Hawaii, providing links researching Hawaii's education, business, and government. This site also happens to have some useful tools for planning a vacation.
- **www.50states.com/hawaii.htm:** This site gives basic facts and figures on Hawaii, with links to travel deals.

The best way to use the websites is to know what you hope to learn from them. Each time you go to a site, stay focused on a particular island or set of events. For example, plan your day trip to **Moloka'i** separately from your four-night stay on **The Big Island.** Visit the website twice, once to focus on Moloka'i and again to center around what Hawaii has to offer. That way you won't get bogged down in multitasking or trying to remember which information was for which island.

Finding the Best Resorts

Everybody likes to vacation a little differently. And for many of us, going to a tropical paradise such as Hawaii conjures visions of mai tais and massages under the palms, golf with a fabulous view, memorable dining, and a slew of inclusive amenities—basically a big dose of general pampering and luxury.

If this sounds like you, then you're in luck because Hawaii is well endowed with world-class resorts. These generally large, dramatically landscaped hotel and timeshare complexes can simplify and streamline your holiday by providing just about everything you need to relax and be entertained right on the premises. They also offer well-informed concierges and connections for must-see tours and local hotspots.

The benefit of a resort is that you choose the level of involvement you want. You can merely book a room and use their resources, or you can buy complete packages—including on-premises history, hula lessons, tours, or rental cars—and have them take care of every detail.

You also have a choice of family-friendly resorts where activities are geared to keep the group together or provide the parents a reprieve from the younger ones through kids-only events. These two websites will help you find the resort that is right for you:

- www.hawaiianhotelsandresorts.com
- www.family-vacations-hawaii.com

Timeshare Resorts

Timeshares, vacation condominiums that you actually purchase for a certain time period each year, have been a major trend in recent years. They're popular with folks who like to take regular vacations (at least once a year) in popular resort areas around the world. These condos are part of both low-rise and high-rise resorts, and vary in size from apartments to three- or four-bedroom units that are rented out when the owners or their families are not using them.

Timeshares generally require a down payment of several thousand dollars, as well as monthly fees, so they can get pricey compared to hotel stays if you don't vacation regularly. Amenities at timeshares vary from moderate to resort-style lavish, and as an owner you usually are enrolled in a network that allows you to trade weeks with other owners in destinations around the world, a perk for which timeshare companies usually tack on a few more bucks.

Timeshare can accommodate individuals of many economic levels, so take some time to see if it is for you. Some well-known vacation clubs that feature timeshares follow.

- **Marriott Vacation Club International:** 407-206-6000, www.vacationclub.com
- **Hyatt Vacation Club:** 1-800-926-4447, www.hyattvacationclub.com
- **Worldmark:** www.wmowners.com
- **Club Sunterra:** 877-258-2786, www.sunterra.com

You can enjoy a fine sunset at the Ka'anapali Beach Club on Maui.

(Photo courtesy of Michael Roney)

Money Matters

Do you want to save some significant bucks on a resort room, while enjoying free meals, discounted lu'aus, and other perks? It's not difficult if you're willing to spend about an hour of your vacation time taking a tour of your resort facilities and listening to a sales pitch. Many timeshare resorts such as the **Ka'anapali Beach Club** on **Maui,** for example, are happy to rent you an oversized room with all of these extras if you'll agree to listen to their timeshare sales pitch while you're there. You might get a $250 nightly room for as little as $125, plus all of those other discounts, so it's an option you should consider. Take the discount and the donuts, but don't feel bound to sign a contract.

Bed & Breakfasts: A Taste of Local Culture

If you're seeking more privacy than a resort hotel, a bed and breakfast may be the right place for you. Blending the comfort of home often with secluded settings, elegant décor, and personalized service from your host, bed and breakfasts truly provide a unique and intimate setting.

In a B&B you may not always have the grand swimming pool, the championship golf course, or the beachside locale, but you'll get to know other travelers and you'll receive "insider's" tips on where to go and what to do from your innkeeper. Oh yeah … there's also the killer gourmet breakfast that these places usually offer. Macadamia nut pancakes, anyone? The following websites will help you find cool B&Bs anywhere in Hawaii:

- **www.bestbnb.com:** This site offers plenty of well-organized photos and information for bed and breakfast accommodations, as well as vacation cottages and boutique hotels.
- **www.bbonline.com/hi:** This national site includes selective, full-page listings for all of the major islands.
- **www.bnbfinder.com:** This resource is well organized with extensive listings for the major islands.
- **www.bedandbreakfast.com:** This is a great site with extensive information and even maps for the listings.

Renting Private Homes

If you're traveling with a lot of people or are just looking to make your trip special, renting a private home is a great option to investigate. Renting a home will provide many amenities that you're used to: a complete kitchen, living room, separate bedrooms for couples or family members, a laundry room, and, most likely, a great view. You can find quaint villas or a fashionable condominium to rent, whatever fits your style and taste.

A few websites you'll find helpful for locating private home rentals are:

- **www.triphomes.com:** This national site allows you to focus in on any Hawaiian island, with hundreds of listings for each.
- **www.eliteprop.com:** This is a good resource for condos and homes on Kaua'i, Oa'hu, Maui, and The Big Island, showcasing bargains and special seasonal deals.
- **www.hawaiianbeachrentals.com:** This well-organized site lets you search among hundreds of condo and home rentals on any island by rate, date, and number of guests.
- **www.cyberrentals.com:** CyberRentals Vacation Properties focus in on any Hawaiian island for information and photos on hundreds of homes and condos.

Hostels

If you're on a very tight budget and don't mind bunking with others—often sharing bathrooms, showers, and other facilities—you might consider a hostel. Generally, hostels offer choices that vary from a private room with an individual bathroom to a bed in a common room with a shared bathroom in the hall. Depending on the type of room you choose, a hostel can be private or dormlike, but is ideal for the budget traveler. Some hostels might provide breakfast; make that part of your research.

A note to romantic couples: most hostels segregate the sleeping quarters of the men from the women, regardless of whether you have benefit of a marriage license.

- **www.hiayh.org:** This extensive site operated by **Hostelling International** is packed with useful hostel vacationing information.
- **www.hostel.com:** This fine commercial site lists over 10,000 hostels around the world.

- **www.hostelworld.com:** This is another commercial site with over 10,000 listings as well as vacation package deals.
- **www.hostelz.com:** This is arguably the largest hostels database on the web, claiming over 21,000 youth hostels and budget hotels listed in over 6,000 cities. (We didn't count them ourselves.)

Camping: The Cheapest Way to Go

The most basic accommodations available on each island is camping in a state park or other designated area. It's quick and easy to throw down a tent or rent a small cottage. Either way, it won't hurt your wallet, but it will require more effort on your part to take care of the rest of the trip, as campsites don't have concierges to lend a hand and some may not even have flush toilets. If camping is the way you go, a car will be a necessity to get you to your campground and to take you where you want to go during the day. One helpful website to understand and learn about Hawaiian campsites is **www.alternative-hawaii.com/accom/dxcc.htm.**

Getting Yourself to Hawaii

Figuring out how you're going to get to Hawaii means competing with the over 2 million other visitors who are doing the same thing in any given year. We've reviewed travel sites, how to use them and what they offer, but how do you decide the best city to leave from and arrive in? What's the best time to catch a flight to Hawaii and who are the major airline carriers? Let's start with the last question and work our way up.

Airlines That Fly to Hawaii

All of the major U.S. airlines fly into and out of Hawaii or are connected to partner airlines that do. The familiar names of **United, American, Continental, Delta, Northwest,** and **American Trans Air** will fly you to Hawaii from just about anywhere on the mainland or Alaska. Other major airlines going into and out of Hawaii include **Air Canada, Aloha Airlines, Air New Zealand, Air Pacific, China Airlines, Hawaiian Air, Japan Airlines, Korean Air, Philippine Airlines,** and **Qantas.**

Major Airlines That Fly to Hawaii

Airline	*Phone Number*	*Website*
American Airlines	1-800-433-7300	www.aa.com
Air Canada	1-888-247-2262	www.aircanada.com
Air Pacific	1-800-227-4446	www.airpacific.com
Aloha Airlines	1-800-367-5250	www.alohaairlines.com
America Trans Air	1-800-435-9282	www.ata.com
China Airlines	1-800-227-5118	www.china-airlines.com
Continental Airlines	1-800-523-3273	www.continental.com
Delta Airlines	1-800-221-1212	www.delta.com
Hawaiian Airlines	1-800-367-5320	www.hawaiianairlines.com
Japan Airlines	1-800-525-3663	www.jal.com
Korean Air	1-800-438-5000	www.koreanair.com
Philippine Airlines	1-800-435-9725	www.phillipineairlines.com
Qantas Airways	1-800-227-4500	www.qantas.com
United Airlines	1-800-864-8331	www.ual.com

HAWAII'S MAJOR AIRPORTS

Here are some basic facts about the major airports in Hawaii. For more information on arriving at these places, see the "Getting Comfortable" chapters in Part 2.

Honolulu International Airport (HNL) O'ahu

HNL is located at 300 Rodgers Boulevard, about five miles west of downtown Honolulu. Call (808-861-1260) for more information.

Airlines: Air Canada, Air New Zealand, Air Pacific Airways, All Nippon Airlines, American Airlines, American Trans Air, Continental Airlines, Continental Air Micronesia, China Airlines, Delta Airlines, Korean Airlines, Japan Air Charter, Japan Airlines, JTB Aloha Service, Northwest Airlines, Philippine Airlines, Quantas Airways, Rich International, and United Airlines.

Inter-Island Terminal: Aloha Airlines and Hawaiian Airlines.

Telephone: 808-836-6413

Hilo International Airport (ITO) The Big Island

ITO is two miles east of the town of Hilo on Hawaii.

Airlines: Aloha Airlines, American Trans Air, Hawaiian Airlines, Island Air, and Pacific Wings.

Telephone: 808-934-5838

Kahului Airport (OGG) Maui

OGG is located three miles east of the town of Kahului on Maui.

Airlines: Air Canada, Aloha Airlines, American Airlines, American Trans Air, America West, Continental Airlines, Delta Airlines, Harmony, Hawaiian Airlines, Island Air, Northwest, Pacific Wings, United Airlines, and West Jet.

Telephone: 808-872-3893

Kaunakakai Airport (MKK) Moloka'i

MKK is a small, two-runway airport in the center of Moloka'i.

Airlines: Aloha Island Air, Commercial Flyer, Inc., Hawaiian Airlines, Molokai Air Shuttle, Pacific Wings, and Paragon Air.

Telephone: 808-567-6361

Kona International Airport (KOA) The Big Island

KOA is seven miles northwest of Kailua-Kona on Hawaii.

Airlines: Air Canada, Aloha Airlines, American Airlines, American Trans Air, Delta Airlines, Hawaiian Airlines, Japan Airlines, Northwest Airlines, North American Airlines, Ryan International Airlines, United Airlines, and US Airways.

Inter-island Terminal: Aloha Airlines, Hawaiian Airlines, and Island Air.

Telephone: 808-329-3423

Lihue Airport (LIH) Kaua'i

LIH is 1.5 miles east of Lihue on the southeast corner of Kaua'i.

Airlines: Aloha Airlines, American Airlines, go!, Hawaiian Airlines, Island Air, Ryan Air, United Airlines, and US Airways.

Telephone: 808-246-1448

Money Matters

Regardless of the length of time you spend on the plane, finding the best fare sometimes means playing around with the arrival and departure airports. The major airports in Hawaii are Honolulu on O'ahu, Lihu'e on Kaua'i, Kaunakakai (Moloka'i Airport) on Moloka'i, Lana'i City on Lana'i, Kahului on Maui, Hilo on Hawaii, and Kona on Hawaii.

Shopping for Cruise Deals

Hey … how about cruising to Hawaii in style? If you have the time, why not? Getting on board a cruise ship and floating into a Hawaiian port is a relaxing alternative to the hubbub of air travel. **Royal Caribbean, Princess Cruises, Norwegian Cruise Lines (NCL),** and **Celebrity Cruises** can take you to Hawaii and even between its various islands.

An important note: because of a set of arcane laws intended to protect the almost nonexistent American shipbuilding industry, foreign-owned cruise lines or companies operating foreign-built ships are not permitted to sail between two American ports without making a stop in a foreign country. For that reason, nearly every cruise originating from the West Coast makes a port call in either Mexico or Vancouver, Canada, on their way to Hawaii. Others just originate in one of the foreign ports and sail direct to the islands. Once you're in Hawaii, you'll find NCL's Project America ships that have a special exemption permitting them to sail circles of the Hawaiian Islands without leaving U.S. waters. You'll also find unusual cruises that circle the Hawaiian Islands but also make a three- or four-day side trip to meet the requirements of the law with a visit to places like the **Republic of Kiribati,** a set of tiny islands and atolls about 1,000 miles south of Hawaii but a foreign nation nevertheless.

Each cruise line offers different amenities on their ships and different routes of travel. Royal Caribbean, for example, provides a journey between O'ahu, Maui, Hawaii, and Kaua'i, while Princess Cruises promotes not only an inter-island trip, but also a trip that includes a visit to Tahiti and Sydney.

Here is a list of the major cruise lines with voyages to Hawaii and around.

Cruise Line Connections

Cruise Line	*Phone Number*	*Website*
Celebrity Cruises	1-800-647-2251	www.celebritycruises.com
Norwegian Cruise Lines	1-866-234-0292	www.ncl.com
Princess Cruises	1-800-PRINCESS	www.princess.com
Royal Caribbean	1-866-562-7625	www.royalcaribbean.com

Inter-Island Transportation

The quickest way to get between islands is to fly. **Hawaiian Airlines** is aptly named, since it flies mainly between the islands. It also offers some flights to California, Australia, America Samoa, and Tahiti. Their headquarters is in Honolulu and they promote themselves as being voted the "best airline to Hawaii." Hawaiian Airlines runs more than 100 flights per day between the islands and has a printable inter-island flight schedule and route grid available on their website, www.hawaiianair.com.

Other well-known companies that offer inter-island flights as well as some trips to California are **Aloha Airlines**, **Pacific Wings (1-888-575-4546;** www.pacificwings.com), **Island Air (1-800-652-6541;** www.islandair.com) and **go! Airlines (1-888-IFLYGO2;** www.iflygo.com). go! Airlines runs a $39 one-way inter-island fare. To get this fare, though, you might need to book up to six months in advance. The tickets are nonrefundable and seats on the flights are limited. There also may be a small service fee associated with the fare price.

Another alternative to commercial airlines is chartering a plane to travel between islands. **Paragon Airlines (808-244-3356;** www.paragon-air.com) is one company that offers chartered flights and guided tours. The benefit to this type of travel is the intimacy of the flight and the ability to travel between islands while also taking a tour of a volcano or another spectacular sight.

The New Inter-Island Super Ferry

A refreshing new inter-island travel option is due to arrive in Hawaii in July of 2007.

The **Hawaii Super Ferry** (www.hawaiisuperferry.com) is scheduled to operate from Honolulu, O'ahu to **Kahului, Maui** or **Nawiliwili, Kaua'i.** Each trip is expected to take about three hours each way. Initial fares for passengers are expected to range from about $42 to $62 each way. If you are taking a car with you, expect to pay an extra $65 to $75.

These spiffy ships are modern, streamlined, and fast. Each double-hulled catamaran has four decks, with a capacity of 866 people and 282 cars. Each offers lounges, restaurants, shops, amusements for the kids, and the freedom to walk around inside or on deck, enjoying the scenery, the occasional whale (in season), and the fresh sea breeze.

In early 2009, **Super Ferry** expects to have daily service from Honolulu to The Big Island, a trip of about four hours. The benefit to traveling on the ferry, as opposed to an airplane, is that you can bring anything you want with you, such as an automobile, surfboard, pet, or kayak. Fares vary depending on if you're traveling during the peak (Friday to Monday) or off-peak (Tuesday to Thursday) days, your age, and what you're bringing with you. Tickets are sold as one-way trips and advanced web purchase can save you some money.

Getting Around on the Islands

Regardless of whether you choose a commercial airline or take a ferry between islands, you'll most likely still need a vehicle to travel around on the islands. Most of the great Hawaiian attractions, like volcanoes and scenic hikes, are not accessible by public transportation in the major cities.

All the major car rental companies offer discounts and run special rates you can take advantage of only by booking ahead of time. Most airlines and travel sites promote car rentals, and it may save you money to book that along with your airfare.

Once a car company runs out of cars slotted with a lower rate, you may end up scrambling to find an affordable rental. Booking ahead of time will not only save you money, but also will take the stress out of figuring out how and where to rent a car upon your arrival. Good deals on "walk-ups" do happen, but you have to get a little lucky.

Major Car Rental Companies in Hawaii

Company	Phone Number
Alamo	1-800-327-9633
Avis	1-800-321-3712
Budget	1-800-527-0700
Dollar	1-800-800-4000
Hertz	1-800-654-3011
National	1-800-227-7368
Thrifty	1-800-847-4389

Planning What to Pack

Once you have your accommodations, flights, and rental car booked, you can sit back and relax until the trip nears. As the hours tick down to your long-awaited departure, you'll get to do the exciting stuff: packing! The beach, the sun, the surf, and the tropical fruits await you, so what should you bring?

As a tropical island, Hawaii doesn't offer too much variation in daytime temperature. In fact, it's always summertime on the coasts, and generally spring or fall (take your pick) at the higher elevations inland on Maui and The Big Island. Also, depending on which side of the island you're on, there will be a good chance you'll see rain.

Here are some tips to think about while packing:

- **Aloha shirts and shorts:** Hawaiians are known for being a relatively casual group of people. Casual wear, including polo shirts, T-shirts, and khaki shorts, is acceptable anywhere. For women, tank tops, T-shirts, lightweight skirts, and shorts will be most comfortable.
- **Keep your feet happy:** With traveling often comes a great deal of walking, so be sure to pack shoes that are appropriate for the activities you'll be doing.
- **Protect yourself from those tropical rays!** Don't get broiled! Be prepared for the tropical sun with brimmed hats and sunscreen (at least SPF 30). If you're tight on space, these certainly are items you can buy once you get there.
- **The ocean is unavoidable:** Going to Hawaii without swimwear? Hey, we won't insult your intelligence by even suggesting such a thing.
- **When you're out on the town:** Hawaiians have a more relaxed dress code than mainlanders for going out at night. Button-up shirts and lightweight pants are acceptable for both sexes. It does get cooler at night, so a light, long-sleeved shirt would be nice to have around. Even Aloha shirts are acceptable almost anywhere. Only a few restaurants in all of Hawaii require jackets, and most of those have a supply on hand if you don't have one with you!
- **When it rains, it pours:** It does rain on the islands, and sometimes an awful lot. Be prepared with a light rain jacket to take with you on hikes or day excursions. If you're going to the windward side of the island, you'll have a greater chance of rain.

How to Budget for Your Trip

Yes, paradise comes at a premium. Overall, you can expect most things to cost you about 20 percent more in Hawaii than they do on the mainland. That can hurt, but if you can find ways to reduce some costs and spend carefully on the rest, you should be able to keep the bottom line within line.

Before beginning any trip, it's important to consider what you can afford. There are places to be frugal and times when splurging is worth it! Creating a rough budget can help you examine your options.

We're not going to include the cost of travel basics: clothing, luggage, medications you already take, and that sort of thing. Buy a bottle or two of sunscreen and pack your sunglasses. And remember, Hawaii is a pretty laid-back place; you don't need to buy a tux and a cocktail gown.

Use the following table. Start with the pre-trip costs: child care, pet care, transportation to the airport. Use the information that we provide in this and other chapters throughout the book, and then calculate the price of paradise.

Budget Worksheet

	Pre-trip costs
Airfare to Hawaii (for your entire group)	__________
Island-to-island transportation	__________
Car rental, taxis, transfers (across entire trip)	__________
Personal care items	__________
Camera supplies	__________
Hotels (per day times number of days)	__________
Food (breakfast, lunch, dinner, and snacks per day, times number of days)	__________
Drinks and entertainment (per day, times number of days)	__________
Excursions (whale-watching, mountain climbing, beachcombing)	__________
Souvenirs and other shopping (if you must, or are overruled by your significant other)	__________
ESTIMATED TOTAL	

Aloha!

In this chapter, we've directed you toward all of the essential resources for researching and booking your Hawaii vacation. Use these resources with the specific information detailed in the following chapters, and you'll be ready to finalize your plans. Are you as psyched as we are?

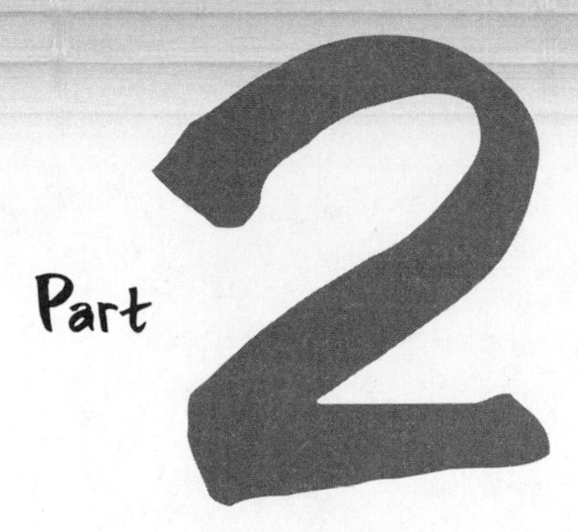

Part 2

Honolulu and O'ahu

Most people who go to Hawaii set down on O'ahu, at least for a while. O'ahu is iconic Hawaii, from Diamond Head to the huge waves of the North Shore. It's also the island that hosts Hawaii's largest city, Honolulu. This part delves deeply into Honolulu, and then provides all you need to know to enjoy the rest of O'ahu.

Relaxing in Honolulu

In This Chapter

- Honolulu's geography and character
- Getting around Honolulu
- Deciding where to stay in the city
- Honolulu's best lodging choices

There's so much to do just in **Honolulu**—everything from world-class nightlife, restaurants, and museums, to incredibly scenic beaches, canyons, rainforests, and waterfalls—that you could easily spend your entire vacation here. Not that we'd expect you to do that. Still, the Honolulu experience is so potentially rich that we give it two chapters all of its own (this one and the next), with the rest of **O'ahu** covered in Chapters 6 and 7.

With Honolulu's massive array of touring options, not to mention the competition from over five million other visitors each year, a bit of savvy planning ahead is definitely in order. This chapter details Honolulu's various neighborhoods, where you might want to stay, and how to move around to see all of the most worthwhile sights.

Honolulu at a Glance

Honolulu is the state capital as well as the center of culture, entertainment, cultural diversity, and all things urban in Hawaii. However, it is also amazingly bright and clean for a city, providing a hefty dose of tropical beauty along with a huge variety of excellent lodgings and restaurants, covering every budget and taste. You can get from Honolulu to most of the best scenic areas on the island of O'ahu in an hour or less.

Snapshot

Honolulu:

Size: 105 square miles

Estimated Metro Population: 905,000

Average Temperature: 65°F to 74°F (18°C to 23°C)

Average Annual Rainfall: 21.6 inches

Elevation: 7 feet

Number of Annual Visitors: 5 million

Situated along a narrow coastal plain rising quickly into rugged green mountains, Honolulu boasts some of the best weather in Hawaii, generally ranging between 75° and 85°F.

As Hawaii's only big city, Honolulu melds tropical beauty with urban amenities.

(Photo courtesy of HVCB/Chuck Painter)

Transportation from the Airport

Honolulu is the easiest place in all the islands of Hawaii to get to, since the state's main airport is located there. **Honolulu International Airport**

(**HNL**) is the main air gateway to Hawaii, and a hub for international air travel across the Pacific. Located near **Pearl Harbor** and adjacent to **Hickam Air Force Base** on a flat peninsula just west of downtown, HNL boasts a well laid-out but busy terminal, and is served by dozens of domestic and international airlines. You can walk from your gate to the baggage claim downstairs, or you can hop on the free airport shuttle, called the **Wiki-Wiki Bus.** For more information on air travel at HNL and elsewhere throughout Hawaii, see Chapter 3.

Rental Cars

To get to and from the airport or to see the area outside of downtown Honolulu, one option is to rent a car; this makes increasing sense if there are several people in your group. Driving yourself does take away the hassle of timetables, locating bus stops, and relying on someone else to take you where you want to go. At HNL you can rent a car from most of the major companies, including: **Alamo Rent-A-Car, Avis, Budget Rent-A-Car, Dollar Rent-A-Car, Enterprise Rent-A-Car, Hertz,** and **National Car Rental.** Rentals run in the range of $44 to $80 a day depending on the type of automobile you choose to rent. To get to the rental lots, grab a shuttle bus at the center island outside of the baggage claim.

If you're looking to save a few bucks by renting a used car, check out **Tradewinds,** 2875-A Koapaka Street in Honolulu (**808-834-1465** or **1-888-388-7368;** www.tradewindsudrive.com). The company is only a few minutes off the airport property, and you can call for a pickup by dialing 80 on the car rental board in any baggage claim area.

Taxis

While there are several options for taxi services in Honolulu, one company to consider is **Star Taxi Hawaii (808-942-7827;** www.startaxihawaii.com). This service promises a $30-or-less ride from the airport to any Waikiki hotel, and they accept reservations ahead of time. Another bonus to this company is their 24-hour service. **AMPCO Express (808-861-8294**) is another option that will run you between $35 to $40 on non-rush hour times.

Shuttle Service

If you're staying in Waikiki, you can use the **Island Express Transport (808-944-1879;** www.islandexpresstransport.com) to get to and from the

Honolulu Airport. It's $10 per person for a one-way ticket. The company also offers a small shuttle service around the **Waikiki** area as well as pre-established or customizable island tours. You can make a reservation online or call the office directly.

Another option is the **Waikiki Airport Express (808-954-8652)**, operated by **Roberts Hawaii.** This shuttle runs every 20–25 minutes between 5 A.M. and 3 A.M. and every hour between 3 A.M. and 5 A.M. It's definitely affordable at $9 per person for a one-way ticket, and $15 round-trip. However, you are only allowed two items of baggage and larger luggage items may have an additional fee attached to them.

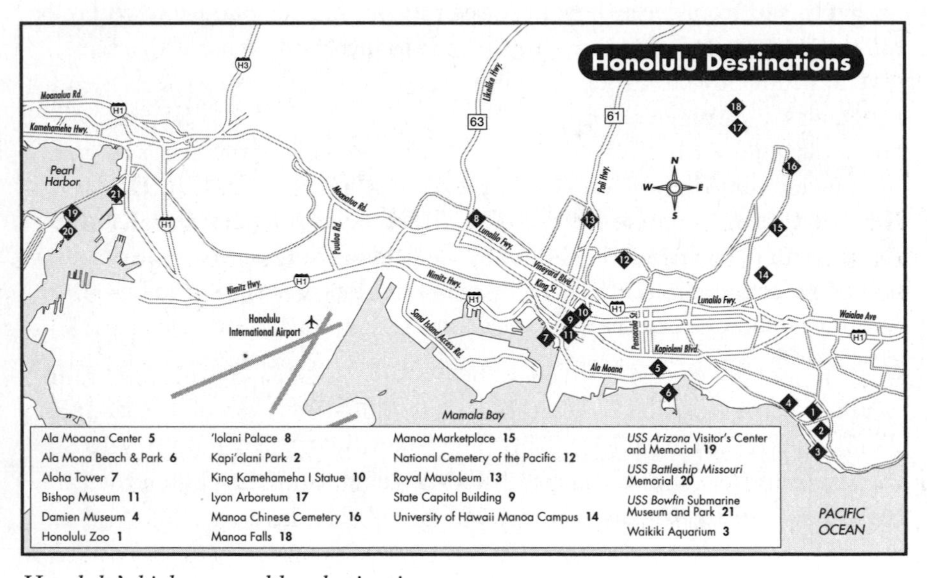

Honolulu's highways and key destinations.

Limousine Services

If public transportation, taxis, or rental cars don't suit your travel needs or won't provide enough room for all the people you're traveling with, you can use a limousine service from the airport to your hotel. **Airport Limo Service (808-946-1001)**, will run you $70 for a 9-passenger limo and $90 for a 12-passenger limo. They also will provide a lei greeting for $10 each.

Another company is **Alpha Limousines (808-955-8898)**. This service will run you around $95 for up to six people and they provide free leis. They have round-trip prices that can save you some cash if you choose it instead of two single one-way fares.

Here's approximately what you can expect to spend for a one-way ride between Honolulu airport and popular destinations around the city:

What Transportation Costs in Honolulu

Destination	*Taxi*	*Limo*	*Shuttle*	*Bus*
Downtown	$35–40	$70–100	$9	$2
Pearl Harbor	$15	$50	$5–10	$2
Waikiki	$35–40	$70–100	$9	$2

Traveling on the Cheap: Buses

Using public transportation within the city limits of Honolulu is an easy and affordable way to get around, not to mention that Hawaii is considered to have one of the best public transportation systems in the United States.

The Oahu Transit System is what you'll find in Honolulu, and it includes **TheBus** and **The Handi-Van.** TheBus has 86 routes and approximately 4,000 stops across Honolulu providing about 70 million rides a year. It is the cheapest mode of transportation per person per mile with a one-way $2 adult fare. Younger folks ages 6–17, high school students up to 19 years of age (with an ID), and seniors and people with disabilities pay only $1 for a one-way pass.

If you'll be in Honolulu for several days, a four-day unlimited ride pass for $20 may be the best way to go, although it excludes rides on the Football Express! and special service buses. You can purchase one of these at any ABC store.

You can call **TheBus Information Center (808-848-5555)** between 5:30 A.M. and 10 P.M. for additional information about the service and stations or visit the website for printable timetables (www.thebus.org).

The **Handi-Van (808-523-4083)** provides curb-to-curb service for those who are unable to take the bus and costs only $2 each way. To take the Handi-Van you need to submit an application, so reviewing the eligibility requirements and submitting an application ahead of time may be necessary in order to get the accommodations you'll need once you're in Honolulu. Consider visiting the website to see if the Handi-Van is right for you: www.honolulu.gov/dts/index.htm.

Consider taking the **Waikiki Trolley (1-800-824-8804;** www.waikikitrolley.com) as a mode of transportation to sightsee in the area. You pay a flat fee of $25 for unlimited rides in one day or $45 for unlimited rides during four consecutive days.

Getting Your Bearings: Honolulu Neighborhoods and Geography

"Downtown" Honolulu lies on a relatively flat coastal plain along O'ahu's southern shore, with Pearl Harbor in the west and **Diamond Head** in the east. Directly behind (or north of) the downtown areas are seven hills and seven valleys that divide the greater part of the city into three distinct residential neighborhoods: **Waikiki, Ala Moana,** and **Manoa Valley.** To the southwest of downtown is **Pearl Harbor.** We'll cover all of these districts in the following pages with the goal of giving you a sense of what to expect and the areas you might want to explore. Like any city, there is some information that is worth knowing before you get there!

HONOLULU VISITORS' INFORMATION

There are two groups in Honolulu that can provide you with a wealth of information whether on the internet, by mail, or in person. Each can give you some insight into Hawaii and Honolulu.

- **Hawaii Visitors and Convention Bureau,** 2270 Kalakaua Avenue, Suite 801, Honolulu; **808-923-1811** or **1-800-464-2924.** www.gohawaii.com.
- **Hawaii Visitors and Convention Bureau Information Office,** Royal Hawaiian Shopping Center, Hibiscus Court, 4th Floor, 2201 Kalakaua Avenue, Waikiki (fronting the Sheraton Waikiki and Royal Hawaiian Hotels). Open 10 A.M.–10 P.M. daily. **808-924-0266.**

Waikiki

There is one picture of Hawaii that almost everyone has seen on TV, on postcards, or in travel brochures—**Waikiki Beach.** The beach itself is actually one of the best in the islands—a long, palm-shaded, gently sloping crescent of sand stretching into rolling blue surf. Behind the beach is a stand of tall, shining buildings, providing a union of nature and, uh … *human* nature. Waikiki is appropriately named a "tourist district," as almost every traveler to O'ahu tries to make a stop there. The people who keep tourism stats say that four out of every five visitors to O'ahu stay in Waikiki. This area is the epicenter of the state's shopping, high-rise hotels (more than 35,000 rooms), and nightlife.

Waikiki Beach and Diamond Head are two of Honolulu's most famous destinations.

(Photo courtesy of HVCB/Joe Solem)

Sure, this high-rise-backed strand and neighborhood is packed with hoards of Aloha shirt–wearing, camera-toting tourists like us, yet somehow it manages to maintain its allure—even after decades of fame. Why? Well, Waikiki is a darn good beach by any standard; the surrounding neighborhood is clean, well manicured, entertaining, and easy to walk. Above all, this area continues to be "where it's happening" in Honolulu.

Snapshot

Waikiki Destinations:

- Damien Museum
- Honolulu Zoo
- Kapi'olani Park
- Waikiki Aquarium

Ala Moana

The area known as Ala Moana is the retail, commercial, and residential district of Honolulu just to the west of Waikiki. Ala Moana also has its own stretch of beautiful sandy beaches. Named **Ala Moana Beach Park,** they were protected by President Franklin Roosevelt in the 1930s. If you want to relax on a fine Honolulu beach that is a bit more low-key than Waikiki, this is the place.

While Ala Moana has great beaches, it was given the crown of Honolulu's retail district for a good reason. Before the Mall of America sprang up in Minneapolis, Minnesota, the **Ala Moana Center (808-955-9517;** www.alamoana.com) was the largest shopping center in the country. Today, the Ala Moana Center still holds a title, but it is now known as the largest *open-air* shopping center in the world. It boasts more than 260 shops and restaurants, with over 56 million visitors a year.

Snapshot

Ala Moana Destinations:

- Ala Moana Beach and Park
- Ala Moana Center
- Kaka'ako Waterfront Park

Downtown

Downtown Honolulu is a district of tall buildings and concrete canyons that can be divided into four neighborhoods: the **Capitol District,** the **Central Business District, Chinatown,** and the **Waterfront.** This area is the commercial center of the city, and the location of the **'Iolani Palace,** the only royal palace in the United States, Honolulu's Chinatown, the modernistic state capital, and numerous other stops of historic and architectural interest. This is a good place for walking tours, the best of which we detail in Chapter 5.

Chinatown is the epicenter of Asian culture in Hawaii, and happens to be the oldest Chinatown in America. Here you'll find intriguing markets and restaurants, reflecting a rich cultural mix from all around the eastern Pacific, covering not only China, but also influences from Japan, Vietnam, Thailand, and other countries. While you're here, you'll also be able to check out the venerable **Hawaii Theater,** a historical landmark designed in neoclassical style, and a popular venue for stage shows and concerts.

Snapshot

Downtown Destinations:

- Aloha Tower
- Bishop Museum
- 'Iolani Palace
- National Cemetery of the Pacific
- Royal Mausoleum
- State Capitol Building
- Statute of King Kamehameha I

Honolulu's waterfront surrounds the **Aloha Tower,** which when built in 1926 was the tallest building in Honolulu. The Aloha Tower kept this designation until 1996 when the more modern **First Hawaiian Center** was built, standing 438 feet tall. While no longer the tallest building, it's now the center of the **Aloha Tower Marketplace** shopping and restaurant complex.

Manoa Valley

This suburban district, just minutes north of Waikiki, is an interesting area that isn't overrun by tourists. It's the home of several notable Honolulu sights, including the **University of Hawaii Manoa Campus,** the **Manoa Marketplace** shopping center, the **Manoa Chinese Cemetery,** the **Lyon Arboretum,** and the 150-foot **Manoa Falls.** Manoa Valley boasts a few B&Bs that will give you a taste of the nontourist life in and around Honolulu.

Pearl Harbor

Situated just a few miles west of downtown Honolulu, this site of the surprise Japanese attack of December 7, 1941, including the **USS *Arizona* Memorial and Museum,** is a moving, must-see destination in the area.

Other than the Pearl Harbor monument, though, there's not much else for the tourist, so you should plan to stay in one of the other parts of Honolulu. For more information on touring Pearl Harbor, see Chapter 5.

Snapshot

Pearl Harbor Destinations:

- Damien Museum
- USS ***Arizona*** Visitors Center and Memorial
- USS Battleship ***Missouri*** Memorial
- USS ***Bowfin*** Submarine Museum and Park

Honolulu Accommodations: Ultimate Places to Stay

Being in the largest city in the state, you won't find a shortage of places to stay in Honolulu. (Heck, there are over 35,000 hotel rooms in Waikiki alone!) The city offers several types of accommodations, most of which cater to the various needs of different types of travelers, from families to the independent visitor. Keep in mind your price tag, location, and type of lodging that you want—if you look around enough you will most likely find it in Honolulu. You can also visit www.visit-oahu.com/directory.aspx for a listing of even more accommodations in all the categories we detail.

Following you'll find a brief overview of a few of our favorite places to stay in Honolulu. Accommodations are organized alphabetically under each lodging category.

Hotels and Resorts

Ala Moana Hotel

Next door to the Ala Moana Center, across the street from the Honolulu Convention Center, and within walking distance of Waikiki, this hotel provides an ideal central location for your visit to Honolulu. The hotel offers single rooms and suites as well as a pool, gym, spa, and several restaurants. *410 Atkinson Drive, Honolulu, HI, 96814.* ***808-955-4811*** *or* ***1-800-367-6025.*** *www.alamoanahotel.com.*

Halekulani

Halekulani has been in operation for about 100 years and is located right on Waikiki Beach. The hotel boasts a five-star restaurant, relaxing spa, a calendar of hotel events, views of Diamond Head, and rooms with understated elegance. This hotel offers an experience even before you step outside. *2199 Kalia Road, Honolulu, HI, 96815.* ***808-923-2311*** *or* ***1-800-367-2343.*** *www.halekulani.com.*

The Equus

This place offers the personal service of a family-run establishment with all of Honolulu's attractions at its doorstep. The Inn underwent extensive renovations in 2006 and now offers a Jacuzzi, tennis courts, pools, and tickets to the Hawaii Polo Club when in season. You can choose to stay in the Inn itself or in the Marina Tower section of the Inn. *1696 Ala Moana Boulevard, Honolulu, HI, 96815.* ***808-949-0061.*** *www.hawaiipolo.com/thehawaiipoloinn.asp.*

Ocean Resort Waikiki

This two-tower hotel offers basic, no-nonsense rooms as well as studio kitchenettes for families and honeymoon suites for those who want more luxury. Located near Waikiki Beach, the Honolulu Zoo, Honolulu Aquarium, and International Marketplace, you won't run out of things to do or see. The hotel offers a pool, banquet hall, beautiful ocean views, and a seafood restaurant. *175 Paoakalani Avenue, Honolulu, HI, 96815.* ***1-800-367-2317*** *or* ***808-922-3861.*** *www.oceanresort.com.*

Pagoda Hotel and Restaurant

Home to the world famous *koi* pond and renowned Pagoda Floating Restaurant, this hotel is just 20 minutes from the Honolulu Airport. The ambiance of the hotel blends Eastern and Western ideals while also incorporating Hawaiian culture. The resort splits 260 rooms among two wings and offers an array of rooms from the basic queen-bed room to a family kitchenette. For amenities, the Pagoda Hotel has two swimming pools, a salon, travel agency, and parking options. *1525 Rycroft Street, Honolulu, HI, 96814.* ***808-941-6611*** *or* ***1-800-367-6060.*** *www.pagodahotel.com*

The Royal Hawaiian

An icon of Honolulu, this "Pink Palace of the Pacific" stands proudly on Waikiki Beach. The hotel offers several selections of rooms from a basic hotel room in the tower to a suite in the main, older section of the hotel. It has a private beach, mai tai bar, spa, ballroom, Internet access, airport shuttles, restaurant, and garden. Truly, this hotel will seem like a palace. *2259 Kalakaua Avenue, Honolulu, HI, 96815.* ***808-931-7098*** *or* ***1-866-716-8109.*** *www.royal-hawaiian.com.*

More Intimate Lodgings and B&Bs

Aloha Bed and Breakfast

This bed and breakfast will require a rental car as it is not located within walking distance to a bus stop. Diamond Head and Waikiki are between 15 to 20 minutes away. The rooms have ceiling fans, TV, and a nice view. The inn offers a pool, large deck, and wireless Internet access. *909 Kahauloa Place, Honolulu, HI, 96825.* ***808-395-6694.*** *www.home.hawaii.rr.com/alohaphyllis.*

Diamond Head Bed and Breakfast

This two-story bed and breakfast is owned by a family of seven and has décor that hints at the typical Hawaiian home of 50 years ago. Each room has a TV, private phone, private bath, mini-fridge, and sliding glass doors that open to an outdoor deck. *3240 Noela Drive, Honolulu, HI, 96815.* ***808-923-3360.*** *www.diamondheadbnb.com.*

J&B's Haven

$

Run by a mother-daughter pair from England (who also speak French), this bed and breakfast is located about 20 minutes from Waikiki Beach and is within walking distance of Hanauma Bay, considered to be "a snorkeler's paradise." The rooms boast a private bath, AC, TV, and a mini-fridge. The bed and breakfast requires a three-night minimum stay or $20 extra per night under the minimum. *P.O. Box 25907, Honolulu, HI, 96825.* ***808-396-9462.*** *www.home.hawaii.rr.com/jnbshaven.*

The Manoa Valley Inn

$ $

Built in 1912, this Inn is on the National Register of Historic Places. It is located within minutes of Waikiki and Honolulu attractions, while providing the distraction of the peaceful Manoa Valley from the hubbub of a day in the city. The Inn offers seven rooms and a small cottage. It's important, depending on your preference, to note if the room you want has a shared or private bath. There is no smoking allowed at the Inn. *2001 Vancouver Drive, Honolulu, HI, 96822.* ***808-947-6019.*** *www.manoavalleyinn.com.*

Best Private Homes

Kahala Beach Villa

$ $ $ $ $

This villa bestows true luxury upon its visitors, but it comes with a hefty price tag. For what you pay, you get a 5-bedroom, 6.5-bath, 4,500-square-foot home that astounds you with a peaceful Japanese garden in the entryway. The home has a fully equipped gym, Jacuzzi-tub, and steam shower. The owners require a seven-night minimum stay and there is a maximum of eight guests allowed. Truly top of the line, this villa will allow you to calmly end each day with a beautiful sunset over the ocean while residing only minutes away from majestic Diamond Head. ***1-800-526-4244.***

Mele Manuku

$ $ $ $ $

This is a two-story, three-bedroom, and three-bath home set on about an acre of tropical land. It is a comfortably furnished home with a pool, ocean views, and a master bedroom that is the entire second floor. Located near Diamond Head and only three miles from Waikiki, staying here won't take you away from the attractions you want to see. There is a minimum stay of seven nights and the home will accommodate up to six guests. ***808-680-05060*** *or* ***1-800-891-4809.***

That's your overview of gleaming Honolulu. Now you more or less know your way around and where to stay. For details on great restaurants, beaches, shopping, outdoor sports, and other activities, take a look at Chapter 5!

Enjoying Honolulu

In This Chapter

- The ultimate itineraries for Honolulu
- The most interesting things to see in Honolulu
- The best places to dine in Honolulu
- The best things to do in Honolulu

Although your mind's eye may picture Hawaii as a place of beaches, surf, and volcanoes, don't overlook the impressive city life in paradise. **Honolulu,** on the southeast coast of the island of **O'ahu,** has plenty to offer to most any traveler: history, culture, dining, and nightlife to rival any metropolis.

Honolulu means "sheltered bay" in Hawaiian, and the large, deep body of water has been inhabited since Marquesans arrived in the fourth century, with Tahitians arriving later, in the twelfth or thirteenth centuries. The first European visit to the island, by England's Captain William Brown in 1794, established the city as an important stop on trade routes between Asia and the Americas. It was host to the court of King Kamehameha I beginning in 1804, and became the permanent capital of the kingdom of Hawaii in 1845. The city grew apace as the commercial and cultural center of the islands.

Today, **Waikiki** is the city's tourist center, but you'll find plenty to pique your interest away from the hotels and beaches, whether it's making visits to the museums, historic buildings, the memorial at **Pearl Harbor,** bargain-hunting your way through the markets in **Chinatown,** or choosing from the impressive selection of theaters and galleries. You'll find botanical gardens, a fascinating maritime center, and blood-soaked historical sites, all in this city of less than a million residents.

All this sits in the shadow of the easily spotted **Diamond Head Crater.** Relax: the volcano's extinct. And don't worry; we'll get to the beaches, too.

Honolulu boasts a good mix of cosmopolitan urbanity and natural beauty.

(Photo courtesy of HVCB/Chuck Painter)

The Top Five Things to Do in Honolulu

Honolulu is a city with real Hawaiian flavor. Be sure to take advantage of the sites and sights you can't get anywhere else!

1. Make a visit to the poignant memorial at Pearl Harbor, one of the iconic sites of Hawaii and the nation.
2. Take a stroll down **Kalakaua Avenue** in Waikiki—you get a classic ocean stroll, landmark hotels, and the Diamond Head crater—all in a two-mile span.

3. Get a taste of royalty in the lavish **'Iolani Palace,** the only state residence for royalty in the United States.
4. Experience Hawaiian and Polynesian science, culture, and history at the renowned **Bishop Museum.**
5. Enjoy sunset drinks at **Duke's Canoe Club.**

Plan My Trip: Ultimate Itineraries for Honolulu

Honolulu has something to offer every visitor, from families to singles, laid-back travelers to ambitious micromanagers. Following you'll find some day-long itineraries to get you started on your trip. You can find more detailed information on sights and restaurants in the "Top Honolulu Attractions" section later in the chapter.

ITINERARY #1: FOR YOUNG FAMILIES

1. **Breakfast:** Try Hawaii's alternative to McDonald's—**Zippy's.** There are plenty of familiar options on the menu.
2. Head downtown and let your little ones burn up some energy oohing and aahing as you walk around the **Chinatown markets.** You'll get your souvenir shopping out of the way, too.
3. **Lunch:** Bring the fresh goodies you picked up in Chinatown to enjoy at the **Liliu'okalani Gardens.** Be sure you have a look at the **Nu'uanu waterfalls** as well.
4. The afternoon will fly by at the **Honolulu Zoo.** Kids of all ages will be fascinated by the Komodo dragon, and it's easy to make a game of looking for critters in the "African Savannah."
5. **Dinner:** Who can say no to delicious, reasonably priced Italian food? Nobody. That's why you'll have dinner at **Auntie Pasto's.**

ITINERARY #2: FOR OLDER FAMILIES

1. **Breakfast:** After breakfast at the hotel, do your best to beat the crowds to **Pearl Harbor;** the **USS *Arizona* Visitors Center, "Mighty Mo,"** and the **USS *Bowfin* Submarine Museum** are worth taking your time through.
2. **Lunch:** Head back into town and negotiate with your picky eaters for a restaurant in the **Ala Moana Center.**
3. As long as you don't have anyone too little, the whole family can enjoy the moderate hike up the **Diamond Head Crater;** and you'll all think it was worthwhile once you see that view!
4. **Dinner:** Everyone should find something to like at **Ninnikuya, the Garlic Restaurant.** Don't be intimidated by the name—garlic also means garlic mashed potatoes.

ITINERARY #3: FOR SINGLES

1. **Breakfast:** Up and at 'em early for breakfast at **Eggs 'n Things,** then enjoy some snorkeling or scuba with **Hanauma Bay Tours.** By the end of your time in the water, you'll wish you could grow gills.
2. **Brunch/Lunch:** Try some local grinds at **Ono Hawaiian Foods.** Even if you stick to familiar territory for the meal, make sure you try the *haupia* (Hawaiian pudding) for dessert.
3. At the **Honolulu Academy of the Arts,** you'll find 30 galleries of art from around the world; be sure to check the **Henry Luce Gallery** for changing exhibitions.
4. **Dinner:** Enjoy live music, good food, and pink beer (that's right!) at the **Mai Tai Bar.**
5. Hit the clubs in the **Ala Moana** area.

ITINERARY #4: A ROMANTIC GETAWAY

1. **Breakfast:** Clichés happen for a reason—sleep in and splurge on breakfast in bed.
2. Enjoy Hawaii's tranquil beauty with a drive out to **Lyon Arboretum** in **Manoa.** Stroll through the grounds and enjoy the soundtrack of native birds; try the easy hike out to **Manoa Falls** before you head back to Honolulu.
3. **Lunch:** When you're feeling warm and fuzzy, comfort food's the only thing for it—and you can enjoy your cuddly mac and cheese in style at the **12th Avenue Grill.**
4. Pretend to admire the architecture and engage in public displays of affection all along the **Nu'uanu Cultural District.** There are galleries, too, you know, if you get tired of staring deeply into each other's eyes.
5. It will feel like the perfect sunset is just for you as you nurse a couple of cocktails at the **Sunset Lanai.**
6. **Dinner:** Nothing says romance like a decadent French dinner at **La Mer.** Just ask the dishes.

ITINERARY #5: EASY-GOING; NONSTRENUOUS

1. **Breakfast:** Do you feel a twinge of guilt at the prospect of enjoying an easy-going hotel vacation? Then there's just one word you should be reminded of: *vacation.* Have some breakfast at the hotel, then …
2. Take the pink **Waikiki Trolley line** over to the **Ala Moana Beach Park.** There's plenty of room to stretch out and enjoy the sun and surf on this idyllic beach.
3. **Lunch:** Head into downtown and try some Asian-style barbecue at **Kiawe Grill.** If you're feeling adventurous, try the ostrich or buffalo burgers—and don't miss the Asian vegetable bar.

continues

continued

4. Spend the afternoon learning about Hawaii's rich past at the world-class **Bishop Museum.** Sports fans might like the **Hawaii Sports Hall of Fame.**
5. **Dinner:** Even in Hawaii, you can enjoy first-rate Tuscan food. **Assaggio's** in the Ala Moana Center has an excellent, varied menu, but we especially recommend the seafood dishes.

ITINERARY #6: CULTURE IN PARADISE

1. **Breakfast:** Try something different for breakfast and head to **Keo's in Waikiki**—Asian and American breakfast foods are available.
2. It's the only royal residence in the United States and just as elegant and extravagant as you'd expect. Spend the morning at **'Iolani Palace** and try to make a tour, if you can. Be sure to check out the throne room and the galleries, which formerly were servants' quarters.
3. Before lunch, you should have time to learn about Christianity's beginnings in the Hawaiian Islands at the **Mission Houses Museum.** The grounds also include one of the earliest examples of American architecture, the **Chamberlain House,** built in 1830.
4. **Lunch:** Locals know best and they know that **Akasaka** is the place to go for fresh, reasonable, and authentic Japanese cuisine. Check out the specials and, if you come right at noon, be prepared for a wait.
5. Completed in 1865, the **Royal Mausoleum** is the final resting place for most of the Hawaiian royal family. It's considered the most sacred burial ground in Hawaii and, indeed, seems to carry a somber reverence in the atmosphere.
6. **Dinner:** Go all out for dinner and enjoy the innovative (and delicious!) island fusion cuisine offered at **Alan Wong's.** Try "da bag," an upscale version of a local favorite with kalua pork.

ITINERARY #7: ADVENTURE IN THE GREAT OUTDOORS

1. **Breakfast:** Skip breakfast or grab something small at the hotel—up and at 'em for surf lessons from **Hans Hedemann Surf School.** Don't worry, even if you're a more experienced surfer, all levels of classes are available.
2. **Lunch:** Fill up after your active moment with some excellent spanakopita from **Marbella's.** Afterwards, enjoy a stroll around the sprawling **Kapi'olani Park,** and if you're really full of energy, hike the Diamond Head Crater.
3. Get back in the water—okay, on the water—and go for an afternoon sail with **Adventure Sail Hawaii.**
4. **Dinner:** Treat yourself with an elegant, hearty dinner at **Hy's Steak House.** Try your cut broiled over *kiawe* wood for a Hawaiian twist!

The Top Honolulu Attractions, A to Z

Bishop Museum & Planetarium Downtown Honolulu

Originally established in 1889 by Charles Reed Bishop to display the artifacts and heirlooms of his late wife, Princess Pauahi Bishop, the last descendent of the royal Kamehameha family. Today it houses artifacts from cultures across the South Pacific, along with the Hawaiian Sports Hall of Fame and the Science Garden, which replicates in miniature the triangular territorial divisions of Native Hawaiians. Also be sure to check out the wonderful Jhamandas Watumull Planetarium for interactive shows and viewings of the night sky. *1525 Bernice Street. Open daily 9 A.M.–5 P.M. Admission is $15.95, $12.95 for children.* ***808-847-3511.*** *www.bishopmuseum.org.*

Chinatown Downtown Honolulu

Located right in the center of the city, Chinatown reflects the diversity of Asian influences in the Hawaiian Islands. Restaurants and nightclubs are set in historic buildings whose distinctive architecture provides a startling contrast to the high-rises nearby. If you're in town, be sure to check out the First Friday or Chinatown After Dark events to fully experience the variety of art and culture in the neighborhood; otherwise, take a stroll down bustling Hotel and Maunakea streets, some of the area's oldest streets. *www.chinatownhi.com.*

Diamond Head Crater Waikiki

Originally called "Leahi," or "brow of the tuna" by Native Hawaiians, this icon of O'ahu is at the end of Kalakaua Avenue east of Waikiki and is perhaps the most famous volcanic crater in the world. Extinct for 150,000 years, the crater is 3,520 feet across and 762 feet at its summit. It received its Western name from English sailors who mistook the glittering calcite in the lava rock for diamonds. The three-quarter-mile hike to the top is well worth the moderate climb for the breathtaking views of Honolulu and the west side of the island and out to sea. On a clear day, you may be able to see Maui to the east. For more Diamond Head hiking information, see Chapter 7. *Take Kalakaua Avenue east to the intersection with Monsarrat Avenue. Turn left onto Monsarrat and follow a bit over a mile until the road becomes Diamond Head Road.*

Hawaii Maritime Center and Aloha Tower Downtown Honolulu

Observe and experience Hawaii's unique maritime history, from Polynesian navigation to Western sailing. The Maritime Center is host to exhibitions on the histories of whaling, surfing, and Polynesian tattoos, as well as home to the *Falls of Clyde*, the world's last fully rigged four-masted sailing ship, and *Hokule'a*, an active voyaging canoe built in the 1970s that is more often abroad, sailing the seas using centuries-old Polynesian navigational methods. Enjoy gazing at the impressive whale skeletons or the 184-foot Aloha Tower, built in 1926 and perhaps the city's best-known landmark of the man-made variety. (Sorry, but you can't go up in it.) *Pier 7, Honolulu Harbor. Museum open daily 8:30 A.M.–5:30 P.M. Admission is $7.50, children are $4.50.* ***808-536-6373.*** *holoholo.org/maritime.*

Honolulu Academy of Art Downtown Honolulu

Founded in 1927 by collector Anna Rice Cooke, and built on the site of her home, the Honolulu Academy of Arts consists of 30 galleries that host a compelling blend of Eastern and Western art; a fitting collection for the Hawaiian islands. Recent additions Southeast Asian & Indian Collections and Arts of the Islamic World complement the large Western collection, featuring well-known artists such as Paul Gaugin. The Henry R. Luce Gallery features changing exhibitions as well as the Hawaiian art collection. *900 S. Beretania Street. Open Tuesday–Saturday 10 A.M.–4:30 P.M.; Sunday 1 P.M.–5 P.M.; Closed Monday. Admission is $7, children under 12 are free.* ***808-532-8700.*** *www.honoluluacademy.org.*

Honolulu Zoo Waikiki

Spread out over 42 acres, the Honolulu Zoo has plenty to offer animal lovers, from their Komodo dragon and nene goose (the Hawaiian state bird) to the recently added 10-acre "African Savannah." If you're in town, make time for the "Zoo by Moonlight" tours, offered every month around the full moon. *The corner of Kapahulu Avenue and Kalakaua Boulevard. Open daily 9 A.M.–4:30 P.M.; Closed Christmas and New Year's Day. Admission is $8 for adults, $1 for children 6–12.* ***808-971-7171.*** *www.honoluluzoo.org.*

ZOO BY MOONLIGHT

It's always disappointing for the kids when they can't see their favorite nocturnal creatures at the zoo—because, well, it's daytime. Honolulu Zoo has come up with a solution, Twilight Tours, which are available each Saturday evening. It's a great chance to see your favorite night critters in action!

'Iolani Palace Downtown Honolulu

The only state residence of royalty in the United States, and the last residence of Hawaiian royalty, the 'Iolani Palace was completed in 1882 and served as the monarch's residence until Queen Lili'uokolani was dethroned in 1893. It then served as Republic and State Capitol until 1969. Don't miss the opulent throne room and Queen Lili'uokolani's room, where she was held captive for eight months after her dethronement. *At the corner of King and Richards streets.* ***808-522-0832.*** *www.iolanipalace.org.*

Kapi'olani Park Waikiki

Host to several other attractions listed in this section, including the Diamond Head Crater and Honolulu Zoo, Kapi'olani Park was dedicated in the 1870s by King Kalakaua. The park stretches over 500 acres and is a great place to spend some time outdoors in the city; on Sunday afternoons you can catch the Royal Hawaiian Band for free in the Kapi'olani Bandstand. *At the east end of Kalakaua Avenue, also bordered by Monsarrat and Paki avenues.*

Kawaiaha'o Church Downtown Honolulu

Built between 1836 and 1842, Kawaiaha'o is the first Christian church in Hawaii and stands out for its New England–style architecture. Its main structure is composed of 14,000 coral slabs, each weighing over 100 pounds. Also located on the church grounds is the mausoleum of King Lunalilo. The church itself seats 4,500 people and still holds services every Sunday. *957 Punchbowl Street. Church Open Monday–Friday from 8:30 A.M.–4 P.M.* ***808-522-1333.*** *www.kawaihao.org.*

Lili'uokalani Gardens Downtown Honolulu

So named because they used to be the property of Queen Lili'uokalani, this seven-and-a-half acre space is devoted to Native Hawaiian plants, as well as a small stream and the Nu'uanu waterfalls. It is a pleasant oasis in the midst of the city and a popular setting for weddings. *N. Kuakini Street. Open daily 7 A.M.–5 P.M., closed on Christmas and New Year's Day.* ***808-522-7060.***

Lyon Arboretum Manoa Valley

See the diversity of plant life Hawaii's tropical climate can support at the Lyon Arboretum, over 200 acres of land managed by the University of Hawaii. The only easily accessible rainforest on O'ahu, the arboretum features heliconia galore, the so-called self-peeling banana and shaving bush tree, and a wide variety of unique and colorful flora from around the Pacific and Southeast Asia. Listen closely on the many trails through the grounds—you might hear the 'amakihi, a bird native to Hawaii. *3860 Manoa Road. Open Monday–Friday, 9 A.M.–4 P.M. Closed Saturday, Sunday, and public holidays.* ***808-988-0456.*** *www.hawaii.edu/lyonarboretum.*

Manoa Chinese Cemetery Manoa Valley

The largest and oldest Chinese cemetery in Hawaii encompasses 34 acres of Manoa Valley. The land for the cemetery was purchased over a period of years, beginning in 1852. The Grave of the Great Ancestor, near the cemetery's highest point, represents all ancestors. The White Mound, just below, contains over 300 remains of early burials before plots were mapped out in the cemetery. These two graves are main sites for rituals during Chi'ing Ming, a Chinese festival to honor the dead which takes place annually on April 5. *2915 East Manoa Road. Open daily dawn to dusk.*

Manoa Falls Manoa Valley

Take an easy mile-and-a-half hike from the end of Manoa Road, through a bamboo rainforest and past the base of the Ko'olau Mountains. The falls themselves tumble 60 feet down a sheer cliff-face into a small pool. Basically, picture an idyllic waterfall in your mind. Yep! This is it! For more Manoa Falls hiking information, see Chapter 7. *Turn left on University from Kapi'olani Boulevard; drive through the University of Hawaii campus and turn right on Manoa Road. Trailhead at end of the road.*

Mission Houses Museum Downtown Honolulu

This museum tells the history of Protestant missionaries in Hawaii from their first journey in 1819 to the written transcription of the Hawaiian language and formal education efforts. The rise of Christianity's foothold in the islands is also chronicled. It is an excellent place to visit to learn more about the Westernization of Hawaii. *553 South King Street. Open Tuesday–Saturday, 10 A.M.–4 P.M. Admission is $10 for adults, $6 for children.* ***808-531-0481.*** *www.missionhouses.org.*

National Memorial Cemetery of the Pacific Downtown Honolulu

This crater was a sacred place, known as the "Hill of Sacrifice" by Native Hawaiians. In 1949 it was dedicated as the National Memorial Cemetery and is today the final resting place for 33,000 men and women who served in the U.S. Armed Forces, including a portion of the dead from Pearl Harbor. The Honolulu Memorial, including a 30-foot statue of the iconic female figure of freedom, "Columbia," was dedicated in 1966 and overlooks the crater. *2177 Puowaina Drive. Open 8 A.M–6:30 P.M. from March 2 through September 29 and 8 A.M–5:30 P.M. from September 30 through March 1.* ***808-532-3720.***

Nu'uanu Cultural District Downtown Honolulu

This community, located between Chinatown and Honolulu's "official" downtown, is the place to be for art connoisseurs, theater junkies, and hipsters of all kinds. Pick up a gallery map and take yourself on a tour, or, if you're in town for First Friday—Honolulu's monthly festival for concerts, art, galleries, and shops—don't miss the late hours, music, special activities and refreshments! *Between Bishop and River/Beretania and Nimitz streets.*

Nu'uanu Pali Lookout Koolau Mountain Range

This site north of the city is famous for more than its great views. In 1795, King Kamehameha sent the O'ahu armies over the steep cliffs of the Ko'olau Mountain Range, claiming his victory in this spot and completing his goal of uniting the Hawaiian islands. From the lookout's impressive height of 1,200 feet above sea level, you can see much of the Windward coast on a clear day. *From Waikiki, take Highway 1 east to the Pali Highway (Route 61) to the crest of the mountains and follow the lookout signs. Open 9 A.M.–4 P.M. daily.*

Royal Mausoleum Downtown Honolulu

Planned by King Kamehameha IV and his wife when their son passed away, the Royal Mausoleum was completed in 1865 and is the resting place for Kings Kamehameha II–V, King Kalakaua and Queen Lili'uokalani. The overseer for the mausoleum is the only hereditary state office, because the duty is based on genealogy by Hawaiian custom. *2261 Nu'uanu Avenue.* ***808-536-7602.***

State Capitol Building Downtown Honolulu

The seat of state government since 1969, the Capitol building is best known for its symbolic representations of the Hawaiian Islands. The water surrounding the building represents the Pacific Ocean, its many pillars stand for palm trees, and the conical shape of the chambers of the legislature are meant to invoke the volcanoes that formed the island chain. *South Beretania Street between Punchbowl and Richards streets. Guided tours are offered Monday–Friday at 1:30 P.M.* ***808-586-0178.***

Statue of King Kamehameha I Downtown Honolulu

This statue is one of four of King Kamehameha the Great. Two others are on the Big Island, and one is in Washington, D.C. This statue—the second made from the same mold by American sculptor Thomas R. Gould, as the first was lost in a shipwreck—was dedicated by King Kalakaua in 1883. It stands eight-and-a-half feet tall and depicts Kamehameha in royal garb, one arm extended in aloha, the other holding a spear to symbolize Hawaii's willingness to defend itself. On June 11, Kamehameha Day, the statue is adorned with flower leis. *957 Punchbowl Street.* ***808-522-1333.***

USS *Arizona* Visitors Center and Memorial Pearl Harbor

On December 7, 1941, 1,177 U.S. soldiers were killed on the USS *Arizona* in the Japanese attack prompting official United States entry into World

War II. The ship today doubles as tomb for 1,100 of those soldiers and a memorial, dedicated in 1962. *One Arizona Memorial Drive (off Route 99). Open daily 7:30 A.M.–5 P.M.. Closed Thanksgiving, Christmas, and New Year's Day.* ***808-422-5664.*** *www.nps.gov/usar.*

The memorials at Pearl Harbor are the top tourist attractions on O'ahu, visited by thousands of people daily. You can beat the worst of the crowds by getting to Pearl Harbor as early as possible in the morning.

USS Battleship *Missouri* Memorial Pearl Harbor

Known as "Mighty Mo," the USS *Missouri* famously hosted the Japanese ministers who signed the Instruments of Surrender in 1945. The memorial opened in 1999, and about half the ship is open to the public. Explore the ship yourself or take a guided tour. *Catch a shuttle to the* Missouri *from the USS* Bowfin *Museum. Open daily 9 A.M.–5 P.M.. Closed Thanksgiving, Christmas, and New Year's Day. Admission: adults $16 and children $8.* ***1-877-MIGHTYMO.*** *www.ussmissouri.com.*

USS *Bowfin* Submarine Museum and Park Pearl Harbor

Known as the "Pearl Harbor Avenger," today the USS *Bowfin* Submarine Museum offers visitors a glimpse of the United States' response to Japanese attacks by sea. Launched on December 7, 1942, exactly one year after the attack on Pearl Harbor, the *Bowfin* completed nine war patrols during World War II. The museum features a variety of exhibits on U.S. submarines, as well as a Poseidon C-3 missile that visitors can examine. *Adjacent to the USS* Arizona *Visitor's Center and Memorial. 11 Arizona Memorial Drive. Open daily 8 A.M.–5 P.M.; admission: adults $10, children (4 and older) are $3, and children under 4 are not admitted.* ***808-423-1341.*** *www.bowfin.org.*

Waikiki Aquarium Waikiki

Founded in 1904, which makes it the third oldest aquarium in the United States, the Waikiki Aquarium focuses on aquatic life around Hawaii and in the tropical Pacific. Featuring over 420 species, the aquarium is a great way to get up-close and personal with reef sharks and the endangered Hawaiian monk seal, along with all the brightly colored reef fish you could ask for. *2777 Kalakaua Avenue. Open daily 9 A.M.–4:30 P.M. Special hours on Thanksgiving and New Year's Day. Closed Christmas. Admission: adults $9, youth ages 13–17 $4, children 5–12 $2, and children 4 and under are free.* ***808-923-9741.*** *www.waquarium.org.*

Honolulu's Top Beaches

There are only two beaches to speak of in Honolulu proper—**Prince Kuhio Beach** in Waikiki and **Ala Moana Beach Park**—but we'd be very remiss not to speak of them. Check out Chapter 7 for more beach options on the island.

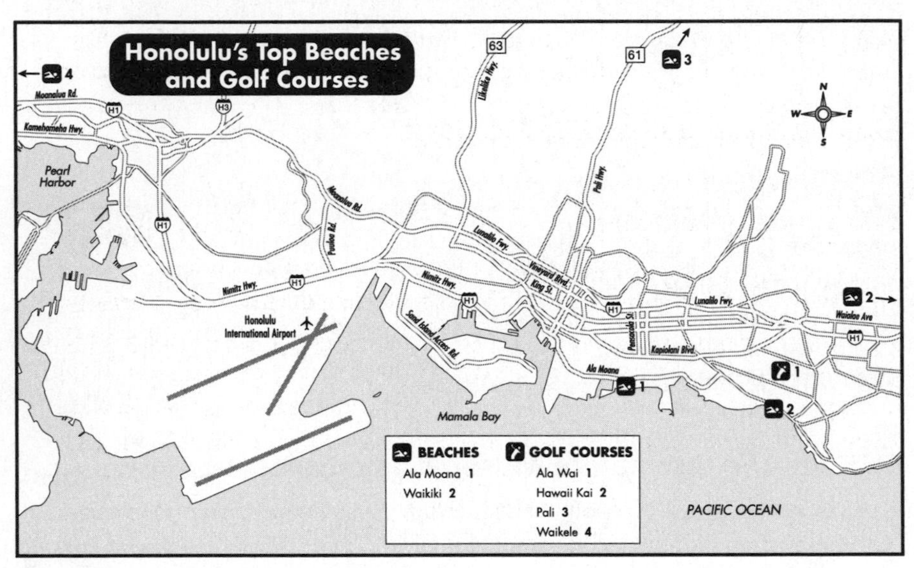

Honolulu's top beaches and golf courses.

Great Dining with Atmosphere: The Best Places to Eat

Gourmands will find more than enough options to satisfy both the sophisticated palate and the empty belly in Honolulu, where designer dining and the backstreet gem are equally at home among the cosmopolitan residents and visitors. Whether your pleasure is some of the most innovative fusion cuisine the Pacific has to offer, authentic Asian dining, "da local grinds," or fine American fare, Honolulu fully lives up to its city status for excellent dining options.

Here are our picks for some of the best restaurants in Honolulu.

Ala Moana

Alan Wong's Ala Moana *Hawaiian/Pacific Rim* $$$$

Reflecting the true melting pot of ethnicities and cultures in the Hawaiian islands, this elegant restaurant's exhibition kitchen prepares some of the freshest, original carnivorous delights on the island—duck prepared three ways, for example, or "da bag," a foil packet with seafood, vegetables, and kalua pork cooked together to succulent perfection. Desserts often feature fresh tropical fruit, so save room! *1857 S. King Street. Open daily 5 P.M.–10 P.M.* ***808-949-2526.*** *www.alanwongs.com.*

Assaggio Ala Moana *Italian* $$$

With four locations, this popular chain has done even better since coming to the big city after its successful start in suburban O'ahu. Giant portions at very reasonable prices make this Sicilian restaurant a good choice after a strenuous day of sightseeing or beach-lounging. The seafood dishes, as with most good restaurants in Hawaii, are the stars, and are served with a wide variety of sauces; but you shouldn't overlook the many lovely chicken and veal options, either. *1450 Ala Moana Boulevard in the Ala Moana Center. Open daily 11 A.M.–3 P.M., Sunday–Thursday 4:30 P.M.–9:30 P.M., Friday–Saturday 4:30 P.M.–10 P.M.* ***808-942-3446.***

Singha Thai Cuisine Ala Moana *Thai* $$

Singha is a great place for Thai, not just Thai food, but the Thai experience. The restaurant, just off of Ala Moana Boulevard, features extravagant statues and a plethora of fresh flowers as its décor along with nightly performances by the Royal Thai Dancers as its entertainment. The food is a combination of Thai and Asian fusion; try the Ahi katsu with wasabi Thai curry sauce for an appetizer, or the Spicy Siamese Fighting Fish for a main. *1910 Ala Moana Boulevard. Open daily for dinner 4 P.M.–10 P.M.* ***808-941-2898.*** *www.singhathai.com.*

Sorabol Ala Moana *Korean* 

This is the place to go for some of the best Korean in Honolulu, with multiple dining options—a cocktail lounge, private dining, and table seating are all available. First-timers rest assured, the menu comes with English translations. And the late-night hours make this a perfect stop for the after-club munchies! Try the steamed butterfish. *805 Ke'eaumoku Street. Open daily 6 P.M.–2 A.M.* ***808-947-3113.***

Zippy's Ala Moana *Hawaiian/American* $

This O'ahu chain is a safe bet for something quick and filling of the "ono grinds" variety. Just hungry? Go for the Teriyaki Meatloaf or the Miso Garlic Chicken. Feeling adventurous? Try the pig feet soup or Zip Min. And, of course, there's always Zippy's famous chili! *In the Sears at the Ala Moana Center, 105 South King. Open Monday–Friday 8 A.M.–5 P.M.* ***808-973-0880.*** *www.zippys.com.*

Downtown Honolulu

Akasaka Downtown Honolulu *Japanese* $$

A little bit off the beaten path in downtown Honolulu, Akasaka is a local favorite, and often crowded with regulars. Small, with a cozy ambience, this is an excellent choice for sushi and daily specials at extremely reasonable prices. This is a great choice for a lunch break during a day of sightseeing. *1646 Kona Street. Open for lunch Monday–Saturday 11 A.M.–2:30 P.M., dinner Monday–Saturday 5 P.M.–2 A.M. and Sunday 5 P.M.–midnight.* ***808-942-4466.***

Auntie Pasto's Downtown Honolulu *Italian* $$

This local favorite has been around for over 20 years and offers "ono" food in a local atmosphere—except instead of chicken katsu and moco loco, you're eating fresh manicotti and eggplant parmesan. The cacciuco (an Italian seafood stew) and gnocchi, house signature dishes, are highly recommended. Also, try the red pepper calamari or gorgonzola bread for starters. On a good night you might have a wait in store—they don't take reservations. *1099 Beretania Street. Open Monday–Thursday, 11 A.M.–10:30 P.M., Friday 11 A.M.–11 P.M., Saturday 4 P.M.–11 P.M., and Sunday 4 P.M.–10:30 P.M.* ***808-523-8855.*** *www.auntiepastos.com.*

Kiawe Grill Downtown Honolulu *Hawaiian* 

Kiawe is a good place to try Asian-style barbecue—or to refresh your memory, if you've tried it before. As the name suggests, kiawe wood is used to grill all the meat served here. If you're not in the mood for barbecue (although you should at least check out the Korean self-serve vegetable bar), try the ostrich and buffalo burgers served on a bed of rice or American style with steak fries. *1311 N. King Street. Open Monday–Saturday 10 A.M.–9 P.M., Sunday 10 A.M.–8 P.M.* ***808-841-5577.***

Marbella Downtown Honolulu *Mediterranean* $$

Try a different kind of sun-inspired menu at Marbella, a restaurant that has received nothing but praise since opening in 2003. While lamb is, of course, well represented, there are plenty of vegetarian options here, too—a relief to herbivores in this meat-heavy dining environment. Try the delectable spanakopita or the puréed lentil soup. *1680 Kapi'olani Boulevard. Open for lunch Monday–Friday 11:30 A.M.–2 P.M.. Open for dinner daily 5:30 P.M.–10 P.M.* ***808-943-4353.***

Ninnikuya, the Garlic Restaurant Downtown Honolulu *Specialty* $$$

The name says it all up front—so if you're not a fan, you've been warned. That said, garlic gorgers will swoon at what's on offer. The chef goes through 20 pounds of garlic a night so that you can enjoy hot-stone filet mignon with garlic mashed potatoes, roasted garlic with blue cheese, and even garlic gelato (you read it right!) in a cozy setting. Outdoor dining available. *3196 Waialae Avenue. Open Tuesday–Saturday 5:30 P.M.–10:30 P.M., Sunday 5:30 P.M.–10:30 P.M.* ***808-735-0784.***

Ono Hawaiian Foods Downtown Honolulu *Hawaiian/American* $

There really is no substitution for Ono Hawaiian Food. If you want kalua pig, spam and poi on the side, and haupia for dessert, there's really only one place to go if you're in Honolulu (and, some would argue, in Hawaii, full stop). If you're an aficionado, go for the tripe stew. *726 Kapahulu Avenue. Open 11 A.M.–7:45 P.M. Monday–Saturday.* ***808-737-2275.***

Roy's Downtown Honolulu *Pacific Rim* 

Chef Roy Yamaguchi's restaurant is not just a less pricey alternative to Alan Wong's; it's got great food in its own right, and an energetic atmosphere. The seafood dishes are guaranteed to excite and satisfy your appetite. Try some of "Roy's Classics," including the Wood Grilled Szechuan Spiced Baby Back Pork Ribs as an appetizer, and for an entrée, the roasted macadamia nut mahimahi. *6600 Kalaniana'ole Highway. Dinner Monday–Thursday 5:30 P.M.–9:30 P.M., Friday 5:30 P.M.–10 P.M., Saturday 5 P.M.–10 P.M., Sunday 5 P.M.–9:30 P.M.* ***808-396-7697.*** *www.roysrestaurant.com.*

12th Avenue Grill Downtown Honolulu *American* $$

This upscale diner offers comfort food in comfortable surroundings—the mac and cheese is rightfully renowned, as is the kim chee steak. For dessert, the sticky toffee pudding cake is your best bet. For those with a lighter appetite, the butter lettuce salad with blue cheese, dried cranberries, and walnuts will do you right. At 12th Avenue Grill you don't need reservations and you don't need to dress up; you just need to come hungry. *1145C 12th Avenue. Open Monday–Thursday 5:30 P.M.–9 P.M., Friday–Saturday 5:30 P.M.–10 P.M.* ***808-732-9469.*** *www.12thavegrill.com.*

Waikiki

Eggs 'n Things Waikiki *American* $

A local breakfast staple, Eggs 'n Things has healthy options—bran pancakes, for example—but you're on vacation, so spoil yourself! The omelets and fruit crepes are a great way to recover from a late night out or to fortify yourself for a busy day. Be sure to try all five of their specialty syrups: guava, boysenberry, coconut, honey, and fresh fruit. This is a great place to get your breakfast on, at 3 A.M. or 9 A.M. *1911 Kalakaua Avenue. Open daily 11 P.M.–2 P.M. Closed afternoons.* ***808-949-0820.*** *www.eggsnthings.com.*

Hy's Steak House Waikiki *European/American* $$$$

You might not be on the mainland anymore, but that doesn't mean you can't get a good steak. In fact, this might be the classiest steak you'll ever have—a dark, intimate interior puts you in mind of Old Europe. Tuxedoed waiters prepare your salad tableside and serve you all the best cuts, from prime rib to T-bone, which you can have broiled over native kiawe wood. There are a few fusion dishes for those less beef-oriented, and mellow live island music from Wednesday to Saturday. An upscale treat for a night off from seafood. *2440 Kuhio Avenue. Open Monday–Friday 6 P.M.–10 P.M., Saturday and Sunday 5:30 P.M.–10 P.M.* ***808-922.5555.*** *www.hyshawaii.com.*

Keo's in Waikiki Waikiki *Thai* $$

Keo's has been serving up reliable pad thai and panang curry for 30 years, turning on locals and celebrities alike to Thai cuisine. Centrally located to Waikiki hotels, Keo's has a casual island ambiance and an extensive menu. All of the fresh herbs and spices at the restaurant are grown on owner Keo Sananikone's farms on the North Shore. *2028 Kuhio Avenue. Open daily for breakfast and lunch 7 A.M.–2 P.M. Open for dinner Sunday–Thursday 5 P.M.–10:30 P.M., Friday–Saturday 5 P.M.–11 P.M.* ***808-951-9355.*** *www.keosthaicuisine.com.*

Kyo-ya Waikiki *Japanese* $$$

For fine Japanese dining in a relaxed, authentic atmosphere, Kyo-ya is your best bet. Conveniently located in Waikiki, Kyo-ya offers delectable sushi and sashimi, and some of the best tempura you'll ever have outside of Japan. You can choose from the Take Niwa dining room on the ground floor or private tatami rooms upstairs. Connoisseurs of Japanese cuisine should be sure to try the simmering nabemono dishes. *2057 Kalakaua Avenue. Open for lunch Monday–Saturday 11 A.M.–1:30 P.M., dinner 5:30 P.M.–9:15 P.M.* ***808-947-3911.*** *www.restauranteur.com/kyoya/index.htm.*

La Mer Waikiki *Pacific Rim* $$$$$

French cuisine with a Hawaiian twist, La Mer is One Big Splurge—but, any real foodie will tell you, it is worth every penny. From the wine list to the ocean view, this dining experience is opulent and will make any special occasion unforgettable. Try the three-fish tartare (salmon, hamachi, and ahi) for an appetizer and the Big Island lobster or roasted venison for an entrée. *2199 Kalia Road, Halekulani Hotel. Open daily 6 P.M.–10 P.M.* ***808-923-2311.*** *www.halekulani.com.*

Entertainment and Nightlife

You want entertainment? We got your entertainment right here! Honolulu is arguably the best destination for admirers of theater and dance, music lovers, and clubgoers in the Hawaiian islands. Take advantage of the close proximity of city hotspots and visit a few in an evening. Why not? You're on vacation. For current listings check out the *Honolulu Weekly* (www.honoluluweekly.com) and the *Honolulu Advertiser* (www.honoluluadvertiser.com), or the free tourist guides *This Week Oahu* and *Spotlight's Oahu Gold.*

Live Music

Most of the Waikiki resort bars listed under "Cocktails with a View" offer quality live music every night, and this is an excellent place to start if you're looking for a little island flavor. Here are a few of our other favorites:

Anna Banana's Downtown Honolulu
2440 S. Beretania Street. ***808-946-5190.***

Brew Moon Ala Moana
1200 Ala Moana Boulevard, Ward Centre. ***808-593-0088.*** *www.brewmoon.com.*

Veranda Waikiki
5000 Kahala Avenue (in the Kahala Mandarin Oriental Hotel), Honolulu. ***808-739-8888.*** *www.kahalresort.com.*

Wave Waikiki Waikiki
1877 Kalakaua Avenue, Honolulu. ***808-941-0424.*** *www.wavewaikiki.com.*

DJs and Dancing

If you just want to get down with your own bad self (and hopefully a friend), Honolulu offers plenty of places where you can shake that booty all evening long. Here are a few of our favorites:

Hula's Bar and Lei Stand Downtown Honolulu
134 Kapahulu Avenue, 2nd Floor. ***808-923-0669.*** *www.hulas.com.*

Nashville Waikiki Waikiki
2330 Kuhio Avenue. ***808-926-7911.*** *www.nashvillewaikiki.com.*

Ocean Club Ala Moana
500 Ala Moana Boulevard, Restaurant Row. ***808-531-8444.*** *www.oceanclubonline.com*

Venus Nightclub Ala Moana
1349 Kapi'olani Boulevard. ***808-955-2640.***

Theater and Performing Arts

Honolulu is the center of the performing arts for the islands. The innovative professional dance troupes **Iona Contemporary Dance Theatre** (**808-262-0110,** www.iona360.com) and **Tau Dance Theater** (**808-227-7718**) often perform in town at the **Hawaii Theatre (808-528-0506,** www.hawaiitheatre.com). This historic theatre is the focal point for performance in the city, with seating for 1,400 people. The Hawaii Theatre also features traditional music revues and modern musicals.

For more local entertainment, try the **Diamond Head Theatre (808-733-0274,** www.diamondheadtheatre.com), Hawaii's oldest performing arts center and host of plays and other community events. Those with kids will enjoy the **Honolulu Theatre for Youth (808-839-9885,** www.htyweb.org), which just celebrated its 50th year in 2005. The HTY puts on everything from reworked fairy tales, to theatrical versions of Polynesian and Asian literature, to an annual local writers' showcase.

If you're in town between February and May, this is officially "Hawaii Arts Season," with plenty of special events around town. Check local listings or www.visit-oahu.com for more information.

The Best Lu'aus

While one of the best lu'aus on O'ahu is at the **Polynesian Cultural Center** an hour away (see Chapter 7 for more details), you can still enjoy the full lu'au experience in or very close to Honolulu. Here are our top recommendations.

Paradise Cove Lu'au Ko'Olina

A short drive west of Waikiki, this lu'au on the Paradise Cove resort also is regarded as one of the best on O'ahu. Set on 10 acres of beachfront property, Paradise Cove is worth the trip for the sunset if nothing else—although the Aloha mai tai you'll receive on your arrival is nice, and the fire knife dance that closes the evening's performance is a real heart-stopper. *Held nightly 5 P.M. to 9 P.M. At the Ko'Olina resort, 92-1480 Aliinui Drive. Free pickup from Waikiki hotels at 4 P.M.* ***1-808-842-5911*** *or* ***1-800-775-2683.*** *www.paradisecove.com.*

Creations: A Polynesian Odyssey Waikiki

You'll find the most impressive performance in Honolulu at the Creations lu'au, at the Sheraton Hotel in Waikiki. This show creatively imagines the origins of Polynesian culture, beginning with recreations of volcanic eruptions and ending in a fire dance. There are cocktail and dinner shows available, so if you're not so keen on the food, you can still enjoy the show. *In the Sheraton Princess Kaiulani Hotel, 120 Kaiulani Avenue. Held Tuesday, Thursday–Sunday.* ***808-931-4660.***

A hula show is standard fare for a Hawaiian lu'au.

(Photo courtesy of HVCB/Joe Solem)

Magic of Polynesia Waikiki

While not a lu'au, strictly speaking, Jon Hirokawa's nightly show belongs in the same category for its exciting, high-energy performance—and, like lu'aus, it is a dinner performance with a Hawaiian-influenced menu. Hula dance and Hawaiian music blend with an illusionist show worthy of Las Vegas. This show sells out, and with good reason; so if you're interested, book ahead of time! *At the Ohana Waikiki Beachcomber, 2300 Kalakua Avenue.* ***808-971-4321.*** *www.waikikibeachcomber.com/magic.html.*

Royal Hawaiian Lu'au Waikiki

With the setting sun over Waikiki Beach and the Diamond Head Crater in the background, it's hard to imagine a more dramatic setting for an evening of large-scale dining and entertainment. The buffet includes island favorites like Teriyaki Beef, and the revue features song and dance from around the South Pacific. The full lu'au experience is right in Waikiki. *At the Royal Hawaiian Hotel, 2259 Kalakaua Avenue. Held every Monday evening.* ***808-661-6655.*** *www.royal-hawaiian.com.*

Shopping in Honolulu

People from all over the Hawaiian Islands come to Honolulu for one thing: the shopping. Here you'll find a quality and diversity sorely lacking on the neighbor islands—and some great deals, too. While the large shopping centers are enticing, make sure to save time for some early-morning shopping in Chinatown before you leave.

Ala Moana Center Ala Moana

This state-of-the-art center has fine dining, daily entertainment ... oh, right, and shopping, lots of shopping. Four department stores and every luxury apparel, jewelry, and shoe store you can think of—from the everyday **Footlocker** to the upscale **Jimmy Choo.** There's even a shopping shuttle, which stops at most resorts and runs about every seven minutes, which means there's no excuse not to go! *1450 Ala Moana Boulevard.* ***808-955-9517.*** *www.alamoanacenter.com.*

Waikele Outlets *Waikele*

Talk about one-stop shopping; this shopping center about 15 miles outside of Honolulu has 50 outlets to choose from, including the **Brooks Brothers Factory Store, Calvin Klein,** and **Barneys New York,** along with Hawaiian stores **Local Motion, Hawaiian Moon,** and **Blue Hawaii Surf.** You can even arrange for a group tour of the outlets for additional savings. *Take the H-1 out of Honolulu for 15 miles; the outlets are at Exit 7. www.premiumoutlets.com/waikele.*

Manoa Marketplace *Manoa*

This shopping center has island staples **Safeway** and **Long's Drugs,** along with 60 other shops and restaurants for your perusal. It makes a good snack stop or a brief shopping trip on your way back to Honolulu. *2756 E. Manoa Road. Take University Avenue north from Waikiki or the H-1 about one mile. Bear slightly right onto O'ahu Avenue, then turn right onto Manoa Road.*

Local Markets

When it comes to browsing local markets, you'll want to check out **Chinatown** in downtown Honolulu. You will find it located between Beretania and King streets, River Street, and Nu'uanu Avenue. Chinatown technically has four markets: the **Maunakea Marketplace, Oahu Market, Kehaulike Market,** and **Chinese Cultural Plaza Open Market.** It's best to come to the markets in the morning to see them at their bustling heights, full of exotic offerings—live eel and fish, chicken feet, kim chee (pickled cabbage), and char siu (roasted pork). Wander further afield and find plenty of specialty shops to tickle your fancy.

Another great spot is the **International Market Place** (2330 Kalakaua Avenue, **808-971-2080,** www.internationalmarketplacewaiki.com), conveniently located in Waikiki, the International Market Place is a well-designed open-air market where you can take care of all your souvenir shopping—T-shirts, jewelry, key chains—in one go. The **Waikiki Town Center,** directly behind the market (2301 Kuhio Avenue) offers more of the same.

Enjoying the Very Best Activities in Honolulu

There are literally thousands of different things to do in Honolulu, and probably 70 percent of those are worthwhile. In fact, we probably could give you an encyclopedia of Honolulu activities … maybe 10 volumes. However, for your convenience we've boiled down and filtered this myriad of choices to a few pages of the essentials—your best options for enjoying your stay in Honolulu. You'll find even more recommended activities for nearby areas in Chapter 7.

Sightseeing Tours

Honolulu could be considered the tourist Mecca. With this in mind, you're spoiled for choices in terms of sightseeing tours on offer, and you'll find plenty to sign up for right out of your hotel. Some of you, however, may want to pick and choose for yourselves, so here are some options. We stick to tours that stay close to Honolulu. For more extensive tours of O'ahu, see Chapter 7.

An outfit called **Hawaii Active (1-866-766-6284**) offers a seven-hour USS *Missouri*, *Arizona* Memorial, and Pearl Harbor tour, offered seven days a week—a must-do for history buffs. The tour also includes a visit to historic downtown Honolulu, passing the 'Iolani Palace and State Capitol. **Aloha Top Ten (1-888-909-0010**) provides **Honolulu's Hidden Waterfall Adventure,** which introduces you to the natural spaces within the city and beyond, along with downtown attractions, on a morning or afternoon tour. For the local touch, try **E Noa Tours (808-591-2561;** www.enoa.com), which has been in business for 30 years. They offer Pearl Harbor and city highlight tours, as well as a shopping tour to Waikele outlets.

Barefoot Tours (1-800-980-0559; www.barefoottours.com) knows O'ahu extremely well and will set you up with a large array of itineraries around the island. In fact, they'll totally customize your vacation for you if you wish, setting you up with local companies for everything from bus tours around the island to helicopter tours, bicycling, horseback riding, surfing, and a myriad of other activities.

Polynesian Adventure Tours (808-833-3000 or **1-800-622-3011;** www.polyad.com) is another of the more economical choices, operating an impeccably maintained fleet of 25 passenger mini-coaches that specialize in one-day island round-trips and more in-depth explorations of Diamond Head, the Polynesian Cultural Center, and other destinations. Rates run from approximately $53 to $79. **Roberts Hawaii (1-866-898-2519;** www.robertshawaii.com) is the Big Daddy of Hawaiian tour companies, with just about every conceivable type of tour you could imagine, on every island, and in every kind of vehicle known to humankind. Roberts is predictable, but also dependable and reasonably priced.

Bicycle Tours

The City and County of Honolulu has been working to make the city a bicycle-friendly place, implementing a Honolulu Bicycle Master Plan that includes several bikeway projects in various stages of completion. These include **Kalakaua Avenue Bike Lane,** the **Paki Avenue Bike Path,** the **McCully Bikeway Promenade,** and others. You can get the latest maps and information by contacting the Honolulu Bicycle Master Plan Bicycle Coordinator at the Department of Transportation Services, 711 Kapiolani Boulevard, #1200 Honolulu, HI 96813, or by calling **808-527-5044.** You also can download maps at www.honolulu.gov/dts/bikeway.

Honolulu and the rest of O'ahu offer some memorable bicycling options.

(Photo courtesy of HVCB/Ron Dahlquist)

Bike Hawaii (1-877-682-7433, www.bikehawaii.com) offers city-wide tours, as well as hike/bike combo tours that range from three hours to all day in length. **Hawaii Fun Tours (1-877-742-7893)** offers a multitude of tours, including a downhill ride that begins at 1,800 feet above Waikiki and descends through cool forests.

Do you just want to do some two-wheeling on your own? You can score a reasonably priced bike rental at **Planet Surf** at 159 Kailulani Avenue in Waikiki (**808-924-9050**).

Enjoying Outdoor Honolulu

Honolulu is a big cosmopolitan city, but it *is* located in paradise, after all. The city is ringed by world-class natural beauty, with manicured parks and semi-wild valleys extending from urban areas into the mountains north of town. And, there's surfing, golf, whale watching, snorkeling, and much more.

The Best Golf Courses

While many of O'ahu's best courses are anywhere from half an hour to an hour's drive from Honolulu (see Chapter 7), there are some options closer to the city:

Ala Wai Golf Course, Honolulu. Located next to Waikiki with views of Diamond Head and the Ko'olau Mountains, this 18-hole municipal course provides quality golf at good prices without having to drive out of town. It also boasts a driving range and a pro shop—and you can't beat the economical greens fees. *18 holes. Par 70, 5,817 yards. 404 Kapahulu Avenue, Honolulu. $42 greens fee (only $12 on weekdays, $16 on weekends, if you have a golf ID card).* ***808-733-7387.*** *www.co.honolulu.hi.us/des/golf/golf.htm.*

Hawaii Kai Golf Course, Hawaii Kai. Located 13 miles away from Waikiki in the suburban area of Hawaii Kai, this facility has both Executive and Championship courses and offers views of the ocean (and even Moloka'i and Maui on a clear day). Ocean winds make for an enjoyable but challenging round. *Executive Course: 18 holes. Par 55, 2,323 yards. Championship Course: 18 holes. Par 72, 6,686 yards. 8902 Kalanianaole Highway, Hawaii Kai. $110 greens fee weekend, $100 weekday.* ***808-395-2358.*** *www.hawaiikaigolf.com.*

Pali Golf Course, Waipahu. This lovely course makes use of the natural terrain with some nice views of the mountains and Kaneohe Bay, and is a pleasure on a sunny day. *18 holes. Par 72, 6,494 yards. 45–050 Kamehameha Highway, Kaneohe. $50 greens fee.* ***808-266-7612.*** *www.co.honolulu.hi.us/des/golf/pali.htm.*

Waikele Golf Club, Waipahu. This 18-hole course, designed by internationally acclaimed course architect Ted Robinson, is about 30 minutes west of Honolulu, and overlooks the ocean, Diamond Head Crater, and the Ko'olau and Waianae Mountains. *18 holes. Par 72. 6,261 yards. 94-200 Paioa Place, Waipahu. Greens fees range from $19 after 3 P.M. on weekdays to $108 on weekends.* ***808-676-9000.*** *www.golfwaikele.com.*

GOLF IN HAWAII: THE BEST

Challenging designs along with awesome mountain and ocean scenery give Hawaii some of the best golf courses in the world. In fact, many of Hawaii's top courses are regularly cited in leading golf magazines, while the PGA Tour, the Champions Tour, and LPGA all make it a point to play here more than once a year. The Sony Open and Mercedes-Benz Championship take place every January or February, while PGA Grand Slam and other contests stop in the islands frequently. All of this makes Hawaii a sort of nirvana for the avid golfer.

Whale-Watching Out of Honolulu

Pacific humpback whales visit Hawaii's waters by the thousands from November to March, migrating close to 3,500 miles from their Alaskan summer feeding waters in order to mate and have their calves. In season you can spot them from many parts of the O'ahu shoreline, and most of O'ahu's whale-watching cruises leave right from Honolulu. For information on the top whale-watching companies, see Chapter 7.

Hiking Near Honolulu

Numerous trails in O'ahu's mountains start right on the edges of the city. You can get complete trail maps, recommendations, and necessary permits by visiting the **Department of Parks and Recreation,** 650 King Street in Honolulu (**808-523-4525**), at the satellite city hall at the **Ala Moana Center,** 1450 Ala Moana Boulevard (**808-973-2600**), or at the **Department of Land and Natural Resources** office at 1151 Punchbowl Street in downtown Honolulu (**808-587-0166;** www.state.hi.us/dlnr). For a rundown on the top trail choices, see Chapter 7.

Surfing, Snorkeling, Fishing, and More

Although the rest of O'ahu is better known for its outdoor offerings, you still can experience some of the best Hawaii has to offer in or very near to Honolulu. Beginners and veterans alike will enjoy the surfing, scuba, and snorkeling.

- **Surfing:** Waikiki, with its gentle surf, is an excellent location for those who want to try surfing for the first time. Lessons are available seven days a week from **Hans Hedemann Surf School (808-924-7778;** www.hhsurf.com) or **Hawaiian Watersports (808-262-5483;** www.hawaiiwatersports.com).
- **Sailing/Parasailing:** If you're interested in sailing while in Honolulu, try **Hawaii Sailing Adventures (808-596-9696)** or **Adventure Sailing Hawaii (808-224-6213;** www.sailinghawaii.com). No, despite the similarity in names, they're not the same place. Both establishments offer package deals, including sunset cruises and refreshments.
- **Snorkeling and Scuba:** Ten miles east of Waikiki along Kalaniana'ole Highway, you'll find **Hanauma Bay** and **Hanauma Bay Dive Tours (808-256-8956;** www.hanaumabaydivetours.com), which takes groups out for snorkeling and diving four days a week. The odds are very good you'll see sea turtles during your underwater adventure.
- **Fishing:** Honolulu has a few good options for fishing within the city. Try **Kuu Huapala Sports Fishing (808-596-0918)** for big game fish, or the **Sea Verse III (808-591-8840)** for more options, including reef fishing.

Many people think they're going to land in Honolulu, spend a day or two, and then high-tail it out of town to more scenic Hawaiian locales. But this gleaming white city backed up against verdant green mountains never ceases to surprise with its varied and rich urban *and* scenic experiences. No doubt, you could spend your whole vacation here. But there's so much more to see!

Chapter 6

Relaxing in O'ahu

In This Chapter

- O'ahu's geography and character
- Getting around O'ahu
- Deciding where to stay on the island
- O'ahu's best lodging choices

The ancient Hawaiians called **O'ahu** "The Gathering Place," and it's an appropriate nickname. Of all of the Hawaiian islands, it is the most populated—home to some 900,000 people, just under three-quarters of all of the residents of the state and all of her islands.

When most people think of O'ahu, they think of Hawaii's big capital city, **Honolulu,** and its famous **Waikiki Beach** (covered in Chapters 4 and 5).

That's the image, but the reality of O'ahu may surprise you. Despite the urbanity of greater Honolulu, the presence of the only "interstate" highways in Hawaii, and the relatively large population, O'ahu is also a place where you actually can relax on a quiet beach under a palm, enjoy the mist of a tropical waterfall, or perhaps take a hike into the mountains.

The world's top surfers flock to O'ahu's North Shore.

(Photo courtesy of HVCB/Kirk Lee Aeder)

Snapshot

O'ahu:

Size: 597 square miles

Population: 903,000

Number of Annual Visitors: 5 million

Coastline: 120 miles

Highest Point: Mt. Ka'ala, 4,040 feet

Number of Public and Resort Golf Courses: 14

Number of Accessible Beaches: 69

Transportation from the Airport

See Chapter 5 for complete information on transportation available at Honolulu Airport.

What Transportation Costs in O'ahu

Destination	*Taxi*	*Limo*	*Shuttle*	*Bus*
Waikiki	$35–40	$70–100	$9	$2
Downtown	$35–40	$70–100	$9	$2

Destination	*Taxi*	*Limo*	*Shuttle*	*Bus*
Pearl Harbor	$15	$50	$5–10	$2
Diamond Head	$35	$80	N/A	$2
Kahalu'u	$85	$120	N/A	$2
Kailua	$45	$100	N/A	$2
Sunset Beach	$85	$100	N/A	$2
Ko'Olina Resort	$45	$65	N/A	$2

Getting Your Bearings: Island Locales

O'ahu is one of the few places on Earth where at any given time you are less than an hour's drive from a palm-lined beach with some of the world's best surf, a rugged extinct volcano, a lavish Victorian royal palace, several tropical waterfalls, a misty rainforest, hot and arid plains, and one of the planet's most cosmopolitan cities.

O'ahu is basically shaped like a wedge, with the narrow end in the east and a broad backside pointing toward the setting sun. It is divided by two low mountain ranges that run roughly northwest to southeast—the **Ko'olau Mountains** along the northern length of the island and the **Wai'anae Mountains** in the west—with a central valley in between.

O'AHU VISITORS INFORMATION

Hawaii Visitor's Bureau, 2270 Kalakaua Avenue, Suite 801, Honolulu; **808-923-1811;** www.gohawaii.com.

O'ahu Visitor's Bureau, 735 Bishop Street, Suite 1872, Honolulu; **808-524-0722;** www.visit-oahu.com.

Metropolitan Honolulu, running from Pearl Harbor in the west to **Diamond Head** in the east, dominates O'ahu's south coast. (See Chapters 4 and 5 for detailed information on Honolulu.) The northeastern coastline faces the moist prevailing trade winds, and is in fact called "Windward O'ahu." The eastern point of the island is generally referred to as "Southeast O'ahu," while the northwest coastal area, site of the famous international big wave competitions, is simply called "The North Shore." The far western side of the island, called "Leeward O'ahu," is usually sunny and dry.

Honolulu

Snapshot

Honolulu:

- Ala Moana
- Aloha Tower
- Bishop Museum
- Diamond head
- 'Iolani Palace
- Pearl Harbor
- Waikiki Beach

Backed by verdant green mountains and extending along a good part of O'ahu's southern coast, Honolulu is Hawaii's largest city at around a million residents. Stretching from such iconic Hawaiian locales as Pearl Harbor in the west, along the famous, hotel-lined Waikiki Beach, to the extinct volcano cone Diamond Head in the east, Honolulu is the center of culture, entertainment, cultural diversity, and all things urban in Hawaii.

Southeast O'ahu

Just a few minutes by car east of Waikiki, this portion of O'ahu is a bit less exotic than other parts of the island, with plenty of typical suburban scenes closer in to the city. It still has plenty to offer, and it is a great direction to head for the afternoon if you're staying around Honolulu. Here you can climb to the rugged heights of the iconic Diamond Head, snorkel through one of Hawaii's best coral reefs at **Hanauma Bay,** hang out while watching whales at lovely Sandy Beach, or check out the 60-foot-high plume of seawater that gushes regularly from **Halona Blowhole.** This area, combined with a trip through the eastern portion of Windward O'ahu, makes for a great circle route. (See the itineraries in Chapter 7.)

Snapshot

Southeast O'ahu Destinations:

- Diamond Head
- Halona Blowhole
- Hanauma Bay
- Kahala

See Chapter 7 for more information and itineraries.

Lanikai Beach in Windward O'ahu is one of the island's best.

(Photo courtesy of HVCB/Joe Solem)

Windward O'ahu

Drive 20 minutes or so northeast from Honolulu through the mountains, and you'll find yourself in a different world—one of verdant green hillsides, a dramatic coastline, and misty—often rainy—weather. From the golf resorts of **Kanuku** in the northwest to beautiful **Kaneohe Bay,** to spectacular **Makap'u Point** in the southeast, this region is O'ahu at its most wild and naturally gorgeous—except for the suburban bedroom communities around **Kane'ohe** and **Kailua.** This area is dotted with scores of scenic B&Bs, as well as resorts and other oceanfront accommodations, making it an easy place to enjoy for a day or a week. From beautiful beaches, golf, and tropical gardens, to **Sea Life Park** (where you can actually swim with dolphins), there are activities for the entire family here. Just be prepared for rainy weather in the winter.

Snapshot

Windward O'ahu Destinations:

- Hoomaluhia Botanical Gardens
- Makapu'u Point
- Nu'uanu Pali Lookout
- Polynesian Cultural Center
- Sea Life Park
- Senator Fong's Plantation and Garden

See Chapter 7 for more information and itineraries.

The North Shore

O'ahu's North Shore is quintessential "surfer Hawaii." In fact, some folks rightly call it "Surfer's Heaven." This coastal area, about 35 miles and an hour's drive from Honolulu, boasts tropical scenery, miles of pristine beach, spectacular sunsets, and—in the winter—some of the biggest surfable waves you'll find anywhere around **Sunset Beach.** (The most famous breaks are the **Banzai Pipeline** and **Waimea Bay,** where they hold the **Hawaiian Triple Crown** competition each December.)

Snapshot

North Shore Destinations:

- Hale'iwa
- Pu'uomakuka Helau
- Sunset Beach
- Waimea Valley

See Chapter 7 for more information and itineraries.

Note to all of you nonsurfers: in the summer, the water calms down considerably, making Sunset and adjacent beaches "family friendly."

Leeward O'ahu

You might just call this region, west of Honolulu, "forgotten O'ahu," since of all the areas of the island, this one has the fewest tourist destinations. That's despite the fact that the geography of O'ahu makes this coastline the sunniest on the island, and in the recent past there has actually been a fair amount of development around the planned community of Kapolei and the upscale **Ko'Olina Resort.** Continue a little farther up the west coast, and you have miles of rural countryside, small towns where Hawaiian culture lives on unabated, and a number of pristine beaches. (Watch out for tricky currents here.)

The road west culminates (and ends, actually) in remote **Ka'ena Point,** a great place to watch a wild sunset, as well as a big wave spot.

Snapshot

Leeward O'ahu Destinations:

- Hawaii Plantation Village
- Hawaiian Waters Adventure Park
- Ka'ena Point
- Makaha Beach Park

O'ahu Driving Times from Waikiki	
Diamond Head	5 minutes
Hanauma Bay	10 minutes
Kahuku	1 hour, 20 minutes
Kailua	30 minutes
Ko'Olina	50 minutes
Pearl Harbor	35 minutes
Sunset Beach	1 hour
Waimanalo	35 minutes

O'ahu Accommodations: Ultimate Places to Stay

Outside the environs of Honolulu, O'ahu offers a large selection of gorgeous beach houses for rent, but only a smattering of five-star resorts and conventional hotels, although you'll find a number of interesting B&Bs in Windward O'ahu. (Note: for suggestions on where to stay in Honolulu, see Chapter 4.)

The accommodation descriptions that follow are organized alphabetically under each lodging category, though we've also included a handy chart that lists them by locale.

Hotels and Resorts

Ihilani Resort & Spa at Ko'Olina $$$$$

This is a place where you can get some five-star treatment away from the crowds of Waikiki. Part of the massive **Ko'Olina Resort and Marina** about

10 miles west of downtown Honolulu, the Marriott-managed **Ihilani Resort & Spa** offers nearly 400 luxurious guest rooms and suites in a white, 17-story tower that faces the blue Pacific. *92-1480 Aliinui Drive, Honolulu, HI 96707.* ***808-679-0079.*** *www.ihilani.com.*

Kahala Mandarin Oriental $$$$$

Set on a secluded beach just 10 minutes from Waikiki, this resort in the Kahala district just east of Waikiki offers 345 rooms and suites furnished in a kind of neo-traditional Hawaiian style. The hotel offers complementary shuttle service to Waikiki and other areas of Honolulu. *5000 Kahala Avenue, Honolulu, HI 96816-5498.* ***808-739-8888*** *or* ***1-800-367-2525.*** *www.kahalaresort.com.*

Turtle Bay Resort $$$$

Located on O'ahu's beautiful North Shore, Turtle Bay has most of the amenities you'd expect from a five-star resort, including good restaurants, two lushly landscaped pools, a couple of championship golf courses, 10 tennis courts, and nearly 5 miles of beachfront. Oh yeah—its 443 guest rooms and beach cottages all boast ocean views, with sunsets (weather permitting). *57-091 Kamehameha Highway, Kahuku, HI 96731.* ***808-293-6000*** *or* ***1-800-203-3650.*** *www.turtlebayresort.com.*

More Intimate Lodgings and B&Bs

Alii Bluffs Windward Bed & Breakfast $

This B&B in a private home is located about 15 minutes from the beach, but offers two double bedrooms overlooking majestic Kaneohe Bay, plus a nice swimming pool with panoramic views of Kaneohe Bay. In addition to the continental breakfast, you'll be offered afternoon tea in the library. This is a comfortable place, and a good value for the price. *46–251 Ikiiki Street, Kane'ohe, HI 96744.* ***808-235-1124*** *or* ***1-800-235-1151.*** *www.hawaiiscene.com/aliibluffs.*

Beach Lane B&B and Studios $$$

Just a few steps from Windward O'ahu's **Kailua Beach,** one of the island's finest, this little place offers an ocean-view beach cottage and a studio done up in Hawaiian style. The proprietors provide boogie boards, beach chairs and beach mats, a "starter supply" tea and coffee and, of course, breakfast! The Bed & Breakfast rate is $125.00 (including breakfast) per night, plus taxes. *111 Hekili Street, Kailua, HI 96734.* ***808-262-8286.*** *www.beachlane.com.*

La'ie Inn

This modest but very comfortable 49-room inn is practically next door to the **Polynesian Cultural Center** in the secluded North Shore town of **La'ie,** and in fact offers a 10 percent discount on Cultural Center tickets to guests. Don't expect anything fancy here—the rooms are pretty basic, but this is a good deal for the price. *55-109 Laniloa Street, La'ie, HI 96762.* ***808-293-9282*** *or* ***1-800-526-4562.*** *www.laieinn.com.*

Lanikai Bed & Breakfast

This quiet and clean family-run establishment across from white-sand Lanikai Beach offers a large upstairs apartment that accommodates four, plus a cottage on the grounds. Both units come with breakfast food and beach equipment. *1277 Mokulua Drive, Lanikai, Kailua, HI 96734.* ***1-800-258-7895*** *or* ***808-261-1059.*** *www.lanikaibb.com.*

Schraeder's Windward Country Inn

This is a cool little mini-resort, nestled right on the shore of magnificent Kaneohe Bay (you can literally fish off the front porch in several of the suites). It offers 30 suites and apartments of one to five bedrooms, with a personalized, friendly atmosphere. The owners not only have free kayaks at the ready for guests, but also offer a complimentary two-hour boat cruise every Saturday, weather permitting. *47-039 Lihikai Drive, Kaneohe, HI 96744.* ***808-239-5711*** *or* ***1-800-735-5071.*** *www.schradersinn.com.*

Best Condos

Kailua Ocean View Condos at Hillside Estate

These three condos will give you privacy with a great view of **Kaneohe Bay,** and are just five minutes from lovely Kailua Beach. The units range from a one-bedroom studio to three-bedroom and five-bedroom villas, all with panoramic views of the ocean. The property also boasts a 9-foot deep heated pool, tennis court. *Located in Kailua, Windward O'ahu.* ***808-330-9526.*** *www.kailuaoceanview.com.*

Turtle Bay Condo Gardenia

Located at the Turtle Bay Resort, this roomy, two-bedroom corner condo has both privacy and panoramic views of the Ko'olau Mountains. Being on the resort property, it's surrounded by 600 acres of landscaped grounds, and includes free use of the pools and tennis courts. *57-091 Kamehameha Highway, Kahuku, Oahu, Hawaii 96731.* ***1-800-345-5277.*** *www.hawaiianbeachrentals.com.*

Ultimate Private Homes

Hang Zen

This awesome four-bedroom oceanfront beach house—raised off the ground to take full advantage of the stunning views—boasts one of the best oceanfront views on the North Shore. The great room, a deck off the kitchen, and three bedrooms are upstairs, with a downstairs studio with a kitchenette and a private *lanai* (balcony) with ocean views. *Located on Sunset Beach, North Shore, O'ahu.* ***1-800-345-5277.*** *www.hawaiianbeachrentals.com.*

Kailua Kai

This newly remodeled five-bedroom beachfront home in Windward O'ahu sleeps eight and is right on the white-sand beach at Kailua. It offers a large, open beachfront living/dining room, a gourmet kitchen, an oceanfront patio, and an upstairs loft bedroom with fabulous views. Relax on the oceanside patio or enjoy day/night outdoor living on the large covered lanai at the back of the house. Requires a minimum seven-night stay. *Located in Kailua, HI.* ***808-261-7895*** *or* ***1-800-258-7895.*** *www.lanikaibeachrentals.com.*

Sunset Beach House

You'll be able to watch surfers tackle the giant waves from this fantasy-quality North Shore house on Sunset Beach—only 1,000 feet from the Banzai Pipeline, one of the world's most famous surfing spots. It boasts four bedrooms and three bathrooms, with a Jacuzzi on the deck overlooking the beach, an outside shower, and its own volleyball/badminton court. *Located on Sunset Beach, North Shore, O'ahu.* ***1-800-454-0443*** *or* ***760-778-3664.*** *www.thesunsetbeachhouse.com.*

Pity the travelers who never venture out of Honolulu to see the rest of O'ahu! It's obviously a world in itself, with a surprising amount of diversity for a relatively small island. For details on great restaurants, beaches, shopping, outdoor sports, and other activities, take a look at Chapter 7!

Chapter 7

Enjoying O'ahu

In This Chapter

- The ultimate itineraries for O'ahu
- The most interesting things to see on O'ahu
- The best places to dine on O'ahu
- The best things to do on O'ahu

O'ahu isn't the largest Hawaiian island, nor does it have the highest mountains or the most beaches. Yet the sights of O'ahu—the **Honolulu** skyline, the iconic mass of **Diamond Head,** the rugged, deeply scalloped mountainsides and waterfalls of **Windward O'ahu,** and the massive waves that pile into the **North Shore** each winter—epitomize Hawaii for most of us.

Why? Maybe it's all of those old television shows that have emanated from these shores that are still showing up on cable in countless reruns. Maybe it's Detective Steve McGarrett barking, "Book 'em Dano," to his Aloha-shirted partner, or a young and buff Tom Selleck driving around the island in a Ferrari in *Magnum P.I.*

Or maybe it's simply the fact that O'ahu is where most people, five million annually, spend all or part of their Hawaiian vacation, thanks to the international airport in Honolulu.

Many of those five million visitors fly directly to other islands, or perhaps spend their time in the immediate environs of Honolulu, missing out on the beguiling variety of sights and memories offered by the rest of this surprisingly diverse and beautiful island.

The fact is that there's a whole tropical playland awaiting you outside of the Honolulu city limits—from waterfalls and knife-edged mountains to brilliant coral reefs; from arid near-desert areas to rainforests; from atmospheric seaside towns fueled on artisans and surf culture, to world-class museums and cultural centers. We give you a taste of all of that in the pages that follow.

The island of O'ahu epitomizes Hawaii for most of us.

(Photo courtesy of HVCB/Kirk Lee Aeder)

The Top Five Things to Do on the Rest of O'ahu

You could probably spend the rest of your life on O'ahu and never run out of cool things to do or great places to enjoy a sunset. However, here's what you must do if you only have a few days on the island:

1. Drive the **loop route** all the way around the island, enjoying the gorgeous beaches, rugged mountains, and island culture along the way.
2. Go snorkeling in Southeast O'ahu's **Hanauma Bay,** where hundreds of tropical fish species abound in an amazing coral reef.
3. Take a **sunset dinner cruise** out of Makaha in Leeward O'ahu.
4. Watch the world's best surfers ride monster waves at the **Banzai Pipeline** on O'ahu's North Shore.
5. Enjoy drinks and a savory dinner at the North Shore's **Hale'iwa Joe's** as you soak in the local ambience.

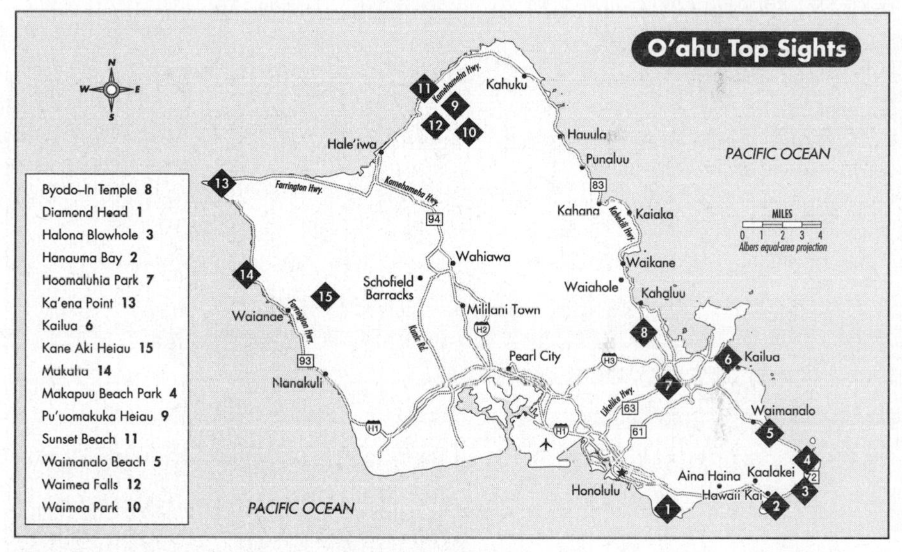

O'ahu's top sights.

Plan My Trip: Ultimate Itineraries for O'ahu

There's plenty to do on O'ahu. Here are several itineraries designed to fit your particular travel mode, complete with good places to eat and to take breaks along the way. Most of these are designed to take about one day, though in several cases we've also included suggestions for stretching the schedule to two days. Of course, you can also mix and match these itineraries, depending on your interests and traveling style.

The descriptions of each stop are generally brief, written to give you a feel for each. You'll find more through write-ups of each place later in the chapter. Be sure to make advance reservations for recommended restaurants and tours!

ITINERARY #1: FOR YOUNG FAMILIES

Day 1

1. **Breakfast:** Enjoy your first meal of the day with the locals at **Jack's** in **Aina Haina,** just a few miles east of Waikiki.
2. Hop back in the car and head for **Sea Life Park** in Southeastern O'ahu to get up-close and personal with the dolphins.
3. **Lunch:** Continue up Routes 72 and 61 into **Kailua** and get a bite to eat at one of the many restaurants in town.
4. Spend the afternoon on beautiful **Kailua Beach,** one of the best in Hawaii.
5. **Dinner:** When the sun starts to get low in the sky, shower off and head just down the beach road to **Buzz's Original Steak House** in **Lanikai.** Enjoy the beverages, good food, and atmosphere as the sun starts to settle in the west.

Day 2

1. **Breakfast:** After an early one at your hotel or condo, head toward O'ahu's North Shore and **Waimea Falls Park.** Spend the morning taking part in one of the many family activities, and watch the professional divers jump off the falls!
2. **Lunch:** head back down the highway into Hale'iwa and try some of the creative tropical burgers and sandwiches at **Kua Aina** right downtown.
3. After lunch, take a **whale-watch/dolphin-watch cruise** out of picturesque Hale'iwa harbor with **North Shore Catamaran Charters,** or just relax on the light brown sand of **Hale'iwa Beach Park.**
4. **Dinner:** Cap off the day with sunset and a fun dinner at **Cholos Homestyle Mexican** restaurant.

ITINERARY #2: FOR OLDER FAMILIES

Day 1

1. **Breakfast:** After breakfast in the condo or hotel, pick up a picnic lunch at the hotel or a local deli and get over to gorgeous **Hanauma Bay** in Southeast O'ahu. Rent a snorkel, mask, and flippers right on the beach. Tour the education center first, and then spend a few hours swimming among the parrotfish at the coral reef.
2. Have lunch on the beach. Make sure you check out the **Toilet Bowl** (the natural wonder, not the restrooms!) while you're there!
3. **Lunch:** After lunch, head west on Route 72 to **Diamond Head.** Take the short, easy hike to the summit and admire the fabulous view.
4. You've been out in the sun and the wind all day, so now it's time for some well-deserved refreshments. Enjoy the awesome pupus and refreshing beverages at the popular **BluWater Grill** overlooking **Kuapa Pond** in nearby **Hawaii Kai.**
5. **Dinner:** You absolutely can't leave Hawaii without having a memorable dinner at **Roy's,** so you might as well head down the road to Hawaii Kai and do it today!

Day 2

1. **Breakfast:** After breakfast at your place, head out for a complete **circle route of the island.** If you're starting from the Honolulu area, we recommend that you head east on the H-1 and **Kalania'ole Highway** (Route 72) toward Diamond Head and Hawaii Kai and travel in a counterclockwise direction from wherever you are. That will put you in certain areas in key points of the day.
2. About 10 miles west of the Honolulu area, stop briefly at beautiful **Sandy Beach** to check out the surfers challenging the heavy break.
3. Continue on Route 72 around the northeastern tip of the island near **Makapu'u Point,** then on **Routes 61 and 83** west through **Kane'ohe** to the beautiful **Byodo-In Temple,** flanked by dramatic mountains and gardens. Spend some time exploring the temple and grounds.

continues

continued

4. **Lunch:** Drive a little further north up the highway from Byodo-In and keep your eye out for **The Shrimp Shack,** a bright yellow lunch wagon parked on the highway outside of **Punalu'u.** Satisfy your cravings on the fresh local shrimp and other delicious island delicacies!
5. Continue up the highway and around the northwest corner of the island to **Waimea Falls Park,** where you can take a short hike, go horseback riding, and watch the professional divers jump off the falls!
6. While you're on the North Shore, cruise over to **Sunset Beach** and spend some time enjoying the surf and watching the expert surfers ride the big waves.
7. Drive several miles south to the cool North Shore town of Hale'iwa. Browse the shops and galleries in the **North Shore Marketplace,** and then walk over to **Jameson's by the Sea** for some late-afternoon pupus and beverages. Try their renowned mai tais, virgin or otherwise!
8. **Dinner:** If it's late, stay for dinner and some live music at **Jameson's,** and then drive south on the Kamehameha Highway (Routes 83 and 99) to the H2 freeway and back into the Honolulu area. If you still have a couple of hours of light left, drive south as directed before, but head west at the junction of H2 to the **Ko'Olina Resort and Marina.** Have dinner at the resort's **Azul** restaurant as you watch the sun set into the Pacific.

ITINERARY #3: FOR SINGLES

1. **Breakfast:** Get up early and drive out to **Wai'anae in Leeward O'ahu.** Take a morning whale-watching and snorkeling cruise on an **Aquatic Safaris** sailboat. Don't worry—a continental breakfast is served on board!
2. **Lunch:** When you get back from snorkeling, enjoy lunch while gazing at the sea at the **Kaiona Restaurant,** in Wai'anae.
3. After lunch, spend a couple of hours on nearby **Makaha Beach,** then drive up into the hills to explore the seventeenth-century **Kane Aki Heiau.**

4. **Dinner:** Head back down to arguably the best lu'au in the islands, the **Paradise Cove Lu'au at Ko'Olina.** You'll be immersed in Hawaiian culture and food as you watch the golden sun set over the water beyond the swaying palms.

Digging up the Imu—a delicious ground-roasted lu'au pig.

(Photo courtesy of HVCB/Kirk Lee Aeder)

ITINERARY #4: A ROMANTIC GETAWAY

1. **Breakfast:** After breakfast at your hotel or condo, drive up Route 61 (the Pali Highway) to the **Nu'uanu Pali Lookout** on the crest of the Ko'olau Range north of Honolulu. Stand in the moist, fragrant wind and gaze upon the sprawling Windward O'ahu panorama.
2. Drive down into Kailua and spend a couple of quiet hours relaxing on beautiful **Kailua Beach,** perhaps the most beautiful strand in Hawaii.
3. **Lunch:** Head north on Route 83 to the **Crouching Lion Inn,** where you can enjoy a Hawaiian lunch with a great view of the ocean and mountains.
4. Backtrack a few miles south on Route 83 to **Senator Fong's Plantation and Garden** near Kahalu'u. Spend a couple of hours exploring some of the 700 acres of exotic tropical gardens set against a dramatic mountain backdrop.

continues

continued

5. **Dinner:** Drop in at the lovely Turtle Bay Resort on O'ahu's northwestern tip. Enjoy cocktails at the resort's open oceanside lounge, the **Hang Ten Bar and Grill.** Stay there for dinner, or repair to dinner at the superb **21 Degrees North** restaurant for a top-end meal as the sun sets into the ocean.

Itinerary #5: Easy-Going; Nonstrenuous

Day 1

1. **Breakfast/Lunch:** Leave your hotel early on a round-island tour with **Polynesian Adventure Tours** in one of their 25-passenger mini-coaches. You'll visit **Diamond Head,** the **Polynesian Cultural Center** (including an "Adventure Canoe Tour," an all-you-can-eat luncheon buffet, and a canoe pageant), as well as a visit to the **Mormon Temple** near La'ie, views of rainforests, mountains, waterfalls, and of course, crashing surf.
2. **Dinner:** Enjoy evening cocktails and a good meal at the **Olive Tree Café** in Kahala, Southeastern O'ahu.

Day 2

1. **Breakfast:** Have breakfast with the locals at **Jack's,** a small and busy local landmark in a shopping center just west of Hawaii Kai.
2. Get in your car and head west and north toward the North Shore. Stop along the way in **Wahiawa** and take a guided tour of the **Dole Plantation.**
3. **Lunch:** Continue north to the fun and funky North Shore town of **Hale'iwa,** stopping for an oceanside lunch at **Jameson's by the Sea.**
4. After lunch, browse the unique galleries and shops in downtown Hale'iwa.
5. Drive a few miles north to Waimea and visit the sacred **Pu'u O Mahuka He,** where you also have great panoramic views of the entire North Shore coastline.
6. **Dinner:** Drive south to the **Ko'Olina Resort and Marina** on O'ahu's southwestern tip. Enjoy a superb meal, a sunset, and live music afterward at the J.W. Marriott's **Azul** restaurant.

Itinerary #6: Culture in Paradise

Day 1

1. **Breakfast:** After breakfast at your hotel or condo, head directly to the **Polynesian Cultural Center** on O'ahu's north shore near the town of **La'ie.** We recommend that you purchase the "Ambassador Lu'au" package, which includes a full day of entertaining and informative activities at the center and its numerous re-created traditional Polynesian villages, lunch, and one of the island's most authentic and lavish lu'aus at night.

Day 2

1. **Breakfast:** After breakfast at your hotel or condo, it's time to do some cultural exploration on your own. First, head over the **Ko'olau Mountains** on the renowned Pali Highway (Route 61). Be sure to stop at the **Nu'uanu Pali Lookout** for a great view of Windward O'ahu.
2. Drive down the hill into **Kane'ohe** and indulge in a sensory experience at the **Ho'omaluhia Botanical Gardens,** where 400 acres of endangered plants, hiking trails, and guided tours will entertain you.
3. Continue down the hill and head north on Route 83 to the beautiful **Byodo-In Temple,** flanked by dramatic mountains and gardens. Spend some time exploring the temple and grounds.
4. **Lunch:** Drive a little farther north up the highway from Byodo-In and watch for **The Shrimp Shack,** a bright yellow lunch wagon parked on the highway outside of Punalu'u. Satisfy your cravings on the fresh local shrimp and other delicious island delicacies.
5. Continue on Route 83 around O'ahu's northern tip to Waimea and visit the sacred **Pu'u O Mahuka Heiau.** While you're there, enjoy the panoramic views of the entire North Shore coastline.
6. **Dinner:** Drive down into the historic North Shore town of **Hale'iwa,** which also holds the studios and galleries of some of O'ahu's and Hawaii's most acclaimed artists. Cap off your day with dinner at **Hale'iwa Joe's,** offering some of the North Shore's best food.

ITINERARY #7: ADVENTURE IN THE GREAT OUTDOORS

Day 1

1. **Breakfast:** Get a hearty breakfast at **Jack's,** just west of Hawaii Kai.
2. After breakfast, pick up some water and lunch at the local deli, then head out for a hike to **Manoa Falls,** one of the most beautiful cascades in Southeast O'ahu. If you're really feeling ambitious, take the rewarding six-mile round-trip hike to **Kuli'ou'ou Ridge** for its sweeping vistas of eastern O'ahu.
3. **Lunch:** Come back down to sea level and recuperate on gorgeous **Sandy Beach** as you watch the locals tackle the rough surf.
4. **Dinner:** Freshen up back at your place, then visit **Roy's** in Hawaii Kai for a memorable dinner.
5. Still have some energy left? Enjoy the live music, refreshments, cool views and good times at the **Kona Brewing Company,** right on the water in Hawaii Kai.

Day 2

1. **Breakfast:** After an early breakfast at **Jack's** in Hawaii Kai, beat the crowds and spend the morning snorkeling at stunning Hanauma Bay in Southeast O'ahu.
2. **Lunch:** Drive on up to the lovely Windward O'ahu town of Lanikai and enjoy a great lunch at the cool place to be: **Buzz's.** Get there by noon and finish lunch by 1:30 P.M.

3a. Spend the afternoon kayaking among the **Mokulua Islands** off **Lanikai Beach,** or ...

3b. Take a short hike out to **Makapu'u Point,** O'ahu's easternmost point.

4. **Dinner:** Get over to **Leeward O'ahu's Ko'Olina Resort and Marina** and take a sunset cocktail cruise on Hawaii Nautical's 53-foot catamaran, the **Ko Olina Cat.** Make sure you book in advance for the 5:30 P.M.–7:30 P.M. excursion.

The Top O'ahu Attractions, A to Z

Byodo-In Temple Windward O'ahu

This beautiful Buddhist temple, a replica of the 900-year-old temple in Uji, Japan, is situated against a dramatic Ko'olau Mountain backdrop and is surrounded by lush Japanese gardens and koi ponds. Inside is a 9-foot Lotus Buddha. Outside is a 3-ton, brass Peace Bell. *Take Kahekili Highway (Route 83) north from Kane'ohe. Turn left into the Valley of the Temples cemetery and proceed up the valley. 47-200 Kahekili Highway.*

Dole Plantation Wahiawa; Interior O'ahu, on the way to North Shore

This is home to one of the world's largest mazes, and it's been created with pineapple! What more could a Hawaiian tourist ask for? The plantation also offers a two-mile, 20-minute fully guided "Pineapple Express" tour; a Plantation Garden; exposure to traditional Hawaiian arts and crafts; and the refreshing Dole Whip at the country store. This is an experience for the whole family. *64-1550 Kamehameha Highway. Open daily from 9:00 A.M.–5:30 P.M. Admission: Free, it's the attractions that cost money.* ***808-621-8408.*** *www.dole-plantation.com.*

Hale'iwa The North Shore

Most visitors adore this area because it has retained its historical and cultural past despite the avid tourism there for several decades. The TV show *Baywatch* was filmed here, and since then Hale'iwa has picked up a reputation as a great place to surf. Not only is Hale'iwa full of some of the most historic buildings on O'ahu, it also is becoming the art mecca of the island. Whether you want to tour a gallery or visit the surf museum, this town will certainly provide something interesting to do. *Take H2 and Route 99 (Kamehameha Highway) northwest from Honolulu.*

Halona Blowhole Southeast O'ahu

This is one of O'ahu's most spectacular natural attractions—the Halona Blowhole. As a result of volcanic eruptions thousands of years ago, tubes developed that run from the ocean to the rock above. When the surf is right, water is shot through the tubes causing the water to funnel out and up to heights of 30 feet. The larger the surf, the larger the spout of water, which is spectacular but also can be dangerous. Beyond the Blowhole itself, this area offers impressive views of Moloka'i and Lana'i. In the winter, you may catch a glimpse of whales playing offshore. The Halona Beach Cove is another component of this site that offers access to a beautiful beach and excellent swimming. The area is part of one of the most dangerous ocean channels in the world, though. There are no life-guards on duty at the beaches, so exercising caution during imperfect weather is recommended. *Take H1 and Route 72 (the Kalaniana'ole Highway) east from Honolulu.*

Hanauma Bay Southeast O'ahu

This scenic bay was formed in a volcanic crater. As one of the most visited sites in O'ahu, it's now a nature preserve dedicated to protecting the natural and beautiful marine ecosystem that makes the bay so special. "Hanauma" means "curved," which accurately describes this long, almost circular beach. Once you've seen this place you will see why it is such an attraction. About 3,000 people visit the Bay each day, where snorkeling, swimming, picnicking, and beach sports are popular. (And you can rent fins, masks, and snorkels right on site.) In 1990, Hawaii put restrictions on how many visitors can be at the Bay at any one time (tour buses are no longer permitted to stop), and an award-winning educational center was completed in 2002.

If you're interested in doing more at the Bay than enjoying the scenery and relaxing on the beach, the Hanauma Bay Education Program hosts events every Thursday night at 6:30 P.M. at the Theater. Events run about an hour and are free to the public. *Open daily except for Tuesdays. $5 admission fee for those who are over 12 years old and aren't Hawaii residents. Summer hours: 6 A.M.–7 P.M. (extended hours until 10 P.M. on the second and fourth Saturday of every month). Winter hours: 6 A.M.–6 P.M. (extended hours until 10 P.M. on the second Saturday of every month). Take the Kalaniana'ole Highway (Route 72) just east of Hawaii Kai.* ***808-397-5840.*** *www.honolulu.gov/parks/facility/hanaumabay/welcome.htm.*

Try to arrive early because once the parking lot is full, you will be turned away from the site. Cost is $1 per car to park.

Aceess to the beach is designed for wheelchair use and the park even provides beach wheelchairs free of charge from 8 A.M.–4 P.M. every day, year-round. Trams and city buses provide wheelchair accessibility as well. Call **808-396-4229** for more information.

Hawaiian Waters Adventure Park Kapolei; Leeward O'ahu

With 25 acres of rides and slides, this attraction promises smiles, screams, and good times for all family members. *400 Farrington Highway, Kapolei. Hours are* *subject to change; check their website or call. Admission: seniors (60+) $14.99, adults $34.99, youths (ages 3–11) $24.99, children (2 and younger) free. Group rates for parties over 20 individuals.* ***808-674-WAVE.*** *www.hawaiianwaters.com.*

Ho'omaluhia Botanical Gardens Kane'ohe; Windward O'ahu

These gardens were designed and built by the U.S. Army Corps of Engineers to provide flood protection for Kane'ohe, providing a beautiful home to 400 acres of endangered plants. With a network of hiking trails and guided walks (offered at 10 A.M. on Saturdays and 1 P.M. on Sundays), exploring the flora can be a sensory experience. The ideal first stop upon arrival is the Visitors Center to learn about the area, pick up a map, and figure out how to spend your time at the site. The Gardens also offer camping Friday through Monday, but a permit must be obtained to stay there. *46-680 Luluku Road. Open Daily from 9 A.M.–4 P.M.* ***808-233-7323.*** *www.co.honolulu.hi.us/parks/hbg/hmbg.htm.*

Ka'ena Point Leeward O'ahu

Ka'ena means "the heat" in Hawaiian, and there's usually plenty of that here on this dry, dramatic, westernmost point of O'ahu. This spear-shaped protrusion of land, lined with jagged sea cliffs, is considered to be, in Hawaiian folklore, a point from which souls leave this world. With beautiful views of western O'ahu and amazing surf, you could understand why this may be the last place anyone would need to see. Extreme caution should be used in and around the ocean during the winter months, as the rip currents and waves become large and dangerous. The point itself can only be reached on foot. *Take Route 930 north from Makaha into Ka'ena State Park. Park in the lot, and from there you will have to hoof it—a five-mile round-trip. You can also walk in from the north side, where an unimproved track extends three miles along the coast from the end of Route 930.*

Kane Aki Heiau Leeward O'ahu

Built in the seventeenth century, this ancient Hawaiian temple was dedicated to Lono, the benevolent god of harvest and fertility. It encompasses restored grass and thatched huts that were used as prayer and meditation chambers. *Take Farrington Highway (Route 93) north along O'ahu's west coast until you see Makaha Valley Road. Turn toward the mountains and follow the signs. Open to visitors Tuesday through Sunday from 10 A.M.–2 P.M., weather permitting.*

Makapu'u Point and Lighthouse Windward O'ahu

Located at the easternmost edge of O'ahu, this spot at 647 feet above the sea offers a spectacular view of the coast and the island of Molokai in the distance. The lighthouse was built in 1909 and automated in 1974. *Follow the Kalanianaole Highway (Route 72) east past Hanauma Bay and Sandy Beach to Hawaii Kai Golf Course. About half a mile past the golf course on the right is a gate marking the entrance to a two-mile trail leading to the lighthouse.*

Mormon Temple La'ie, Windward O'ahu

Mormonism was a key part of Hawaiian immigration in the nineteenth and twentieth centuries, and is still quite prevalent in Hawaii today. In 1865, the church purchased a 6,000-acre plantation on Oahu's North Shore in La'ie, and by 1919 had created this impressive temple near the Polynesian Cultural Center—a sight quite unlike anything else on O'ahu. It's also part of the Brigham Young University Hawaii Campus. You can't enter the temple itself, but there is a visitor center that provides some history and context. *Open from 9 A.M.–8 P.M. daily, admission is free and tours are available. Kamehameha Highway (Highway 83).*

Nu'uanu Pali Lookout Pali Highway

Nu'uanu Pali means "windward cliff," and this location at 1,200 feet above the sea offers one of O'ahu's best panoramic views. Showing the expanse of the northeast coast of O'ahu, the Lookout can be reached by taking Route 61 (the Pali Highway) out of Honolulu. Once the site of some of the bloodiest battles in Hawaii's history, the area now offers sweeping and peaceful views of Windward O'ahu, including Kailua and the coastline. A series of four tunnels, two in each direction, provide access to this majestic area that should not be missed. *At the crest of Route 61 (the Pali Highway).*

Polynesian Cultural Center La'ie; Windward O'ahu

About a one-hour drive from Waikiki, the Polynesian Cultural Center boasts seven native villages set up on its premises and endless cultural activities to explore, including guided tours and canoe tours. The Center also hosts a large nightly lu'au that features authentic rituals performed before hundreds of camera-toting tourists. *55-370 Kamehameha Highway (Route 83), La'ie. Parking is $5. Admission prices range from $55–$200 for adults ($40–$150 for kids), depending on package/ticket choice.* ***1-800-367-7060*** *or* ***808-293-3333****. www.polynesia.com.*

Pu'u O Mahuka Heiu The North Shore

Located near the North Shore town of Pupukea, this well-preserved ancient temple with great views overlooking Waimea Bay is the largest heiau on O'ahu, covering over five acres. It was considered a powerful place and may also have been a site of human sacrifice. *Take Kamehameha Highway (Route 83) north past Waimea Beach Park, turn right onto Pupukea Road, and follow the signs.*

Sea Life Park Waimanalo; Windward O'ahu

Sea Life Park is Hawaii's only marine park and is one of O'ahu's most spectacular displays of sea life, offering close encounters with dolphins, sea lions, and penguins, as well as daily programs and shows. *41-202 Kalanianaole Highway (Route 72). Open daily from 9:30 A.M.–5 P.M. Admission: adult $29, child (4–12 years old) $19. If you want to swim with the dolphins, it will set you back $199.* ***1-866-365-7446*** *or* ***1-866-DOLPHIN****. www.sealifeparkhawaii.com.*

Senator Fong's Plantation and Garden Kane'ohe, Windward O'ahu

Named after the former U.S. Senator Hiram Fong, this popular Windward O'ahu destination is a family-owned establishment that provides tours and lei-making classes and hosts events on its 700-acre tropical garden. *47-285 Pulama Road. Open daily 10 A.M.–2 P.M., tours at 10:30 A.M. and 1 P.M. Tour fee: seniors (65+) $13, adults $14.50, children (ages 5–12) $9.* ***808-239-6775.*** *www.fonggarden.net.*

Sunset Beach Park Waimea; The North Shore

Sunset Beach Park is best known for its big wave surfing competitions in the winter months, when the swells sometimes rise to 30 feet or more. The actual competitions take place on a strand directly adjacent to Sunset: Ehukai Beach, called "The Banzai Pipeline" by the surfing world. *59-104 Kamehameha Highway (Route 83).*

Toilet Bowl Hanauma Bay; Southeast O'ahu

Located on the left side of Hanauma Bay, the so-called Toilet Bowl is a natural pool connected to the ocean by an underground channel. The pool rises and falls precipitously—up to five feet at a time, each time a wave surges into the tunnel below. Quite a lot of fun, and the view is great! *Take the Kalaniana'ole Highway (Route 72) just east of Hawaii Kai.*

Waimea Valley Audubon Center Waimea; The North Shore

Part of Waimea Falls Park (see below), this center offers several paths and sanctuaries for relaxation and the enjoyment of nature. It also boasts a small waterfall and swimming hole at one end of the Center. As a host to countless bird, plant, and animal species, this Center is an amazing place to catch a glimpse of what O'ahu has to offer. *59-864 Kamehameha Highway (Route 83). Open daily, closed Christmas and New Year's Day. Admission: child/senior (60+) $5, adults $8. www.audubon.org/local/sanctuary/Brochures/Waimea.html.*

Waimea Falls Park Waimea; The North Shore

Yet another lovely sight on the North Shore is Waimea Falls, located in a tropical forest as part of 1,800-acre Waimea Falls Park. Ancient Hawaiians once brought wounded soldiers to the waterfall with the hope that they would be healed. Now professional cliff-divers climb the rock wall alongside the falls and then dive from 45 and 60 feet into the deep, cold pool below. The park offers four theme areas: adventure, Hawaiian culture, and a children's play center, as well as horseback riding, hiking, kayaking, and mountain biking. *59-864 Kamehameha Highway (Route 83).* ***808-638-8511.***

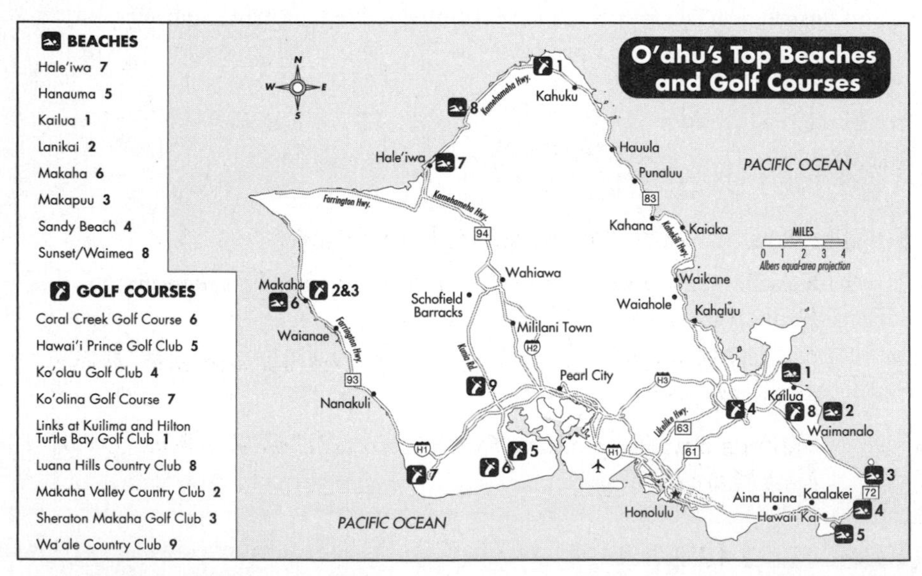

O'ahu's top beaches and golf courses.

O'ahu's Top Beaches

Why go to Hawaii if you aren't going to check out the beaches? The sand and surf is what makes Hawaii one of the vacation hotspots in the United States. A tropical paradise for relaxation or play, O'ahu has some of Hawaii's premier beaches. Some have facilities such as picnic tables, restrooms, and showers. Others don't, and we've tried to note those below. You can get daily surf information by calling the O'ahu Surf Report phone at **808-596-7873.**

Southeast O'ahu

Hanauma: *Take Kalaniana'ole Highway (Route 72) about 10 miles west of Waikiki.*

Makapu'u: *From Honolulu take H1 and Route 72 east a couple of miles past Sandy Beach.*

Sandy Beach: *Full facilities. From Honolulu take H1 and Route 72 east for about 13 miles.*

Windward O'ahu

Kailua: *Full facilities. 450 Kawailoa Road. Take Route 61 (the Pali Highway) north from Honolulu.*

Lanikai: *No facilities. Kailua Road.*

The North Shore

Hale'iwa: *Take H1 west to H2 and Route 99 north.*

Kawela: *No facilities. Take H1 west to H2 north to Kamehameha Highway (Route 83).*

Sunset: *No facilities. Take H1 west to H2 north to Kamehameha Highway (Route 83).*

Waimea Bay: *Full facilities. Take H1 west to H2 north to Route 83 (the Kamehameha Highway).*

Leeward O'ahu

Ma'ili: *Full facilities. Take H1 west out of Honolulu to Route 93 (the Farrington Highway).*

Makaha: *Full facilities. 84-369 Farrington Highway.*

Great Dining with Atmosphere: The Best Places to Eat

Not being a particularly large island, you might think that all of the best restaurants on O'ahu are located in cosmopolitan Honolulu. *Au contraire!* There actually are an amazing number of quality eateries—from *haute cuisine* establishments to awesome sandwich shops—scattered all around the island.

Here are our picks for some of the best dining spots on O'ahu, outside of Honolulu.

Southeast O'ahu

BluWater Grill Hawaii Kai *Hawaiian* $$

Located in a shopping center, but right on the edge of scenic Kuapa Pond, the reasonably priced BluWater Grill serves creative, well-prepared cuisine in a high-ceilinged, large-windowed, often crowded room with colorful artwork and a curved, open kitchen area. Try the pan-seared scallops with soy-mustard butter sauce, or maybe the macadamia nut-crusted prawns with Thai coconut aioli. Yum. *Hawaii Kai Shopping Center, 377 Keahole Street. Open Monday–Thursday 11 A.M.–11 P.M., Friday and Saturday 11 A.M.–midnight, Sunday brunch 10 A.M.–2:30 P.M.* ***808-395-6224.*** *www.bluwatergrillhawaii.com.*

Jack's Aina Haina *American* 

A small and busy local landmark in a shopping center a few miles east of Waikiki and Diamond Head, Jack's is a family-owned place that serves up tasty and inexpensive food. It's a breakfast favorite for area residents. Try the honey biscuits and/or the large variety of pancakes! They offer lunch items as well. *Aina Haina Shopping Center, 820 W. Hind Drive. Open daily 6 A.M.–2 P.M.* ***808-373-4034.***

Olive Tree Café Kahala *Greek* 

In the mood for some savory Mediterranean specialties, expertly prepared and offered at great prices? You owe it to yourself to check out this cool and casual place, featuring an open kitchen, counter ordering, and tables inside and out. Try the tabule salad, the signature souvlaki kebabs (fish, chicken, lamb, served with a house salad), or rotating nightly specials. *4614 Kilauea Avenue behind Kahala Mall. Open Monday–Thursday from 5 P.M.–10 P.M., Friday–Sunday 11 A.M.–10 P.M.* ***808-737-0303.***

Roy's Hawaii Kai *Pacific Rim* $$$

This lively and crowded establishment probably is one of the best chain restaurants you'll ever experience—made famous by Hawaii's most successful celebrity chef, Roy Yamaguchi. The secret of Roy's success is the savory Euro-Pacific fusion cuisine, fresh local ingredients, a good wine list, highly efficient service, and surprisingly reasonable prices! There's also a Roy's in Kapolei. *6600 Kalaniana'ole Highway. Dinner Monday–Thursday 5:30 P.M.–9:30 P.M., Friday 5:30 P.M.–10 P.M., Saturday 5 P.M.–10 P.M., Sunday 5 P.M.–9:30 P.M.* ***808-396-7697.*** *www.roysrestaurant.com.*

Windward O'ahu

Ahi's Restaurant Punalu'u *Hawaiian* $$

This family-owned place is down-home Hawaii at its most comfortable and delicious. Set on a rolling green lawn in a rural setting, Ahi's specializes in shrimp at good prices—prepared scampi, cocktail, tempura, or deep-fried style. They also have steak, mahimahi, chicken, and various salads and sandwiches. *53-146 Kamehameha Highway (Route 83). Open Monday–Saturday 11 A.M.–9 P.M.* ***808-293-5650.***

Buzz's Original Steak House Lanikai *Steak & Seafood* $$$

Right on Kailua Beach in trendy Lanikai, this rustic and popular place boasts rattan furniture and a koa bar to put you in that old-school tropical frame of mind. Once you've perused the many celebrity photos on the walls, you can get down to enjoying the dependable food, which includes steak-and-lobster combos, fresh fish, and excellent burgers. *413 Kawailoa Road. Open daily 11 A.M.–3 P.M. and 5 P.M.–10 P.M., pupus from 11 A.M.–10 P.M. Cash only.* ***808-261-4661.***

Crouching Lion Inn Ka'a'awa *Hawaiian* $$$

Stopping at this Windward O'ahu dining institution for either lunch or dinner is standard procedure for many folks driving the circle island route around the island. Here you can get steak, seafood, burgers, and Hawaiian specialties, in a country inn atmosphere. Add in the great ocean view and—if you're lucky—live Hawaiian music on most nights, and you have a great dinner location. Try the mahimahi with papaya sweet and sour dressing. *51-666 Kamehameha Highway (Route 83). Open daily 11 A.M.–11 P.M.* ***808-237-8511.***

Jameson's by the Sea Hale'iwa *Hawaiian* $$$

Atmosphere is king at the harborside establishment in Hale'iwa. And the food is great, too. Offerings include fresh seafood direct from Hawaiian waters, plus stuffed shrimp, scallops, lobster tails, New York steak, and filet mignon. You can eat indoors or out. *62-540 Kamehameha Highway (Route 83). Lunch Monday–Friday 11 A.M.–2:30 P.M., dinner nightly 5 P.M.–9 P.M.* ***808-637-4336.***

Lucy's Grill 'n Bar Kailua *Hawaiian* $$$

One of the best restaurants in Windward O'ahu, this open-air Kailua hot spot will keep you in that ultimate Hawaiian mood with its Tiki torches, surfboards, colorful paintings on the wall, and buzzing crowd of happy clientele, all energized by superb food served in large portions. Try the "spicy ahi tower," the coconut-crusted mochiko moi, or the always-popular pan-seared, pepper-crusted ahi with a wasabi-miso beurre blanc! Lucy's also offers a great Sunday brunch, including seafood omelets, rib-eye steak and eggs, Eggs Benedict, Belgian waffles, and much more. *33 Aulike Street, Kailua. Open daily 5 P.M.–10 P.M.* ***808-230-8188.*** *www.lucysgrillnbar.com.*

The Shrimp Shack Punalu'u *Hawaiian* $

A drive up the Windward O'ahu coast wouldn't be complete without a stop at the bright yellow lunch wagon on the Kamehameha Highway in Punalu'u, where "shrimp lady" Irene Theofanis will inspire you to "pig out" on fresh local shrimp and other island delicacies such as mahimahi and mussels. *53-352 Kamehameha Highway (Route 83). Open daily from 11 A.M.–5 P.M.* ***808-256-5589.*** *www.alternative-hawaii.com/shrimp/index.html.*

The North Shore

21 Degrees North Turtle Bay *Pacific Rim* $$$$

It's a little pricey, but this place is the premiere fine-dining choice on the North Shore. Part of the swank Turtle Bay Resort, the multi-level dining room features floor-to-ceiling windows looking out on the Pacific and the setting sun. And the food is excellent, offering such delicacies as braised Kona lobster and rosemary-crusted Colorado lamb rack. *Turtle Bay Resort, 57-091 Kamehameha Highway. Dinner served Tuesday–Saturday 6 P.M.–9:30 P.M. Closed Sunday and Monday except for Christmas and New Year's Eve.* ***808-293-8811.*** *www.turtlebayresort.com.*

Cholos Homestyle Mexican Restaurant Hale'iwa *Mexican* $$

Cholos is a hip little place where the homestyle Mexican offerings are made from fresh ingredients every day. You can eat inside and groove to the tunes playing loudly from the jukebox, or dine out front on the lanai. Cholos also sells authentic artwork from Oaxaca, Mexico, as well as hats and T-shirts. Check out the excellent ahi tacos! Good margaritas, too! *66-250 Kamehameha Highway (Route 83). Open daily for breakfast, lunch, and dinner from 8 A.M.–9 P.M.* ***808-637-3059.***

Hale'iwa Joe's Hale'iwa *Hawaiian* $$

Situated next to the famous 1921 Anahulu Stream Bridge (Rainbow Bridge) in groovy Hale'iwa, this award-winning establishment offers harbor-view seating and some of the best food on the North Shore. Try the crunchy coconut shrimp, the grilled scallops on cilantro-lime greens, and the well-named Paradise Pie (Kona coffee ice cream on a bed of Oreo cookies, with Belgian bittersweet chocolate sauce, whipped cream, and toasted almonds). *66-011 Kamehameha Highway (Route 83). Open daily for lunch 11:30 A.M.–4:15 P.M., with dinner offered Sunday–Thursday 5:30 P.M.–9:30 P.M., Friday–Saturday 5:30 P.M.–10:30 P.M.* ***800-637-8005.*** *www.haleiwajoes.com.*

Kua Aina Hale'iwa *American* $

Situated in the heart of Hale'iwa, this North Shore favorite offers great burgers and sandwiches, which you can enjoy inside or out. In fact, the burgers are so good that there is often a line for service during lunch and dinner hours. Try a beef burger with grilled hunk of pineapple and guacamole. The fries also rock. Kua Aina also serves as a great place to pick up something for a beach picnic. *66-160 Kamehameha Highway (Route 83). Open daily 10:30 A.M.–9 P.M.* ***808-637-6067.***

Leeward O'ahu

Azul Kapolei *American/Hawaiian* 

Here you'll enjoy a savory dinner selection of popular meat and fish dishes in what you might call nouvelle American style, prepared skillfully with fresh island ingredients. However, if you're willing to splurge, you've really got to come for the Champagne brunch on Sundays—one of the best you're going to find on O'ahu, or anywhere for that matter. Cost: a mere $45 per person the last time we were there. Outdoor tables offer a garden view. *JW Marriott Ihilani Resort & Spa, 92-1001 Olani Street. Dinner served daily 6 P.M.–10 P.M. Closed Sunday evening through Monday. Sunday Champagne brunch 9:30 A.M.–2 P.M. (The hours tend to change seasonally, so call ahead!)* ***808-679-0079.*** *www.ihilani.com.*

Hapa Grill Kapolei *Hawaiian* 

This small eatery offers modern, delectable versions of popular Hawaiian specialties such as Mochiko chicken and hamburger steak, as well as grilled mahimahi sandwiches with fresh mango salsa, and basil pesto eggplant parmesan, and more. The restaurant is even building a reputation around Honolulu, and the prices are very reasonable. *91-590 Farrington Highway. Open Sunday–Monday 8 A.M.–9 P.M., Tuesday–Saturday 8 A.M.–10 P.M.* ***808-674-8400.*** *www.hapagrill.net.*

Kaiona Restaurant Wai'anae *American* 

One of the better places to eat in Leeward O'ahu, spectacular ocean views and sunsets await you here, along with a great selection of American/continental food at this restaurant of the Makaha Golf Resort. *Makaha Resort & Golf Club, 4-626 Makaha Valley Road. Open for breakfast daily 7 A.M.–11 A.M, dinner daily 5:30 P.M.–9 P.M.* ***808-695-9544*** *or* ***1-866-576-6447.***

Mom's Soul Food Waipahu *Southern* $$

Yes, Virginia, there's a Southern soul food place a few miles outside of Honolulu—a place where you can get mouthwatering country-fried steak with collard greens and garlic mashed potatoes, catfish, pulled pork, hush puppies, corn muffins, and all the rest. *94-226 Leoku. Open Tuesday–Saturday 11 A.M.–7:30 P.M., Sunday from 1 P.M–6 P.M., and for dinner daily from 5:30 P.M.–9:30 P.M. Closed Monday.* ***808-678-8201.***

Roy's Ko'Olina Kapolei Pacific Rim 

Savory Euro-Pacific fusion cuisine, fresh local ingredients, a good wine list, highly efficient service, and surprisingly reasonable prices! There's also a Roy's in Hawaii Kai. (See that listing for a full description.) *92-1220 Ali'inui Drive. Lunch daily 11 A.M.–2 P.M., pupus daily 2 P.M.–5:30 P.M., dinner daily 5:30 P.M.–9:30 P.M.* ***808-676-7697.*** *www.roysrestaurant.com.*

Entertainment and Nightlife

Needless to say, there's more nightlife than you can shake a stick at in Honolulu. What may be surprising is that there's also a decent selection of things to do elsewhere around the island, as many restaurants and lounges feature live music in the evenings—usually a mix of Hawaiian, folk, and pop.

To get the lowdown on the most local of community events around O'ahu, including entertainment at local clubs, check out **http://oahu.alllocalevents.com.** Also, there are tons of handout pamphlets published weekly in nearly every part of the island, highlighting restaurants, entertainment, and events. All hotels have stands, and the hotel desks are liberal with information and reservations help.

Live Music and Karaoke

No matter where you travel around the island of O'ahu, music is in the air catering to people like you who want to soak in the full ambience of being in paradise while sipping a mai tai. Just about all of the resort lounges, as well as many of the island's independent restaurants and bars, offer live music of varying quality, ranging from traditional Hawaiian and slack-key guitar, to rock, jazz, and the Hawaiian-style reggae called "Jawaiian."

Close to Honolulu in Southeastern O'ahu, check out the **Kona Brewing Company**, at Koko Marina, 7192 Kalaniana'ole Highway in Hawaii Kai (**808-394-5662,** www.konabrewingco.com), a large bar and restaurant right on the water, with an Hawaiian entertainment lineup Wednesday through Sunday. If you're in a mellow mood, head over to the **Honu Bar and Terrace** at the Kahala Mandarin Oriental Hawaii, 5000 Kahala Avenue, Kahala (**808-739-8888**). Enjoy being in the shadow of Diamond Head while you listen to light jazz and island musicians.

If you're in Windward O'ahu and want to check out the "big game" in the company of friendly strangers, drop in at **The Shack,** 1051 Keolu Drive in Kailua (**808-261-1191;** www.shackhawaii.com), a sort of sports and burger bar with seven or eight televisions showing highly paid professional athletes doing what they do best.

If you're on the North Shore, enjoy live music at **Jameson's by the Sea** at 62-540 Kamehameha Highway in Hale'iwa (**808-637 6272**) or **The Bay Club** at the Turtle Bay Resort, 57-091 Kamehameha Highway in Kahuku (**808-293-8811**), where local bands play contemporary Hawaiian tunes on weeknights, with DJs and dance music taking over on weekends.

A Waialua civic group presents free performances and family programs on the first Sunday of every month from 4 P.M.–5:30 P.M. at the **Waialua Bandstand** on Kealohanui Road adjacent to the Waialua Sugar Mill, about a block west off the highway at Waialua District Park. Bring a picnic supper or pupus and enjoy the entertainment (**808-637-9721;** www.sugarmillhawaii.com/bandstand).

The Best Lu'aus

Attending a lu'au is a mandatory part of visiting Hawaii—especially if it's your first time. Unfortunately, this traditional feast with Polynesian-style entertainment has become very commercial in most cases, almost to the point of kitsch. Even through the commercialism, the better shows will provide an evening of entertainment and some real insight into the Polynesian culture.

With the exception of the Paradise Cove lu'au, most lu'aus on O'ahu are inferior to those you'll find on other Hawaiian islands. So if you plan to travel to Kaua'i, Maui, or The Big Island, you might want to plan a big night at a lu'au during one of your itineraries there. For details, see the respective "Enjoying" chapters for those islands.

Lu'aus generally last three or four hours and charge $75 to $100 for adults, about 25 percent less for children. All feature an all-you-can-eat Hawaiian feast, an open bar, and entertainment. Here, then, are a few of the better lu'aus on Oahu:

Ali'i Lu'au at the Polynesian Cultural Center La'ie

Set in Windward O'ahu, this lu'au gets high marks for authentic culture and overall quality, but expect to share your experience with about 700 other people. It's held in the Center's Hale Aloha Theater, with several serving stations for food. The fire dances are especially notable. It's somewhat pricey, with adult ticket prices starting at just over $100. *55-370 Kamehameha Highway (Route 83). The Ali'i Luau is served Monday–Saturday (closed Sundays) from 5:15 P.M.–6:30 P.M.* ***808-293-3333*** *or* ***1-800-367-7060.*** *www.polynesia.com.*

Germaine's Lu'au Kapolei

Located on private land near Barber's Point Lighthouse on the southwest tip of O'ahu, this lu'au is generally regarded as the most authentic on O'ahu. It's kind of like a backyard barbecue, but with hundreds of people. It offers the usual tropical cocktails; lavish entertainment featuring music and dances of

Tahiti, Samoa, Fiji, New Zealand, and Hawaii; a tasty buffet-style banquet; and an awesome tropical sunset (weather permitting, of course). *Take H1 to Kalaeloa Boulevard and follow that south to Olai Street. Turn right and continue until the end of the road. Held nightly at 6 P.M. Gates open at 5:15 P.M.* ***808-949-6626*** *or* ***1-800-367-5655****. www.germainesluau.com.*

Paradise Cove Lu'au Ko'Olina

The Paradise Cove lu'au at the beautiful Ko'Olina Resort and Marina in Leeward O'ahu (about 10 miles west of Honolulu) is hands-down the best lu'au on the island. You'll be greeted with a mai tai and live Hawaiian music, stroll through a replica Hawaiian village, attend a beach ceremony, and enjoy a huge feast and award-winning show with a spectacular Hawaiian sunset as a backdrop. *From Waikiki, take H-1 west toward Waianae and continue on Farrington Highway (Route 93). Take the Ko'Olina exit to Aliinui Drive and continue past the guard shack. The Paradise Cove parking lot will be on your right. Held nightly 5 P.M. to 9 P.M. 808-842-5911 or 1-800-775-2683. www.paradisecovehawaii.com.*

Shopping Around O'ahu

Cosmopolitan Honolulu is the center for shopping in O'ahu and all of Hawaii, of course (see Chapter 5), but the rest of the island also has some excellent shopping choices, especially if you're on the lookout for authentic arts and crafts. You not only can choose from small shops and galleries in the smaller towns, but from the many open-air markets that take place across O'ahu on a regular basis throughout the week. Here is a rundown of some of the most interesting places to shop around O'ahu.

Southeast O'ahu

In Southeast O'ahu, you're basically in the Honolulu suburbs, specifically the rather upscale towns of Kahala and Hawaii Kai. Being close-in to the big city, there is **Kahala Mall,** 4211 Waialae Avenue (**808-732-7736**), boasting over 90 shops and an eight-plex movie theater. You'll find all of the major brands and plenty of quality shopping around here, just as you would at home, including **Macy's, Banana Republic, Barnes & Noble, Starbucks, Ann Taylor,** and the rest. Mall hours are Monday–Saturday from 10 A.M.–9 P.M., and Sunday from 10 A.M.–5 P.M. The nearby **Kahala Hotel and Resort,** 5000 Kahala Avenue (**808-739-8888**) has a sort of mall of its own, featuring such higher-end stores and boutiques as **Fendi** and **Hildgund Jewelers,** the latter renowned for its custom designs and Hawaiian jewelry.

TOP SHOPPING DISTRICTS AWAY FROM HONOLULU

Serendipity is a big part of traveling. As you cruise around O'ahu you're going to stumble upon open-air markets and little stands offering exquisite handmade items you would never have thought of on your own. So, ironically, you've got to "plan" on that happening. Nevertheless, if you're looking for specific items, here are the primary locales outside of Honolulu worthy of your focus:

- **Hawaii Kai and Kahala:** Primarily malls and mainstream shopping opportunities, but with a small assortment of "discovery" opportunities.
- **Hale'iwa:** This North Shore town is a great shopping destination if you're looking for creative arts and crafts, as well as relics of contemporary surf culture.
- **Kailua:** This Windward O'ahu settlement definitely has some cool shops and interesting items, but doesn't offer the sheer variety of choices that you'll find in Hale'iwa.

In Hawaii Kai, the **Koko Marina Center** at 7192 Kalanianaole Highway (**808-395-4737**) offers a variety of specialty and gift shops. These include **Local Motion,** selling cool surfwear and accessories for adults and kids; and **Island Treasures At The Marina** (formerly known as Island Treasures Art Gallery), which boasts a selection of local artists' creations in artwork, Koa Wood furniture, ceramics, jewelry, Hawaiian quilts, specialty foods, and stationery items.

Windward O'ahu

You'll find interesting shops all over Windward O'ahu, with the highest concentration in the towns of Kailua and Kane'ohe. Kailua's funky little downtown offers a small but eclectic selection of shops, boutiques, galleries, and antique stores that are fun to explore and are often the sources of unique special treasures you can take back to the folks at home. One such place is **Ali'i Antiques of Kailua,** 9-A Maluniu Avenue (**808-261-1705**), which is loaded with all kinds of cool island relics that you definitely won't find on the mainland. You also can check out **Global Village,** 539 Kailua Road

(**808-262-8183**), offering more unique Hawaiian jewelry, clothing, and gifts; as well as **Manuheali'i**, 629 Kailua Road (**808-261-9865**), featuring an excellent collection of Hawaiian apparel and accessories.

The **Windward Mall** at 46-056 Kamehameha Highway (Route 83) in Kaneohe (**808-235-1143;** www.windwardmall.com) is another one of those familiar shopping experiences, much like home, with over a hundred stores that represent nationally recognized brands (**Hot Topic; Jeans Warehouse, Radio Shack**), as well as about 15 homegrown shops and galleries such as **Gallery Haiku,** offering an impressive selection of handcrafted Hawaiian artwork and gifts.

The North Shore

Browse the galleries and pick up a piece of art in Hale'iwa on the North Shore—the center for unique purchases on that part of the island. You can begin at the **Northshore Marketplace,** 66-250 Kamehameha Highway (Route 83), offering a nice selection of stores. A few of the standouts are **Oceans In Glass (808-637-3366**), offering beautiful glass sculptures of sea creatures such as dolphins, humpback whales, and colorful reef fish; **Wyland Galleries (1-888-435-6691**) selling beautiful artwork and bronze work; and **Polynesian Treasures (808-637-1288**). Nearby you might enjoy **Oogenesis Boutique,** 66-249 Kamehameha Highway (**808-637-4580**), filled with vintage-style dresses that flutter prettily in the North Shore breeze.

Local Markets

Hawaii is known for its outdoor farmers markets, where you can get your hands on some super-authentic Hawaiian fresh produce, arts and crafts, and food. These occur most days of the week in different parts of O'ahu.

One of the most well-known events is the **North Shore Country Market** (www.northshorecountrymarket.com), which takes place every day across from the post office in Hale'iwa from 8 A.M.–2 P.M. (**808-638-0151**). On Saturdays you can drop by the **Waialua Farmers' Market** (www.sugarmillhawaii.com/farmer/), at the Waialua Sugar Mill from 8 A.M.–12 noon.

The Honolulu Department of Parks and Recreation sponsors island-wide farmers markets offering fresh fruits, vegetables, and fish. These take place in Hawaii Kai on Saturdays, in Leeward O'ahu on Tuesdays, Fridays, and Sundays, and in Windward O'ahu on Thursdays. Call **808-522-7088** or go to www.co.honolulu.hi.us/parks/program/pom for more information. You also can check in at the individual local town halls for information on upcoming markets. Here's a sampler of ongoing markets:

Saturdays in Hawaii Kai:

- Banyan Court Mall, 800 North King Street, 6:15 A.M.–7:30 A.M.
- Kalihi Valley District Park, 1911 Kam IV Road, 10 A.M.–10:45 A.M.
- Salt Lake Municipal Lot, 5337 Likini Street; 11:15 A.M. –12 noon
- Hawaii Kai Park-n-Ride, 300 Keah'ole Street, 1 P.M.–2 P.M.

Sundays in Leeward O'ahu:

- Kapolei Community Park, 91-1049 Kamaaha Loop, 7 A.M.–8:30 A.M.
- Royal Kunia Park-n-Ride, Kupuohi Street, 9:30 A.M.–11 A.M.
- Waikele Community Park, 94-870 Lumiaina Street, 11:30 A.M.–12:30 P.M.

Tuesdays in Leeward O'ahu:

- Waiau District Park, 98-1650 Kaahumanu Street, 6:30 A.M.–7:30 A.M.
- Waipahu District Park, 94-230 Paiwa Street, 8:15 A.M.–9:15 A.M.
- Wahiawa District Park, North Cane Street and California Avenue, 10 A.M.–11 A.M.

Thursdays in Windward O'ahu:

- Waimanalo Beach Park, 41-741 Kalanianaole Highway, 7:15 A.M.–8:15 A.M.
- Kailua District Park, 21 South Kainalu Drive, 9 A.M.–10 A.M.
- Kaneohe District Park, 45-660 Keaahala Road, 10:45 A.M.–11:45 A.M.

Fridays in Leeward O'ahu:

- Halawa District Park, 99-795 Iwaiwa Street, 7 A.M.–8 A.M.
- Ewa Beach Community Park, 91-955 North Road, 9 A.M.–10 A.M.
- Pokai Bay Beach Park, 85-037 Pokai Bay Road, 11 A.M.–11:45 A.M.

Enjoying the Very Best Activities on O'ahu

As Hawaii's most populated and most visited island, O'ahu offers plenty of activities to suit your vacation style—whether your thing is a sedate bus ride or windsurfing.

Sightseeing Tours

A huge variety of sightseeing tours on vehicles of all types can be booked from the front desk or concierge station in your hotel, and almost all operate out of Honolulu. Please refer to the "Sightseeing Tours" section of Chapter 5 for our recommendations.

Enjoying Outdoor O'ahu

When people consider O'ahu they think of a big city, Honolulu. But even in Waikiki nature starts to take over, and by the time you get a few miles outside of town, there are great things to do amid mountainous green landscapes and turquoise seas. That's the beauty of O'ahu: drive a few minutes and you're amid nature's bounty. Of course there's surfing, but also golf, whale watching, snorkeling, horseback riding, hikes into rainforests, and much more.

Best Golf Courses in O'ahu

Playing golf in Hawaii is an experience unto itself. With the gorgeous scenery and wonderful climate, you're practically guaranteed a good time. Courses on O'ahu, though, may not be as exciting as those on other Hawaiian islands. They do, however, promise a challenging and great game even if they lack some of the thrilling sights. With over 30 courses that vary from public to military, you can absolutely find a course that fits your needs.

Here are a few of O'ahu's golf courses that we think are worth checking out:

> **Coral Creek Golf Course,** Ewa Beach. With natural coral rock formations and beautiful cliffs, this course promises a serene setting. It was designed in 1999 and was the first course to use seashore *paspalum grass. Thirteen of the holes provide water views. 18 holes. Par 72, 6,808 yards. Nonresident greens fees range from $56–$130, depending on*

time of day and package. 91-1111 Geiger Road. ***808-411-GOLF or 1-888-TO-TEEUP.*** *www.coralcreekgolfhawaii.com.*

Hawaii Prince Golf Club, Ewa Beach. This public course was designed by Ed Seay and Arnold Palmer in 1992 on 270 acres. Lakes and palm trees dot the predominantly flat landscape. *27 holes. Par 72, 7,117 yards. 91-1200 Fort Weaver Road. $140 greens fee.* ***808-944-4567.*** *www.princeresortshawaii.com.*

Ko'olau Golf Club, Kane'ohe. Considered the toughest course in America, this course promises an adventure for any player. Wrapped by looming mountains and traveling through three climate zones, this course will not disappoint. *18 holes. Par 72, 7,310 yards. Greens fees are $135, $85 after 12 noon. 45-550 Kionaole Road.* ***808-236-4653 ext. 223.*** *www.Koolaugolfclub.com.*

Ko'Olina Golf Course, Kapolei. As part of Ko'Olina Resort, this course is home to the newest LPGA tournament, the Fields Open. It promises beautiful coastal views and all the luxury of the resort that you may desire. *18 holes. Par 72, 6,867 yards. Greens fees are $170, $110 for twilight rate at 2 P.M. If you stay at the resort it's $145/$95. 92-1220 Aliinui Drive.* ***808-676-5300, ext. 1.*** *www.koolinagolf.com.*

Luana Hills Country Club, Kailua. Between Kailua and Waimanalo lies the Luana Hills Country Club. Surrounded by towering mountains and lush rainforest, this course promises a breathtaking and unforgettable round of golf. Designed by Pete Dye, it's challenging, but accessible to all levels of players. *18 holes. Par 72, 6,164 yards. 770 Auola Road. $125 tee fee.* ***808-262-2139.*** *www.luanahills.com.*

Makaha Resort Golf Club, Wai'anae. Boasting views of the Pacific in a more compact course, the public Makaha Resort Golf Club is the cousin of the Makaha Valley Resort Course. This course claims to be a championship course that will give all your clubs a run for their money. *18 holes. Par 72, 6,369 yards. $80 tee fee. 84-627 Makaha Valley Road.* ***808-695-9578*** *or* ***808-695-7111.*** *www.makahavalleycc.com.*

Turtle Bay Resort Golf Club, Kahuku. This is the only course in O'ahu where you will find 36 holes spread out over two distinct courses: the Arnold Palmer and the George Fazio. *The PGA Champions Tour even takes place here. Palmer Course: 18 holes. Par 72, 7,199 yards. 57-091 Kamehameha Highway, Kahuku. $145–175 tee fee.* ***808-293-9147.*** *Fazio Course: 18 holes. Par 72, 6,535 yards. 57-049 Kuilima Drive. $115–$155 tee fee.* ***808-293-8574.*** *www.turtlebayhotel.com.*

Wai'alae Country Club, Waipahu. You can see Pearl Harbor from this Ted Robinson–designed course, which is located 30 minutes west of Waikiki. You'll enjoy the three waterfalls dotting the landscape. *18 holes. Par 72, 5,874 yards. 94-200 Paida Place. $85–$125 tee fee.* ***808-676-9000.*** *www.golfwaikele.com.*

Hiking in O'ahu

O'ahu is often thought of as Hawaii's urban island—at least in the minds of those who have not actually dropped in for a visit, or who maybe have spent all their time on the sands of Waikiki. However, O'ahu actually has hundreds of miles of scenic, and sometimes rugged, hiking trails, ranging from cliff-side walks to deep valleys to lofty mountain ridges with panoramic views.

It rains quite a bit on O'ahu, especially on the windward coast and up in the mountains. It's therefore smart to take along a walking stick to help with those slick, muddy trails that you're almost sure to encounter, as well as rain gear.

MAP CENTRAL FOR O'AHU HIKING

You can get complete trail maps, recommendations, and necessary permits by visiting the **Department of Parks and Recreation,** 650 King Street in Honolulu (**808-523-4525**), at the satellite city hall at the **Ala Moana Center,** 1450 Ala Moana Boulevard (**808-973-2600**), or at the **Department of Land and Natural Resources** office at 1151 Punchbowl Street in downtown Honolulu (**808-587-0166**). You also can download a Hawaii State Parks brochure at www.hawaii.gov/dlnt/dsp/dsp.html.

These descriptions will give you a sense of the best hikes on O'ahu, but you can't use them for navigation. Be sure to pick up a map before you set out!

Diamond Head Southeast O'ahu

Hiking this ancient volcanic cone and crater, located just east of Honolulu, isn't exactly a backcountry experience. The trail to the top involves a good deal of concrete, a bunch of dusty switchbacks, some metal fittings, a whole lot of stairs, and scores of other tourists. But hey … Diamond Head is the symbol of O'ahu and there's a fabulous

360-degree view from the top. The trail starts at the parking area with a concrete walkway, then turns into a rocky footpath that rises 540 feet (sometimes relying on metal stairs) to top out at Diamond Head's highest point: the Leahi Benchmark (elev. 762 feet). On a clear day, you may be able to see Maui from the top. ***Distance: 0.75 mile.*** *Diamond Head State Monument, $1 per person for entry for walk-in and $5 per private vehicle.*

Ka'ena Point Leeward O'ahu

Ka'ena means "the heat" in Hawaiian, and there's usually plenty of that here on this dry, dramatic, westernmost point of O'ahu. This spear-shaped protrusion of land, lined with jagged sea cliffs, is considered to be, in Hawaiian folklore, a point from which souls leave this world. With beautiful views of western O'ahu and amazing surf, you could understand why this may be the last place anyone would need to see. Extreme caution should be used in and around the ocean during the winter months, as the rip currents and waves become large and dangerous. ***Distance: 5 miles.*** *The point itself can only be reached on foot. Take Route 930 north from Makaha into Ka'ena State Park. Park in the lot and from there you will have to hoof it. You also can walk in from the north side, where an unimproved track extends three miles along the coast from the end of Route 930.*

Kaunala Loop The North Shore

This trail above the Waimea Valley offers a moderate climb with panoramic views of the North Shore all the way to Ka'ena Point and the Wai'anae Mountains. ***Distance: 4.5 miles.*** *Drive to the end of Pupukea Road, which junctions with Kamehameha Hwy (Route 83) near the Foodland between Waimea Valley and Sunset Beach. The dirt portion of Pupukea Road, about 0.8 miles from the end of the paved road.*

Kealia Trail The North Shore

Starting at near sea level, this trail entails 19 switchbacks climbing 1,040 feet to the top of sea cliffs, then turns into a jeep road the rest of the way to the junction with the Kuaokala Ridge Trail. You can then walk a bit further up the Waianae ridgeline to a viewpoint (elev. 1,960 feet) of Makua Valley and the Waianae coast. From there you also can see the summit of Mt. Ka'ala (4,025 feet), Oahu's highest point. ***Distance: 5 miles.*** *The trail starts about 0.3 miles behind the air traffic control building parking lot on the mauka (inland) side of Dillingham Airfield in Mokule'ia.*

Kuli'ou'ou Ridge Southeast O'ahu

Climbing to the crest of the southeastern Ko'olaus Mountains, this graded trail climbs 1,700 vertical feet and ends at a windswept summit with sweeping coastal views of the Windward O'ahu coastline. It's very popular, so expect company. ***Distance: 3.4 miles.*** *Along Kalanianaole Hwy (Route 72) just west of Hawaii Kai, turn at the traffic light onto Kuliouou Road. Follow the road around a park and just before the road ends take a right onto Kala'au Road.*

Manoa Falls Southeast O'ahu

This trail is second in popularity only to Diamond Head. Why? It's a short hike at the end of the lush Manoa Valley outside of Honolulu, and it leads to a lovely 60-foot waterfall and pool in which you can cool off. ***Distance: 0.8 miles.*** *Follow Punahou Road and Manoa Road out of the Waikiki area and north toward the mountains. Go all the way to the end, park your vehicle, and follow the signs.*

Waimano Trail Leeward O'ahu

This is the longest public hiking trail on Oahu, taking you through some great wilderness country and ending at an elevation of 2,160 feet between two peaks along the Ko'olau Mountains crest. There you'll have fabulous views of the bowl-like Waihee Valley directly below as well as Kaneohe Bay, Chinaman's Hat (Mokolii Island), and other landmarks along the leeward and windward coasts. Due to the length of this trail, you should start by 8 A.M. ***Distance: 7 miles.*** *From H-1, exit at the Pearl City/Waimalu exit. Turn right on Moanalua Road at the end of the ramp. Take that to Waimano Home Road, and then to a guard shack with a parking area on the left.*

Surfing and Windsurfing in O'ahu

O'ahu is world-famous for surfing, mainly because of the huge 30-foot waves that pound into the North Shore's Sunset Beach and Banzai Pipeline each winter. But other parts of O'ahu are also prime surfing spots, including Makaha in Leeward O'ahu, Kailua in Windward O'ahu, and the smaller, perfect swells of Waikiki—perfect for beginners. If you're into **bodyboarding,** You might want to check out Sandy Beach in Southeast O'ahu, which the locals like but has very dangerous rip currents (surf there at your own risk!). The North Shore's Waimea Beach is also good for bodyboarding in the calmer summer months.

In Waikiki, lessons are available seven days a week from **Hans Hedemann Surf School** (**808-924-7778;** www.hhsurf.com) or **Hawaiian Watersports** (**808-262-5483;** www.hawaiiwatersports.com), where you also can rent a board. Most private lessons are generally around $100 or more an hour; about $50 an hour for group lessons.

If you're headed for the leeward coast, **Hale Nalu Surf & Bike** in the Makaha/Wai'anae area, 85-876 Farrington Highway, Wai'anae (**808-696-5897;** www.halenalu.com), will rent you a range of surfing, diving, and kayaking equipment—heck, they'll even rent you a beach chair and umbrella. Longboard rates start at about $22 per day, $80 per week. You can get a bodyboard for approximately $11 per day; $38 per week. On the North Shore, check out **Barnfield's Raging Isle Surf & Cycle** (**808-637-7707;** www.ragingisle.com), located in the North Shore Marketplace in the center of town. Owner Bill Barnfield is a legend in these parts as a renowned surfboard designer, surfer, and avid bicycle racer.

Windsurfing, Hang Gliding, and Paragliding

Windward O'ahu is a great place for windsurfing and paragliding, especially around Kailua Beach. **Gravity Hawaii,** 44-116 Kauinohea Place, Kane'ohe (**808-220-6302;** www.gravityhawaii.com) is ready to set you up with gear for windsurfing, wave surfing, and paragliding, and they run a school for these pursuits. **North Shore Hang Gliding,** located at Dingham Airfield in Hale'iwa (**808-637-3178**) will also teach you how to fly like a bird. In Windward O'ahu, check out **Kailua Sailboards and Kayaks,** 130 Kailua Road in the Kailua Beach Center (**808-262-2555**).

Sailing and Snorkeling

The near-constant trade winds make all of the Hawaiian Islands nearly perfect for sailing, and O'ahu is no exception, with sailboat charters leaving from the Ko'Olina Marina in Leeward O'ahu, and Hale'iwa and Waimea on the North Shore. Most of these outfits offer a full range of activities. Of course, gorgeous and placid **Hanauma Bay** in Southeast O'ahu is one of the top snorkeling sites in Hawaii, home to over 450 species of tropical fish, and is in fact a state underwater park. You can rent masks, snorkels, and fins at a concession stand there.

TOP WATERSPORTS LOCATIONS AROUND O'AHU

Feel like getting wet? You can partake in all of these activities almost anywhere along the O'ahu coast, but geographical and weather-related factors make these the preferred spots for those in the know.

Surfing

- Leeward: Makaha
- North Shore: Kawela Beach, Sunset Beach, Waimea Beach
- Windward O'ahu: Kailua Beach

Snorkeling

- Leeward: Off Wai'anae
- North Shore: Kawela Beach, Waimea Beach (summer)
- Southeast: Hanauma Bay
- Windward: Lanikai

Bodyboarding

- North Shore: Waimea (summer)
- Southeast: Sandy Beach

Windsurfing

- North Shore: Kawela
- Windward: Kailua

Outside of Hanauma Bay, a great deal of sailing and snorkeling goes on off O'ahu's west coast. In Leeward O'ahu, **Hawaii Nautical (808-234-SAIL;** www.hawaiinautical.com) runs a 53-foot catamaran, **the Ko Olina Cat,** out of the Ko'Olina Resort and Marina for cruises along the Wai'anae Coast to view dolphins, turtles, and other Hawaiian sea life. For around $100, you can take a three-hour morning or afternoon snorkeling sail, including a light meal. A cocktail sunset cruise from 5:30 P.M.–7:30 P.M. (5 P.M.–7 P.M. in the winter) is especially nice, including two free alcoholic drinks per adult and the cruise for just $45. Hawaii Nautical also offers dinner cruises, and charters mono-hull sailboats and motor boats for sightseeing, diving for $125, including equipment, and whale-watching for $50.

Aquatic Surfaris in Wai'anae (**808-306-7273;** www.sailhawaii.com) and **Ocean Joy Cruises** in Ko'Olina (**808-678-8477** or **1-888-677-1277;** www.oceanjoycruises.com) also offer a full menu of pleasure cruises, snorkeling, and dolphin-, turtle-, and whale-watching cruises about their boats. On the North Shore, go to **North Shore Catamaran Charters** in Hale'iwa (**808-351-9371;** www.sailingcat.com) for sailing charters, whale-watching cruises, snorkeling, and sunset cruises, including a pupu platter and non-alcoholic beverages.

Kayaking

O'ahu's windward coast from Waikane to Kailua and Lanikai is da' place for sea kayaking, especially around Kailua Bay, which is protected by a reef, and the beautiful Mokulua Islands off Lanikai Beach. Paddling quietly in your kayak, you'll commune with native sea turtles, whales, and dolphins. **Kailua Sailboards and Kayaks,** 130 Kailua Road in the Kailua Beach Center (**808-262-2555;** www.kailuasailboards.com), will outfit you with a safe polyethylene two-seater, as well as provide tours, lessons, and rentals for kayaking, windsurfing, snorkeling, boogieboarding, sailing, kite surfing, surfing, and other watersports.

Whale-Watching and More

Pacific humpback whales visit Hawaii's waters by the thousands from November to March, migrating close to 3,500 miles from their Alaskan summer feeding waters in order to mate and have their calves. In season you can spot them from many parts of the O'ahu shoreline—including Makapu'u Point in Southeast O'ahu and Turtle Bay on the North Shore.

These same areas are also rife with dolphins and giant Hawaiian sea turtles, and there's nothing quite like getting up-close and personal with these intriguing creatures.

Paradise Cruises (**808-983-7827** or **1-800-334-6191;** www.paradisecruises.com) sails out of Aloha Tower Marketplace in Honolulu on three separate boats, ranging in capacity from 150 passengers to 1,500 passengers, to view humpbacks with a naturalist crew. Prices range from $33 to $50.

For a more intimate experience, check out **Wild Side Specialty Tours** (**808-306-7273;** www.sailhawaii.com). Wild Side offers four-hour morning "wildlife adventures" out of Leeward O'ahu's **Waianae Boat Harbor** to view whales, dolphins, and Hawaiian sea turtles on a 16-passenger catamaran.

Tours include a continental breakfast, refreshments, drinks, snorkel gear, and instruction.

Fishing

The waters around O'ahu offer world-class deep sea fishing, and there are scores of charter companies ready to provide everything you need to cast for blue marlin, ono, mahi-mahi, and tuna with an experienced captain and crew. On the North Shore, **Ku'uloa Kai Charters,** 66-195 Ka'amooloa Road, Waialua (**808-637-5783;** www.kuuloakai.com) runs a well-equipped 31-foot Bertram Sportfisher. In Leeward O'ahu, **Boom Boom Sportfishing** at the Wai'anae Boat Harbor (**808-306-4162;** www.boomboomsportfishing.com) offers 50-foot or 40-foot luxury Sportfisher boats.

Whew! There's really a lot to do around O'ahu, with only an hour of driving time separating the far ends of the island. That's what we call a concentrated vacation experience.

Part 3

Maui

Maui is first in the hearts of most visitors to Hawaii. That's probably because of its magical scenery and incredible variety of resorts, shopping, sports, history, culture and performing arts, adventure, and pampered luxury. You name it, Maui's got it.

Chapter 8

Relaxing in Maui

In This Chapter

- Maui's geography and weather
- Transportation options
- Deciding where to stay on Maui
- Maui's best lodging choices

Is **Maui** number one in the Hawaiian Islands? The locals certainly think so. They boast: "Maui no ka oi," which means "Maui is the best!"

Let's look at the facts. Maui has more miles of swimmable beaches than any other Hawaiian Island. Depending on elevation, it has climate zones ranging from tropical to alpine. It has both rainforests and deserts and ferns and cacti.

And then there is **Haleakala,** the huge dormant volcano that makes up the main part of the island. The cone reaches to 10,023 feet above sea level. If it wasn't surrounded by deep water, Haleakala would rise more than 30,000 feet above the ocean floor. As large as it appears when you're standing in its shadow, something like 97 percent of its volume lies below the surface of the ocean.

Whatever is on its surfaces or surrounding, Maui certainly has something special to offer.

Maui Is King

Maybe Maui is king because it's the only Hawaiian Island named after a deity: the demigod Maui, who, as legend has it, hid in the crater of Haleakaka, snared the fierce sun god, and made him promise to travel more slowly over Maui.

Snapshot

Maui:

Size: 727 square miles

Population: 135,605

Average Temperature: 72°F to 78°F (22.2°C to 25.5°C); colder at higher elevations)

Coastline: 120 miles (193 kilometers)

Number of Golf Courses: 16

Highest Elevation: 10,023 feet (Haleakala)

Size of Haleakala Crater: 25 square miles

Home of gorgeous palm-fringed beaches, world-class resorts and restaurants, white-sand beaches, dramatic sea cliffs, funky surfer towns and historic whaling villages, tropical waterfalls, rocky vistas above timberline, waving fields of sugar cane, and innumerable rainbows, Maui's just got that magical and supremely satisfying "certain something."

Maui almost owns the top spot in annual magazine surveys of the world's most bodacious islands. All we know is, like most people, we want more Maui and the sooner the better.

Airport Transportation Options

All major flights to Maui arrive at the modern airport in **Kahului,** the island's main town situated in the flat, sugar cane–blanketed isthmus between the mountains of western and eastern Maui. You also have the option of flying from other Hawaiian Islands to the much smaller **West Maui airport** in the hills above **Ka'anapali.** To research a trip to Maui, see Chapter 3.

After you make your way down to the open-air lobby and baggage area, your senses will most likely be assaulted by a mild tropical breeze and the pervasive scent of flowers. Aloha! It's time to secure some transportation and start experiencing the magic of Maui.

Rental Cars

All of the major car rental companies maintain offices on the Maui airport property, with small booths in the terminal area itself. You can find them by walking toward the north end of the terminal (to the right as you're facing the street). You can confirm your reservations at these booths and from there catch a company van for the very short ride to the rental office and lot. As on most of the other Hawaiian islands, you can pick from a wide range of vehicles, including cars, trucks, vans, and SUVs. Rates begin at about $44 to $54 per day and $264 to $300 per week for subcompacts, with unlimited mileage.

You can save some significant bucks on car rental if you're willing to settle for an older, used vehicle. Outfits such as **Maui Car Rentals (1-800-567-4659)** or **Word of Mouth Car Rentals (808-877-2436)** will give you a clean, well-maintained car for as little as $15 per day and $130 per week.

Taxi Service

There are several taxi services that will pick you up right at Kahalui Airport curbside and take you anywhere on the island. Among these are **Maui Airport Taxi (808-877-0907)** and **Alii Cab Company (808-661-3688)**. With a metered rate of about $3.50 per mile, any taxi on Maui will be pretty pricey. A taxi to **Lahaina** will set you back about $74; to **Kihei** you'll spend about $45.

Shuttles

Maui offers several shuttle services that can get you where you want to go at a lower cost than a cab or limo. All run frequently, and you can call them to arrange for a pickup. **Speedi Shuttle (808-242-7777** or **1-877-521-2085)** will take you to Kihei or Wailea for about $16, while **Kapalua Executive Transportation Services (808-669-2300)** goes all over the island. With these outfits, the more people you squeeze into the van, the less it will cost per person, with additional passengers in your party charged only about $5. One-person rates to Lahaina are about $36; $26 to Kihea. The **Airporter Shuttle (808-877-7308** or **1-800-231-6984)** specializes in runs to West Maui all day, charging about $15.

Limousine Services

If you want to travel in a little more comfort and style, or just need a lot of room and want someone else to do the driving, you can make a reservation with one of Maui's limousine companies, including **Aloha Maui Limousine Service** (**808-873-2034** or **1-877-877-2034**) or **Star Maui Limousine** (**808-875-6900** or **1-877-875-6900**). A limo ride in any of these to any part of the island will cost you about $100.

Traveling on the Cheap: Buses

Maui public buses (**808-871-4838**) provide service between **Central, South,** and **West Maui** Monday through Saturday. And yes, the white motor coaches with green stripes do stop at the airport. A system-wide all-day pass costs about $10 per person, with one-way fares only $1 for short routes and $2 for longer runs.

A separate transportation service, **Holo Ka'a Public Transit** (**808-879-2828**), runs comfortable, air-conditioned shuttle buses to just about all of the major locations in West Maui and South Maui (look for the white, pink, and purple buses). Within the resort areas of **Kaanapali, Kapalua,** and **Wailea,** the coaches are free. Between these resort areas, they'll cost you a measly $1 to $2, which may be one of the best bargains in the Hawaiian Islands.

Group Tours

If you're just stopping in Maui for a day, or prefer someone else manage your itinerary, you can let a tour company chauffer you to notable sites. Check out one of the Lahaina-based operators, **Barefoot Cashback Tours** (**808-661-8889;** www.tombarefoot.com), which operate vans, or **Fantasy Island Activities and Tours** (**808-667-9740**). If you don't mind riding one of those large coaches, call **Roberts Hawaii** (**808-871-6226** or **1-800-831-5541**). There is more information on sightseeing tours in Chapter 9.

Here's about what you can expect to spend between Kahului airport and popular destinations around Maui:

What Transportation Costs on Maui

Destination	*Taxi*	*Limo*	*Shuttle*	*Bus*
Hana				
Kaanapali	$87	$100	$38	$1

Destination	*Taxi*	*Limo*	*Shuttle*	*Bus*
Kapalua	$105	$100	$50	$1
Kihei	$45	$100	$16–$25	$1
Lahaina	$74	$100	$36	$1
Makena	$65	$100	$35	$1
Wailea	$57	$100	$30–$206	$1
Wailuku	$20	$100	$20	Free

Getting Your Bearings: Island Locales

Maui is made up of two mountainous landmasses joined by a low, fairly narrow isthmus in the middle (hence the nickname, **"The Valley Isle"**). Because the prevailing trade winds blow from northeast to southwest, the eastern and northern sides of the island tend to be damp and lush; the western and southern sides, sunny and dry—at least along the coast. Elevation is a major factor in Maui weather, and the higher you go, the more likely it is that you'll experience clouds and rain.

West Maui is classic Hawaii, a land of green hillsides, pineapple fields, and palm-fringed beaches—all of which surround the central massif of the deeply eroded and precipitous **West Maui Mountains** that rise to a respectable 5,788 feet at the summit of **Puu Kukui.** The southern and western coasts of West Maui are home to the New England–style former whaling village of Lahaina and (mostly) tasteful landscaped resorts, while the north coast is wild, rocky, and mainly undeveloped.

East Maui is dominated by the incredible mass of 10,023-foot Haleakala, to which the land rises from all directions. The broad flanks of Haleakala, called **Upcountry Maui,** is a rural area of farmland and orchards. Along the southwest coast of East Maui are the resort towns of **Kihei, Wailea,** and **Makena,** where the weather is almost always sunny, the hillsides arid. The northern shore of East Maui is wild, lush, and rainy, the rugged coastline followed by the famous **Hana Highway.** At the far eastern tip of the island is the quiet, green town of **Hana.**

West Maui's scenic 'Iao Valley.

(Photo courtesy of HVCB/Ron Dahlquist)

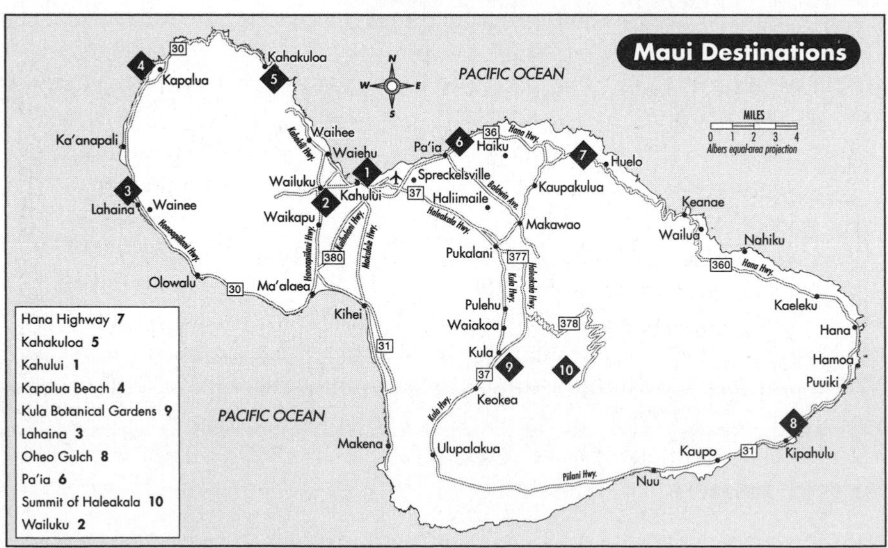

Maui's regions, highways, and key destinations.

The isthmus joining the two sides of the island was formed by a lava flow from Haleakala; the region is relatively flat, and is where you'll find Maui's largest town, **Kahului** (home of the main airport) as well as the county seat of **Wailuku** and the windy fishing port of **Ma'alaea.**

Central Maui: Kahului and Wailuku

Let's get right to the point: Kahului is probably not where you want to spend your vacation on Maui. Located on the north shore of Maui's central isthmus, it's the island's commercial center, and you'd never know you're in Hawaii while you're cruising through most of it. When you pull out of the airport road and onto the main drag, what you see is **Home Depot, Target,** car dealerships, fast-food joints, and other monuments of American culture. Unless you need to do some shopping at the **Maui Mall,** move on to better places.

Immediately west of Kahului is the town of Wailuku, which has a bit more character, including some historic buildings and a number of funky antique shops. You could have a worthwhile lunch here on the way to elsewhere, but there are many more interesting places on Maui.

On the south shore of the central isthmus, several miles down Route 30 or 380, is the fishing port of **Ma'alaea.** This is one of the windiest places on Maui, thanks to the funneling effect of the **West Maui Mountains** and **Haleakala** on either side of the valley. Obviously, the windsurfers like it here, and it's also a good area from which to view whales November through April.

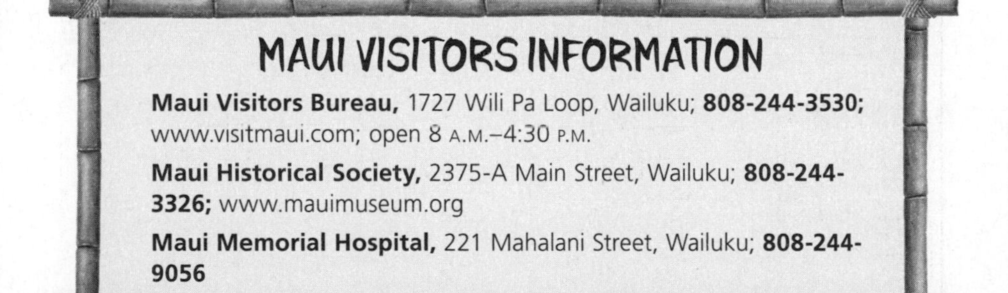

MAUI VISITORS INFORMATION

Maui Visitors Bureau, 1727 Wili Pa Loop, Wailuku; **808-244-3530;** www.visitmaui.com; open 8 A.M.–4:30 P.M.

Maui Historical Society, 2375-A Main Street, Wailuku; **808-244-3326;** www.mauimuseum.org

Maui Memorial Hospital, 221 Mahalani Street, Wailuku; **808-244-9056**

West Maui

There's nothing quite like sitting out under the palms on a West Maui afternoon, a relaxing beverage in hand, the strong, mild trade winds rustling the fronds above you, and the steep mountains beyond bathed in rainbows. The sun glints off the sea to your side, where you can see humpback whales breaking the surface of the water and the hulk of Moloka'i on the near horizon.

This western part of the island is the Maui of your mind's eye. And once you're settled in around here, the island's other top sights are within easy reach.

The quaint, if somewhat touristy, town of Lahaina on West Maui's southern coast was settled by whalers from Nantucket and elsewhere in New England in the early 1800s. There was, for those who had survived the long trip down the coast of South America and around Cape Horn, "No God west of the Horn" and they lived it up while in port, enjoying the charms of the beautiful local girls and imbibing plenty of grog.

Alas, after a while, missionaries and preachers arrived in Lahaina to put a stop to all of the merrymaking. Today, Lahaina still carries a New England feel in its architecture, museums, and churches.

Lahaina also boasts a nice little yacht harbor from which you can depart on sightseeing cruises. However, parking can be difficult, so allow yourself a few extra minutes if you have booked a cruise and are driving into town from elsewhere.

Further west from Lahaina are miles of resorts, condos and golf courses, covering the areas of **Ka'anapali, Napali,** and **Kapalua.** These are for the most part tastefully designed, with lush, green landscaping. In fact, the entire Ka'anapali resort area was designed in the 1980s under a master plan. There are superb beaches throughout this part of Maui, including the four-mile-long **Ka'anapali Beach** and the beautiful tropical crescent of **Kapalua Beach.** Further on along the coast, past Kapalua, the land along the sea road starts to climb, often rising into the mist that hangs around the northwestern tip of Maui.

The north coast of West Maui is a totally different scene of wild beauty, composed of rocky headlands, a stormy ocean, and the quintessential Hawaiian village of **Kahakuloa.**

plumeria

Snapshot

West Maui Destinations

- Lahaina
- Kahakuloa
- Kapalua Beach

East Maui

East Maui is the large part of the island, dominated by the hulking presence of Haleakala.

With its summit often in the misty clouds, Haleakala is one of the most jaw-dropping features of Maui. No trip to Maui would be complete without witnessing sunrise from its summit.

Haleakala's physical features of broad slopes and a sprawling crater above treeline also significantly affect the weather throughout East Maui.

The northern and eastern slopes of Haleakala catch the trade winds and rain, making East Maui's north shore and the eastern tip around Hana green and junglelike, broken by glimpses of many black-sand beaches. This is where you'll find the scenic Hana Highway, which winds its way through 600 curves, past sea cliffs and cascading waterfalls, from **Pa'ia** to **Hana.** Although Hana has some nice accommodations, it's a quiet place and hours by car from most of Maui's other destinations.

The western slope of Haleakala is generally dry and sunny. That means that the coastline running south of Maui's central isthmus has guaranteed sunny weather most days of the year. It also happens to have miles of beautiful golden beaches, a fact not lost on the developers who have focused on this region for the past couple of decades.

In fact, this coastline's **Kihei** area is a testament to unregulated planning, resulting in miles of sprawling condo complexes and mini-malls.

While Kihei is not exactly idyllic Hawaii, the beaches are good and here you can find more good deals on accommodations than anywhere else on the island.

The next town down, **Wailea,** is a different world from Kihei. It is quite expensive, featuring some of the most luxurious resorts on Maui, including the **Wailea Four Seasons** and the **Grand Wailea Resort and Spa.**

A bit further south is **Makena,** the end of the road along this coastline. It's an area where you're just as likely to see a cactus as a palm tree, with a few resorts, a nice beach, and a relatively quiet atmosphere.

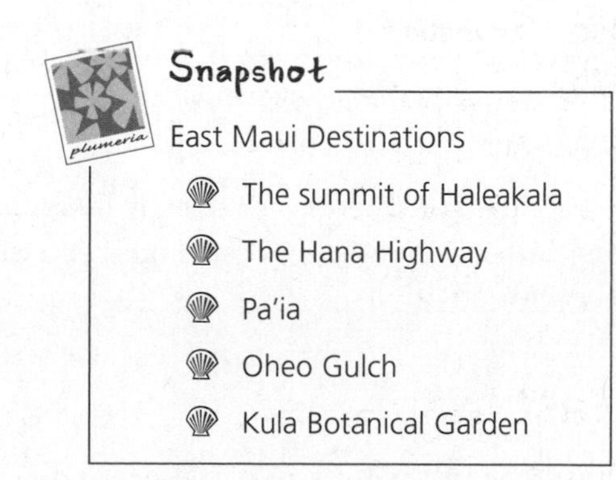

Snapshot

East Maui Destinations

- The summit of Haleakala
- The Hana Highway
- Pa'ia
- Oheo Gulch
- Kula Botanical Garden

The interior portion of East Maui, the highlands on the slopes of Haleakala, is generally called **Upcountry Maui.** It's a land of wineries, orchards, generally rural landscapes, and, of course, the summit of Haleakala.

Driving Times from Kahului Airport

Halealaka	1 hour, 45 minutes
Hana	3 hours (with stops)
Ka'anapali	50 minutes
Kapalua	1 hour
Kihea	20 minutes
Lahaina	40 hour
Makena	35 minutes
Pa'ia	15 minutes
Wailea	30 minutes
Wailuku	10 minutes

Comfortable Accommodations: Ultimate Places to Stay on Maui

Maui's accommodations can't be beat for variety, from B&Bs, to private homes, to condos of all shapes and sizes, to the utmost in pampered luxury at world-class resorts. There's only one little problem: accommodations here tend to be a little on the pricey side, even compared to the other Hawaiian Islands.

Following you'll find a few of our favorite places to stay on Maui, organized alphabetically under each lodging category. All have cable TV, telephone, overhead fans, and a private lanai.

Keep in mind that you can usually better any of these prices, especially during Hawaii's "low" season (summer) and through special timeshare and Internet promotions.

Hotels and Resorts

Ka'anapali Beach Club Lahaina $$$

Right on the beach, this pleasant all-suite high-rise resort is built around a huge open-air atrium and boasts large one- and two-bedroom suites with kitchenettes and good views. Amenities include a one-acre pool with water-slide and a hot tub, restaurants, and lounges. Rates include a daily breakfast buffet for two and complimentary cocktails each evening. You can save a bundle by taking the timeshare promotional package. *104 Ka'anapali Shores Place, Lahaina, HI, 96761.* ***808-661-2000.*** *www.sunterramaui.com.*

Hyatt Regency Maui Lahaina 

If you feel like splurging on a top resort, and you want to be in atmospheric West Maui, the Hyatt is worth serious consideration. Featuring a tree-filled atrium, fine restaurants, plenty of high-end shops, and extensive landscaped grounds right on beautiful Ka'anapali beach, you may not want to put down your mai tai to go sightseeing anywhere else. *200 Nohea Kai Drive, Lahaina, HI 96761.* ***808-661-1234.*** *www.maui.hyatt.com.*

Grand Wailea Resort Hotel and Spa Wailea $$$$$

If you like luxurious excess, you'll love this place, which is quite possibly the most over-the-top resort on Maui, and maybe in all of Hawaii. Just the swimming pool alone will blow your mind, with its myriad landscaped canals and passageways, faux rock chutes, waterfalls, waterslides, and swim-up bars. Then there are the sumptuous rooms, each with a private lanai, at least a partial ocean view, and an Italian marble bathroom with oversized bathtub. Add in six restaurants and lovely Wailea Beach and you've found a worthy place to stay. *3850 Alanui Drive, Wailea, HI 96753.* ***808-875-1234*** *or* ***1-800-888-6100.*** *www.grandwailea.com.*

Ma'alaea Surf Resort Ma'alaea $$$

This quiet retreat with one- and two-bedroom oceanfront condos is spread out over five acres of tropical gardens and a white sandy beach. It's close to bustling **Kihei,** closer to Ma'alaea, and even relatively close to Kahului and Maui's upcountry. *12 South Kihei Road, Kihei, HI 96753.* ***808-879-1267.*** *www.maalaeasurfresort.com.*

More Intimate Lodgings and B&Bs

The Inn at Mama's Fish House Pa'ia $$$$

This atmospheric inn is set on the beach amid coconut palms at a quiet location on Maui's spectacular north shore. It's also right next door (and associated with) one of the best restaurants on the island. It's only about 15 minutes from Maui's main airport in Kahuli, and about 5 minutes from cool and funky downtown Pa'ia. You have your choice of a one-bedroom duplex (which sleeps four) or a two-bedroom cottage right on the beach. *799 Poho Place, Pa'ia, Hawaii 96779.* ***808-579-9764*** *or* ***1-800-860-HULA (4852).*** *www.mamasfishhouse.com.*

Malu Manu Kula $$

Try this for a different kind of Maui experience: a two-bedroom home and log cabin on seven acres at the 4,000-foot level on the broad slopes of Haleakala, with all of Maui spread out beneath. This unusual accommodation serves as a romantic getaway anytime, and is the perfect base for sightseeing and hiking on the upper reaches of the mountain. *446 Cooke Road, Kula, HI 96790.* ***808-878-6111*** *or* ***1-888-878-6161.*** *www.mauisunrise.com/.*

Old Wailuku Inn at Ulupono Wailuku $$

When you visit Maui, you generally don't want a place "in town" and far from the beach. However, this former plantation house, called "the queen of historic Wailuku homes," offers leisurely comfort, real 1920s Hawaiian atmosphere, and large guest rooms with rare Hawaiian ohia wood floors and Hawaiian quilts. What's more, it's close to historic neighborhoods and museums. This is a great place if you want to spend a single night near Kahului and the airport. *2199 Kaho'okele Street, Wailuku, HI 96793.* ***808-244-5897*** *or* ***1-800-305-4899.*** *www.oldwailukuinn.com.*

The Plantation Inn Lahaina $$$

This 19-room Victorian-style inn is elegant, eminently comfortable, and right in the middle of historic Lahaina. Soundproof rooms keep out the touristy bustle of town, and you get a pool with Jacuzzi thrown into the mix. The award-winning Gerard's Restaurant is right on the premises, and breakfast is included in the room rates. If you're into B&Bs, you'll find this place classy and cool. *174 Lahainaluna Road, Lahaina, HI 96761.* ***808-667-9225*** *or* ***1-800-433-6815.*** *www.theplantationinn.com.*

Best Condos

Hale Napili Napili $$$

Located near the beautiful western tip of Maui, and only about 20 minutes from Lahaina, this intimate (18 units), pretty, and clean condo retreat will put you right on the beach without causing spontaneous combustion of your wallet. (There's no swimming pool, however.) The waves will soothe you to sleep at night, and you'll see the islands of Moloka'i and Lana'i on the horizon outside your window. Did we mention the sunsets? Accommodations at Hale Napili include studio units and one-bedroom units—each with a full kitchen and microwave. *65 Hui Drive, Napili Bay, Maui, HI 96761.* ***808-669-6184*** *or* ***1-800-245-2266.*** *www.halenapilimaui.com.*

Kapalua Villas Kapalua $$$$

If you like great views, golf, and country club ambience, check out these modern villas, located in one of the most beautiful and exclusive areas of Maui. It's part of a 23,000-acre master-planned resort community set amidst Maui's only working pineapple plantation. These units aren't cheap, but you can get real value if you're staying with another couple or a family and you opt for one of the many packages offered by the rental company for one of the two-bedroom, 2,400-square-foot villas. *800 Kapalua Drive, Lahaina, HI 96761.* ***1-800-545-0018.*** *www.kapaluavillas.com.*

Maui Kamaole Kihei $$

Located directly across the road from one of Maui's best public beaches, Kamaole Beach III, this low-rise complex offers nice views, good rates, and spacious one- and two-bedroom accommodations—all of which come with two bathrooms. *2511 South Kihei Road, Kihei, HI 96753.* ***808-879-5445*** *or* ***1-800-822-4409.*** *www.mauikamaole.com.*

Puamana Townhomes Lahaina $$$$

These lovely one-, two-, or three-bedroom homes are located on a great beachfront setting within walking distance of downtown Lahaina. Some of the rooms are oceanfront and all come with equipped kitchens. And there's a pool right by the beach. They are great accommodations for the price, especially if you're vacationing with the family and are rented by an outfit called Hawaii Vacation Condos. *Homes available at several addresses in Lahaina.* ***1-800-207-3565.*** *www.hawaii-maui-vacation-rental.com.*

Punahoa Beach Apartments Kihei $$$

This is the kind of place to which you want to return again and again. And many people do just that. Why? Maybe it's because it is on a secluded side street with an intimate 15 units. Or maybe it's because every unit is right on the ocean with a lanai facing the sunset. It's not overly fancy, but Punahoa Beach is a true oasis in the sometimes crass hubbub of the Kihei sprawl. *2142 Ili'Ili Road, Kihei, HI 96753.* ***808-879-2720*** *or* ***1-800-564-4380.*** *www.punahoabeach.com.*

Ultimate Private Home

Ekena Hana $$$

Are you ready to totally chill out—to be transported to a higher state of mind? "Ekena" means Eden in Hawaiian, which is more than apt for this place. A unique beauty, elegance, and seclusion await those who rent this hilltop villa outside of Hana, which boasts 360-degree views of the rainforest and coastline across nine acres of property. Only one floor is rented at a time to ensure privacy. The rooms are spacious and open onto Hawaiian-style decks that extend the length of the house. The home accommodates anywhere from one to eight people, with up to four bedrooms and two master bedroom suites with baths. Rooms in the home take advantage of the awesome ocean and coastal views, but have all of the modern conveniences, including a high-tech kitchen, DVD player, and more. *Off the Hana Highway just north of town, Hana, HI 96713.* ***808-248-7047.*** *www.ekenamaui.com.*

Hana Oceanfront Hana $$$

These romantic cottages right on Hamoa Bay are beautifully furnished, with large lanais and expansive views out to sea. Best of all, staying here won't break the bank. During the day there is a little traffic on the road that runs behind the cottages, but at night, the only sound you're likely to hear is that of the waves just beyond your front door. *Haneoo Road, Hana, HA 96713.* ***808-248-7558.*** *www.hanaoceanfrontcottages.com.*

Ahhh … Maui! It is really the best, in our humble opinion. Now that you more or less know your way around and where to stay, check out some of its best restaurants, beaches, shopping, outdoor sports, and other activities, as described Chapter 9!

Enjoying Maui

In This Chapter

- The ultimate itineraries for Maui
- The best places to dine on Maui
- The most interesting things to see on Maui
- The best things to do on Maui

Maui is the second largest of the Hawaiian Islands (at 727 square miles, a distant second behind the 4,028 square miles of **The Big Island,** Hawaii), but first in the hearts of most visitors.

The Island of Superlatives

Maui is also an island of superlatives: It's the whale-watching capital of Hawaii, and it boasts more miles of swimmable beaches than any other island. It also has one of the world's largest dormant volcanoes, Hawaii's first building, arguably the world's top windsurfing beach, and the largest Banyan tree in America.

Life's a beach on Maui.

(Photo courtesy of HVCB/Ron Dahlquist)

Maui was once two islands formed by separate volcanoes. Haleakala later spewed lava into the channel between them, creating Maui more or less as we know it now. The ancients built Hawaii's largest *heiau* (shrine) in 1400 C.E. in **Hana.** Much, much later, in 1802, King Kamehameha made **Lahaina** the capital of Hawaii when he united all of the Islands. Maui also has served as a port of call for whaling vessels from New England, a center for Christian missionaries, and the locale for Hawaii's top sugar cane and pineapple plantations.

Now Maui waits in all of its rainbow-crowned glory to delight and enchant everyone, from sunbathers, golfers, surfers, historians, art lovers, and spa aficionados, to hikers, naturalists, and birdwatchers.

The Top Five Things to Do on Maui

Maui is at once spectacular and soothing, rugged and pampering. Here are our "must dos" for this unique part of the world.

1. Watch the sun rise over the clouds from Maui's highest point, 10,023-foot **Halealaka.**
2. Drive the **Hana Highway** past sea cliffs, waterfalls, and lush rainforest along Maui's spectacular north coast.
3. Experience some world-class snorkeling at **Molokini Island,** located just out from **Wailea** and **Makena Beaches.**
4. Take a cruise on the ***America II*** racing sailboat out of **Lahaina.**
5. Enjoy dinner at sunset while gazing at the vast **Pacific** and **West Maui Mountains** from **Mama's Fish House,** near **Pa'ia.**

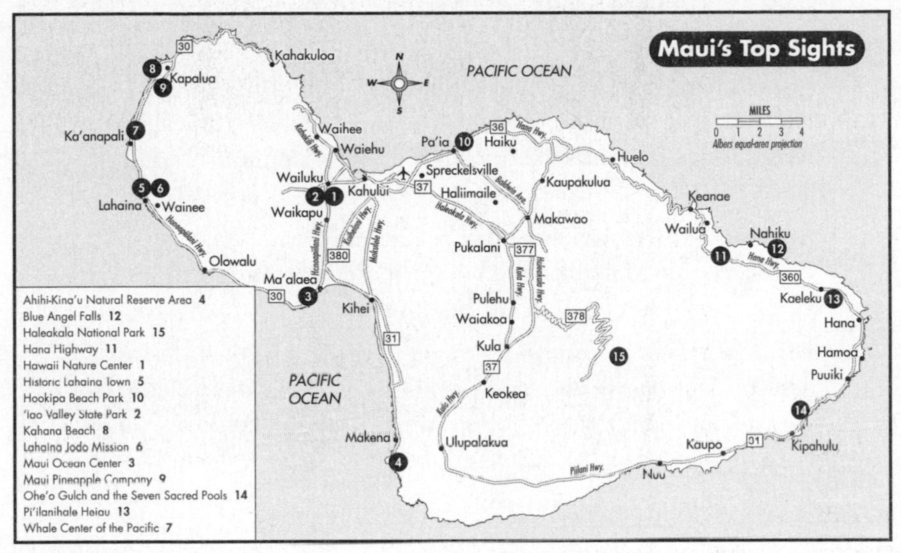

Maui's top sights.

Plan My Trip: Ultimate Itineraries for Maui

Perhaps more than any of the other Hawaiian islands, Maui has something for everybody. Here are several itineraries designed to fit your life and lifestyle, complete with good places to eat. Most of these are designed to take about one day, though in several cases we've also included suggestions for stretching the schedule to a second day.

The descriptions of each stop are generally brief, written to give you a feel for each. You'll find more thorough write-ups of each place later in the chapter.

It's usually worthwhile to make advance reservations for recommended restaurants and tours.

ITINERARY #1: FOR YOUNG FAMILIES

Day 1

1. **Breakfast:** Have breakfast at the condo or hotel, then hop in the car and head to the **Maui Ocean Center** in Ma'alaea, which opens at 9 A.M. Spend a few hours looking at the amazing variety of sea life.

continues

continued

2. **Lunch:** After hanging out at the aquarium, head down south Kihei Road a few miles to **Maui Tacos,** where you can enjoy some scrumptious fare that should appeal to both your and the kids' palettes.
3. At this point you're right at lovely **Kalama Beach Park,** so grab the towels, chairs, umbrella, and boogieboard from the trunk and enjoy an afternoon on the sand. No hassles here!
4. **Dinner:** When the sun starts to get low in the sky, shower off and head back up to Ma'alaea and the family-run **Ma'alaea Waterfront Restaurant.** Here you can watch the sun sink into the sea while enjoying beverages, food, and atmosphere the entire family will appreciate.

Day 2

1. After breakfast in the condo or hotel, get over to the stunning **'Iao Valley** just outside of Wailuku. Visit the fun, interactive **Hawaii Nature Center** museum, then take a walk through the rainforest in the valley!
2. **Lunch:** Follow Route 30 south and west from Wailuku to the historic whaling village of Lahaina. If it's Saturday, check out the **Hula show at Lahaina Cannery Mall,** usually scheduled for 1 P.M. Otherwise, head directly to the **Aloha Mixed Plate** restaurant, where you can have a real Hawaiian lunch while enjoying the view.
3. Finish lunch before 2:30 P.M. so that you can take a whale-watching cruise on the Island Marine Institute's **Whale Watch Maui** from Lahaina's main dock. This is one of the best outfits in the islands, and kids under 12 ride for free.
4. After the cruise (or in its place if it's not whale season), chill out at **D.T. Fleming Beach Park** a few miles north of Lahaina off Route 30. Bring your own drinks and snacks. Or you can just do some economical shopping at **Hilo Hattie** or hang out under the islands' **largest Banyan tree** in downtown Lahaina.
5. **Dinner:** Cap off the day with sunset and dinner at the fun **Bubba Gump Shrimp Company** in Lahaina. It's not a local place, it's part of a chain, but it's in … Lahaina.

ITINERARY #2: FOR OLDER FAMILIES

We suspect that you don't really enjoy getting up at 2:30 or 3 in the morning, but you've got to humor us just this one time, okay? You won't be sorry, honest!

To help ease the pain, plan your drive up Haleakela for one of your first days on the island, when your body is still on mainland time!

Day 1

1. Rouse your sleepy head from the pillow, grab some warm jackets, and leave the hotel by 3 A.M. on your way to the view the sunrise from **Haleakala,** Maui's massive 10,023-foot mountain. Take Route 311 or 36 to the **Haleakala Highway,** drive up the fiendishly twisting road in the dark, and stake out a spot in the summit parking lot by 5 A.M. Sometime before 6 A.M. the sky will start to lighten, at which point you should walk up the stairs to the summit viewing platform. Try to keep your jaw off the ground as the cloudbank just below you explodes in impossible shades of crimson and orange while the sun rises into view.
2. **Breakfast:** Drive back down the Haleakala Highway in the daylight and enjoy the views. Stop for breakfast at the **Kula Lodge,** which looks out upon all of Central and West Maui from 3,000 feet.
3. Proceed further down the flanks of Haleakala on Routes 377 and 390, though **Makawao,** all the way to the cool and funky town of **Pa'ia.** Spend some time checking out the shops and people on Baldwin Avenue.
4. **Lunch:** Pick up box lunches at the **Moana Bakery & Café** and head straight to the North Shore's stunning **Ho'okipa Beach Park,** where you can relax on the sand, cool off in the shallow water within the reef, and watch the world-class windsurfers and surfers further out.
5. **Dinner:** Cruise back into Pa'ia for dinner with the windsurfing crowd at the **Café des Amis,** and then call it a night early!

Day 2

1. **Breakfast:** After breakfast at your place, head for the Whalers Village shopping center in Ka'anapali to visit the **Whale Center of the Pacific.**

continues

continued

2. Head south on Route 30 to the historic whaling town of Lahaina and take a whale-watching cruise on the Island Marine Institute's **Whale Watch Maui** from Lahaina's main dock. This is one of the best outfits in the islands. If you're off season (the whales are only around November–March) opt for a thrilling ride on the former Americas Cup racing sailboat, ***America II***.
3. **Lunch:** Grab a real Hawaiian lunch while enjoying the view at the **Aloha Mixed Plate** restaurant in downtown Lahaina.
4. After lunch, head north on Route 30 for a drive clockwise all the way around **West Maui.** Drive with care, as the road gets extremely narrow and twisting past **Kahakuloa.** The entire excursion should take about two and a half hours.
5. On the dramatic north coast, near mile marker 20, stop at the turnoff and walk down the hill to a view of **Nakelele Blowhole**, where the wild waves of the Pacific shoot up through the rocks. This is also an excellent location for tracking whales out at sea.
6. Stop in the picturesque town of Kahakuloa and buy some of "the best banana bread on the planet" at the green roadside stand.
7. Continue on past Kahakuloa, up the hill, Stop at the **Kaukini Gallery** to peruse its beautiful and sophisticated collection of local arts and crafts.
8. **Dinner:** Continue to drive carefully and enjoy the view as you make your way back into Wailuku, where you can grab some dinner at one of the island's best "local" eateries: **A Saigon Café.**

ITINERARY #3: FOR SINGLES

1. **Breakfast:** Get up early and take a half-day snorkel cruise from Ma'alaea to the island of **Molokini** on Lani Kai Friendly Charters. A continental breakfast is served on board.
2. **Lunch:** When you get back from snorkeling, have some drinks and pupus oceanside at the **Ma'alaea Waterfront Restaurant.**
3. Take a tour of the working plantation of the **Maui Pineapple Company** near Kapalua. While you're there, admire the dramatic views of West Maui.

4. **Dinner:** Head back down to Ka'anapali and enjoy the song, dance, food, and open bar of the evening-long **Drums of the Pacific lu'au** at the Maui Hyatt. Advanced reservations are required. Trade vacation stories and tips with the other people sitting at your long table.

Molokini Island is one of Hawaii's top snorkeling destinations.

(Photo courtesy of HVCB/Ron Dalhquist)

WHALE-WATCHING FROM MAUI

Whatever you do on Maui, you're likely to see Pacific humpback whales almost every day from November through March, when they frequent Hawaiian waters to give birth. Of the approximately 7,500 humpback whales in the North Pacific Ocean, about 5,000 of them hang out in Maui's waters at some point during the winter. You don't even need to take a whale-watching cruise, especially during February. You can spot their flukes and plumes from the comfort of your hotel lanai, and they can often be spotted from the many roadside lookouts on Maui's highways—especially around Ma'alaea.

ITINERARY #4: A ROMANTIC GETAWAY

Day 1

1. Spend the night at one of the luxuriously rustic chalets of the atmospheric **Kula Lodge** on the flanks of Haleakala, which looks down upon all of Central and West Maui from 3,200 feet.
2. **Breakfast:** In the morning, take a before-breakfast stroll around the landscaped grounds, then have one of Kula's renowned breakfasts while enjoying the view in the dining room.
3. Head down the mountain on Routes 377 and 390 to the North Shore town of **Pa'ia.** Pick up a box lunch at **Café Mambo** on Baldwin Avenue and head east on Routes 26 and 360, the **Hana Highway.**
4. Just beyond mile marker 16, Route 36 turns into Route 360 and you're on the Hana Highway proper, the path to dramatic views and about 600 hairpin turns. Stop at the **Twin Falls** overlook at mile marker 2. Take a short hike to the falls if it's not raining. On the way back to the car, stop to buy a refreshing, fresh fruit **smoothie** from the roadside stand that is usually there.
5. **Lunch:** Continue on another 40 or so miles to tropical, lush Hana and the easternmost point on Maui. On the way, stop frequently to admire the views, as well as historic **Kaulanapueo Church** just off the road at mile marker 4, and the picturesque village of **Ke'anae,** right on the crashing Pacific. This is a good place to eat that boxed lunch.
6. **Dinner:** In Hana, check into the romantic **Hana Oceanfront Cottages** and then go for dinner at the upscale **Hotel Hana-Maui.**

Day 2

1. **Breakfast:** Have breakfast at the **Hana Ranch Restaurant,** then drive 40 minutes south on Route 31 to **Ohe'o Gulch** and the **"Seven Sacred Pools."** Spend some time frolicking in the waterfalls and natural pools.
2. While you're in the area, you can drive just a bit further down the road to pioneer aviator Charles Lindbergh's grave at **Palapalo Hoomau Church.**
3. **Lunch:** Turn the car around and head back down the Hana Highway, stopping briefly at **Tutu's at Hana Bay** for a Hawaiian plate lunch.

4. Drive back toward Pa'ia, stopping along the way to admire the waterfalls and westward views. When you get to the parking lot on the bluffs above **Ho'okipa Beach Park,** pull over for a few minutes and watch the world-class windsurfers and surfers.

5. **Dinner:** Treat yourself with cocktails, dinner, and a fabulous view of the ocean and the **West Maui Mountains** from **Mama's Fish House,** about a mile east of downtown Pa'ia.

Itinerary #5: Easy-Going; Nonstrenuous

Day 1

1. **Breakfast:** Have breakfast at the hotel. Leave your hotel or condo at 7 A.M. to ride a van, run by **Temptation Tours,** to the top of **Haleakala** for stupendous views of Maui.

2. **Lunch:** On your way down the mountain, your tour company will stop at a scenic upcountry restaurant for lunch.

3. Spend the afternoon at the **Bailey House Museum** in Wailuku.

4. **Dinner:** Enjoy evening cocktails and a good meal with live music at the **Hula Café** at **Whaler's Village** in **Ka'anapali.**

Day 2

1. **Breakfast:** After breakfast at your place, head for the Whalers Village shopping center in Ka'anapali to visit the **Whale Center of the Pacific.**

2. **Lunch:** Enjoy a lunch at the award-winning **Gerard's Restaurant** in the same building as Lahaina's Victorian **Plantation Inn.**

3. After lunch, take a whale-watching cruise on the **Island Marine Institute's Whale Watch Maui** from Lahaina's main dock.

4. Upon your return, relax under Lahaina's giant Banyan tree, or perhaps do a little shopping in the many stores nearby.

5. **Dinner:** For your evening's diner and entertainment, make your way to Lahaina's far south side and attend the **Feast at Lele Lu'au,** notable for its intimate atmosphere, fine food, and table service (no waiting in buffet lines).

ITINERARY #6: CULTURE IN PARADISE

Day 1

1. **Breakfast:** After breakfast at your hotel, spend the morning tooling around historic Lahaina, visiting the **Baldwin Home Museum, Hale Pa'i,** the **Lahaina Jodo Mission,** the 1858 Courthouse, the **Holy Innocents Episcopal Church,** the **Old Prison,** and the **Waihee Cemetery.**
2. **Lunch:** Have lunch at **Gerard's Restaurant** at the Victorian-style Plantation Inn.
3. After lunch, drive about half an hour along Routes 30, 380, and the Haleakala Highway to the upcountry town of **Makawao,** where you'll find the renowned **Viewpoints Gallery,** where you can peruse some of Maui's best homegrown art.
4. **Dinner:** Later in the afternoon, proceed further up the Haleakala Highway to the elegantly rustic **Kula Lodge**, where you can enjoy cocktails and dinner while overlooking all of West Maui from an elevation of 3,200 feet above sea level.

Day 2

1. **Breakfast:** Grab a bite to eat at your hotel or condo, then drive to the **Haleki'i and Pihana Heiau,** an ancient human sacrifice site, located on Route 340 in the **Wailuku-Kahului** area.
2. Continue west on winding Route 340 along West Maui's northern coast until you come to the **Kaukini Gallery,** home of a beautiful and sophisticated collection of local arts and crafts.
3. **Lunch:** Proceed down the hill past the gallery to the picturesque village of **Kahakuloa**, which hasn't changed much in the past 100 years. Buy some fruit for a light lunch and see if you agree with the roadside stand's claim that it is the home of "the world's best banana bread."
4. Past Kahaluloa going west, Route 340 widens and becomes Route 30, offering more staggering views of the West Maui coastline. Proceed several more miles to the lovely Kapalua area and if it's still mid-afternoon, take the **Maui Pineapple Company Plantation Tour.**
5. **Dinner:** Cruise further along Route 30 to Lahaina, and spend the evening at the **Old Lahaina Lu'au,** the most authentic lu'au on the island.

ITINERARY #7: ADVENTURE IN THE GREAT OUTDOORS

1. Get up early, get to the Ma'alea dock by 6:30 A.M., and take a half-day snorkel cruise to the island of **Molokini** on Lani Kai Friendly Charters. A continental breakfast is served on board.
2. **Lunch:** After returning to Ma'alaea, drive south on Route 31 (Pi'ilani Highway) about 9 miles to Wailea and treat yourself to a fine lunch at **Sarento's on the Beach.**
3. After lunch, continue driving south on Route 31 past Makena and the Maui Prince Hotel until you reach the **ahihi-Kina'u Natural Reserve Area,** where the last eruption of Halaekala poured lava into the ocean in 1790. Here you can explore fascinating rock formations and enjoy some of the best snorkeling on Maui amid dramatic scenery.

4a. **Dinner:** Drive back north on Route 31, stopping at **Kamaole Beach Park III** to shower and change. Then head for the fabulous **Humuhumu** restaurant at the **Grand Wailea Resort Hotel.** Chill out the rest of the evening.

4b. **Dinner:** If you're staying in West Maui, head all the way back to your place to freshen up, then enjoy dinner while watching the sun set from the porch dining room of **Mala** in Lahaina.

Day 2

1. **Breakfast:** After an early breakfast, grab some water and a packed lunch at your condo or hotel. Then take Routes 30 and 340 around to the north side of West Maui to Maluhia Road. Turn up that road to the Boy Scout camp and hike up the **Waihee Ridge Trail** for spectacular views.
2. **Lunch:** In the afternoon, drive back down Route 340, proceed through Kahului to Pa'ia and beautiful **Baldwin Beach,** where you can relax for the afternoon.
3. **Dinner:** Enjoy diner and entertainment at the **Moana Bakery & Café** in Pa'ia.

The Top Maui Attractions, A to Z

Ahihi-Kina'u Natural Reserve Area Makena; East Maui

This moonlike area of jagged black volcanic rocks is the site of Haleakala's last lava flow into the ocean in 1790, making it the youngest part of Maui. It also happens to be the site of some of the best snorkeling on the island. As a protected area, the sea life here is both varied and bountiful, and includes coral, sea turtles, and tarpons. *Makena Alanui Road about three miles south of Makena. Open daily dawn to dusk.*

Alexander and Baldwin Sugar Museum Puunene; Central Maui

Hawaii's sugar industry and the culture that evolved around it in the 1800s is showcased in this museum housed in a former plantation superintendent's residence outside of Kahalui. The museum depicts plantation life and industrial sugar production through such displays as photo murals and artifacts, an authentic scale model of the plantation, and a working model of factory machinery. *Located at the intersection of Puunene Avenue (Routes 331 and 350) and Hansen Road, half a mile from Dairy Road (Route 380). Open Monday–Saturday, 9:30 A.M.–4:30 P.M. Admission: adults $4, children 6–17 $2, children 5 and under are free.* ***808-871-8058.*** *www.sugarmuseum.com.*

Bailey House Museum Wailuku; West Maui

This 150-year-old historic home surrounded by lush gardens was originally the residence of missionaries in the 1800s, and was built on the site of the royal compound of Kahekili, last ruling chief of Maui. The house served as the Mission station for the Wailuku Female Seminary for Girls until 1847, then was occupied by early Maui settler and painter Edward Bailey and his family until 1888. It now showcases the culture and art of Maui and all of Hawaii with paintings of nineteenth-century Maui, ancient tools, woven work, and clothing. *2375-A Main Street. Open Monday–Saturday 10 A.M.–4 P.M., closed Sundays, Fourth of July, Thanksgiving, Christmas, and New Year's Day. Admission: $4 seniors, adults $5, children 7–12 $1, children under 6 are free.* ***808-244-3326.*** *www.mauimuseum.org.*

Baldwin Home Museum Lahaina; West Maui

Dwight Baldwin, the first doctor and dentist in Hawaii, lived in this house with his wife Charlotte and eight children from the mid-1830s until 1868.

The house's thick walls are made of cut lava; the mortar from crushed coral. The house served as a medical office, boarding house, and gathering place for missionary activity, and is now filled with period furniture and documents from the good doctor's practice. *Located at the corner of Front Street and Dickenson Street in downtown Lahaina. Open daily. Admission: seniors $2, adults $3, children free.* ***808-661-3262.***

Blue Angel Falls Hana Highway; East Maui

These impressive falls pour into a deep blue pool (called the "Blue Pool," strangely enough) right next to the ocean, and are a "must-see" stop when you're cruising down the Hana Highway. Keep an eye out for wild pigs as you admire the stunning scene! There are no facilities. *Drive down the Hana Highway a quarter-mile beyond mile marker 31, then turn toward the ocean onto unpaved 'Ula'ino Road. Follow that about three miles, park and walk the final 200 yards to the site.*

Charles Lindbergh's Grave Palapala Ho'omau Church, Kipahulu; East Maui

In his prime, "Lucky Lindy" lived a life of fame, some of it spectacularly good, some horribly bad. After withstanding the public spotlight for most of his adult life, he spent his last days on the remote and lush Hana coast, dying on August 26, 1974. His remains are buried on the grounds of the Palapala Ho'omau Church (circa 1857) eight miles south of Hana in the village of Kipahulu. *Drive south of Hana to mile marker 41. A small road on the ocean side leads to the church.*

Haleakala National Park West Maui

The massive slopes and 10,023-foot summit of Haleakala dominate the view from almost anywhere in Central and East Maui, making this huge mountain unquestionably the most striking feature of the island. There's a road all the way to the top, which winds for 38 miles and over two hours through five distinctly different climate zones to a parking area and lookout. From the summit you can watch a spectacular sunrise on most days, or embark on any of the numerous hikes through the crater. A number of bicycle tour companies will drive you to the top and provide bikes specially equipped with oversize brakes so that you can admire the scenery while coasting all the way back down.

From the rocky slopes on top you can see all of West Maui, as well as The Big Island of Hawaii in the distance. The mind-boggling crater just below the summit looks a bit like the surface of Mars and is 3,000 feet deep, 7.5 miles long, and 2.5 miles wide, a total of 22 miles in circumference. *Follow Route 378 (Haleakala Highway), which begins at Route 311 near the Kahului Airport. Call for information and weather conditions before driving, hiking, or biking up. Admission: vehicles $10, hikers and bikers $5. Campgrounds are available free on a first-come basis. Cabins in the crater are by reservation only.* ***808-871-5054.***

Hikers enjoy rugged trails in Haleakala Crater.

(Photo courtesy of HVCB/Ron Dahlquist)

Haleki'i and Pihanakalani Heiau Wailuku; Central Maui

Haleki'i and Pihanakalani Heiau are two of Maui's most accessible archeological sites—the remains of temples that were used to perform human sacrifices. In fact, archeologists believe that Pihanakalani Heiau is probably the last site where Kamehameha I performed sacrifices on Maui. *Drive past the Wailuku Industrial Area on Route 33 (Market Street) toward Waihe'e, turn left on Kuhio Place and then left on Hea Place. Admission is free.*

Hale Pa'i Lahaina; West Maui

This authentic period building is the restored site of the Lahainaluna Seminary, which was founded in 1831 as the first school west of the Rockies. It's now on the campus of Lahaina High School. The name means "the house of printing," because it was here that, beginning in 1834, students were taught how to set type, operate a printing press, create copper engravings, and bind books. The original press printed the first newspaper west of the Rocky Mountains on February 14, 1834, a four-page weekly school paper called *Ka Lama Hawaii*. An original 1838 copy is on display in the museum. *980 Lahainaluna Road. On the mountainside above downtown Lahaina. Open Monday–Friday by appointment only. Admission is free.* ***808-661-3262.***

Hawaii Nature Center Wailuku; Central Maui

This kid-oriented nature museum is a good first-day activity, featuring interactive exhibits and educational programs to foster awareness and appreciation of Hawaii's natural environment. Take the Rainforest Walk, which includes more than 30 museum exhibits and a guided introduction to the Hawaiian rainforest (reservations required). *875 'Iao Valley Road. Open daily 10 A.M.–4 P.M. Admission: adults $6, children $4, members free. Rainforest Walks can be booked at 11:30 A.M. or 1:30 P.M. Monday–Friday, 11 A.M. or 2 P.M. on Saturdays and Sundays. Walkers must be 5 years old or older. Cost for the Rainforest Walk is $29.95 for adults and $19.95 for children and includes a visit to the museum.* ***808-244-6500*** *or* ***1-888-244-6500.*** *www.hawaiinaturecenter.org.*

'Iao Valley Wailuku; Central Maui

The dramatic, deep valley hosts a state park as well as the Hawaii Nature Center, and is the site of the 1790 battle in which King Kamehameha I destroyed the Maui army in an effort to unite the Hawaiian Islands. Right in the middle of the valley is the 'Iao Needle, a dramatic 2,250-foot stone pinnacle that towers over its surroundings and was once used as a natural altar. The valley has four converging streams and is a great place to take some interesting and easy hikes while admiring the tropical landscape. The ridgetop lookout offers a fantastic view of the valley and Kahului Harbor. *Follow Route 32 (Kaahumanu Road) west from Wailuku until it becomes Route 320, which leads directly to the State Park.*

Kahakuloa Head East of Kahakuloa; West Maui

Located just east of the old-style Hawaiian village of Kahakuloa, this dramatic 636-foot-high hill rising from the sea is one of the most prominent natural landmarks of West Maui. It's said that the eighteenth-century Maui King Kahekili used to climb over 200 feet up the hill and leap into the water below, and that was before breakfast! *Located on Route 30 just east of Kahakuloa.*

Kepaniwai Heritage Gardens Wailuku; Central Maui

Located next the Hawaii Nature Center in the lush 'Iao Valley, these gardens were established in 1952 as a showcase for Maui's diverse heritage. Garden and architectural displays represent eight cultures that contributed to modern Maui: Chinese, Japanese, New England, Portuguese, Native Hawaiian, Korean, Puerto Rican, and Filipino. *Take Highway 32 west out of Kahului toward 'Iao Valley. The Gardens are located before you reach the town of Wailuku. Open daily 7 A.M.–7 P.M. Admission is free.*

Lahaina Jodo Mission Lahaina; West Maui

The Lahaina Jodo Mission is one of those must-see sites on Maui, encompassing an authentic Buddhist Temple with a 90-foot high Pagoda and a 12-foot-tall copper and bronze statue of Amida Buddha, the largest of its kind outside Japan. The entire property is beautifully framed by the West Maui Mountains. The temple itself blends Japanese and Western styles. *12 Ala Moana Street.* ***808-661-4304.*** *www.lahainajodomission.com/.*

Lahaina Heritage Museum Lahaina; West Maui

This museum showcases Hawaiian history and culture through engaging videos, interactive displays, live demonstrations, exhibits, and artifacts. *648 Wharf Street. Open daily 9 A.M.–5 P.M.* ***808-661-1959*** *or* ***1-888-310-1117.***

Maui Ocean Center Ma'alaea; Central Maui

This is a cool place for (pardon the expression) kids of all ages—really! As the largest aquarium in Hawaii, it lets you view thousands of marine animals and plants in living coral reefs, and also features a clear acrylic underwater tunnel that lets you walk through a 750,000-gallon open ocean tank. *192 Ma'alaea Road. Follow Route 30 past the Ma'alaea Harbor and turn right on Ma'alaea Road. The Maui Ocean Aquarium is on the left-hand side. Open daily, 9 A.M.–5 P.M. Admission: adults $18.50, children $12.50.* ***808-270-7000.***

Nakelele Blowhole West Maui

This amazing site along the "West Maui loop" on Route 30 features ocean waves shooting dramatically into the air like some misplaced Yellowstone geyser. It was made by the ocean creating a hole in the lava shelf, where waves are funneled up and out! The "eruption" is even better during high tide and strong surf! *Located on Route 30 just west of Kahakuloa near mile marker 38.*

O'heo Gulch O'heo Gulch; East Maui

See the description under Seven Sacred Pools.

Old Lahaina Courthouse Lahaina; West Maui

Here's another bit of history under Lahaina's swaying palms. It was built by King Kamehameha III, who gave Hawaii its first constitution and proclaimed the Great Mahele land ownership system, and then served as a customs house during the town's colorful whaling era. Located right across from the harbor on Wharf Street, and right next to the giant Banyan tree (a worthy destination in itself), it actually serves as a visitor's center today. This is a good first stop in Lahaina—a place where you can pick up a walking map of the town and generally get oriented. *648 Wharf Street. Open daily 9 A.M.–5 P.M.* ***808-667-9193.***

Old Lahaina Prison Lahaina; West Maui

Back in Lahaina's boisterous whaling era, sailors who had consumed way too much grog were unceremoniously thrown into this rather small and nondescript prison. (Locals called this Hale Pa'ahao or "stuck in irons.") Other typical offenses included deserting ship, working on the Sabbath, and "reckless horse riding." Today the building is often used for parties and other community functions. *187 Prison Street. Open daily 10 A.M.–4 P.M. Admission is free.* ***808-667-1985.***

Pi'ilanihale Heiau Hana Highway; East Maui

If you enjoy a sense of mystical history, this is a must-stop on your cruise down the Hana Highway. This is Hawaii's largest and most magnificent ancient site that is still intact. Created by the powerful King Pi'ilani way back in the fourteenth century and maintained by his heirs, the heiau includes a stone platform measuring 340 feet by 415 feet. Just standing here quietly for a few minutes will transport you to another time and place. *Located in the Kahanu Garden. Follow Route 360 (Hana Highway) east toward Hana to mile marker 31 and turn right onto Ulaino Road. Kahanu Gardens is on the left past the Hana Caverns. Open Monday–Friday, 10 A.M.–2 P.M. Admission: adults $10, children free.* ***808-248-8912.***

Seven Sacred Pools O'heo Gulch; East Maui

About 40 minutes south of Hana on Maui's eastern shore sits one of the most famous sites on Maui—a series of several beguiling waterfalls and natural pools formed by Pipiwai Stream as it pours over countless lava rocks from the broad slopes of Halealaka. Part of Halealaka National Park, these actually number more than seven, and they're not sacred. In fact, the place is really called Ohe'o Gulch, but was named "The Seven Sacred Pools" by the Hotel Hana back in 1947 in an attempt to attract visitors to the area. Nevertheless, you should really block out an entire afternoon to visit this lovely area as long as you're all the way out here. It's truly a great place to spend some time hiking while taking tropical-style dips in the pools from time to time, as long as rain is not pouring from the skies. A few of the pools are only about 10 minutes from the parking area; others are a bit further away, but along hikes with truly picturesque settings. *Follow Route 30 to Hana, after which it turns into Route 31. Follow to the parking lot just past Mile Marker 42 on the ocean side of the road.*

The "Seven Sacred Pools" are a sacred (and worthy) tourist lure.

(Photo courtesy of HVCB/Ron Dahlquist)

Tropical Gardens of Maui Wailuku; Central Maui

This four-acre tropical garden and nursery features foliage from tropical climates throughout the world. Among the scores of species here are orchids, palms, and other rare and exotic plants. *200 'Iao Valley Road. Admission $5. Open Monday–Saturday 9 A.M.–4:30 P.M.* ***808-244-3085.*** *www.tropicalgardensofmaui.com.*

Whale Center of the Pacific Lahaina, West Maui

Located on the mezzanine level of Ka'anapali's Whalers Village shopping center, this small but interesting museum will give you a good sense of the seafaring life of the nineteenth century, a rough time for both men and whales. Here you can learn about all of the whale species, view films about whaling history, gaze upon harpoons and scrimshaw, see what the inside of a whaling ship looked like, and even gape at the skeletal remains of a 40-foot Sperm Whale. *2435 Ka'anapali Parkway. Located off of Ka'anapali Road, north of Lahiana near Ka'anapali Beach. Open daily 9:30 A.M.–10 P.M. Admission is free.* ***808-661-5223.***

Maui's Top Beaches

Life's a beach, right? Yeah, we've heard that one before, too. Still, that particular sentiment is more true in Maui than most other places in the world. Maybe it's because of Maui's 120 miles of coastline and scores of swimmable beaches, ranging from fine white sand to black rock. The variety is a bit mind-boggling, but depends on your location. Unless noted, most of these beaches have changing and bathroom facilities, as well as lifeguards. You can get daily beach information for the beach parks (the guarded beaches) by calling the Maui Division of Parks and Recreation at **808-270-6137.**

Central Maui

Baldwin Beach: *Full facilities. One mile west of Pa'ia on Route 36 (Hana Highway).*

Ho'okipa Beach: *Full facilities. No lifeguards. Follow Route 36 (Hana Highway) two miles west of Pa'ia.*

West Maui

D.T. Fleming: *Full facilities. Head northwest from Lahaina on Route 30 (Honoapi'ilani Highway) to mile marker 32 and turn left.*

Honolua Bay: *No facilities. Travel north on Route 30 (Honoapi'ilani Highway) to mile marker 33 and turn onto the small access road dropping off to your left.*

Ka'anapali Beach: *Outdoor showers. If you're not staying at one of the adjacent hotels, go to the northernmost Ka'anapali exit on Route 30 (Honoapi'ilani Highway), near Maui Ka'anapali Villas, and park next to the public access signs.*

Kapalua Beach: *Full facilities. Follow Route 30 north approximately 10 miles from Lahaina. Turn left onto Office Road and left again onto lower Honoapolani Highway. Follow signs to beach.*

East Maui

Big Beach/Little Beach: *From the Kihei take Route 31. Take Highway 31 south into Wailea. Turn left at the Alanui Dr. intersection. Continue on past the Maui Prince Hotel to the State Park sign. Turn right into the parking lot.*

Hamoa Beach: *No lifeguard. Follow Hana Highway one mile south of Hana, park on the road, and take the stairs down to the beach.*

Kamaole Beach III: *Full facilities. 2800 South Kihei Road.*

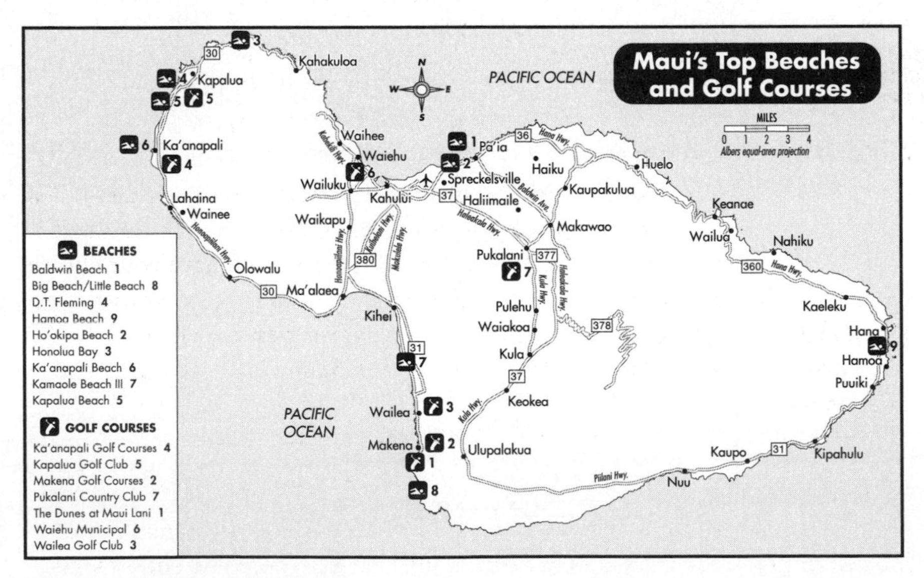

Maui's top beaches and golf courses.

Great Dining with Atmosphere: The Best Places to Eat

Thanks to its international reputation as one of the best vacation destinations, Maui has some of the best food in Hawaii, with a large number of gourmet restaurants, often in spectacular locations that cater to discriminating travelers willing to spend their hard-earned money for a memorable meal. Of course, there are plenty of good restaurants in all price ranges, and to suit every taste.

You can "chill" in warm Maui, where an Aloha shirt and slacks are usually sufficient for even the top-end establishments.

West Maui

Aloha Mixed Plate Lahaina *Hawaiian* $$

This place combines the traditional Hawaiian dinner menu with some outdoor tables and the kind of lovely view that travelers like us love. Try the traditional Hawaiian-style plate lunches of pork, beef, chicken, or fish, with two scoops of rice, and a scoop of macaroni salad. However, for a special treat, start with their award-winning Coconut Prawns pupu! *1285 Front Street, right across the street from the Lahaina Cannery Mall. Open daily 10:30 A.M.–10 P.M.* ***808-661-3322.***

Cascades Ka'anapali *Hawaiian; Pacific Rim* $$$

Don't let the setting sun and the swaying palms distract you from that grilled mahi-mahi steaming on your plate! It would be all too easy in this candlelit indoor/outdoor restaurant in the Hyatt. Each evening you'll have your choice of three or four kinds of fresh Hawaiian fish in any of four preparation styles (they've got meat, too), and the sushi bar is one of the best on Maui. *200 Nohea Kai Drive. Dinner: 5:45 P.M.–10:00 P.M. Sushi: 5:00 P.M.–10:00 P.M.* ***808-667-4727.***

Chez Paul Olowalu *French* $$$$

This is one of the more famous restaurants on Maui—a little French place located on the side of the highway south of Lahaina. There's no sunset view (or any view) here; you come for the food, which is classic French and expertly prepared. *Honoapillani Highway (Route 30). Open daily 6 P.M.–8:30 P.M., closed on Sundays in the summer.* ***808-661-3843.*** *www.chezpaul.net.*

David Paul's Lahaina Grill Lahaina *American* $$$$$

This is one of the most popular restaurants on Maui, even though it's somewhat pricey and also lacks a view. That's no doubt because the food is fresh and delicious, the service is prompt, and the presentation is such that your dinner looks like a work of art. Try the seared lion paw scallops with celery root mash, lobster Champagne essence, and crisp pancetta chips. *127 Lahainaluna Road. Dinner served nightly from 6 P.M.* ***808-667-5117.*** *www.lahainagrill.com.*

Hula Grill Ka'anapali *Pacific Rim* $$$

Sure, you could sit indoors at this oh-so-popular restaurant on the beach side of Ka'anapali's Whaler's Village shopping center, but where you're really going to want to be is at one of those umbrella tables, with your feet literally in the sand! The food is excellent but not too expensive, and you'll be able to enjoy the beach scene and sunset while listening to live Hawaiian music. Bottom line: casual and lots of fun. *2435 Ka'anapali Parkway, Building P.* ***808-667-6636.*** *www.hulagrill.com.*

Mala, An Ocean Tavern Lahaina *Pacific Rim* $$$

This little place is one of Lahaina's best-kept secrets, a mile north of the crowded "downtown" area and actually overhanging one of the narrower sections of Ka'anapali Beach. The locals and veteran Maui visitors know that Mala is great—quiet, with a nice bar, excellent tapas (small plates), and a great view. Try the flatbreads (pizza in disguise)! *1307 Front Street. Open Monday–Friday 11 A.M.–10 P.M., Saturday 9 A.M.–9 P.M., Sunday 9 A.M.–9 P.M. with brunch from 9 A.M.–3 P.M.* ***808-667-9394.***

Maui Brewing Co. Kahana *American/Hawaiian* $$$

In this fun brew pub you'll certainly enjoy the eight handcrafted beers along with some quality contemporary cuisine, including fresh seafood, delectable steaks, and other meats roasted in a rotisserie over red-hot kiawe wood coals. *Kahana Gateway Plaza at 4405 Honoapi'ilani Highway (Route 30). Open daily 11 A.M.–1:30 A.M.* ***808-669-3474.***

Pacific'O Lahaina *Pacific Rim* $$$

This atmospheric place is right on the beach, so you can sit on the torch-lit patio outside and watch the sunset if you wish. The food is creative Pacific

Rim using fresh Hawaiian ingredients, and it's some of the best on Maui. We're rather partial to the catch of the day, crusted with coconut and macadamia nuts, but the menu features creative vegetarian dishes as well. *505 Front Street. Open daily 11 A.M.–5 P.M., and 5:30 P.M.–10 P.M.* ***808-667-4341.*** *www.pacificomaui.com.*

Plantation House Kapalua *Pacific Rim* $$$$

Pinch yourself. You're sitting at a teak table, eating one of the most magnificent meals of your life, gazing out upon literally miles of golf course, pineapple fields, mountains, the Pacific Ocean, the islands of Moloka'i and Lana'i, and maybe a rainbow or two. Yes, you could get used to this. *2000 Plantation Club Drive on the Plantation Golf Course. Open daily 8 A.M.–3 P.M., and 5:30 P.M.–9 P.M. Opens 6 P.M.–9 P.M. May 1 to September 30.* ***808-669-6299.*** *www.theplantationhouse.com.*

Central Maui

Haliimaile General Store Haliimaile *Hawaiian* $$$

Don't let the name fool you. This is one sophisticated restaurant, featuring an exhibition kitchen, superb Hawaiian contemporary cuisine, and fine local artwork around the premises. Check out the Hunan rack of lamb, tinged with sesame oil and hoisin sauce. *900 Haliimaile Rd. Open Monday–Friday 11 A.M.–2:30 P.M. and 5:30 P.M.–9:30 P.M.* ***808-572-2666.***

Kula Lodge Kula *Pacific Rim* $$$

Hey, do you think you could handle some progressive contemporary cuisine seasoned with homegrown herbs and spices, all while gazing out upon all of West Maui from over 3,000 feet up? Try the Barbados rum and pepper-painted Ono with vanilla-scented mango-habenero "mojo," Cuban black beans, and grilled rum-soaked bananas. Uh huh. Breakfasts are good, too. It is a great place to stop on your way to or from Halealaka. *Route 377* (Haleakala Highway). *Open from 6:30 A.M.–11:15 A.M., 11:45 A.M.–4:15 P.M., 4:45 P.M.–9 P.M., and Sunday brunch served from 6:30 A.M.–1:00 P.M.* ***808-878-1535.*** *www.kulalodge.com.*

Moana Bakery & Café Pa'ia *American* $$$

This friendly place has stylish booths, superb local artwork on the walls, and generally hip décor, keeping with the groovy vibe in Pa'ia. And guess what?

The food is excellent, consisting of a slew of creative, reasonably priced dishes made with fresh ingredients. Also try the French pastries while enjoying the live music. *71 Baldwin Avenue. Open daily 7 A.M.–9 P.M.* ***808-579-9999.*** *www.members.aol.com/moanacafe.*

The Saigon Café Wailuku *Vietnamese*

This hole-in-the-wall in downtown Wailuku ain't fancy (it isn't even labeled with a proper sign outside), but it's the real thing. Here you can get tasty, authentic Vietnamese food, served quickly and at good prices. Try the beef noodle soup or one of the stir-fry dishes. *1792 Main St. Open 10 A.M.–10 P.M.* ***808-243-9560.***

The Waterfront Ma'alaea *American* 

This family-run place has a view of scenic Ma'alaea harbor, is friendly and casual, and has some of the freshest food on Maui. Try the fresh sea scallops sautéed and served with a Thai peanut sauce, macadamia nut and coconut risotto, and tobiko caviar. Then watch the whales and the sunset out beyond the yachts. *50 Hauoli Street. Open daily 5:30 P.M.–8:30 P.M.* ***808-244-9028.*** *www.waterfrontrestaurant.net/.*

East Maui

Bubba Gump Shrimp Co. Lahaina *American* 

You're gonna like sitting right by the beach, perhaps watching whales offshore or enjoying the sunset, and digging into Bubba's Po' Boy Peel 'n' Eat Shrimp—or maybe the fresh fish, rib eye steak, hamburgers, and other favorites. Bubba even offers a *keiki* menu for the kids. It is casual and fun. 889 Front Street. ***808-661-3111.*** *www.bubbagump.com.*

Café Des Amis Pa'ia *Pacific Rim* 

Hang with the windsurfers in this crowded and fun little place while you enjoy the savory Asian-infused crepes, seafood, and salads. We especially recommend the bowl of curried shrimp. Truly some of the best food in Maui, without any fuss, is here. If you come here once, you'll be back. The café also offers a good selection of beer and wine. *42 Baldwin Avenue. Open 8:30 A.M.–8:30 P.M.* ***808-579-6323.***

Hana Ranch Restaurant Hana *American/Hawaiian* $$

There's slim pickings for good restaurants—make that any restaurants—in Hana. It's just not that kind of place. However, the light and airy Hana Ranch Restaurant offers dependable, decent eats from hamburgers, steaks, and pork chops, to Hawaiian-style fresh fish and chicken. For dessert, check out their cookie dough sundae or macadamia nut pie! *Hana Highway. Open 11 A.M.–4 P.M. daily. On Wednesdays, Fridays, and Saturdays also open 6 P.M.–8:30 P.M. for dinner.* ***808-248-8255.***

Humuhumunukunukuapua'a (Humu) Wailea *Fusion, Pacific Rim* $$$

Named after the unofficial Hawaiian state fish, this thatched-roof establishment on the lagoon in the Grand Wailea Hotel is simply referred to as "Humu" by folks in these parts (and actually in most other parts as well). You'll enjoy the setting and the fresh, expertly prepared Pacific Rim cuisine. *Located at the Grand Wailea Resort Hotel & Spa, 3850 Alanui Drive. Open daily 5:30 P.M.–9 P.M.* ***808-875-1234.*** *www.grandwailea.com/dining.*

Mama's Fish House Pa'ia *Hawaiian, Pacific Rim* $$$$

You should make a reservation several days early for this place, which could be the most popular restaurant in Maui. It's so popular for several good reasons, including top-notch dishes that use local fish and produce (the menu even tells who caught the fish), a south-seas atmosphere of flowers and bamboo, and spectacular views westward across Kuau Cove and the Pacific toward the mountains of West Maui. *799 Poho Place, just off Route 36 (Hana Highway). Open daily 11 A.M.–9:30 P.M.* ***808-579-8488.*** *www.mamasfishhouse.com.*

Maui Tacos Kihei and other locations *Mexican* $$

Start with one takeout counter. Add a few tables and some paper plates, then dress with garlicky fresh-fish tacos, "surf burritos" of fresh fish, black beans, and salsa, and other concoctions. Don't charge too much, and you've got a winning restaurant chain, catering to everyone from surfers to families from Kansas. *Located in the Kamaole Beach Center at 2411 S. Kihei Road. Also in Lahaina, Napili, and other locations around Maui. Open daily 9 A.M.–9 P.M.* ***808-879-5005.***

Roy's Bar & Grill Lahaina and Kihea Pacific Rim $$$

This lively and crowded establishment is probably one of the best chain restaurants you'll ever experience—made famous by Hawaii's most successful celebrity chef, Roy Yamaguchi. The secret of Roy's success is the savory Euro-Pacific fusion cuisine, fresh local ingredients, a good wine list, highly efficient service, and surprisingly reasonable prices! *4405 Honoapi'ilani Highway (Lahaina) or 303 Piikea Ave., Building 1 (Kihei). Open daily beginning at 5:30 P.M. In Lahaina call **808-669-6999**, in Kihei call **808-891-1120**. www.roysrestaurant.com.*

Entertainment and Nightlife

Thanks to the fact that Maui has garnered a reputation as one of the world's top vacation destinations, there's plentiful nightlife here. In fact, Maui rivals the more urban O'ahu when it comes to partying into the night, boasting a handful of trendy clubs, complete with the occasional celebrity or two, located in Lahaina, Ka'anapali, Kahului, Wailea, Kihei, and Makawao. It's also a hotbed of good local musicians, who play at many of the more popular island restaurants each night.

To find out what's happening where, check the local *Maui News*, published three times a week and available all over the island, as well as the free visitor publications. You can also go to **www.mauinews.com** to see the latest nightlife calendar.

Live Music

Maui has some of the best musicians in Hawaii, playing traditional Hawaiian and slack-key guitar, to rock, jazz, and the Hawaiian-style reggae called "Jawaiian." In addition to the resort lounges, which have live music of varying quality almost without exception, a great many of the island's independent restaurants and bars feature quality live music each night.

Lahaina is one of the island's hotspots, with plenty of musical venues. Among these are **Kimo's** at 585 Front Street in Lahaina (**808-661-4811**), which is a restaurant by the sea that also offers very good drinks, the **Cool Cat Café** at 685 Front Street (**808-667-0909**), the **Hard Rock Cafe** at 900 Front Street (**808-667-7400**), and the **Pioneer Inn** at 658 Wharf Street (**808-661-3636**). If you like jazz, check out the **Pacific 'O** restaurant, 505 Front Street (**808-667-4341**) on Friday and Saturday nights.

Up the road in Ka'anapali, you can't go wrong at the **Hula Grill** in the Whaler's Village shopping center (**808-667-6636**), where every night you can put your feet in the sand while listening to some of the island's best players. Just down the beachside promenade is **Leilanie's** (**808-661-4495**), which has a similar scene.

In the Kehei/Wailea area, stop by the **Blue Marlin Harborfront Grill & Bar,** at Ma'alaea Harbor (**808-244-8844**), **Henry's Bar & Grill** at 41 E. Lipoa Street (**808-879-2849**), the **Life's A Beach Club,** 1913 S. Kihei Road (**808-891-8010**), **Lulu's** at 1945–H S. Kihei Road (**808-879-9944**), or the Tradewinds Poolside Café, 2259 S. Kihei Road (**808-874-6284**).

If you're up around Pa'ia, check out the nightly musical fare at the **Moana Bakery & Café,** 71 Baldwin Avenue (**808-579-9999**) or **Charley's** at 142 Hana Highway (**808-579-8085**). In Central Maui, the place to peruse is **Café Marc Aurel** at 28 North Market Street in Wailuku (**808-244-0852**).

DJs and Dancing

Maui is just so darn mellow during the day that a lot of us feel compelled to work off some energy when the sun goes down. For that reason, the DJ/ dance scene is out in full force on Maui, and there's even more than a smattering of karaoke at some of these places.

In West Maui, check out **Moose McGillycuddy's,** 844 Front Street in Lahaina (**808-667-7758**), **Spats,** an Italian restaurant at the Ka'anapali Hyatt or **Paradise Bluz** at 744 Front Street in Lahaina (**808-667-5299**).

A few of the hotter spots on the Kehei/Wailea coast include the **Bocalino Bistro & Bar** at Azeka Place II, 1279 South Kihei Road (**808-874-9299**) or **Hapa's Nightclub** at 41 E. Lipoa Street (**808-870-6105**). If you feel like doing your own warbling, call for the karaoke schedule at the **Sansei Seafood Restaurant & Sushi Bar** in the Kihei Town Center at 1881 South Kihei Road (**808-879-0004**).

Upcountry, you can shake that body most nights at **Casanova,** 1188 Makawao Avenue in Makawao (**808-572-0220**).

Theater and Performing Arts

The **Maui Symphony Orchestra** is the premiere classical music ensemble on the island, with a season that runs through fall and spring, including a performance of Handel's Messiah once every December. You can call the

Maui Arts and Cultural Center at **808-242-7469** or check its website, **www.mauiarts.org,** for calendar information on the symphony and many other cultural and performing arts events, including live theater, dance concerts, film festivals, and concerts by internationally acclaimed performers.

The Best Lu'aus

If you go to Hawaii, you've got to go to a lu'au, right? Yes, this traditional feast has become very commercial in most cases, but attending a lu'au is still something that every visitor to Hawaii has got to do at least once. These generally last three or four hours, and charge $50–$75 for adults, half-price for children. All feature an all-you-can eat Hawaiian feast, an open bar, and Hawaiian-themed entertainment.

Feast at Lele Lahaina

This is an "upscale" Maui lu'au, with intimacy and a price to match. However, it's one of the best—more romantic than some of the others, and in a spectacular oceanfront setting. Guests receive their own table, and a five-course, sit-down dinner. *505 Front Street. Held daily.* ***808-667-5353*** or ***1-866-244-5353.*** *www.feastatlele.com.*

Hyatt Lu'au Ka'anapali

The "Drums of the Pacific" lu'au in a specially designed terrace/theater at the Hyatt features a master of ceremonies and show that might make you think you're in Vegas, but hey … the view is nice and there's lots of Hawaiian food, updated to contemporary tastes. In all fairness, this is one of the better lu'aus on Maui. There's a huge buffet, and the show itself covers a variety of Polynesian cultures, from New Zealand to Tonga, to … Maui! *The Sunset Terrace at the Hyatt Regency Maui. Held daily. Check-in starts at 4:30 P.M., gates open 5 P.M.* ***808-661-6655*** *or* ***1-877-661-6655.***

Legends of Makena Lu'au Makena

Located at the Maui Prince Hotel south of Wailea, this lu'au offers family-style table service with a full Hawaiian feast of laulau, kalua pig, island fish, poi, fresh fruits, and much more. *South of Wailea on Route 31. Sunday evenings only, starting at 5:30 P.M.* ***808-875-5888.***

Old Lahaina Lu'au Lahaina

Located right on the ocean with incredible views of Lana'i and Moloka'i, this is one of the most authentic and enjoyable lu'aus on the island. You'll be greeted with a fresh tropical flower lei and a mai tai, after which you'll enjoy kalua pig, baked mahi-mahi, and other Hawaiian specialties, along with entertainment and local arts and crafts available for purchase. *1287 Front Street. Held daily 5:45 P.M. April 1–September 30, 5:15 P.M. October 1–March 31.* ***808-667-1998*** *or* ***1-800-248-5828.*** *www.oldlahainalu'au.com.*

Renaissance Wailea Beach Lu'au Wailea

This is one of the more authentic lu'aus in East Maui, held in the Wailea Beach Resort's lovely oceanfront gardens—a great place to be drinking a mai tai at sunset. This lu'au is known for the breathtaking fire knife dance that closes the show, its proximity to the ocean, and the open bar available throughout the evening. *Held Tuesday, Thursday, and Saturday beginning about 5:30 P.M.* ***808-356-1800*** *or* ***1-888-349-7888.*** *www.renaissancewaileabeachlu'au.com.*

Shopping on Maui

You can shop until you drop in Maui, with hundreds of options for every conceivable product, from fine art, jewelry, and authentic crafts, to those cheesy little cedar boxes with the laminated photo of the surfer on the top.

For a wide variety of basics—books, clothes, and services—your best bet is to shop in **Kahului,** which is like any other large town in America and even has a couple of malls. For a selection of more unique items, you can peruse the shops of **Lahaina, Pa'ia,** and **Kihei.** Of course the major resorts all have their own gift shops, jewelry stores, and art galleries, which are pricey but usually have high-quality, authentic goods.

Kahului and Central Maui

This is Maui's commercial center. As a visitor, you probably won't have much need for a 2 × 4 at the **Home Depot** on the Kahului strip (100 Pakaula Street; **808-893-7800**), though there are plenty of "basics" available in the area from major chains. Your best bet for most useful items is Maui's largest mall, the **Queen Ka'ahumanu Center,** located at 275 W. Ka'ahumanu Avenue in Kahului (**808-877-3369**), which is jam-packed with all of the usual stores and restaurants you see in these places, including Macy's, Sears, Waldenbooks, and scores of other establishments. The **Maui Marketplace Mall,** 70 E. Kaahumanu Avenue (**808-877-7559**), is a newer construction, with Borders Books, OfficeMax, and The Sports Authority.

Of course, if you're looking for something more original, you should avoid the malls like the plague. In Wailuku, walk down Market Street, where you'll find such shops as **Bird of Paradise Unique Antiques**, 56 N. Market Street (808-242-7699), featuring real Hawaiian furniture, china, pottery and glass, **Brown-Kobayashi**, 160-A N. Market Street (**808-242-0804**), full of rare and fascinating Asian antiques, or the **Bailey House Gift Shop** (2375-A Main Street (**808-244-3326**), where everything is of good quality and made in Hawaii.

In Ma'alaea, visit the **Ma'alaea Harbor Village,** 300 Ma'alaea Road (**808-244-4500**), which has a small assortment of gift shops and decent restaurants.

West Maui

Lahaina and the resorts of Ka'anapali are loaded with shopping opportunities. On the north side of Lahaina, check out **Lahaina Printsellers** or **Na Mea Hawaii** in the **Lahaina Cannery Mall,** 1221 Honoapi'ilani Highway (**808-661-5304**), where you can find all manner of prints, paintings, and clothing that are quintessential Hawaii. In downtown Lahaina, the **Lahaina Center,** 900 Front Street (**808-661-5304**), has a number of shops worthy of a look.

Up the road in Ka'anapali, you'll find plenty to peruse at the **Whaler's Village** shopping center, 2435 Ka'anapali Parkway (**808-661-4567**), which offers a mix of Hawaiian merchandise and global brands such as Prada, Tiffany, and Ferragamo.

Finally, if you're driving the West Maui loop around the northwest side of the island, be sure to stop off at the acclaimed hilltop **Kaukini Gallery** on Route 340 just up the hill east of Kahakuloa (**808-244-3371**), where you'll find a superb collection of handmade works of over 100 local artists from Maui and other parts of Hawaii.

East Maui

Most East Maui shopping goes on along the Kehei-Wailea coast, where there are hundreds of hotels and condos, thousands of people, and tourist-based shopping infrastructure to match. **Azeka Place** at 1280 S. Kihei Road

(**808-879-5000**) is a rather nondescript but utilitarian place, though it happens to be Kihei's largest shopping center, claiming over 50 stores and restaurants (we haven't counted).

The East Maui interior known as "Upcountry" is where you'll find the settlement of **Makawao**. It's usually described as a "former cowboy town," but happens to have some of the most interesting and sophisticated shopping on Maui.

Makawao shopping includes the **Hui No'eau Visual Arts Center,** 2841 Baldwin Avenue (**808-572-6560;** www.huinoeau.com), Maui's most respected arts organization, offering a range of workshops and classes, as well as a killer gift shop with some of the top Maui-produced artwork.

The sun-bleached former sugar mill town of **Pa'ia,** situated on the north coast of East Maui, is filled with twenty-something windsurfers, as well as funky arts and crafts shops—perfect for a morning of shopping and observing the local scene before heading to the beach yourself.

There's not much shopping out in Hana, but when you're there, do make it a point to stop by the **Hana Coast Gallery,** a high-end affair devoted almost entirely to the very best Hawaiian artists. Here you'll find not only superb paintings and prints in a variety of media, but also stonework, carvings, koa-wood furniture, hand-turned bowls, and more.

Local Markets

Hawaii is known for its community markets, usually set outdoors, and Maui is no exception. Call ahead for all of these to make sure they're happening.

On Saturdays, check out the more-than-100 booths at the **Maui Swap Meet,** held in Kahului every Saturday from 7 A.M.–noon on South Pu'unene Ave. next to the Kahului Post Office. Here you can get local baked goods, ethnic foods, local fruits and vegetables, fresh tropical flowers, resale goods and household items—all at low prices.

Ohana Farmers Market at the Kahului Shopping Center (**808-871-8347**), is a fine place to revel in a fresh, inexpensive selection of locally grown produce, as well as local arts and crafts. It's open Fridays from 9 A.M.–5 P.M.

The **Kihei Open Market,** Piilani Highway (Route 31) at Ohukai Street (**808-874-0978**) is held every Sunday from 9 A.M.–4 P.M., and features flowers, arts and crafts, tropical silks, and a farmer's market. If your timing is right, you can take in the **Keanae Open Market** in the Kaenae Peninsula along the Hana Highway (**808-248-7858**), where the communities of Keanae and Wailua Nui gather together for a monthly market on the scenic Keanae Peninsula. Here you'll find taro and poi, fruit, flowers, crafts such as Hawaiian seed leis, lauhala weaving, fabric creations, jewelry, and much more.

Enjoying the Best Activities on Maui

Being the tourist mecca that it is, Maui has no shortage of activities to suit your vacation style—whether your thing is a sedate bus ride or extreme windsurfing.

Sightseeing Tours

If you'd rather hop on a bus, helicopter, or boat and let others do the actual driving, flying, or sailing, you have plenty of choices of tour companies in Maui. This is a savvy option for two of Maui's most popular activities, the long, winding drive to Hana, and the equally taxing drive up Haleakala.

All of these can be booked from the front desk or concierge station in your hotel, though we've also provided some numbers in case you'd at least like to handle that part of the planning yourself.

Keep in mind that the cheaper tours often use bigger vans with more people. All of these outfits will pick you up at your hotel or condo.

Family-owned **Ekahi Tours** (**808-877-9775** or **1-888-292-2422**) will be happy to show you around the island in vans, not buses, whether your preferred destination is Hana, Haleakala, or a road trip covering most of the important sacred sites on Maui. Tours run around $75 to $105.

Polynesian Adventure Tours (**808-877-4242**) is a bit more economical, operating an impeccably maintained fleet of vans, including 25 passenger mini-coaches and full-size buses to Haleakala, Hana, and other parts of Maui. Rates run from approximately $70–$90.

Akina Aloha Tours (**808-879-2828**) runs sedans, limos, vans, minibuses, and the big motor coaches to Hana, Halealaka, and other parts of the island, including various museums and cultural centers. Rates run around $90. **Temptation Tours** (**808-877-8888**) goes to all of the same places with vans that hold only six to eight people, allowing a more personalized experience at $170–$200.

Bicycle Tours

For many visitors to Maui, the ultimate ride is a bicycle descent 38 miles down from the summit of 10,023-foot Halealaka, which can be accomplished after witnessing sunrise from the summit. **Maui Downhill (808-871-2155 or 1-800-535-BIKE;** www.mauidownhill.com) is one of the top bike outfitters offering this tour, with free round-trip transportation from over 150 hotels and destinations around Maui.

Enjoying Outdoor Maui

Maui is a fabulous island for those who appreciate the great outdoors, offering everything from world-class golf, surfing, and snorkeling, to rugged hikes through rainforests and through the barren, Mars-like wilderness of Haleakala. Here you can be trudging through snow in the morning and diving through a tropical reef by afternoon.

The Best Golf Courses

Maui is definitely one of the world's premier golf destinations, with over 20 spectacular courses, several of which are ranked worldwide. Despite all of this quality, tee times aren't all that hard to come by compared to the norm in metropolitan areas around the rest of the United States. However, you should still call well ahead.

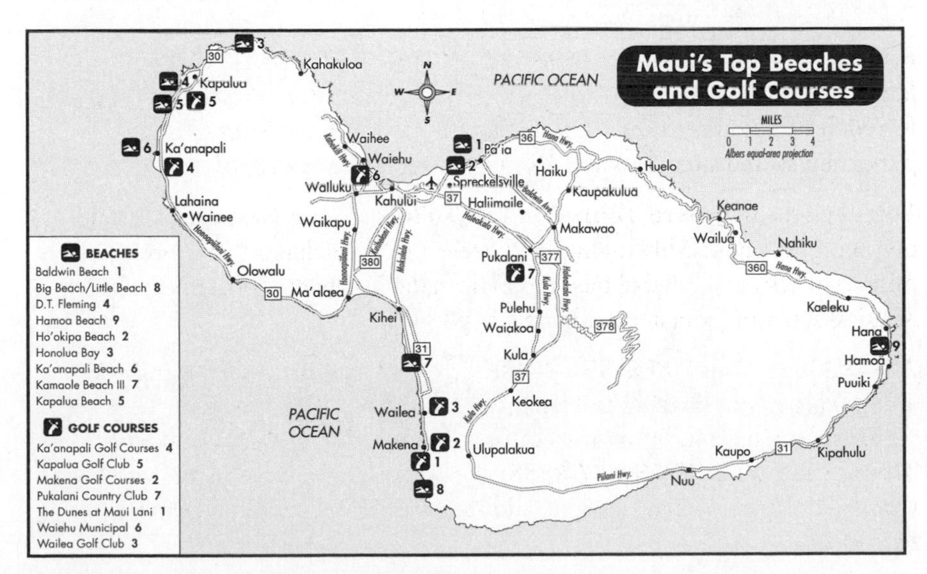

Maui's best beaches and golf courses.

The Dunes at Maui Lani Makena

This links-style, 6,800-yard course is one of the most acclaimed anywhere—*Golf Digest* called it "One of the Five Best Kept Secret Golf Courses in America," so it's obviously a "must play" on Maui. It's got lots of natural sand dunes, large lakes, and one of Maui's toughest finishing holes. *1333 Maui Lani Parkway. Greens fees are only about $95 after 2 P.M.* ***808-873-0422.*** *www.dunesatmauilani.com.*

Ka'anapali Golf Courses Ka'anapali

Offers a north (Tournament) and south (Resort) course, covering 6,994 and 6,555 yards respectively. Both allow you to play through the beautiful foothills of the West Maui Mountains with sweeping panoramas of the coastline. *Ka'anapali Beach Resort, 2290 Ka'anapali Parkway. Greens fees are around $140.* ***808-661-3691.*** *www.Ka'anapali-golf.com/.*

Kapalua Golf Club Kapalua

The Kapalua Golf Club offers three courses between the sea and the West Maui Mountains. The 18-hole Plantation Course is home to the annual Mercedes Championship and is guaranteed to challenge your game, with 7,263 yards of golf. The Kapalua Bay Course offers 6,600 yards, while the Village course sprawls over 6,632 yards. *300 Kapalua Drive. Greens fees are $195 to around $295 for the Plantation Course.* ***877-527-2582.*** *www.kapalua.com/golf.*

Duffers and golf pros alike enjoy Maui's scenic courses.

(Photo courtesy of HVCB/Kirk Lee Aeder)

Makena Golf Courses Makena

Two more Robert Trent Jones Jr. creations, a North Course (6,539 yards) and South Course (6,633 yards) offer the typical (yawn) awesome views of mountains and sea, and are particularly integrated into the natural geography. *5415 Makena Alanui. Greens fees range from $125 after 1 P.M. to around $185.* ***808-879-3344.*** *www.makenagolf.com/.*

Pukalani Country Club Pukakani

This upcountry course at 1,500 feet elevation is fun and not as expensive as most of the other courses on Maui—though it can get windy. It boasts 6,927 yards of golfing and nice views of West Maui and Haleakala. Play early to avoid the winds. *360 Pukalani Street. Greens fees are only about $68, and a thrifty $53 after 1:30 P.M.* ***808-572-1314.*** *www.pukalanigolf.com.*

Waiehu Municipal Golf Course Waiehu

Known as the poor man's Pebble Beach, this 6,330-yard course may be the best golfing deal on Maui, with a front nine along the ocean, and a hilly back nine. The course gets about 400 players a day, so progress can be slow at times. *Off Kahekili Highway (Route 340), two miles north of Wailuku. Greens fees start at an amazing $25, plus an $8 per player cart fee.* ***808-243-7400.***

Wailea Golf Club Wailea

There are three championship courses here: Blue (6,758 yards), Emerald (6,825, yards), and Gold (7,070 yards). The Gold Course is the home course of The Senior Skins Game, with numerous mountain and ocean vistas, and has been ranked among the country's best new courses by *Golf Magazine* and *Golf Digest. 100 Wailea Golf Club Drive, Wailea. Greens fees are around $200.* ***808-875-7450*** *or* ***1-888-328-6284.*** *www.golfbc.com/courses/gold.*

Whale-Watching off Maui

Pacific humpback whales visit Maui's waters by the thousands from November to March, migrating close to 3,500 miles from their Alaskan summer feeding waters in order to mate and have their calves. Sure, there are so many whales that you can usually see them at a distance from your own lanai, but there's nothing quite like getting up-close and personal with these intriguing creatures. Here are the best whale-watching tours on Maui:

Whale Watch Maui Lahaina

The two-hour cruises offered by this major outfit feature big, comfortable boats with an enclosed main cabin and upper observation deck. You can buy food on board, and there's even a "whale cam" that lets you observe the activity underwater. A naturalist is on board to provide information on the whales. *The boats leave four times a day from Lahaina Harbor. Adult prices ranging from $26–$35, depending on the time of day. Kids under 12 are free.* ***1-877-500-6284.*** *www.mauiprincess.com.*

Pacific Whale Foundation Lahaina

The Pacific Whale Foundation runs two-hour "Eco-Cruises" at 10:30 A.M. every day from Lahaina Harbor on two high-tech power catamarans. A marine naturalist is on board, and guests can listen to whale songs on hydrophones. Beverages and snacks are available for purchase on board. *Cruises are $29.95 for adults and $15 for kids over 6. Kids under 6 ride for free.* ***808-249-8811*** *or* ***1-800-942-5311.*** www.pacificwhale.org.

Hiking in Maui

Maui boasts easy and scenic walks, as well as some of the most challenging trails you'll find anywhere. Climates can range from extremely hot to freezing; from arid rock fields above timberline to humid rainforests. If you're on the trails, make sure you've brought along clothing and footwear appropriate for the terrain and climate.

You can get complete trail maps, recommendations, and necessary permits by contacting the **State of Hawaii Department of Land and Natural Resources** offices at **808-587-0400** or **808-873-3501.** You can even download a Hawaii State Parks brochure at www.hawaii.gov/dlnr/dsp/dsp.html.

These descriptions will give you a sense of the best hikes on Maui, but you can't use them for navigation. Be sure to pick up a map before you set out!

Haleakala Crater East Maui

If you can handle high-altitude hiking (up to 10,000 feet), then the trails that crisscross the otherworldly Haleakala Crater in Haleakala National Park are "must dos" before you leave Maui—especially since you can actually reserve overnight stays in any of three wilderness cabins located along the routes ($40 per night; book early). Make sure you obtain a permit at Park Headquarters before entering the crater wilderness on an overnight trip. If you're only doing a day trip, sign the register at the trailhead. The 10-mile **Halemauu Trail** crosses the crater from west to east over a series of switchbacks descending to the crater floor, traversing 4 miles before reaching the Holua cabin at 7,000 feet. The trail then continues another six miles across the crater floor to Paliku cabin. The 10-mile **Sliding Sands Trail** runs from the summit into the crater, beginning near the Visitor Center at 10,000 feet and following the base of the south rim of the crater for six miles to the Kapalaoa cabin at 7,400 feet. From there the trail descends gradually another 4 miles to the easternmost end of the crater and Paliku cabin at 6,400 feet.

Kula & Kahikinui Forest Reserve Trails on Haleakala East Maui

Within the Kula and Kahikinui Forest Reserves are several good trails beginning at 6,400 feet on the western flanks of Haleakala. Get a four-wheel-drive vehicle and follow Route 37 out of Kahului to just before mile marker 14. Turn left on Route 377 for 0.3 miles and then turn right onto Waipoli Road. Follow that through a long series of switchbacks until it enters the forest at an elevation of 6,400 feet. From there you can hike the 7-mile **Upper Waiakoa Trail** to a rocky and barren 7,800-foot elevation, where you'll have excellent views of Central and West Maui. In the same area you can also take the **Skyline Trail (6.5 miles),** beginning at 9,750-foot elevation at the lowest point on the Science City Road, passing through an iron gate and down the ridge till it ends at Skyline switchback at 6,500 feet at the upper end of Haleakala Ridge Trail. The terrain is rugged and barren in a primitive, volcanic way, with expansive views.

Waihee Ridge Trail West Maui

This is the best trail in West Maui, climbing the windward (northern) slopes of the West Maui Mountains 2.5 miles to a peak overlooking Wailuku. At the top you can see Wailuku and Central Maui, with Mount Eke inland and high in the clouds. The trail is well marked but steep at times, climbing from 1,000 feet to 2,563 feet in elevation. Although the area is damp, there is no drinking water along the trail, so be sure to bring your own! Camping is not permitted.

Waikamoi Ridge Trail East Maui

This short 0.8-mile loop trail off the Hana Highway starts at a picnic shelter and climbs through a lush forest of native and planted trees to a grassy clearing with another shelter and picnic site, and is a scenic way to stretch your legs on the way to Hana. *Follow Route 360 (Hana Highway) 3.5 miles past Kailua Village toward Keanae. Pull into the parking area with picnic shelters above the road.*

Waimoku Falls; Seven Sacred Pools East Maui

The **Ohe'o Gulch** area, 40 minutes south of Hana on Route 31, is a starting point for an awesome 2-mile trek upstream to the 400-foot **Waimoku Falls,** and along the way you can take side trips to the pools. To avoid the crowds, spend the night in Hana and get here early! You can camp down at the grassy sea cliffs below, but only for three nights, and there is no water and no open fires are permitted.

Surfing, Snorkeling, Fishing, and More

This island is nothing less than a world destination for such things, so you might as well take full advantage, whether your thing is surfing (including windsurfing), snorkeling, fishing, or sailing.

Surfing: World-renowned big-wave surfer Laird Hamilton is from Maui, as are plenty of other pros, but you can enjoy the waves without being an expert. However, be extremely careful, as Maui's waves are generally big and the undertow strong. The shores from Ka'anapali south through Kihei and Wailea are generally the best for beginning to intermediate surfers, with Lahaina breakwall, Launiopoko Park, and Kihei's Cove Park being some of the best spots. The northwest and northern coasts are generally for experts only. If you're planning ahead, **Mauisurf.com** (Internet access only) will connect you with any one of several surf schools around the island, with rates starting at about $60 for a two-hour lesson. **Maui Waveriders** at 3353 Keha Drive in Kihei (**808-875-4761**) is also a good bet at $55 to $85, as is the North Shore–based **Rivers to the Sea** (**808-280-8795** or **808-280-6236**), at $70.

Windsurfing: Ho'okipa Beach on Maui's North Shore near Pa'ia is one of the world's best windsurfing spots, with Kealia Beach Park near Kihei another prime spot. To rent equipment or take a lesson, get in touch with **Maui Windsurf Company (808-877-4816** or **1-800-872-0999;** www.maui-windsurfcompany.com), which will rent you a board for $30 a day. You can also check in with **Sailboards Maui (808-871-7954;** www.sailboardsmaui.com).

Sailing: You can take an exciting two-hour sailing cruise out of Lahaina Harbor on the ***America II*** **(1-888-667-2133)**, a 65-foot racing boat that was second only to Dennis Connor's *Stars and Stripes* in the 1987 America's Cup Race. It's a great sail out into the Paiolo Channel between Maui, Lana'i, and Moloka'i, with whales and dolphins swimming beside the boat as you heel over and the spray comes over the bow! The boat goes out several times a day, including romantic sunset cruises. Snacks and beverages are included in the $40 fare.

Snorkeling: Maui is surrounded by vibrant coral reefs, often accessible by simply wading out into the water in front of your hotel. What's more, the island of Molokini, just off the Kehei coast, is one of Hawaii's top snorkeling destinations. **Lani Kai Friendly Charters (808-244-1979** or **1-888-983-8080;** www.mauisnorkeling.com) and the **MV Prince Kuhio (808-242-8777** or **1-800-468-1287;** www.mvprince.com) both leave Ma'alaea Harbor at 6:45 A.M. daily, returning at noon, for a trip to Molokini Marine Preserve, where the crew will pass out complimentary snorkel gear and flotation devices, and then provide brief snorkeling instruction to anyone who requires it. The trips also include a cruise to observe green sea turtles, moray eels, and other exotic marine life. The trip includes a continental breakfast and lunch, as well as beer, wine, and mai tais. These outfits charge about $90 for adults and $58 for kids over 5 years of age.

Fishing: The waters around Maui offer world-class fishing for marlin, mahimahi, ono, and tuna, with charters sailing out of Lahaina and Ma'alaea charging $100–$180 for a half day of group fishing. There are a wide variety of boats and packages, so you should shop around. In Lahaina, call **Lucky Strike Charters (808-661-4606)** or **Sport Fishing Lahaina (808-667-6672)**. In Ma'alaea, check out **Rascal Charters (808-874-8633)**. Another way to ensure you get the best boast at a good price and time is to call **Sportfish Hawaii (808-396-2607** or **1-877-388-1376)**, the top booking desk for fishing trips in the state.

With all that there is to do, you could not only spend your vacation in beautiful Maui, you could even spend your life there. Well ... we could, anyway.

The Big Island

The island of Hawaii, most often referred to as "The Big Island," is the largest and the youngest island in the Hawaiian chain. There's an amazing diversity of climates and landscapes for you to enjoy, not the least of which is the spectacular and very active Ki'lauea volcano. For those of us who enjoy a less commercial experience—at least for a day or two—it might be the best bet of all.

Chapter 10

Relaxing on The Big Island

In This Chapter

- The Big Island's geography and weather
- Transportation options
- Deciding where to stay on the Big Island
- The Big Island's best lodging choices

Let's get something straight right up front: the state's name is Hawaii, and in the State of Hawaii there is an island named Hawaii. It's kind of like New York, New York, except for the palm trees and the whales and the volcanoes. But you knew that, didn't you?

But to avoid confusion between the state and the island (and the subject of this chapter), we're going to do as the locals do and call the island of Hawaii by its more popular nickname: **The Big Island.**

It's an apt name, anyway. The Big Island is indeed the largest in the entire Hawaiian archipelago, with more land area than all of the other islands combined. If that doesn't tickle your fancy, consider some of these additional superlatives:

- The Big Island boasts Hawaii's highest mountains, with snowcapped **Mauna Kea** and **Mauna Loa** rising to almost 14,000 feet above sea level. Mauna Kea could be considered the highest mountain in the world (more than 30,000 feet) if you were to measure its height from the ocean floor.
- The Big Island offers the only snow skiing in Hawaii.
- It's the youngest Hawaiian island, a real punk at just under one million years of age, and it's still growing.
- Like most punks, it's a little wild: it's home to the most active volcano on Earth and the only currently erupting volcano in Hawaii, **Ki'lauea.**
- The west side of the island includes the driest land in Hawaii, and what is claimed to be the United States' largest privately owned cattle ranch, **Parker Ranch.**
- The southern tip of The Big Island, called **South Point** or **Ka Lae,** is the southernmost point in the United States.

Snapshot

The Big Island:

Size: 4,038 square miles

Coastline: 266 miles

Population: 137,500

Average Temperature: 71° (21.6°C) to 77° F (25°C) (much colder at high elevations)

Average Annual Rainfall: 10 inches at Kawaihae (near the Kohala coast); 128 inches at Hilo Airport

Highest Elevation: 13,796 feet (Mauna Kea)

Favorite Endangered Species: Giant Pacific Green Sea Turtle (which can grow to 400 pounds)

Number of Golf Courses: 17

Oh, we could go on, but that should give you a flavor of what you're dealing with in terms of drama and variety. Because of its size, The Big Island is like a mini-continent, with widely varying landscapes and lifestyles. It's got rugged mountains in the middle, a rainforest in the east, arid "cowboy country" in the west, and stunning white and black (and even green) sand beaches along the coasts. Add to that the state's oldest city (**Hilo**), lava flows that occasionally swallow entire neighborhoods, world-class luxury resorts, and a smattering of hippie towns.

The sheer size of The Big Island means that unless you're planning on spending a week or more, it would make the most sense for you to focus on a couple of different areas rather than trying to tour the entire thing.

Airport Transportation Options

Unlike the other Hawaiian islands, The Big Island has two international airports: one in Hilo on the rainy east coast and close to **Hawaii Volcanoes National Park;** and one in the **Kailua-Kona** area, in the sunny west, where most of the resorts are located. A third airport, **Waimea-Kohala Airport,** near **Waimea,** is a small airstrip that services private and chartered planes only.

Kona International Airport at **Keahole** is located about 7 miles northwest of Kailua-Kona, about 35 to 40 minutes by car from the upscale resorts along the North Kona-Kohala Coast. Kona has two terminals, North and South, with open-air pavilions, swaying coconut palms, and lush tropical greenery.

Hilo International Airport is located about 2 miles outside of town, with an open-air ticket lobby area. It's only a few minutes by car from downtown Hilo, and about 40 minutes from Hawaii Volcanoes National Park.

In either airport, you'll find rental and ground transportation desks right outside the baggage area, with shuttles to the car rental lots available on the terminal roadway.

Rental Cars

All of the major car rental companies maintain offices at the Kona and Hilo airports. Kona International is located about 7 miles northwest of the town of Kailua-Kona, while Hilo International lies about 2 miles east of Hilo. At both airports, you'll find the car rental stands on the roadway opposite the baggage area. You can pick from a wide range of vehicles, including cars, trucks, vans, and SUVs. Rates begin at about $65 to $75 per day and about $300 per week for subcompacts, with unlimited mileage.

Note that some of these agencies have restrictions on where on the island you can drive their cars, especially if you're planning to motor all the way up to the 13,796-foot summit on **Mauna Kea.** In the latter case, you may want to consider renting a vehicle cleared for the drive with an engine that has been adjusted for the high altitude. You can get such a vehicle at **Harper Car & Truck Rental,** which has offices in both Kona and Hilo (**808-969-1478** or **1-800-852-9993** for both locations; www.harpershawaii.com).

Taxi Service

At both Kona and Hilo, you can pick up taxis right at the terminal.

From Kona, taxi fares start at about $20 for transport to **King Kamehameha's Kona Beach Hotel** and are slightly more expensive for other Kailua-Kona hotels and condos. Taxi fares to Kohala Coast resorts range from $45 to $65. Several taxis offer guided tours. A few of the more popular taxi services are **Aloha Taxi (808-325-5448), Elsa Taxi (808-887-6446), Kona Airport Taxi (808-329-7779)**, and **Paradise Taxi (808-329-1234)**.

Hilo is served by a number of cab companies that charge a metered rate of $3 plus $.30 per ⅛th mile and $.30 per minute for waiting time, plus $1.00 per bag. Taxis from the airport to Hilo's Banyan Drive hotels charge about $10–$12 for the 2-mile ride. Popular taxi companies around Hilo include **A-1 Bob's Taxi (808-959-4800)** and **Hilo Harry's Taxi (808-935-7091)**.

Shuttles

SpeediShuttle (808-329-5433 or **877-521-2085**) provides shared rides from Kona International Airport to major area resorts, and charges about $18 per person around Kailua-Kona, approximately $46 to resorts further north along the Kohala Coast, and about $40 to the Captain Cook area to the south.

Private shuttle services are offered by the various Kohala Coast resorts to the north. The rates for these rides vary, but are similar to those charged by other shuttles. Contact the **Kohala Coast Resort Association (808-886-4915** or **1-800-318-3637** or e-mail info@kohalacoastresorts.com), or check in at the counters located in the Aloha Airlines or Hawaiian Airlines arrival areas.

Hilo offers no regularly scheduled public shuttle service, but you can get a quote by going to www.airportshuttle.com. You also can secure private shuttle rides from **Arnott's Lodge (808-969-7097)**, the **Hawaii Naniloa Hotel (808-969-3333)**, and others. Call your hotel to assess their offerings.

Limousine Service

Limousine service around the island tends to cost around $60 or more an hour, with a two-hour minimum. There are no limousine companies based in Hilo, which makes any kind of limo transportation from there prohibitively expensive, since the cars have to come from Kona. In the Kona area,

Classic Hawaii: Honolulu's Waikiki and Diamond Head.

Sunset in an urban paradise—in this case, Honolulu.

Maui's dramatic Haleakala Crater may remind you of Mars.

Just off the coast of busy Maui, Molokini Island offers some great snorkeling.

The Blue Pools are one of the less-visited scenic treasures of Maui's East Coast.

One of the most dramatic sights in all of Hawaii is Kaua'i's Na Pali Coast.

The Big Island is still growing, as evidenced by Ki'lauea's lava pouring into the sea.

You'll find some scenic links at The Big Island's Mauna Kea Golf Course.

Sunset on Moloka'i is truly an "away from it all" experience.

Moloka'i's Halawa Valley combines beautiful scenery with historic sites.

Lana'i's Experience at Ko'ele is one of Golf Magazine*'s favorite courses.*

Heading home after a vacation in Hawaii may be tough.

Principle Limousine Service (808-325-5466) or **Gold Coast Town Car Service (808-325-5530)** will take you from the airport to area resorts for between $60 and $130, depending on exactly where you're going and what size vehicle you need.

Traveling on the Cheap: Buses

The Big Island's public bus system, **Hele-On Bus (808-961-8744)**, operates all over the island, but from the town centers rather than the airports. But the fares can't be beat: they're free on any scheduled route, though you do have to pay $1 for each piece of luggage or backpack or to carry a bike. The buses run Monday through Saturday with at least once-daily connections between major towns. The ride between Kona and Hilo takes about three hours each way and makes numerous stops. You can review complete schedules at http://www.hawaii-county.com and click on the bus schedule link.

For transportation from between Keauhou Bay and Kailua-Kona and places in between, check out **Alii Shuttle (808-775-7171)**, which runs a bus service stopping at hotels and shopping districts Monday through Saturday from 8:30 A.M.–7 P.M. The cost is $3.

What Transportation Costs on The Big Island

From Kailua-Kona Destination	*Taxi*	*Limo*	*Shuttle*	*Bus*
Hilo	$250	$180	N/A	$1 for each item
Kailua-Kona	$20	$70	$18	$1 for each item
Keauhou Kona	$20	$120	$40	$1 for each item
Kohala	$70	$110	$46	$1 for each item
Waimea	$95	$130	N/A	$1 for each item
From Hilo Destination	*Taxi*	*Limo*	*Shuttle*	*Bus*
Kailua-Kona	$250	N/A	N/A	$1 for each item
Volcano	$70	N/A	N/A	$1 for each item

Group Tours

Of course, you don't have to go to all of the trouble of driving around The Big Island yourself, or even planning your own itinerary, especially if you're just visiting for a day or two. You can let a professional tour company do all of the work, chauffeuring you to the island's top sights with a minimum of hassle on your part. **Tom Barefoot's Tours (808-661-8889;** www.tombarefoot.com), will take you anywhere you want to go in vans, including a trip to the glowing lava fields of **Ki'lauea,** while **Polynesian Adventure Tours (808-356-1800** or **1-888-349-7888;** www.hawaiiantours.org) will transport you in 25-passenger "mini-coaches" on a circle tour all the way around the island for about $75. An old standby, **Roberts Hawaii (1-866-898-2519;** www.robertshawaii.com), probably has the largest selection, ranging from a grand circle tour to dinner cruises.

Getting Your Bearings: Island Locales

The Big Island is a very large, somewhat circular, volcanic massif poking nearly 14,000 feet above the sea. It's still growing, thanks to nearly continuous lava flows. This means that nearly all parts of the island are dominated by volcanic features to an extent not seen on the other Hawaiian islands. This includes barren lava deserts and black-sand beaches. You'll also spot a few snowcapped summits.

The Big Island's landmass is dominated by three primary volcanoes: Mauna Kea and Mauna Loa in the middle, and Ki'lauea along the southeast coast. These major mountains capture the moisture borne by trade winds from the northeast, making the northern and eastern coasts very rainy and green, with plenty of lush tropical foliage to cover the volcanic rocks in those areas. The southern and western coasts are generally sunny and dry.

The majority of resorts are found, not surprisingly, in the sunny west and south, and this part of the island is generally called the Kona Coast. It includes the overgrown fishing village of Kailua-Kona, and the resort areas of the Kohala Coast to the north and Keauhou Kona to the south.

The Big Island's damp northern shoreline is called the Hamakua Coast, and includes the small towns of **Hawi, Kukuihaele,** and **Honomu.** It's characterized by tropical foliage, towering cliffs, waterfalls, and beautiful seascapes, but because of the weather it is not a big resort area.

The island's largest and oldest town, Hilo, sits in the rainy east, and is the settlement closest to **Hawaii Volcanoes National Park,** where Ki'lauea continues to spew lava down its slopes and into the sea on a daily basis.

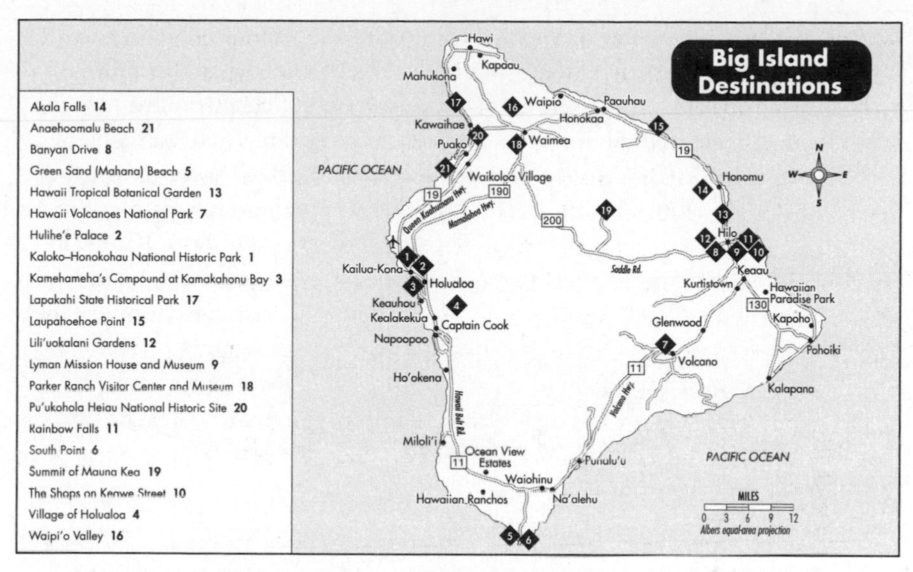

The Big Island's regions, highways, and key destinations.

The Kona Coast in the West

"Kona" means "leeward side" in Hawaiian, and this western part of The Big Island certainly benefits from its location in the rain shadow of the big volcanoes inland. In fact, the weather report here is nearly the same every day of the year, which is to say "sunny."

Much of the near-coastal area here is composed of black, lava desert, giving the landscape a feel somewhere between "American West" and "otherworldly." However, the multiple resorts that sit beside the ocean have spared little expense bringing in green, tropical landscaping fed by extensive irrigation systems. So if you're sitting on the beach with a drink in your hand, you're still going to feel like you're in a tropical paradise, but without any of that pesky rain.

A bit inland, however, as the land rises toward the volcanoes, the weather become cloudier and usually includes afternoon showers. This makes inland Kona a fertile region for growing world-renowned coffee, macadamia nuts, tropical fruit, and flowers.

The beaches along the Kona Coast, and everywhere on The Big Island for that matter, are often composed of black and (sometimes) even green sand. For details, take a look at our beach descriptions in Chapter 11.

The town of **Kailua-Kona** serves as the commercial center of this region. It used to be a quiet fishing village, but now serves the tourism industry with the island's primary airport and all manner of fine restaurants and convenient services. To the immediate south is the resort-lined coastline of **Keauhou** and the artists' community of **Holualoa.** Further south down the coastline from there is a string of interesting towns—**Honalo, Kainaliu, Kealakekua, Captain Cook,** and **Honaunau**—where those looking to get away from the touristy hubbub can find some beauty and peacefulness among the pristine beaches and macadamia groves.

Further south still is the somewhat remote region called K'au, home of a few small towns, a green-sand beach (**Papakolea**), and the southernmost point in the United States, creatively named *Ka Lae*, or **South Point.** (By the way, when Key West, Florida, claims to be the southernmost place in the country, read the fine print: that spit of sand is the southernmost place in the *continental* United States.)

Snapshot

Here are the top Kona Coast destinations:

- Honaunau National Historic Park
- Hulihe'e Palace (Kailua-Kona)
- Kamehameha's Compound at Kamakahonu Bay
- Kula Kai Caverns and Lava Tubes
- Papakolea Beach
- South Point
- Village of Holualoa

Snapshot

Here are some important phone numbers to remember while on The Big Island.

Big Island Visitors Bureau, 808-961-2126, 250 Keawe Street, Hilo, and **808-886-1652** 250 Waikoloa Beach Drive, Waikola; www.bigisland.org.

Kohala Coast Resort Association, 808-318-3637, 69-275 Waikoloa Beach Dr., Kamuela; **1-800-318-3637** or **808-886-4915;** http://kohalacoastresorts.com

Hilo Medical Center, 808-974-4700, 1190 Waianuenue Avenue, Hilo.

Kona Community Hospital, 808-322-9311, 79-1019 Haukapila Street, Kealakekua

North Hawaii Community Hospital, 808-322-9311, 67-1125 Mamalahoa Highway, Waimea.

The Kohala Coast in the Northwest

The western coast north of Kailua-Kona is the primo resort area of The Big Island. It also happens to be seasoned with numerous ancient historical sites such as the **Pu'ukohola Heiau** and ancient fishing village at **Lapakahi State Historical Park.** Called the Kohala Coast, this area is a land of contrasts, from flat, black lava plains in the southern portion, to a lush, misty coastline around the funky New-Age town of **Hawi** on the northwest tip of the island, and green rolling hills around the upcountry town of **Waimea,** home of the **Parker Ranch** visitor center and museum.

The resorts tucked away below the arid plains along the rocky coastline between Kailua-Kona and Kawaihae are among the best on the island, including **The Four Seasons** and **Kona Village Resorts** not far from the airport at Hualalai, and the beautifully landscaped **Mauna Kea Resort** a bit further up the coast. The beaches here tend to be black sand, and the sun is nearly always shining.

Snapshot

Here are our top Kohala Coast destinations:

- Anaehoomalu Beach
- Lapakahi State Historical Park
- Parker Ranch Visitor Center and Museum
- Pu'ukohola Heiau National Historic Site
- Summit of Mauna Kea
- Village of Hawi
- Village of Waimea

Some of the world's top observatories sit on top of Mauna Kea at nearly 14,000 feet elevation.

(Photo courtesy of HVCB/Kirk Lee Aeder)

From anywhere on the Kohala Coast you can see the lofty, often snowcapped summits of Hawaii's two largest mountains, **Mauna Kea** (13,796 feet) and **Mauna Loa** (13,677 feet). Mauna Kea boasts a glacial lake and several of the world's top observatories near its peak, with an auto road that you can take to the top in a four-wheel-drive vehicle.

Hilo in the East

Hilo is The Big Island's oldest and largest town, a lovely settlement of 40,000 people between the **Wailuku River** and the **Pacific Ocean.** It boasts lush foliage, Victorian homes, and beautiful parks, and is located only an hour's drive from **Hawaii Volcanoes National Park.** Hilo probably would have become the number-one destination on The Big Island, and maybe even the top destination in all of Hawaii, if it were not for one thing: rain!

Unfortunately for the tourist trade, Hilo is considered to be the wettest city in America, checking in at over 130 inches of precipitation annually. And with all of the corrugated metal roofs around town, there's no other place where we've *heard* it pour as hard as in Hilo. (Can you hear it now?) These little details have kept down Hilo's popularity as a place to hang out for any length of time. Still, it's a great walking town, full of history, and when it rains the streetscapes can look almost like an Impressionist painting. On those odd days when the sun actually makes an appearance, you'll almost always see a rainbow or two in the sky high above the snow-capped summit of Mauna Loa.

Snapshot

Here are our top Hilo destinations:

- Banyan Drive
- Lili'uokalani Gardens
- Lyman Mission House and Museum
- The Shops on Keawe Street
- Rainbow Falls

Hawaii Volcanoes National Park

If you're going to The Big Island, you can't afford to miss Hawaii Volcanoes National Park, about 30 miles southwest of Hilo and home of the world's most active volcano, **Ki'lauea.** At an elevation of 4,091 feet, this mountain is dwarfed by Mauna Loa (13,677 feet) and Mauna Kea (13,796 feet) to its north, but what it lacks in stature it makes up for in lava production. This is the life source and youngest part of the island. Every day, and night, you can view glowing, steaming molten rock sliding down Ki'lauea's flanks.

A drive along the summit caldera and along **Chain of Craters Road** will put you in a bizarre foreign world—a place of cinder cones, lava tubes, steam vents, sulfur banks, and barren craters. Within walking distance from the road you'll be able to gaze upon ancient petroglyphs and creeping, bubbling lava flows—some of which pour dramatically into the Pacific.

Just outside of the park, you visit the town of Volcano (elevation 4,000 feet above sea level), where you can shop at a number of interesting shops, have an excellent meal, and enjoy the evening at the famed **Volcano House** or another quaint inn beside a roaring fireplace.

Snapshot

Top Volcanoes National Park destinations include:

- Chain of Craters Road
- Crater Rim Road
- Pu'u Loa Petroglyphs
- Volcano Art Center
- Volcano House
- Volcano Winery
- Waha'ula Heiau

The Big Island is constantly growing, thanks to lava pouring into the ocean along the southeast coast.

(Photo courtesy of HVCB/Kirk Lee Aeder)

Hamakua Coast in the North

This northern coast is a side of The Big Island that a lot of people don't see—a region of green cliffs, gorges, waterfalls, and awesome coastline. It can be approached from either Kona or Hilo, though the latter is a bit closer. This is also an interesting route to drive between Kona and Hilo.

The drive along the coast should take you about an hour and a half, plus stops. You also can stay in these parts, but it's not really necessary. It's best to

Snapshot

Here are our favorite Hamakua Coast destinations:

- Akala Falls
- Hawaii Tropical Botanical Garden
- Laupahoehoe Point
- Waipi'o Valley

simply start from Hilo and set aside a day to explore this unique part of the island, which includes **Hawaii Tropical Botanical Garden** on Onomea Bay, **Akala Falls** (the highest in all of Hawaii), dramatic **Laupahoehoe Point,** the verdant **Waipi'o Valley** (once a retreat of Hawaiian royalty), and the atmospheric town of **Waipi'o.**

Driving Times from Kona International Airport

Hapuna	40 minutes
Hilo	2 hours 15 minutes
Kailua-Kona	10 minutes
Volcano	2 hours 30 minutes
Waimea	50 minutes

Driving Times from Hilo International Airport

Kohala	1 hour 45 minutes
Volcano	45 minutes
Waimea	1 hour 15 minutes

Comfortable Accommodations: Ultimate Places to Stay on The Big Island

Because of its size and diversity of landscapes and destinations, The Big Island has a very large selection of accommodations, ranging from ultra-luxurious resorts on sprawling landscaped grounds, to comfortable condos and small B&Bs that will give you a taste of authentic Hawaii living.

Hotels and Resorts

Fairmont Orchid Kohala $$$$$

With a daily visit of giant green sea turtles, a 36-hole champion golf course, and 32 acres of lush tropical grounds, including waterfalls, this Fairmont resort will pamper you almost to excess. In fact, you may have to pinch yourself to make sure you're not dreaming—or maybe the $300-plus nightly room rates will bring you to your senses. Check out their package deals, which can save you some bucks. *1 N. Kaniku Drive, Kohala Coast, HI 96753.* ***808-885-2000.*** *www.fairmont.com/orchid.*

Four Seasons Resort Hualalai $$$$$

If you want the top luxury available on The Big Island, and you are willing to part with up to $600 per night, this may be the place for you. If you don't think about the money, you can really relax in one of several individual bungalows scattered among lovely gardens, ponds, and pools. Or when you're not in your bungalow, you can swim in one of five pools, work out at the fitness center, or perhaps play a round or two on the Jack Nicklaus–designed golf course. *Hualalai, Kaupulehu Kaupulehu, HI 96740.* ***808-325-8000.*** *www.fourseasons.com/hualalai.*

Hilton Waikoloa Village Waikoloa $$$

Ah! Now here's a deal. This posh, 60-acre property is inland several miles from the beach areas in northern Kohala, but will give you a well-appointed guest room on beautiful grounds, with a fancy swimming pool, tennis courts, two golf courses, and even a dolphin play area—all without breaking the bank. *425 Waikoloa Beach Drive, Waikoloa, HI 96738.* ***808-886-1234.*** *www.hiltonhawaii.com/hilton-waikoloa-village.*

King Kamehameha's Kona Beach Hotel Kailua-Kona $$

This place is located in the heart of Kailua-Kona, right on a white-sand beach and next to fishing pier. The rooms are comfortable if not spectacular, and you can have a fine ocean view if you wish. You also can enjoy the pool and hot tub, and then enjoy drinks and pupus from the poolside Billfish Bar. The room rates are quite reasonable, especially if you can grab one of their Internet specials. *75-5660 Palani Road, Kailua-Kona, Hawaii, 96740.* ***808-329-2911.*** *www.konabeachhotel.com.*

Sheraton Kailua-Kona Kailua-Kona

Recently remodeled to the tune of about $80 million, this top resort hotel has all the amenities to both delight and soothe, with view-heavy oceanfront rooms, spectacular landscaped grounds, and a great swimming pool. There's no real beach here—just black rock—but sand beaches aren't far away. *78-128 Ehukai Street, Kailua-Kona, HI 96740.* ***808-930-4900.*** *www.sheratonkeauhou.com.*

More Intimate Lodgings and B&Bs

Areca Palms Bed & Breakfast Captain Cook

Picture a country estate near beaches and just outside the historic Captain Cook area, with beautiful landscaping, great views up and down the south Kona coast, immaculate guest rooms, creative gourmet breakfasts, and a hot tub from which you can gaze at the setting sun—all for a most reasonable nightly rate. It's real, and it's here at the Areca Palms. *Off Route 11, P.O. Box 489, Captain Cook, HI 96704.* ***1-800-545-4390.*** *www.konabedandbreakfast.com.*

Kilauea Lodge Volcano

This rustic lodge, dating from 1938 and just a mile from Hawaii Volcanoes National Park, used to be a YMCA camp and is now one of the most interesting and satisfying places to stay on The Big Island. You can stay in the main lodge, but an even better experience can be had in the two cottages on the property. All the rooms have been totally renovated with fireplaces, balconies, original artwork, and stained-glass windows. The restaurant's food is superb, so have some dinner and then relax by the fireplace. *Old Volcano Road, Volcano, HI 96785.* ***808-967-7366.*** *www.kilauealodge.com.*

Shipman House Bed & Breakfast Hilo

This early twentieth-century Victorian inn is probably the coolest place to stay in Hilo, and a place where Jack London used to spend the night. Listed on the National Register of Historic Places, it's located just a few minutes from downtown. Hula is offered on the veranda twice a week, and continental breakfast buffets are served each morning. *131 Kaiulani St., Hilo, HI 96720.* ***808-934-8002*** *or* ***1-800-627-8447.*** *www.hilo-hawaii.com.*

Best Condos

Kanaloa at Kona Kailua-Kona

This is an excellent find for couples or families: a moderate high-rise of big, comfortable condos, most with ocean views and big bathrooms, sweeping views, flowering gardens, and tide pools where you can observe giant sea turtles and colorful reef fish. There's also a spa and tennis courts, with the 36-hole Kona Country Club just a mile away. *78-261 Manukai Street, Kailua-Kona, HI 96740.* ***1-800-688-7444.*** *www.outrigger.com.*

Kona Magic Sands Kailua-Kona

The Kona Magic Sands literally hangs over the ocean, with all condos facing the sea. There's a pool on the main level and a good snorkeling beach next door. Plus, the rates here are incredibly reasonable. So what's the catch? Well, the units are nothing more than large studios, so they only accommodate two people. So if you're feeling romantic and want to save money, this may be the place for you. *77-6452 Alii Drive, Kailua-Kona, HI 96745.* ***1-800-244-4752.*** *www.konahawaii.com.*

Outrigger Royal Sea Cliff Kailua-Kona

With a dramatic ocean view on a black lava beach, these one- and two-bedroom condos on seven landscaped acres by the sea are large and quite reasonably priced for the area. Located between Kailua-Kona town and the Keauhou Golf Course, the resort setup includes two swimming pools, tennis courts, sauna, whirlpool spa, tropical gardens, and a waterfall. *75-6040-Alii Drive, Kailua-Kona, HI 96740.* ***1-866-733-0659*** *or* ***1-800-OUTRIGGER.*** *www.outriggerroyalseacliffcondo.com.*

Ultimate Private Home

The Cliff House Kukuihaele (Waipi'o)

In the mood for something different? Dramatically situated on the edge of the lush, green cliffs adjacent to historic Waipi'o Valley, this romantic private home will lull you into a higher state of mind, with unobstructed, breathtaking views of the ocean, coastal cliffs, and valley waterfalls. The House has two bedrooms with queen beds, one full bath, a fully equipped kitchen and living/dining room. It's only an hour and a half from Kona and an hour from Hilo. *Off Route 240, P.O. Box 5045, Kukuihaele, HI, 96727.* ***808-775-0005*** *or* ***1-800-492-4746.*** *www.cliffhousehawaii.com.*

The Big Island is truly a world in itself, whether you're looking for beach or mountains, ranch country or rainforest, city or country. For details on dining and activities, see Chapter 11.

Enjoying The Big Island

In This Chapter

- The ultimate itineraries for The Big Island
- The best places to dine on The Big Island
- The most interesting things to see on The Big Island
- The best things to do on The Big Island

The island of Hawaii, most often referred to as **"The Big Island,"** is the largest and the youngest island in the Hawaiian chain. There's an amazing diversity of climates and landscapes for you to enjoy, not the least of which is the spectacular and very active **Ki'lauea Volcano.** In many ways, The Big Island is the unsung island, but for those of us who enjoy a less commercial experience—at least for a day or two—it might be the best bet of all.

You can explore the haunting, lush rainforest of **Puna** and the **Kohala lava desert** in the same day. On much of the island you may feel completely remote from the rest of the world, but head to **Kailua-Kona** and you'll find a bustling town with all the comforts of home and one of the best lu'aus in the state.

Rainbow Falls, near Hilo, will immerse you in tropical beauty.

(Photo courtesy of HVCB/Kirk Lee Aeder)

Like many a youngest child, The Big Island is impetuous and unpredictable. In October of 2006, islanders experienced the largest earthquake in 30 years, with a magnitude of 6.7, causing rockslides and structural damage across the island. That was a big one, but according to the U.S. Geological Service, the various islands of Hawaii typically experience several small to mid-sized tremors a day.

And of course, there are the volcanoes. The Big Island has five volcanoes: **Kohala, Mauna Kea, Hualalai, Mauna Loa,** and **Ki'lauea.** Only two currently are active—Mauna Loa, which last erupted in 1984, and Ki'lauea, which has been continuously erupting since 1983, adding at least 568 acres to the eastern coastline during that time.

The Top Five Things to Do on The Big Island

The Big Island has something for every traveler: idyllic beaches, geological wonders, significant and fascinating cultural sites. Here's what you can't miss.

1. Learn the natural meaning of the word "lush" driving on **Route 137** in **Puna,** stopping often to explore the black-sand beaches and impressive coastline.

2. Drive above the clouds and spend a night stargazing at the **Mauna Kea Visitors Information Station.**
3. Nothing compares to the thrill of a lava hike at **Hawaii Volcanoes National Park,** home of Pele, goddess of the volcano.
4. Save a long afternoon for some of the best, and least crowded, snorkeling you'll experience in **Honaunau Bay.**
5. Treat yourself to the perfect sunset over the ocean at **'Anaeho'omalu Beach** in Kohala.

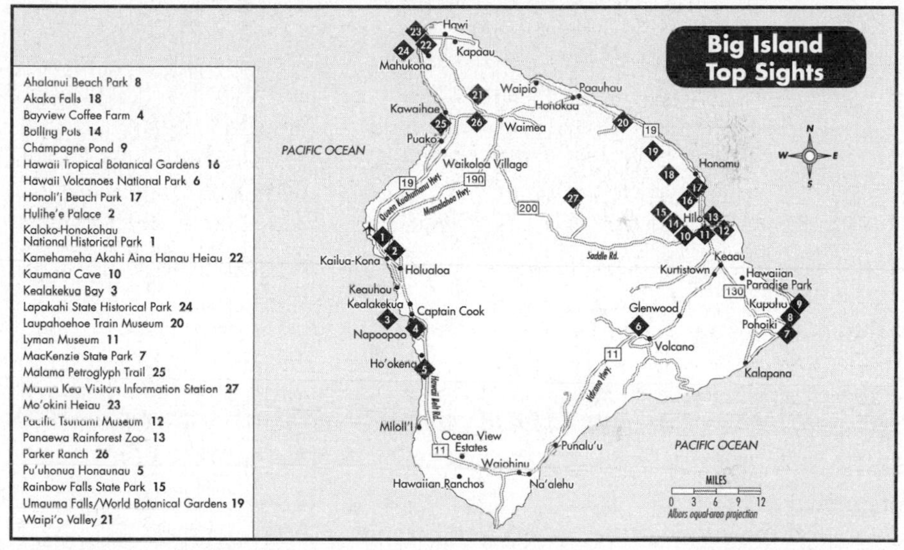

The Big Island's top sights.

Plan My Trip: Ultimate Itineraries for The Big Island

Note: Because of the shear size of the aptly named Big Island, where you eat breakfast depends entirely on which end of the island you're staying. Therefore, we're leaving breakfast up to you in the following itineraries. Check the restaurant listings later in the chapter for a suggested place near you.

The Big Island is truly an adventurer's destination, but don't worry, there are adventures for all ages and lifestyles. In this section you'll find itineraries designed for all travelers (including good eats and rest stops). Most of these itineraries originate on the **Kona Coast** in the western part of the island where most hotels/resorts are based. They are designed to take about a day, although we couldn't help but suggest how to stretch out your time in case you fall in love with an area or activity. It's easy to do!

In this section, we've kept the descriptions of each stop brief; you'll find more through write-ups of each place later in the chapter. *It's usually worthwhile to make advance reservations for recommended restaurants and tours.*

ITINERARY #1: FOR YOUNG FAMILIES

Day 1

1. **Breakfast:** Have breakfast at the condo or hotel, then head to **Hulihe'e Palace in Kailua-Kona,** once a vacation spot for Hawaiian royalty. Adults can take in a little light history and kids should love the collection of artifacts.
2. **Lunch:** Head down the highway into Kona and grab a quick lunch at **Buns in the Sun,** which features a great selection of sandwiches to satisfy any picky eater.
3. Just north of Kailua Pier you'll find the **'Ahu 'ena Heiau,** King Kamehameha's personal *heiau* (temple) which features several *ki'i akua* (statues) to admire, as well as a beach with calm water for an afternoon swim.
4. **Dinner:** Pizza time at the **Kona Brewing Company,** right in Kailua-Kona. If you've worked up an appetite at the beach, make sure to get there on the earlier side of dinner. The specialty pizzas can be a bit esoteric for little ones, but there are plenty of made-to-order options.

Day 2

1. **Breakfast:** Up and at 'em early this morning. Grab a quick breakfast on your way toward Waimea. Stop at nearby **Parker Ranch** for a wagon tour of the grounds and a fun history of the pani'olo.
2. **Lunch:** Follow Highway 19 east from Waimea and stop at **Tex's Drive-In.** Fast, no-frills dining, and everyone will love their famous *malasadas*, a donut-like Portuguese confection. Grab it and go, you don't want to rush this drive.
3. After about an hour in the car—and a million photoopportunities—steer yourself toward the **Panewa Rainforest Zoo** on Highway 11

right outside of Hilo. Enjoy the tropical setting and be sure to say "Hi" to Namaste, the resident white Bengal tiger.

4. Before it gets dark, drive back through town and have a look at **Rainbow Falls** and **Boiling Pots** waterfalls. And, if you still have energy before dinner, make sure you stop and check out the natural skylight at **Kaumana Cave.** Bring your flashlights!
5. **Dinner:** Before you drive back to the west side of the island, try breakfast for dinner over at **Ken's House of Pancakes.** They have a special keiki menu—and some pretty grown-up sized portions, too. Two words: Sumo Loco.

ITINERARY #2: FOR OLDER FAMILIES—KONA COAST

Day 1

1. **Breakfast:** Wake up, throw on your bathing suits, and head to Keauhou Bay for a Deluxe Morning Luncheon Cruise with **Hawaii Snorkel Cruise** in Kailua-Kona, which takes you to a snorkeling site by the **Captain Cook Monument** in **Kealakekua Bay.** Even beginners can enjoy the world-class snorkeling, and breakfast and lunch are included!
2. **Lunch:** After you've dried off, head a couple of miles north of Kailua to **Kaloko-Honokohau National Historical Park.** The impressive array of wetland birds should provide a fun contrast to the sea life you witnessed in the morning. The fishponds provide some insight into the sophistication of Hawaiian culture that you might miss at the ABC Store.
3. **Dinner:** After your busy day, sit down and enjoy some major chow at **Quinn's Almost By the Sea** back in town. It has great patio seating, a friendly atmosphere, and most importantly, big, delicious portions.

Day 2

1. **Breakfast:** After breakfast in the hotel, enjoy a relaxing morning and get some of your souvenir shopping out of the way at **Keauhou**

continues

continued

Shopping Center. Or, if you're early risers, head further up to the **Kings' Shops** in Waikoloa.

2. **Lunch:** Experience a more local-style "fusion" the whole family should enjoy at **Killer Tacos** back in Kailua. May we recommend the kalua pig burrito?
3. **Dinner:** You might be ready to get away from the crowds, so it's time to move on up, literally, with **Mauna Kea Summit Adventures.** You'll get picked up in the afternoon from several central locations in Kailua-Kona or Waikoloa and drive 13,000 feet above sea level. Explore world-class observatories, enjoy a gorgeous sunset above the clouds, and stick around for the best stargazing you'll ever experience. Don't worry, dinner is included.
4. When you come back to Earth, you'll probably be exhausted; the altitude change will do that to you. Make sure to drink plenty of water, and call it an early night.

ITINERARY #3: FOR SINGLES

1. Wake up early in Kona or the Kohala area and head down the Kona coast to **Honaunau Bay** for snorkeling. You'll find a laid-back local atmosphere and a dazzling array of aquatic life just offshore. If you're in the mood, cough up the $5 or so for admission and have a look at **Pu'uhonua o Honaunau,** a Hawaiian place of refuge, next door.
2. Driving back up toward Kailua-Kona, stop off at the **Bayview Coffee Farm,** only a few minutes away in Honaunau off Highway 160. Enjoy a fresh-brewed cup and the fabulous view of **Kealekekua Bay** below.
3. **Lunch:** Stop at **Manago** in Captain Cook as you continue the drive back to Kona; this joint has all the local food and none of the tourist flavor.
4. Keep going past Kona and enjoy a leisurely drive up the Kohala Coast; stop off at the **Malama Petroglyph Trail.**
5. **Dinner:** Enjoy a light dinner and live music at the **Beach Tree Bar** back in Kailua-Kona.

ITINERARY #4: A ROMANTIC GETAWAY—TO HILO

Day 1

1. **Breakfast:** Nothing says romance better than breakfast in bed—room service it is.
2. If your morning is getting off to a late start, no worries, just throw on bathing suits and lounge around at **Kahalu'u Beach Park,** just a few minutes south of Kailua-Kona. Plenty of sun, shade, and snorkeling—whatever you're in the mood for.
3. **Lunch:** After your beach jones has been satisfied, grab a real Hawaiian lunch at **Kona Mix Plate** in Kailua-Kona, then head north on Highway 19 and make sure to take the 270 extension through the Kohala Coast. There are plenty of places to stop and savor this drive; make sure you stop at **Waipi'o Lookout** over Honoka'a and save time to admire tropical beauty at **Hawaii Tropical Botanical Gardens.**
4. Bypass Hilo for today and head out to Puna, where you can enjoy another scenic drive (with hardly any people) along Route 137 between Kapoho and Puna. If you time it right, you can watch the sun set over the lava flow.
5. **Dinner:** Finish up your day with an intimate dinner for two at **Paolo's Bistro** in Pahoa Village. The fresh flowers and impeccable Italian cuisine are the perfect finish to a day in paradise.

Day 2

1. **Breakfast:** Enjoy brunch at **Café Pesto,** in Hilo, and before you head back to the west side of the island, take some time to explore the growing number of galleries and boutiques in a classic seaside setting.
2. On your way up to the Saddle Road to drive back to Kona, stop and enjoy the spectacular **Rainbow Falls** and **Boiling Pots** waterfalls.
3. **Lunch:** Once you're back on the western side of the island, head to **Huggo's** to enjoy friendly, but not obtrusive, service and a gorgeous view of Kailua Bay.

continues

continued

4. Head back up the Kohala Coast to watch the sun set over **A-Bay.** No need for sunset cocktails tonight. This intoxicating view is the best sunset on the island, hands down.
5. **Dinner:** Enjoy locally farmed lobster, prepared New England style, and an award-winning Wine Flight in Waikoloa at the **Kamuela Provision Company,** Hilton's Waikola Village restaurant and wine bar. Relax together over this sumptuous dinner with laid-back live music in the background.

Itinerary #5: Easy-Going; Nonstrenuous

1. **Breakfast:** If you missed the hotel breakfast, never fear, **U Top It** is near. This local favorite, right on Ali'i Drive in Kailua-Kona, gives you breakfast with a Hawaiian flavor—taro pan crepes with your choice of topping. Spam anyone?
2. **Lunch:** Take a look around **Hulihe'e Palace,** right in central Kailua, for a taste of culture in the middle of town. You're only minutes away from lunch at **Bubba Gump Shrimp Co.,** an imported chain from the mainland.
3. Head up to Kohala for a sunny, relaxing afternoon on **Mauna Kea Beach.** There's great snorkeling on the south side if you're in the mood—and plenty of beach to stretch out on if you're not.
4. **Dinner:** Spend the evening enjoying one-of-a-kind performances and an excellent traditional Hawaiian buffet at the **Kamaha'o Lu'au** at **Keauhou Resort.**

Itinerary #6: Culture in Paradise

Day 1

1. **Breakfast:** After breakfast at the hotel, drive up the Kohala Coast to explore the **Mo'okini Heiau,** once a sacrificial site for Native Hawaiians and today a place of stark beauty.

2. **Lunch:** Enjoy a picnic lunch close by at the **Lapakahi State Historical Park,** a 600-year-old Hawaiian village, many structures of which still remain. It's spread over 200 acres, so give yourself time to enjoy the coastal setting, and keep your eyes peeled for daily cultural demonstrations.
3. You're already in the area, so before the sun sets, make your way to **Kaloko-Honokohau National Historical Park.** You'll learn much about Hawaiian culture from the ancient fishponds which ingeniously use the ocean's tides as an integral part of the lure. Watching the sun set over this part of the coastline is simply incredible.
4. **Dinner:** Why not enjoy a bit of culturally influenced cuisine at the **Daniel Thiebaut** restaurant in Waimea? This restaurant's focus is Pacific Rim dining with an emphasis on local ingredients and influences.

Day 2

1. **Breakfast:** Hawaiians stress the importance of the *'aina,* the land, and everyone's connection to it and the creatures in it. With this in mind, wake up early to sight some humpbacks with **Captain Dan McSweeney's Whale Watch,** which leaves from Honokohau Harbor right in Kailua-Kona. Even if it's after April and before December, Captain Dan promises whale sightings; and with several other species making their home off the coast of The Big Island, he can deliver!
2. **Lunch: Kona Mix Plate** on Kopiko Street in Kailua-Kona is a great place to eat a fast lunch as you start the second half of your day, with a local flavor, for *very* reasonable prices.
3. Enjoy an old beach that's newly accessible at **Kua Bay Beach Park,** a few miles north of Kona on Highway 19. The road to this beach was just finished in October 2005. This is a great location to enjoy the Hawaiian beach experience minus a commercialized presence.
4. **Dinner:** Spend your evening at the fantastic **Kona Village Lu'au** at the Kona Village Resort. Not only will you experience the same beautiful sunset that's graced Kona's shores for millennia, but you also can witness the night's "royal party" entering from the sea by canoe.

Itinerary #7: Adventure in the Great Outdoors

Day 1

1. **Breakfast:** Head straight over on Highway 19 for a trip into Waipi'o Valley with **Waipi'o Na'alapa Trail Rides (808-775-0419)**. This two-hour journey will take you over streams, past waterfalls and taro patches, and deep into a part of The Big Island that few visitors make time to see.
2. **Lunch:** Grab a late lunch at one of the several restaurants in Waimea's **Parker Square** on your way back to Kona.
3. Book a manta ray snorkel trip in Kailua for the evening. Where? In Kailua? This is a double treat, as you get to enjoy a rare night snorkel experience, as well as close proximity to these beautiful and very large creatures.
4. **Dinner:** What a day! Treat yourself to one of the best dinners on the island at **Pahu i'a** in Kohala.

Day 2: Interior–Volcanoes National Park

1. **Breakfast:** This morning it's off to the east side of the island. Grab a quick breakfast at **Buns in the Sun** in Kailua-Kona and drive up Route 190 to the Saddle Road (Route 200) between Mauna Loa and Mauna Kea. With all of its climbs, dips, and turns, it could be classified as an adventure in and of itself.
2. **Lunch:** Aim to get to **Hawaii Volcanoes National Park** by early afternoon. Start with the **Kilauea Iki Crater hike** (great for a picnic lunch), then check in at the Visitors' Center and make your way down Chain of Craters Road. If there's surface lava, hike out to the flow—bring lots of water—and wait for the sun to set. Flashlights will come in handy on the hike back, unless you've got a full moon on a clear night.
3. **Dinner:** The **Kilauea Lodge**, only a few minutes from the park, is a great way to unwind after an invigorating day at the volcano. Take advantage of their great wine list, but don't get too stuffed on their homemade bread before dinner!

The Top Big Island Attractions, A to Z

Ahalanui Beach Park Puna, Hilo, and East Hawaii

You'll find this crystal-clear pool just next to the ocean, tucked behind a manmade wall. Believe it or not, it is volcanically heated to 90° F or higher! This park is right on Route 137, so it's quite convenient for a quick dip … but don't be surprised if you stay longer once you're in! *Route 137 just past mile marker 10.*

Akaka Falls Hamakua, Hamakua Coast in the North

A convenient stop on the Hilo-Hamakua Heritage Drive toward Waimea, Akaka is arguably the most impressive falls on the island, a stark 400-foot-plus fall surrounded by misty clouds, lush ferns, and canopies of bamboo. A quite pleasant (paved) walk through the forest can take you directly to Akaka or, the long way and highly recommended, past another beautiful fall. *Turn-off is on Route 19 between the 13 and 14 mile markers.*

Bayview Coffee Farm Honaunau, Kona Coast in the West

If you want to learn about Kona Coffee, this is one of the best places to do it. Open for more than 20 years, Bayview boasts a great facility, knowledgeable staff, and great coffee. Summer visitors get the added treat of watching workers rake fresh-picked, sun-dried coffee berries. The view of Kealakekua Bay deserves more than a mention, too. Aficionados shouldn't miss this stop! *Off Route 160 on Painted Church Road. Open daily from 9 A.M.–5 P.M.* ***808-328-9658*** *or* ***1-800-662-5880.*** *www.bayviewfarmcoffees.com.*

Boiling Pots Hilo and East Hawaii

You'll find the impressive Boiling Pots waterfall about 2 miles upstream from the more famous Rainbow Falls on the Wailuku River. Its name comes from the separation of the river water by an old lava flow—some runs beneath the lava flow, then resurfaces suddenly, bubbling to the surface and giving the appearance of boiling water. The lovely **Pe'epe'e Falls**—a great place to picnic—are to the left, accessible by a short trail if the falls' volume is not too high. *On Pe'epe'e Falls Street, about 2 miles north of Hilo Hospital.*

Champagne Pond Kapoho, Hilo, and East Hawaii

At the end of Route 132 in Kapoho you'll find a dirt road leading out to the sea. Where the road ends, at an old flow, you'll find a light tower and a well-trod four-wheel-drive (4WD) lava road (about a 15-minute walk if you're on foot) that will take you to a clear, heated inlet similar to Ahalanui. This pond, though, isn't walled off, which means on the right day you can find a variety of fish and sea turtles sharing the warm waters with you. This is a great place to enjoy a secluded soak—it's almost always deserted during the week—with the coastline in full view. *Drive toward Kapoho on 132 and take the dirt road straight ahead where the paved road ends. Dirt road ends at the light tower; stay on the lightest gray (most traveled) lava road from that point for about 1.2 miles.*

Hawaii Tropical Botanical Gardens Hamakua, Hamakua Coast in the North

You might balk initially at the $15 fee to explore these Botanical Gardens on Onomea Bay, but once you're walking among the many varieties of palm trees, ti plants, orchids, and especially the heliconia, you'll realize you're only paying for the best. There are more than 2,000 varieties of tropical plants in the gardens, which opened in 1984 and take about an hour to walk through—or even closer to two, if you really take your time. More likely than not, you'll find this stretch of the coast to be rainy, but don't worry, complimentary umbrellas are provided and the rain only makes Onomea Falls (within the garden) more impressive. *Take the scenic route from Route 19, just past mile marker 7. 9 A.M.–5 P.M. daily, last admission 4 P.M.* ***808-964-5233.*** *www.htbg.com.*

Hawaii Volcanoes National Park Volcano, HI

The active volcanic activity in this park is what sets The Big Island apart from its neighbors. There is so much to explore here, you could easily spend a day (or two!) wandering within park limits. Check out the **Thurston Lava Tube** or **Devastation Trail,** overlooks of several massive craters, and if you have time, hike the **Kilauea Iki Crater,** or **Napau Crater Trails.** If the lava flow is active during your visit, drive down to the end of Chain of Craters Road to where the road comes to an end. Barricades stop cars, but you can walk a bit closer and catch a whiff of sulfur and a hint of heat in the air. *Route 11 in between mile markers 28 and 29, Volcano. Open 24 hours a day.* ***808-985-6000.*** *www.nps.gov/havo.*

DON'T TAKE THE LAVA!

At some point during your visit to The Big Island, it's likely you'll hear tales of horrible calamities that befell unfortunate tourists who stole lava rock from Volcanoes National Park and invoked Pele's wrath. Guess what? This local legend is only about 50 years old and was invented by park rangers and tour guides to stop the heavy outflow of rock from the island. The only real guaranteed punishment for taking a souvenir is a strong scolding at the airport—although that doesn't stop thousands of tourists from mailing contraband lava back each year. And the volcanoes keep erupting … perhaps there is some truth to the legend, after all.

Honoli'i Beach Park Hamakua, Hamakua Coast in the North

Honoli'i is just a few quick turns (and a flight of stairs) off Route 19, and is the best place to head for serious surfing (or boogieboarding) action. There's a decent black-sand beach, but really, this spot's all about the waves—as the weekend crowds will attest. *Route 19 heading north out of Hilo; make a right on Nahala Road just past the 4 mile marker and a left at the T.*

Hulihe'e Palace Kailua-Kona, Kona, and West Coast

Built by the second governor of Hawaii in 1838, and once the vacation place of Hawaiian royalty in the nineteenth and early twentieth century, today Hulihe'e features some interesting artifacts, royalty's personal memorabilia, and a truly impressive collection of koa furniture. The museum is run by the Daughters of Hawaii, who offer brief, informative tours of the palace and grounds. This is a family-friendly stop and a great way to spend a morning. *75-5718 Ali'i Drive, Kailua-Kona. Open Tuesday–Saturday, 9 A.M.–4 P.M., Sunday 10 A.M.–4 P.M. Closed Sunday, Fourth of July, Thanksgiving, Christmas, and New Year's Day. Admission: $6.* ***808-329-1877.*** *www.huliheepalace.org.*

Kaumana Cave Saddle Road, Hilo, and East Hawaii

This "cave" a few minutes from Hilo is actually an old lava tube from an 1881 flow originating at Mauna Loa, and offers a short walk to a gorgeous rainforest "skylight" with 2 miles of tube to explore. Bring a flashlight and allow yourself a couple of hours to study the one-of-a-kind formations formed by lava over 100 years ago. This site often is overlooked but should not be missed! *Just before mile marker 4 on Route 200. Cave entrance is well marked and accessible by stairs.*

Kealakekua Bay Kona Coast and the West

This is quite possibly the place to go for water activities on The Big Island. The snorkeling and kayaking (particularly by the Captain Cook monument) are hard to beat, and the whole bay is a great place to watch for spinner dolphins. If you've never snorkeled before, this is the place to start. For history buffs, you can find the actual spot of Captain Cook's death in 1779 commemorated by a plaque to the left of the more obvious white obelisk. *Take Napoopoo Road off Route 11 just past mile marker 111; turn right at the intersection with Middle Ke'ei Road and head toward the ocean.*

Kaloko-Honokohau National Historical Park Kona Coast and the West

This park highlights the stark lava fields of the Kona coastline, its surprising diversity of wildlife, and the sophistication of Hawaiian aquaculture. That's right, all in one place! Check out the Kaloko and Aimakapa fishponds, hundreds of years old and today a great place to spot wetland birds of native and migratory varieties. Only a few miles from Kona, this makes an easy stop on your way in or out of town. *3 miles north of Kailua-Kona on Route 19. Visitor contact station and other public buildings open from 8:30 A.M.–4 P.M. daily; visitors may stay later but cars must be removed from visitor station parking lot before closing time. Admission: free!* ***808-326-9057****. www.nps.gov/kaho.*

Kamehameha Akahi Aina Hanau Heiau Kohala Coast in the Northwest

Recognized as the birthplace of King Kamehameha I in 1758, this site is not well marked but well worth the search. The stone walls surrounding the site impress a feeling of solemnity, heightened by the dramatic contrast between the coastline to the west and green hills to the east. *Take Route 270 north from Kawaihae. Turn left at the sign to Upolu Airport, near mile marker 20. Just before the airport, turn left on the unmarked dirt road. Drive for approximately 2 miles. The site is on hill to the left.*

Lapakahi State Historical Park Kohala Coast in the Northwest

This park features an ancient (over 600 years old) Hawaiian village, which is larger in scale than other similar sites on the island, stretching over 200 acres.

While some of the structures have been restored, many of the walls are original. Call ahead for daily cultural demonstrations and storytelling. *On Akoni Pule Highway (Route 270), 12.4 miles north of Kawaihae.* ***808-889-5566.***

Laupahoehoe Train Museum Hamakua Coast in the North

This small museum chronicles the history of the Hilo Railroad, which ran from 1899 until 1946, when a tidal wave brought the railroad to an abrupt end. There's a good selection of train photographs and memorabilia, which should satisfy any railroad enthusiasts. A good stop to break up the Hamakua Coast drive if you're traveling with kids. *Route 19, just past mile marker 24. Open 9 A.M.–4:30 P.M. weekdays; 10 A.M.–2 P.M. weekends. Admission: $3; $2 students and seniors.* ***808-962-6300.*** *www.thetrainmuseum.com.*

Lyman Museum Hilo and East Hawaii

Right in downtown Hilo, this museum is a good place to spend an hour—maybe more if you're really into geodes, because there's an outstanding mineral collection. Guided tours of the mission house next door (original home of the Lyman missionary family) are worthwhile if you've got the time. *276 Haili Street, Hilo. Open Monday–Saturday 9:30 A.M.–4:30 P.M. House tours at 11, 1, and 3. Closed Sundays, New Year's Day, Memorial Day, July 4, Labor Day, Thanksgiving, and Christmas.* ***808-935-5021.*** *www.lymanmuseum.org.*

MacKenzie State Park Puna, Hilo, and East Hawaii

You won't see this park in most guidebooks, but it's the perfect place to stop for a picnic or a short hike while enjoying the sights along Route 137. The surf against the black cliffs, while totally inaccessible, is absolutely stunning; and the ironwood forest feels like a delightful secret in the midst of such dense jungle. *Route 137 just after mile marker 137.*

Malama Petroglyph Trail Kohala Coast and the Northwest

This archaeological site, an easy 25-minute walk through kiawe forest, has over 3,000 ancient rock carvings scattered through an old pahoehoe (smooth and glassy) lava flow. It makes an excellent complement to the larger Pu'u Loa petroglyph field at Hawaii Volcanoes National Park. *Take Route 19 north from Kona, and take the left between mile markers 74 and 73. At the main intersection turn right. Go to the "Y" in the road and bear to the left and take the next right. You'll find the trailhead on your right.*

Mauna Kea Visitors Information Station Mauna Kea

Sure, you can pay for a summit tour, but why not get your own 4WD (on this island, you should have one anyway), drive up yourself, and get an expertly guided tour for free? The volunteers and staff at the Mauna Kea Visitors Information station are knowledgeable on the mountain's cultural and scientific history—not to mention the great array of telescopes to view an unparalleled night sky. The **Keck Observatory** even has visitors' galleries from which the telescope may be viewed at certain times. *From Saddle Road, take the Mauna Kea Access Road just past mile marker 28; the station is 6 miles up the road on your right. Open daily from 9 A.M.–10 P.M.; stargazing from 6 P.M.–10 P.M. Summit tours at 1 P.M. on Saturday or Sunday.* ***808-961-2180.***

HAWAIIAN HEIAUS

The Hawaiian islands are well known for their heiaus, ancient temples built by the original Hawaiians who settled the islands from Polynesia. These range from small shrines to much larger structures. Many heiaus have been dated by archeologists to the thirteenth century, and were used to perform human sacrifices to pay homage to the ancient gods. Heiaus are often located in dramatic settings, and are excellent places from which you can learn a little history while getting a spiritual feel for the islands and their people.

Mo'okini Heiau Kohala Coast and the Northwest

If you want to be spooked, this is the place to go. This site, built by Tahitian priest Pa'ao in the eleventh or twelfth century, has hosted thousands of human sacrifices. Today the setting is picturesque and the architecture still impresses (the walls of the heiau are over 30 feet high in places). It's only about a kilometer away from the Kamehameha Akahi Aina Hanau Heiau, so it's easy enough to combine both stops in one visit. *Take Route 270 north from Kawaihae. Turn left at the sign to Upolu Airport, near mile marker 20. Just before the airport, turn left on the unmarked dirt road. Drive for slightly more than a mile.*

Pacific Tsunami Museum Hilo and East Hawaii

This museum combines oral histories and scientific data to give visitors an idea of what a tsunami is really like. Photos, a movie, and other permanent exhibits supplement a guided tour. Tsunamis are a big part of local eruptions, and since most of the tour guides have lived through one, odds are you won't find a better account. *130 Kamehameha Avenue, Hilo. Open Monday–Saturday, 9 A.M.–4 P.M. Admission: seniors $6, adults $7, students $2, children five and under are free.* ***808-935-0926.*** *www.tsunami.org.*

Pana`ewa Rainforest Zoo Hilo and East Hawaii

This zoo can not only boast its being the only tropical rainforest zoo in the United States, it also has over 80 endangered species, including a white Bengal tiger. The grounds themselves are considered a botanical garden and are constantly being improved. *Open daily 9 A.M.–4 P.M., except Christmas and New Year's Day. Admission: free! Located off Highway 11 south of Hilo.* ***808-959-9233.*** *www.hilozoo.com.*

Parker Ranch Waimea, Hamakua Coast in the North

Parker Ranch, a 35,000-acre area of land in central Hawaii, has a lot to offer for those interested in the history of the paniolo (Hawaiian cowboy). The visitors' center and museum provides a good overview of the ranch's history—at one time, it was the largest privately owned ranch in the United States—as well as offering wagon tours and ATV and horseback tours. The Parker Ranch Historic Homes are also worth a look. *Located just past the light in Waimea at the Parker Ranch Center. Visitor Center open Monday–Saturday 9 A.M.–5 P.M. Admission: adults $7.* ***808-885-7655.*** *www.parkerranch.com.*

Pu'uhonua Honaunau National Historic Park Kona Coast in the West

Pu'uhonua means "place of refuge," and that's certainly how you'll feel upon entering this restored cultural site. Amongst the palm trees and the blue water, you'll find the Great Wall, which was built in the 1500s and is over 1,000 feet long. Commoners sentenced to death could be pardoned if they made it over the wall and performed certain rites before the *ali'i* got to them. The contemporary visitor can instead enjoy a leisurely stroll, some impressive structures (including the Hale-o Keawe mausoleum), and basking sea turtles on most days. There's also great snorkeling just around the corner in Honaunau Bay. *Open daily 7 A.M.–8 P.M. Visitors' Center open 8 A.M.–5 P.M. Admission: $5 per noncommercial vehicle, $3 per individual (on tours), or free with National Parks pass.* ***808-328-2288.***

Rainbow Falls State Park Hilo and East Hawaii

One of The Big Island's top attractions, Rainbow Falls is conveniently located just a few minutes' drive from Hilo. The falls themselves vary pretty dramatically depending on rainfall, but are always worth stopping for. The trail off to the left leads to an impressive grove of banyan trees—be sure to check them out while you're there. *Take the right fork after mile marker 1 on Waianuenue Avenue heading out of Hilo and follow the well-marked signs.*

Umauma Falls/World Botanical Gardens Hamakua Coast in the North

Although this waterfall is hidden behind an entrance fee, we think it's worth it. It's a multi-tiered waterfall nestled in lush rainforest ... which only can be accessed via the World Botanical Gardens. The gardens themselves are relatively new, but coming along nicely—plus, visitors get free fruit! Does the price tag seem more appealing? *Take the first turn (inland-side) after mile marker 16. Open daily 9 A.M.–5:30 P.M. Admission: adults $13, teens 13–17 $6, children 5–12 $3, children under 5 free.* ***808-963-5247****. www.wbgi.com.*

Waipi'o Valley Hamakua Coast in the North

Another reason to spring for that 4WD vehicle (or a tour shuttle). This valley could easily eat up two or three days of your time. Once home to thousands of people, Waipi'o was left mostly deserted after the 1946 tsunami and today is still almost bereft of residents—but is chock-full of waterfalls, beaches, and camping opportunities. *From Route 19, take the road into Honoka'a Town, just past mile marker 42, and follow the signs to Waipi'o Lookout.*

The Big Island's Top Beaches

Sure, the beaches on Maui and Oahu are incredible, and well worth the visit. Guess what else they can be? Crowded. The Big Island has some of the most beautiful beaches in the world, over 80 beaches overall (and growing—you can thank Ki'lauea volcano for that!), and many of them, though easily accessible, are off the beaten tourist track. You've come all this way, so why pass up the chance to stretch out, bring a picnic, snorkel mask, and surfboard, and enjoy living the postcard? White sand, black sand, green sand—take your pick or try all three.

Some beaches have facilities such as picnic tables, restrooms, and showers. Others don't, and we've tried to note those. You can get daily beach information for the beach parks, the guarded beaches, by calling the Hawaii County Division of Parks and Recreation at **808-961-8311.**

Time for the specifics. Here's where to get your beach on The Big Island of Hawaii.

The Kona Coast in the West

Kahalu'u Beach Park: *Full facilities and lifeguards. On Ali'i Drive, about 5½ miles south of Kailua.*

Kua Bay Beach Park: *Partial facilities, no lifeguard. Located off Route 19 between mile markers 87 and 88.*

Makalawena Beach: *Limited facilities at the park; no lifeguards. Take the turnoff to Kekaha Kai between mile markers 90 and 91 on Route 19.*

Kohala Coast in the Northwest

'Anaeho'omalu Bay Beach Park: *No lifeguards. Follow the signs at Waikoloa Beach Drive (at mile marker 76 on Route 19).*

Hapuna Beach State Park: *Full facilities, occasional lifeguards. Located in the Kohala resort area 30 miles north of Kailua, near mile marker 69 on Route 19.*

Kauna'oa Beach (Mauna Kea Beach): *Kohala Resort area, 30 miles north of Kailua. Turn off at mile marker 68 and follow signs.*

Spencer Beach Park: *Full facilities and lifeguards. Located on Route 270 in Kohala, between mile markers 2 and 3.*

Hilo and East Hawaii

Leleiwi Beach Park: *Partial facilities, no lifeguards. Take Kalanianaole Street (where Routes 19 and 11 meet in Hilo) east toward the ocean. Leleiwi is the last beach park.*

Near Hawaii Volcanoes National Park in the South

Green Sand Beach: *No facilities. No lifeguards. Take South Point Road (between 69 and 70 mile markers on Highway 11), go left at the fork, and either follow 4WD roads or take the walking path.*

Punalu'u Beach: *Partial facilities, no lifeguards. In South Ka'u, off Route 11 between mile markers 55 and 56.*

Great Dining with Atmosphere: The Best Places to Eat

While The Big Island is comparatively sleepy compared to the bustling tourist centers of **Maui** and **O'ahu,** you shouldn't be fooled into thinking your dining options will be a snore. Fans of *haute cuisine* and local food alike will find plenty to feast on here. Similarly, although Kona is at first glance the best place to head for diverse dining options, "Hilo-side" (the eastern side of the island, where Hilo is located) should not be ignored for some *ono* meals at reasonable prices. For more information on Hawaiian cuisine, see Chapter 2.

Here are our picks for some of the best restaurants on The Big Island.

The Kona Coast in the West

Bubba Gump Shrimp Co. Kailua-Kona *American* $$

You're gonna like sitting right by the beach, perhaps watching whales offshore or enjoying the sunset, and digging into Bubba's Po' Boy Peel 'n' Eat Shrimp—or maybe the fresh fish, rib eye steak, hamburgers, or other favorites. Bubba even offers a *keiki* menu for the kids. Casual and fun. *75-5776 Ali'i Drive. Open daily.* ***808-331-8442.*** *www.bubbagump.com.*

Buns in the Sun Kailua *American* $

A great, quick place to stop for lunch in the middle of a busy day, this sandwich shop in the Lanihau Shopping Center is reasonable and offers a wide selection, plus their bread is baked fresh on-site. A good choice for breakfast on the go as well. *75-5595 Palani Road. Open for breakfast and lunch daily.* ***808-326-2774.***

Killer Tacos Kailua-Kona *Mexican* 

Talk about *ono* grinds! Mexican fans will find what they're looking for here—with a Hawaiian twist: you can get your tacos and burritos with kalua pork and fried cod along with the usual beef and chicken. *74-5483 Kaiwi Street #145.* ***808-329-3335.***

Kona Brewing Company Kailua *American* $$

A popular choice, and with good reason. Besides the fine beer selection (try the Hula Hefeweizen), the Brewing Company is well known for its specialty pizzas and *ono* appetizers. The atmosphere is lively and family-friendly, but be prepared for a long wait on the weekends. *75-5629 Kuakini Highway. Open daily from 11 A.M.–10 P.M.* ***808-334-BREW(2739).*** *www.konabrewingco.com.*

Kona Mix Plate Kailua-Kona *Hawaiian* $

If you're sick of scarfing your meals with other hungry tourists, try Kona Mix Plate for the real local lunchtime experience. As with most local places, the loco moco is a good bet, as is the katsu or the teriyaki burger. Sorry, vegetarians, not many options for you here! 75-5660 Kopiko St., Suite B6. *Open daily.* ***808-329-8104.***

Kona Village Kailua *Pacific Rim* $$$$$

At the Kona Village Resort you can choose from two restaurants, Hale Moana or the smaller Hale Samoa. Both offer fixed-price meals that are among the most elegant offerings on the island. Seafood dominates the selection, and with good reason, but landlubbers and herbivores won't be disappointed. **If you are not staying at the resort, reservations are required.** *Queen Ka'ahumanu Highway, north of Kona. Open daily, dinner starts at 6 P.M.* ***808-325-4273.*** *www.konavillage.com.*

Manago Captain Cook *Hawaiian* $

This homey restaurant, located in a hotel by the same name, is arguably *the* place to go for local food Kona-side. Speaking of sides, they'll get brought to you first, so be sure to get plenty to share with your group—remember, you haven't dined Hawaiian until you've had "choke" (plenty of) macaroni salad and two scoops of rice. Carnivores shouldn't miss the teriyaki steak and pork chops. *82-6155 Mamalahoa Highway. Open Tuesday–Sunday from breakfast through dinner.* ***808-323-2642.***

Pahu i'a Kailua *Pacific Rim* $$$$$

The beachside setting and excellent sunset view make this restaurant at the Four Seasons resort a top pick for a romantic dinner. And did we mention the food? Seafood lovers are in for a treat here, with a variety of creative options—and the steak's worth a second trip. Even vegetarians can relax and enjoy a creative, rewarding selection. Remember to save room for the decadent desserts! Reservations recommended. *72-100 Kaupulehu Drive, 14 miles north of Kona on Route 19. Open daily, dinner starts at 5:30 P.M.* ***808-325-8000.*** *www.fourseasons.com.*

Quinn's Almost By the Sea Kailua-Kona *American* $$$

While you may not get a seaside view at Quinn's, you'll still get great seafood and a secluded patio seating area. You'll find the usual array of seafood choices and landlubber options—we recommend the fish and chips and the Huge (no kidding!) Prawns. *75-5655 Palani Road, Suite A. Open daily, 11 A.M.–midnight.* ***808-329-3822.***

U Top It Kailua-Kona *American/Hawaiian* $

This place is a favorite for locals and visitors alike. Make sure you try the taro pancrepes, a great on-the-go breakfast with plenty of local toppings for you to try. *75-7559 Ali'i Drive. Open daily for breakfast and lunch.* ***808-329-0092.***

The Kohala Coast in the Northwest

Daniel Thiebaut Waimea *Pacific Rim* $$$$

The price tag is significant at this upscale Waimea restaurant, but so is the dining experience. You can look forward to some of the most creative fusion cuisine on the island, with an emphasis on fresh, seasonal ingredients—and the elegant décor reflects the same philosophy. *65-1259 Kawaihae Road. Open for lunch and dinner.* ***808-887-2200.*** *www.danielthiebaut.com.*

The Grill Kohala *Pacific Rim* $$$$$

Like many of The Big Island's high-end restaurants, The Grill can be found in the Fairmont Orchid in Kohala's resort area. The portions are small; however, they have one of the most creative seasonal menus and possibly the best lobster on the island. Reservations are required. *1 North Kaniku Drive. Open 6 P.M.–9:30 P.M. Tuesday–Saturday.* ***808-887-7320.*** *www.fairmont.com/orchid.*

Hilo in the East

Café Pesto Hilo *American* $$$

Café Pesto actually has two locations, one in Hilo and one in Kawaihae. They have excellent gourmet pizzas, a decent wine selection, and a wide variety of local seafood. The atmosphere is relaxed and family-friendly at both locations.

308 Kamehameha Avenue. Open daily for lunch and dinner. ***808-969-6640.*** www.cafepesto.com.

Garden Snack Club Hilo *Thai* 

You know you're in a town on The Big Island when you see a Thai restaurant; however, the Garden Snack Club sets itself apart. Located on a side street right in downtown Hilo, the relaxed, intimate atmosphere is complimented by several unique dishes, in particular "Tina's Spaghetti," featuring noodles and tofu in a delectable peanut sauce. Service is among the friendliest in town. *82 Kilauea Avenue. Open Tuesday–Saturday from 5:30 P.M.* ***808-933-9664.***

Harrington's Hilo *American* 

Harrington's offers a tranquil, open-air setting, overlooking the Ice Pond at Reeds Bay at the start of the Keaukaha beach area. Standard but well-prepared steak and seafood on offer. Try the house specialty of thinly sliced Slavic steak. *135 Kalanianaole Avenue. Open daily for lunch and dinner Monday–Friday.* ***808-961-4966.***

Ken's House of Pancakes Hilo *Hawaiian/American* 

Voted time and again "Best Breakfast on The Big Island" by locals, Ken's is absolutely not to be missed. Plenty of familiar breakfast favorites are available, but you must try the macadamia nut pancakes and the "local flavor" syrups—coconut, guava, and lilikoi (passion fruit). Breakfast is served all day, along with well-prepared local foods. Try the "sumo loco" (local dish "moco loco" on a sumo scale), and you'll know when it's ready. The wait staff bang a gong and yell "Sumo!" before they bring it to your table. *1730 Kamehameha Avenue. Open 24 hours a day!*

> **Money Matters**
>
> You can usually save a few bucks with all-you-can-eat specials, such as the ones offered at Ken's House of Pancakes. Four days a week Ken's offers such deals, including tacos, prime rib, spaghetti, and Hawaiian dishes—all served for as long as they last.

Maui Tacos Hilo *Mexican* 

Start with one takeout counter, add a few tables and some paper plates, and dress with garlicky fresh-fish tacos, "surf burritos" of fresh fish, black beans, and salsa, and other concoctions. Don't charge too much, and you've got a winning restaurant chain, catering to everyone from surfers to families from Kansas. Also a good choice for a quick breakfast stop. *111 E. Puainakoo Street, in the Prince Kuhio Plaza. Open daily 9 A.M.–10 A.M.* ***808-959-0359.*** *www.mauitacos.com.*

Nihon Restaurant and Cultural Center Hilo *Japanese* $$$

Overlooking Liliuokalani Gardens and Hilo Bay, this Japanese restaurant is reasonably priced and offers innovative sushi and outstanding poke. The presentation is just as lovely as the setting. *123 Lihiwai Street. Open Monday–Saturday for lunch and dinner.* ***808-969-1133.***

Paolo's Bistro Pahoa *Italian* $$$

This intimate, cozy venue is the perfect place to ease your transition back into civilization after several hours in Pahoa's untamed wilderness. Chef Paolo brings the old country to The Big Island with elegant offerings such as spinach ravioli in gorgonzola sauce, a "seafood pasta" that exceeds all expectations, and a potato gnocchi appetizer that's not to be missed. One of the top restaurants on the island. *333 Pahoa Village Road. Open Tuesday–Sunday from 5:30 P.M.* ***808-965-7033.***

Hawaii Volcanoes National Park Region

Kilauea Lodge & Restaurant Volcano American $$$$

This cozy, welcoming restaurant offers a touch of rustic charm as a contrast to the fine, though sometimes haughty, seaside dining The Big Island has to offer. For those with a hunter's palate, venison and rabbit are often available as entrées. Don't miss their daily soups or the fabulous homemade bread, and be sure to admire the International Fireplace while you sip your aperitif. *19-3948 Old Volcano Road. Open daily from 5:30 P.M.* ***808-967-7366.*** *www.kilauealodge.com.*

Hamakua Coast in the North

Tex Drive In Honokaa *American/Hawaiian* $

Tex's is famous for a reason, and that's the *malasada*, a Portugese filled pastry. It's a good reason, and you won't be disappointed. However, this is a great stop for people en route from one side of the island to another, and it's easy enough to grab-and-go if you're in a hurry. *45-690 Pakalana St. Open daily 6:30 A.M.–8 P.M.* ***808-775-0598.***

What's Shakin' Pepeekeo *Health food* 

There are smoothies and then there are What's Shakin' smoothies. This smoothie and healthy snack shop is conveniently located close to Akaka Falls, but is almost worth the several miles' trip out of Hilo for its own sake. Try the Papaya Paradise smoothie for the full assortment of fresh island fruits, and don't miss the guacamole if it's available when you go! *27-999 Old Mamalahoa Highway. Open daily 10 A.M.–5 P.M.* ***808-964-3080.***

Entertainment and Nightlife

Let's be honest: The Big Island can't compete with Lahaina or Honolulu for a lively nighttime scene. That said, you're not trapped in your hotel after dark unless you want to be. Kona's your best bet, followed by Kohala for the resort crowd, and Hilo for real local flavor. Your best bet for finding a listing of after-dark activities is the *Hawaii Island Journal*, published weekly (www.hawaiiislandjournal.com), or the daily *Hawaii Tribune Herald* (www.hilohawaiitribune.com) or *West Hawaii Today* (www.westhawaiitoday.com).

Live Music

Kona is the island's best spot for live music, with far and away the most venues. Among these are: **Durty Jake's Café and Bar** for bluegrass at 75-5819 Ali'i Drive (**808-329-7366;** www.dirtyjakes.com) and the **Hard Rock Café** for rock at 75-1855 Ali'I Drive (**808-329-8866;** www.hardrock.com).

Farther north, in Waikoloa and Kohala, you'll find good music at the **Blue Dolphin,** 61-3616 Kawaihae Road (**808-882-7771**), a restaurant that features big band, swing, jazz, and Hawaiian tunes Wednesday to Saturday, the **Clipper Lounge** at the Marriot Waikoloa, 69-275 Waikoloa Beach Drive (**808-886-6789**), and the **Beach Tree Bar,** 72-100 Ka'upalehu Drive (**808-325-8000**).

In Hilo, you can find live music at **Nichols Public House** at 776 Kilauea Avenue (**808-934-8782**), **Kope Kope Espresso Café** at 1261 Kilauea Avenue (**808-933-1221;** www.kopekope.net) and **Café Pesto** at 308 Kamehameha Avenue (**808-969-6640;** www.cafepesto.com).

DJs and Dancing

You're not exactly spoiled for choice for dancing on The Big Island, but you do have options. In Kona check out **Huggo's on the Rocks** at 75-5828 Kahakai Road (**808-329-1493;** www.huggoss.com), **Durty Jake's Café and Bar** at 75-5819 Ali'i Drive (**808-329-7366;** www.dirtyjakes.com), or the **Mask Bar** at 75-5660 Kopiko Street (**808-329-8558**).

Hilo side, check out **Uncle Mikey's** at 400 Hualani Street (**808-933-2667**), **Shooters Bar and Grill** at 121 Banyan Drive (**808-969-7069**), and **Fluid Ultralounge at Detour** at 124 Makaala Street (**808-920-8687**).

Theater and Performing Arts

In Kona, the **Aloha Theatre** at 79-7384 Malamahoa Highway (**808-322-2323;** www.alohatheatre.com) presents films, plays, concerts, and other performing arts from local and national groups. In Hilo, you'll find its counterpart in the **Palace Theatre** at 38 Haili Street (**808-934-7777;** www.hilopalace.com), as well as the **East Hawaii Cultural Center** at 141 Kalakaua Street (**808-961-5711;** www.ehcc.org).

The Best Lu'aus

It's tricky stuff finding a good lu'au these days, but they do exist, and are truly one-of-a-kind experiences with lots of entertainment, some Hawaiian culture, and "choke" food. Here are "the better lu'aus" on The Big Island. These generally last three or four hours, and charge $50 to $100 for adults, half-price for children. All feature an all-you-can-eat Hawaiian feast, an open bar, and Hawaiian-themed entertainment.

Kona Village Lu'au Kona

This is the oldest continuously running lu'au on The Big Island (almost 30 years old!), and once you go you'll know why. The Kona Village Resort gets right what so many other big resort lu'aus seem to miss, from the preparation for the kalua pua`a (roasted pig) to the Polynesian Revue. Don't miss it. *Queen Kaahumanu Highway. Held Wednesdays and Fridays at 5:30 P.M.* ***808-325-5555*** *or* **1-800-367-5290.** *www.konavillage.com.*

Island Breeze Lu'au Kona

The Island Breeze Lu'au is very popular and located at the King Kamehameha's Kona Beach Hotel, the site of which is also known as Kamakahonu, the first capital of Hawaii. They've got good food, a great Polynesian revue, and a super location on the beach—the "Hawaiian Royal Court" arrives by canoe. *75-5660 Palani Road at the Kona Beach Hotel. Held every Sunday, Tuesday, Wednesday, Thursday, and Friday beginning at 5 P.M.* ***808-329-8111.*** *www.islandbreezeluau.com.*

Kamaha'o Lu'au Kailua-Kona

For those most interested in the performance aspect of a lu'au, as opposed to the kalua pua`a aspect, this is the one for you. Ka'ike puts on the show, which features elaborate costumes and presentations and depicts local myths and legends. This is also the right lu'au for those who might prefer tableside service to a buffet. The sunset ain't shabby, either. *78-128 Ali'i Drive. Held Mondays and Fridays beginning at 5:30 P.M.* ***808-930-4900.*** *www.sheratonkeauhou.com.*

Royal Lu'au Waikoloa

This lu'au at the Royal Kona Resort, while very entertaining, is mainly recommended for its proximity to the 'Anaeho'omalu Bay, one of the best sunset-viewing spots on the island. Match that with a dynamic show and an ample buffet, and you've got a winner. *69-275 Waikoloa Beach Drive. Held Sundays and Wednesdays beginning at 6 P.M. (doors open at 5 P.M.).* ***808-886-6789.***

Shopping on The Big Island

There's something for everyone on The Big Island, and that applies to visitors' shopping tastes, too. From the **ABC Stores** (www.abcstores.com) on every corner in Kailua to the specialty galleries in Holualoa to the large farm markets across the island, you're sure to find something special for friends and family back home—as well as plenty of reasons to spoil yourself.

Kona and West Hawaii

Close to Kailua you'll find the **Keauhou Shopping Center** on 76-6831 Ali'i Drive (**808-322-3000**), an open-air complex with more than forty shops and restaurants and a state-of-the-art movie complex. For gift items in particular, check out the **Showcase Gallery** (**808-322-9711**); for women's clothing, try **Borderlines** (**808-322-5003**). At the North end of Ali'I Drive you can find the **Made on The Big Island Outlet** (**808-326-4949**) at the King Kamehameha Beach Hotel, 75-5660 Palani Road; the name should be self-explanatory.

As you might expect, Kohala has the more upscale shops, particularly the **Kings' Shops,** 69-250 Waikoloa Beach Dr., (**808-866-8811**) in Waikoloa, with over 35 shopping and dining options. Just west of Kailua-Kona in **Holualoa** (www.holualoahawaii.com) you'll find a great collection of galleries and boutiques with wares varying from fine art to custom-crafted ukuleles.

Waimea and Central Hawaii

In Waimea you can find the **Parker Ranch** and **Parker Square Center** (**808-885-7178**), and **Waimea Center** (**808-885-4139**), all right along Highway 19, that offer a lot of the familiar big-box options as well as smaller local shops such as **Kamuela Goldsmiths** and **Silk Gallery.** It's also worth stopping in at Honoka'a for the shops on Mamane Street, particularly **Mary Guava Designs** and **Mary Guava Boutique** (**808-775-8255**).

Hilo and East Hawaii

Downtown Hilo has a burgeoning gallery scene that's worth taking advantage of, as well as some good boutique shops. Check out the shops on Kamehameha Avenue, especially **Sig Zane** (**808-935-7077;** www.sigzane.com) for original, locally made island print clothes and **Basically Books** (**808-961-0144;** www.basicallybooks.com) for their Hawaiiana collection and excellent maps. Of course, you could head south on Highway 11 to the **Waiakea Center** (www.princekuhioplaza.com), which has **Borders Books,** or to the **Prince Kuhio Plaza** across the street, which has **Hilo Hattie** (**808-961-3077;** www.hilohattie.com), if you're in the mood for more one-stop shopping.

Local Markets

In Kona, check out the **Ali'i Gardens Marketplace** (www.aliigardens.com), open Wednesday through Sunday, the **Kaiwi Square Market** (www.konafarmersmarket.com), open Saturday & Sunday, and the **Kona Farmers' Market,** at Old Industrial Park in Kaiwi Square, open Wednesdays through Sundays. These are great places to pick up cheap produce to take on day trips, as well as longer-lasting purchases to take home.

One of the best markets on the island, the **Maku'u Farmers' Market,** is on the other side of the island. Just outside Pahoa, and held every Saturday and Sunday along Highway 130. Like the **Hilo Farmers' Market** held Wednesdays and Saturdays at the corner of Kamehameha Avenue and Mamo Street, this market offers an impressive array of fresh produce and locally made artesan treats, a greenhouse's worth of flowers, and plenty of crafts and kitsch.

Enjoying the Very Best Activities on The Big Island

With so much to do and usually a week (or less!) of time budgeted, it can be hard to fit it all in. Relax, there's plenty of expert help to guide you and just as many opportunities to trailblaze your own Big Island experience.

Sightseeing Tours

Sometimes you just want someone else to do the hard work of organizing your day. On The Big Island, with so much to see, this isn't a bad plan. Check with your hotel—they might have special tour rates (especially if you're willing to sit through a timeshare presentation). If you'd like to forego the recommendations of the concierge, your best bets are:

Arnott's Lodge (**808-969-7097; www.arnottslodge.com**) has cheap, no-frills tours in addition to budget accommodations; their friendly guides know what they're doing, but don't expect a plush tour bus and a gourmet meal en route. A great choice for backpackers.

The **Mauna Kea Summit Adventures** (**1-800-322-2366** or **1-888-322-2366;** www.mauakea.com) guided tour gives you the best of the mountain—a tour of the observatories as well as another "tour" of the unbeatable night sky after watching the sunset. The price is a bit steep ($185), but you'll probably say it's worth it.

Horseback Tours

For would-be paniolos (Hawaiian cowboys), try a horseback ride at **Parker Ranch** (**808-885-5006;** www.parkerranch.com) in Waimea, or in the same area with **Dahana Ranch** (**808-885-0057;** www.dahanaranch.com), which is Native Hawaiian owned and operated. Exploring Waipi'o Valley is an unforgettable experience, and doing so by horseback makes it that much better. Your best option is **Waipi'o Na'alapa Trail Rides** (**808-775-0419;** www.naalapastables.com/waipio.html), which gives you a ride in and out of the valley (your front-wheel-drive rental car will you thank you) and two hours on horseback once you're down there.

Enjoying the Outdoor Big Island

Maui fans will argue, but The Big Island is really the top choice for outdoor enthusiasts—you could snorkel, hike a volcanic crater, and make a snow angel all in one (long) day, if you really wanted. Did we mention the outstanding beachfront golf courses? What about the surfing? Or the rainforest hikes ... you get the idea.

The Best Golf Courses

These days The Big Island is the place to go if you're serious about golf, and with good reason. It's hard to go wrong with any course here, particularly in Kohala, but here are a few the avid enthusiast shouldn't miss.

Big Island Country Club Kailua-Kona

This course, located 2,000 feet above sea level on the slopes of Mauna Kea, is generally considered a masterpiece. The 17th hole, a par three, is the only green golf hole on The Big Island and a great challenge for any golfer. Just try not to be too distracted by the scenery and you're in for a great game. *71-1420 Mamalahoa Highway. Greens fees are $169 ($109 after 12 noon).* ***808-325-5044.***

Kona Country Club Kailua-Kona

There are two courses at the Kona Country Club. First, the Ocean Course, has great views of (surprise!) the ocean and a superb lava hazard at hole 17. Second, the Mauka Course is more molded to the landscape and sports some great views of its own. *78-7000 Alii Drive. Greens fees are $155 for the Ocean Course, and $140 for the Mauka.* ***808-322-2595.*** *www.konagolf.com.*

Makalei Golf Club Kona

Like The Big Island Country Club, this course is located upslope, although slightly higher, between 2,000 and 3,000 feet. The elevation means less wind, which, with the views, makes this course a treat. *Route 190, 7 miles north of Kailua-Kona. Greens fees are $110.* ***808-325-6625.*** *www.makalei.com.*

Mauna Kea Resort Kohala

While the resort hotel may be closed for repairs after the earthquake on October 15, 2006, the course is still open, and thank goodness, because this is *the* place to golf on The Big Island. The Mauna Kea course (**808-882-5400**) opened in 1964 and is good, open terrain that hugs the shoreline. The newer Hapuna Golf Course (**808-880-3000**), opened in 1992, is well kept but far narrower than Mauna Kea. *32 miles north of Kona on Route 19 off the 68 mile marker. Green fees are $195 for Mauna Kea and $145 for Hapuna.* ***808-325-6625.*** *www.maunakeabeachhotel.com.*

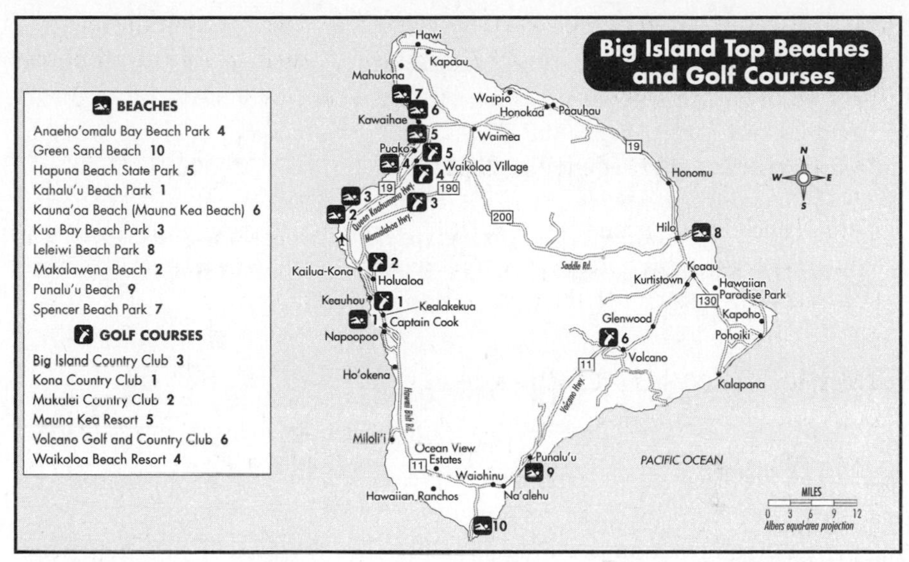

It may be hard to keep your eye on the ball amid the spectacular terrain of the Mauna Kea course.

(Photo courtesy of HVCB/Kirk Lee Aeder)

Volcano Golf and Country Club Volcano

Located next to Volcanoes National Park and 4,000 feet above sea level, this course is straightforward and a decent challenge with (usually) low winds. *On Golf Course Road, off Highway 11 by Hawaii Volcanoes National Park. Greens fees are $63.50.* ***808-967-7331.*** *www.volcanogolfandrestaurant.com.*

Waikoloa Beach Resort Waikoloa

Again, at this resort you have two courses to choose from: the Waikoloa Kings' Course (**808-886-7888**) uses lava to increase the difficulty considerably. The view of Maui and several Big Island volcanoes, make this course unforgettable. Waikoloa Beach (**808-886-6060**) is closer to the ocean and a bit easier, and thus more popular. However, don't underestimate the wind, particularly on the ninth hole. *On Golf Course Road, off of Highway 11 by Hawaii Volcanoes National Park. Greens fees are $195. www.waikoloabeachresort.com.*

Whale-Watching off The Big Island

Humpback whale season, when the whales come to mate and give birth, runs November through April or December through May depending on who you're asking.

If you're lucky you can spot a whale or three during the season while enjoying an oceanside view, but if you want a guaranteed whale sighting, your best bet is to take a tour. Most tours are located in and around Kona. We recommend **Living Ocean Adventures (808-325-5556;** www.livingoceanadventures.com) and **Captain Dan McSweeney's Whale Watch** (**808-322-0028** or **1-888-942-5376;** www.ilovewhales.com)—they both do whale-watching year-round and are small, owner-operated outfits. **Captain Zodiac** (**808-329-3199;** www.captainzodiac.com) runs a whale rafting expedition in the morning and afternoon that gives you that up-close-and-personal feeling.

Hiking on The Big Island

Did you say hiking? There's something for everyone here, from an easy scamper over some lava rack to a real huff-and-puff affair up to the summit of Mauna Loa—with plenty of rainforest and beach hikes along the way. There are five different climates on the island, so make sure you read up on where you're going and bring adequate clothing and footwear.

You can get complete trail maps, recommendations, and necessary permits by contacting the **State of Hawaii Department of Land and Natural Resources** offices at **808-587-0400,** or **808-587-0166** for hiking permits. You can even download a Hawaii State Parks brochure at www.hawaii.gov/dlnr/dsp/dsp.html.

These trail descriptions of the best hikes on The Big Island should help you plan accordingly.

Mauna Loa Summit Hike Mauna Loa, Central Hawaii

Warning: This hike is serious stuff! There's a three-to-five-day version up the Ki'lauea side of the mountain; however, most visitors will only have time for the 8-mile hike starting from the Mauna Loa Weather Observatory. The hike starts at 11,000 feet, so be wary of altitude sickness. It's steep, but the view is worth it if you can stomach it (literally!). Get an early start and bring cold-weather clothes. *Take Saddle Road to Mauna Loa Observatory Road, between mile markers 27 and 28. Drive up this road for about 18 miles. About a mile up the road a white line appears—straddle it with your car because it helps for driving during low visibility.*

Pu'u O'o (Ka-ha-a-Le'a) Trail Glenwood, East Hawaii

This trail, located just a few minutes outside of Volcano, is an open secret on the island. About a 4.5-mile moderate hike each way through almost pristine rainforest, the trail ends at a lava field, with a clear view—even on rainy days, which is almost all of 'em—of the Pu'u O'o vent, source of the current eruption. This is The Big Island at its best! Your best bet is to get here as early as possible in the morning to avoid the rain, which comes, inevitably, in the afternoon. It goes without saying that waterproof shoes are preferable. Note: Don't leave anything valuable in your car! *Take South Glenwood Rd. between mile markers 19 and 20 on Highway 11 for about 3.5 miles until it ends.*

Kalopa Native Forest State Park Honokaa, North Hawaii

About 5 miles southeast of Honoka'a, this native *'ohi'a* forest is considered a budding arboretum of native plants. There are two hiking options—an easy, 0.7-mile hike that's perfect for families, or a 2-mile loop hike around the park. *On Kalopa Road, 3 miles off of Highway 19 by Honoka'a.*

Hawaii Volcanoes National Park Volcano, East Hawaii

There are many trails worth exploring in the park, but we highly recommend two in particular. One, the Kilauea Iki trail, is about 4 miles and descends down to the calderas floor of the Kilauea Iki Crater, which filled with lava during the eruption of 1959, and ascends back up again, through lush green forest.

The Napau Crater trail, which leads out to Pu'u O'o, the source of Ki'lauea's current eruption, is much longer at 14 miles and is a very challenging hike. If you're going farther than Pu'u Hululu, you need to register for a permit with the Visitors' Center.

A shorter hike and a great treat is the Wild Lava Tube (Pu'o Po'o) Hike. The tube was discovered in 1990 and in order to preserve the state of the tube, hikes are limited-guided groups of 12 on Wednesdays and Saturdays. For more information, call **808-985-6017.** *Route 11 between mile markers 28 and 29, Volcano. Open 24 hours a day. www.nps.gov/havo.*

Captain Cook Monument Hike Kona, West Hawaii

You can kayak to the Captain Cook monument, you can take a snorkel cruise, you can ride a horse—and yes, you can hike there, too. It's a 2-mile hike each way, almost 1,500 feet down to the water—more than an hour each way; drink lots of water. Start out early to beat the crowds in the Bay, and don't forget your snorkel mask. *Trail near intersection of Highway 11 and Napoopoo Road, across from three large palm trees.*

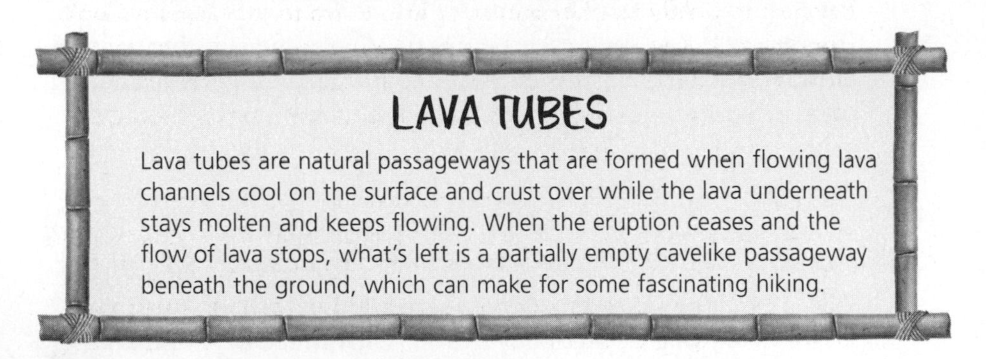

LAVA TUBES

Lava tubes are natural passageways that are formed when flowing lava channels cool on the surface and crust over while the lava underneath stays molten and keeps flowing. When the eruption ceases and the flow of lava stops, what's left is a partially empty cavelike passageway beneath the ground, which can make for some fascinating hiking.

Surfing, Snorkeling, Fishing, and More

Hawaii's the place for water sports, and The Big Island has plenty to offer. While the west side of the island has a better variety of offerings, don't leave the eastern side out of your plans.

- **Surfing:** Accessibility to good surf spots can be a dilemma without a 4WD vehicle—the best places to look are along the Kohala Coast or at South Point. Kahalu'u Beach Park in Kona is a good spot for beginners. On the eastern side of the island, Honoli'i Beach Park, just outside of Hilo, is a local favorite, and consequently jam-packed on the weekends. If you'd like something a bit less busy, try **Hilo Bayfront, Kalapana,** or **Pohoiki.** You can find up-to-date information at www.hawaiisurfnews.com.

- **Windsurfing:** Have you heard of Kona winds? Then you know which side is your best bet for windsurfing. A-Bay with **Ocean Sports (808-886-6666 (ext. 1)** or **1-888-724-5234;** www.hawaiioceansports.com) is a great spot, although nearby bays along the Kohala coast are almost as good. If you have prior experience you might want to give Hilo Bay a try.

- **Sailing:** There's first-class sailing all along the Kohala Coast, where you have the Kona winds but are buffered from the more haphazard northeastern trade winds by the volcanoes. There are plenty of opportunities to combine snorkeling and sailing, particularly in Pawai Bay. For this treat get in touch with **Honu Sailing Charters (808-896-HONU,** www.sailkona.com) or **Kamanu Charters (808-329-8424** or **1-800-348-3091**).

- **Snorkeling and Scuba:** If you're an experienced snorkeler, you can find some truly breathtaking snorkeling all on your own at Honaunau Bay next to Pu'uhonua Honaunau, or hike down to the Captain Cook monument in Kealakekua Bay (see the **Hiking** section). For beginners or those who'd like to go farther out in the water, we'd recommend **Ocean Sports (808-886-6666), Big Island Watersports (808-324-1650;** www.bigislandwatersports.com).
- **Fishing:** The Big Island has some great fishing spots for mahi mahi, marlin, wahoo, ahi, and more, and if you're running on limited time it's best to let the experts lead you to them. Try **Kona Deep Sea Fishing (808-329-1806;** www.konadeepsea.com) and **Legend Sportfishing (808-987-7312** or **808-987-7311,** http://www.hawaii-bnb.com/legend.html) for affordable fun, around $80 to $100 per person, both of which sail out of Kailua-Kona.

There's so much to do on The Big Island that it can be daunting, especially considering the driving time from end to end. Still, if you're willing to spend several days there, you should be able to experience the best of what the island has to offer while staying mellow. Just don't overcommit. Schedule regular beach time, drink in the beauty of the land and local culture, and chill!

Part 5

Kaua'i

Kaua'i is the westernmost, northernmost, and most isolated of the inhabited Hawaiian Islands, with stunning beaches, rugged cliffs rising from the sea, cascading waterfalls, and lush tropical vegetation. It has more native bird species than anywhere else in Hawaii, a gash in the earth comparable to the Grand Canyon, and several iconic locations that were made famous in major motion pictures. These attributes make The Garden Isle a place where you can enjoy the best of all worlds.

Relaxing in Kaua'i

In This Chapter

- Kaua'i's geography and weather
- Transportation options
- Deciding where to stay on Kaua'i
- Kaua'i's best lodging choices

They call **Kaua'i "The Garden Isle"** and it's impossible to argue with that description.

Think of an idyllic tropical place and you're imagining Hawaii's westernmost major island, especially along its lush northern coast. In fact, the place may already be ingrained in your mind: Hollywood directors have been using Kaua'i's stunning tropical beaches, mountains, and waterfalls as backdrops for classic films such as *South Pacific*, *Blue Hawaii*, *Jurassic Park*, *King Kong*, and many others.

The Garden Isle's natural charms don't end on the beach: it is also home to dramatic **Waimea Canyon,** dubbed by local boosters as "The Grand Canyon of the Pacific," and the stunning **Na Pali Coast,** where rugged 4,000-foot mountains descend precipitously to the blue sea.

Kaua'i Paradise

Although Kaua'i may be the most beautiful Hawaiian island, all that greenery is there for a reason: it is also the rainiest island, with **Mount Wai'ale'ale** claiming the distinction as the wettest spot on earth due to its average of 486 inches of precipitation annually. In the winter months, it can rain for a week or more without pause on Kaua'i's north coast, though summers are generally sunny.

The island's abundance of natural beauty makes Kaua'i a paradise for hikers, kayakers, outdoorsy types, and the rest of us who simply appreciate stunning tropical scenery, exotic birds, heady fragrances, awesome beaches, and fewer fellow tourists. (Not that there's anything wrong with being a tourist!)

Snapshot

Kaua'i:

Size: 522 square miles

Population: 58,303

Average Temperature: 75°F (23.8°C) to 85°F (29.4°C)

Coastline: 90 miles

Number of Golf Courses: 9

Number of Native Mammals: 2 (hoary bat and monk seal)

Highest Elevation: 5,243 feet (Kawaikini)

Lovely Kaua'i is less developed than **O'ahu, Maui, or Hawaii,** but it is certainly not lacking in such worldly pleasures as great lodging, fine restaurants, enticing shops and galleries, and a range of transportation and sightseeing choices.

Airport Transportation Options

Most folks flying into Kaua'i arrive at the airport in **Lihu'e,** the island's main settlement on the southeastern coast. You also have the option of flying from other Hawaiian islands to Kaua'i's tiny north-coast airstrip at **Princeville.** Once you touch down in Lihu'e, make your way into the modern, open-air terminal, and collect your baggage, you'll need to walk out to the roadway, where you'll find the following options.

Rental Cars

As on the other Hawaiian Islands, you'll find desks for major car rental companies right on the airport property. A few booths are located across the street from the baggage area, but it's best to catch the company van at the pick-up roadway for the very short ride to the rental office and lot. Here you can rent a wide range of vehicles, including cars, trucks, vans, and SUVs.

Rates begin at about $40 per day and $120 per week for subcompacts, with unlimited mileage.

Taxi Service

The **Kaua'i Taxi Company (808-246-9554)** has a phone inside the terminal, and several other companies have cabs available at curbside of baggage claim areas. There's a start-up fare of about $2.50, and about $2.40 a mile after that. You'll pay about $10 into Lihu'e, $40 to the **Po'ipu** resort area, and up to $100 to Princeville on the north coast.

Limousine Service

If you have a large family or special needs, or you simply like to travel with more style and fewer hassles, you can call one of Lihu'e's limousine companies, including **Any Time Shuttle (808-927-1120), Custom Limousine (808-246-6318)**, or **Kaua'i Limousine (808-245-4855)**. A limo ride to Kapa'a will set you back $25 to $30. Riding in style all the way to Princeville will cost about $70.

Hotel Shuttles

The **Kaua'i Marriott Resort and Beach Club (808-245-5050)** offers shuttle service for guests, picking up every 15 to 30 minutes at the group tour areas outside of the baggage claim. The **Radisson Kaua'i Beach Resort (808-245-1955)** also provides guest pick-up services from the airport.

Here's about what you can expect to spend between Lihu'e and popular Kaua'i destinations:

What Transportation Costs on Kaua'i

Destination	*Taxi*	*Limo*	*Bus*	*Rental Car*
Po'ipu	$35–$40	$45	$1.50	$17–$40/day
Wailua	$17–$20	$30	$1.50	$17–$40/day
Waimea	$60–$70	$65	$1.50	$17–$40/day
Princeville	$75–$95	$70	$1.50	$17–$40/day

Traveling on the Cheap: Buses

There is no public bus transportation from Lihu'e Airport. However, the **Kaua'i Bus Company (808-241-6410)** does serve the entire island from the Lihu'e Courthouse and other stops downtown, and the fare is only about $1.50 no matter where you're going. The buses don't go to any resorts, but you can get from town to town if you're traveling with only one small bag (maximum size 7" x 14" x 22"). The company operates two main routes: one up the eastern and northern coasts to **Kapa'a** and **Hanalei,** and one west to **Waimea** and **Kekaha.** The buses don't run on Sundays.

Group Tours

If you're just stopping in Kaua'i for a day, or you prefer to let the local experts manage your island itinerary, you can let a tour company chauffeur you to notable sites. **Kaua'i Island Tours (808-245-4777), Roberts of Hawaii (808-245-9101, 808-241-7255)**, or **Polynesian Adventure (808-246-0122)** would all be happy to pick you up at the airport and show you the sights—for a fee, of course.

Getting Your Bearings: Island Locales

There's something for everyone in beautiful Kaua'i. Overall, it is the classic tropical island, but like most of its siblings in the Hawaiian chain, its windward side is rainy (the northeast), while its leeward side is relatively dry (the southwest). Kaua'i's annual rainfall averages 40 inches. However, Princeville on the north coast receives 85 inches, while Waimea in the southwest receives an average of only 21 inches.

This variety in weather, combined with elevation and the level of development in a particular location, means that your own experience can vary greatly depending on what part of The Garden Isle you're visiting.

On Kaua'i's north coast near **Hanalei,** you can be standing amid ferns under a waterfall on the edge of a lush rainforest as one squall after another challenges the seams of your poncho. In another part of the island at exactly the same time—say, near **Kekaha** in the west—you would be surrounded by miles of flat, white-sand beach, dry grasses, and the occasional cactus as a relentless sun broils the top of your head. In **Wailua,** on the eastern **"Coconut" Coast,** you could easily find yourself in a commercial strip, with stores, hotel rooms, and swaying palms extending nearly as far as the eye can see.

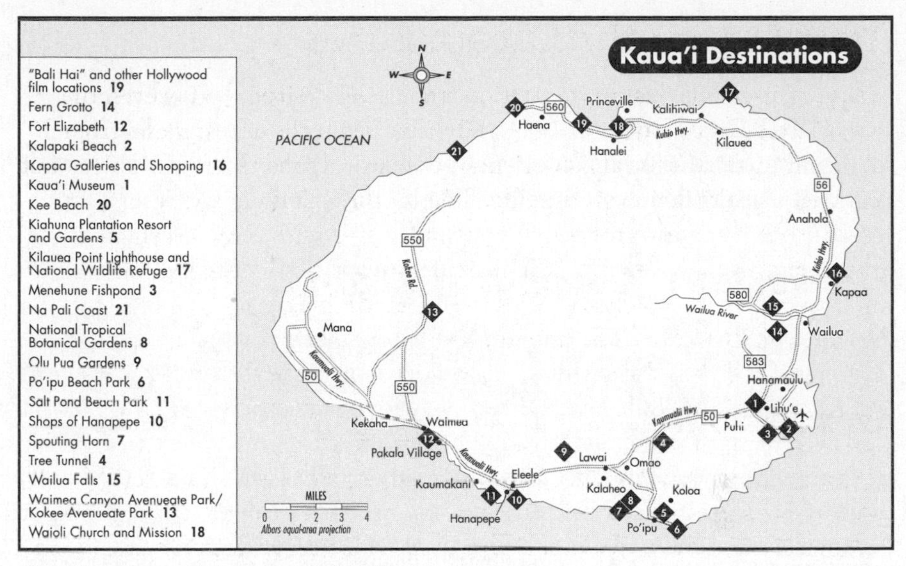

Kauai's regions, highways, and key destinations.

All of this variety is good, of course. On Kaua'i, you're guaranteed beautiful beaches, intriguing local food and culture, comfortable accommodations, and natural beauty no matter where you spend your time. Beyond that, you can pick your sights and sounds according to your mood and vacation goals.

Lihu'e and Vicinity

Lihu'e, on Kaua'i's southeastern coast, is the main arrival point for tourists, the county seat, and the island's major commercial center. That doesn't make it a big place, however. With a population of about 5,500, it's essentially a former plantation town that has grown up a bit over the years. There's nothing particularly beautiful or dramatic about downtown Lihu'e—it's mostly composed of nondescript storefronts and the occasional strip mall, though its Spanish Revival/ Classical Revival courthouse is rather grand.

Snapshot

Visitor's Information:

Kaua'i Visitors Bureau: 4334 Rice Avenue, Suite 101. **808-245-3971** or **1-800-262-1400.** www.Kauaivisitorsbureau.org or www.Kauaidiscovery.com.

Kaua'i Historical Society: 4396 Rice Avenue. **808-245-3373.** www.Kauaihistoricalsociety.org

Kaua'i Medical Clinic: 3420 Kuhio Highway. **808-822-3431.**

Although Lihu'e isn't very picturesque, it does have its good points. Not only is it close by the airport and centrally located for most of Kaua'i's best sights, it's got plenty of decent restaurants, inexpensive lodgings, and great shopping deals. Two of Kaua'i's top resorts—the **Kaua'i Marriott Resort and Beach Club** and the **Radisson Kaua'i Beach Resort**—are just outside of town, and nearby **Kalapaki Beach** is considered one of the island's best.

The Eastern "Coconut" Coast

The eastern shore of Kaua'i just north of Lihu'e along Route 56 is called the Coconut Coast; you'll see why when you drive between the towns of Wailua and Kapa'a and find mile after mile of swaying coconut palms. The scene along the main road isn't exactly idyllic Hawaii, but there's plenty to do here. There is shopping galore, including interesting galleries and markets, a wide range of places to eat, and plenty of places to stay. Here you are literally within minutes of many of eastern Kaua'i's most notable natural and historical sites, and once you get off the main drag and into some of the seaside properties, you can find quiet beaches fronting an azure sea. And the Coconut Coast often sees the sun when rain showers are pelting Kaua'i's northern shore.

Snapshot

Here are the top destinations on Lihu'e and the Coconut Coast:

- Fern Grotto
- Kaua'i Museum
- Kalapaki Beach
- Kapa'a Galleries and Shopping
- Wailua Falls

This is a land of B&Bs and relatively inexpensive vacation rentals, definitely worth a serious look if you're on a budget. The village of Kapa'a's wooden storefronts, rebuilt after the devastation of 1992's Hurricane Iniki, offer some real character, and there are several good restaurants in town.

The North Shore

There are few who would argue with a declaration that Kaua'i's northern shore is its most beautiful area. This land of jagged mountains, lush vegetation, plunging waterfalls, and dramatic coastlines has served as the shooting location for more than 40 Hollywood movies. Remember *Bali Hai*? This is it.

The North Shore is generally the wilder, quieter, and cloudier side of Kaua'i. You'll love it if you want a "getaway" feel to your vacation and are looking to do more than just lie on a beach. The planned community of Princeville, sitting on a bluff above the sea, is a golfer's paradise of low-rise condos and resorts, its highly manicured acres flanked by misty mountains and a stormy sea. The laid-back village of **Hanalei** is classic Hawaii, with its down-home shops and surfer's esthetic. The **Na Pali Coast,** accessible only by boat or on foot, provides some of the most dramatic scenery in all of the Hawaiian Islands, while **Kilauea Point** is Hawaii's northernmost point, a refuge for rare birds, and a favorite spot for whale-watching during the winter months.

Snapshot

North Shore Destinations:

- *Bali Hai* and other Hollywood film locations
- Kee Beach
- Kilauea Point Lighthouse and National Wildlife Refuge
- Na Pali Coast
- Wai'oli Church and Mission

Kauai's Na Pali coastline is one of the world's most famous sights.

(Photo courtesy of HVCB/Robert Coello)

Now for the downside: the North Shore is at least an hour's drive from Lihu'e and points south and west. There's also that pesky overcast sky and rain, which is most prevalent in the winter.

But back to Bali Hai: it would take months to run out of things to do on the North Coast, and any extra driving (and dampness) is a modest price to pay for the experience of this special land.

Po'ipu and the South Coast

Do you like plenty of sunshine, fine beaches, outstanding restaurants, and a wide variety of comfortable accommodations? If that's your vacation style, then Kaua'i's **Po'ipu** area south and west of Lihu'e may be the ticket for you. In fact, this is Kaua'i's most popular resort region, with low-rise hotels and resorts situated alongside beautiful golden-sand beaches.

The Po'ipu area was developed over the past 10 years as part of a master plan, so the scene here tends to be tasteful, not tacky. You'll find water sports of every kind, as well as plenty of options for golf, tennis, and other outdoor activities. You'll be able to watch plenty of young, buff surfers here, especially in the summer, when the south coast gets its largest waves. You'll see plenty of middle-aged guys from the mainland boogieboarding or trying to "hang ten" the rest of the time.

Snapshot

Po'ipu and South Coast Destinations:

- Kiahuna Plantation Resort and Gardens
- Menehune Fishpond
- National Tropical Botanical Gardens
- Po'ipu Beach Park
- Spouting Horn
- Tree Tunnel

Po'ipu is only half an hour from the airport and services of Lihu'e, as well as from points west, including **Waimea Canyon.** However, it is about an hour and a half from the attractions on the North Shore.

Waimea and West Kaua'i

West Kaua'i is more remote, drier, and less touristy than other parts of the island. A series of sleepy plantation towns along the highway don't appear to offer much for the visitor, but this region certainly has its unique charms. Those include one of Hawaii's most spectacular wonders and a "must-see" destination, **Waimea Canyon.** They call this place the Grand Canyon of the

Pacific, which is a bit of an overstatement, but not by much. In fact, it looks amazingly like the "real thing" in Arizona, albeit on a slightly smaller scale. Think red-rock buttes and dizzying 3,000-foot ravines, but with waterfalls and more greenery. Either way, it's certainly a grand canyon to see, and you don't have to worry about rattlesnakes.

Waimea Canyon is called "The Grand Canyon of the Pacific."

(Photo courtesy of HVCB/Ron Dahlquist)

There's also the handsome **Koke'e State Park,** encompassing a cool, forested upland that offers impressive overlooks of the **Na Pali Coast.**

The small coastal town of **Waimea** was the place where Capt. James Cook made his first landing in Hawaii in 1778. Cook, who had explored Australia, New Zealand, Alaska, Newfoundland, and most of the virtually unknown points between and betwixt, was on his third and final voyage. In 1779 he had an unpleasant encounter with some of the natives at **Kaawaloa** on **Kealakekua Bay** on the island of Hawaii and it was there he met a violent death.

The Russians, who were also exploring the area, built a fort at Waimea in 1815, and the remnants are still there for your viewing pleasure today.

Atmospheric **Hanapepe** was one of the most scenic and well-preserved historical towns on

plumeria

Snapshot

West Kaua'i Destinations:

- Fort Elizabeth
- Olu Pua Gardens
- Salt Pond Beach Park
- Shops of Hanapepe
- Spouting Horn
- Waimea Canyon/Koke'e State Park

Kaua'i before it was seriously roughed up by Hurricane Iniki in 1992. Fortunately, about half its period buildings survived and local residents rebuilt most of the others, preserving a quaint setting of art galleries, antique stores, and funky curiosities. Nearby is **Salt Pond Beach Park,** where native Hawaiians have harvested salt from ocean waters since ancient times, and is also the departure point for boat and helicopter tours of nearby Niihau, the "forbidden" Hawaiian island.

Driving Times from Lihu'e Airport	
Ha'ena Avenueate Park	1 hour, 15 minutes
Hanalei	1 hour, 5 minutes
Kapa'a	20 minutes
Kilauea	45 minutes
Po'ipu	25 minutes
Princeville	1 hour
Wailua	15 minutes
Waimea	45 minutes
Waimea Canyon	1 hour, 5 minutes

Comfortable Accommodations: Ultimate Places to Stay

Sure, Kaua'i is a bit of a world apart, with less development than Oahu or Maui, but The Garden Isle still offers a full complement of great places to stay, no matter what your style. Want to be pampered at a luxury resort? No problem. Looking for a quiet ocean-view condo next to a golf course? They've got you covered. How about some down-home "true Hawaiian" lodgings close to a waterfall? Your wish will be fulfilled.

Following you'll find a few of our favorite places to stay on Kaua'i.

Hotels and Resorts

Aloha Beach Resort Kapa'a

Make no mistake about it: this is a real resort right on the Coconut Coast of Kaua'i's eastern shore, but here you can get an ocean-view room for as little as $135, which is a pretty good deal by Hawaiian standards. Recently renovated, with 216 rooms and 26 beach cottages, this place features fine views and a protected swimming and snorkeling beach, which is somewhat rare in this part of Kaua'i. It also boasts two swimming pools, Jacuzzi, fitness room, tennis, volleyball, and shuffleboard, as well as a full-service restaurant, a poolside snack bar and grill, and the all-important lounge. *3-5920 Kuhio Highway (Route 56), Kapa'a, HI 97646.* ***800-367-5004*** *or* ***1-888-823-5111.*** *www.alohabeachresortkauai.com.*

Garden Island Inn Lihu'e

This centrally located inn just north of Lihu'e is reasonably priced, and will put you less than an hour's drive from all of Kaua'i's best sites. A two-floor motel-style place about two minutes' walk from Kalapaki Beach, it offers 21 cheery and comfortable mini-suites with exotic tropical flower arrangements. The top-floor rooms have their own lanais, and all rooms include full amenities, including refrigerators, microwave ovens, coffeemakers, and more. The owners will supply you with all manner of beach equipment, along with plenty of "insider" touring suggestions for seeing the island. *3445 Wilcox Road, Lihu'e, HI 96766.* ***808-245-7227*** *or* ***1-800-648-0154.*** *www.gardenislandinn.com.*

Hanalei Colony Resort Ha'ena

This laid-back but sublimely comfortable little resort offers a taste of real Hawaii. Located on a quiet portion of the two-lane highway just west of downtown Hanalei on the North Shore, and directly on a quiet beach lined with coconut palms, this refuge will assure that you're able to decompress from the worries of the everyday world. Here you're in the heart of the "Bali Hai" coast, just minutes from cascading waterfalls, caves, hiking trails, beautiful Kee Beach Avenueate Park and the incomparable Na Pali coast. *5-7130 Kuhio Highway, Ha'ena, HI 96714.* ***808-826-6235*** *or* ***1-800-628-3004.*** *www.hcr.com.*

Kaua'i Marriott Resort & Beach Club Lihu'e $$$$$

This oceanfront resort is only a mile from the airport in Lihu'e, but in a world of its own. It sits on a lush 800-acre property with myriad lagoons and gardens, and is also right on one of the best beaches in Kaua'i: Kalapaki. The resort is large—over 300 rooms and another 200 or so condos, but Marriott has done a good job in blending it into the surroundings. The public rooms and corridors boast gorgeous bouquets everywhere, and the open-air lobby has ponds and gardens. It's a pricey place, but guests have the use of two 18-hole golf courses, one of the largest swimming pools in Hawaii, two restaurants, 12 tennis courts, extensive children's programs, plenty of water sports, and many other amenities. Marriott also runs a lower-key sister property in the Po'ipu resort area. *3610 Rice Street, Kalapaki Beach, Lihu'e, HI.* ***808-245-5050*** *or* ***1-800-220-2925.*** *www.marriott.com/property/propertypage/lihhi.*

Princeville Hotel Princeville $$$$$

Overlooking beautiful Hanalei Bay on the North Shore, this is truly a five-star luxury resort, with stunning "Bali Hai" views of the mountains and Hanalei Bay. In fact, as you're enjoying an expensive cocktail on the veranda here, you may need to pinch yourself to make sure that the panorama spread out before you is not some kind of technicolor dream. Some might say the atmosphere here is a little stuffy, but if total luxury is your thing, you'll be pleased. *5520 Ka Haku Road, Princeville, Kaua'i, HI 96722.* ***808-826-9644*** *or* ***1-800-826-4400.*** *www.princevillehotelhawaii.com.*

Waimea Plantation Cottages Waimea $$$

Here you'll find the best of all worlds: a little history, beach life, and proximity to backcountry hiking. Originally built in the early 1900s, this converted plantation features historically restored and updated private cottages in a 27-acre coconut grove. Located on a black-sand beach near the gateway to spectacular Waimea Canyon, its one-, two- and three-bedroom cottages have complete kitchens and large lanais with grove or ocean views, and you also can book a room in the "Manager's House." You'll enjoy the property's pool, wireless Internet hotspot, a restaurant, and a spa. *9400 Kaumualii Highway, Waimea, HI 96796.* ***808-338-1625.*** *www.waimea-plantation.com.*

More Intimate Lodgings and B&Bs

Kaua'i Cove Koloa $$

These three attached studio cottages each offer a full kitchen, private lanai, cathedral ceilings, and four-poster beds, and are walking distance to the beach, a favorite snorkeling spot, Whalers Cove, and other spots in town. You'll feel at home here. *2672 Puuholo Road, Koloa, HI 96765.* ***808-624-9945.*** *www.kauaicove.com.*

Princeville Bed and Breakfast Princeville $$

Sitting on the sixth hole of Princeville's Makai Golf Course, this airy home offers spacious suites and sparkling single rooms with beautiful views of both the mountains and the sea. The honeymoon suite features a Jacuzzi, and all guest rooms have cable TV, VCR, and refrigerator. The penthouse affords you a 360-degree view and even includes a washer and dryer. Of course, hosts Gary and Billie will serve you a full breakfast each day. (Macadamia nut pancakes, anyone?) *3875 Kamehameha, Princeville, HI 96722.* ***808-826-6733*** *or* ***1-800-826-6733.*** *www.pixi.com/~kauai.*

Best Condos

Kapa'a Sands Kapa'a $$

Reasonably priced, directly on the beach, and centrally situated between all of Kaua'i's best destinations, this Coconut Coast establishment offers 20 nicely furnished studio and two-bedroom rentals—all with either a full or partial ocean view. In addition to its convenient proximity to island points, the Kapa'a Sands is also within walking distance of Kapa'a's Coconut Plantation Marketplace, as well as minutes from hiking trails, scenic waterfalls, and other local delights. *380 Papaloa Road, Kapa'a, HI 96746.* ***808-822-4901*** *or* ***1-800-222-4901.*** *www.kapaasands.com.*

Kuhio Shores Po'ipu $$$

Only a few feet from a white-sand beach on the sunny southern Po'ipu coast, these beautifully outfitted one- and two-bedroom units are a great choice if you like snorkeling, swimming, observing sea turtles and whales, or just kicking back with a beverage on the lanai while watching the sun sink into the water. The Beach House Restaurant is right next door. *5050 Lawai Beach Road, Koloa, HI 96756,* ***808-823-6625.*** *www.kuhioshores.net.*

Sea Lodge Princeville $$

The crashing waves of the South Pacific will lull you to sleep at night at these one- and two-bedroom units on Kaua'i's North Shore, and each condo features fantastic views of both the ocean and the Bali Hai mountains. Part of the Princeville planned community, Sea Lodge sits on a 130-foot-high bluff above the ocean, providing a sense of remoteness while just minutes from great restaurants, entertainment, golf, hiking, and other outdoor activities. *3700 Kamehameha Road, Princeville, HI 96722.* ***1-866-264-7954.*** *www.sealodge-Kauai.com.*

Ultimate Private Home

House of Views Princeville

Yes, you can live like a modern-day Hawaiian king or queen without breaking the bank! This gorgeous private home sleeps up to eight in four bedrooms, with panoramic views of both the ocean and mountains on Kaua'i's north coast. It also features a large living room with hardwood floors and floor-to-ceiling windows, furnished decks from which to enjoy the spectacular views, and wireless Internet access. At $550 per night and $2,700 weekly, this works out to a great deal if you're traveling with other families. *Kaua'i Vacation Rentals and Real Estate, Inc. 3-3311 Kuhio Hwy., Lihue, HI 96766.* ***1-808-245-8841*** *or* ***1-800-367-5025.*** *www.kauaivacationrentals.com.*

Kaua'i is truly South Pacific come to life. If you stay here, you'll love the tropical ambience, as long as you can handle a little rain. For details on great restaurants, beaches, shopping, outdoor sports, and other activities, take a look at Chapter 13.

Chapter 13

Enjoying Kaua'i

In This Chapter

- The ultimate itineraries for Kaua'i
- The best places to dine on Kaua'i
- The most interesting things to see on Kaua'i
- The best things to do on Kaua'i

Kaua'i is the westernmost, northernmost, and most isolated of the inhabited Hawaiian Islands, with only a string of small, low-lying atolls extending further north and west. The vast majority of Kaua'i's 58,000 residents live along its coastline, which has left the island's interior in a pristine, almost prehistoric, natural state. Even the populated areas along the coasts feature stunning beaches, rugged cliffs rising from the sea, cascading waterfalls, and lush tropical vegetation.

The Top Five Things to Do on Kaua'i

Kaua'i's rich bounty of history, natural beauty, and culture makes it a place where you can indulge nearly every tropical fantasy. You really shouldn't leave The Garden Isle without checking out these activities. Here's our list of the best things to do in Kauai:

1. Tour **Waimea Canyon,** the "Grand Canyon of the Pacific."
2. Observe migrating whales, rare sea birds, and miles of dramatic Pacific coastline from **Kilauea Point.**
3. Enjoy cocktails at sunset while gazing at the "Bali Hai" mountains from the patio at the **Princeville Resort.**
4. Take a sunset cruise along the spectacular **Na Pali Coast.**
5. Spend an afternoon on beautiful **Ke'e Beach,** where you can gaze at both mountains and monk seals.

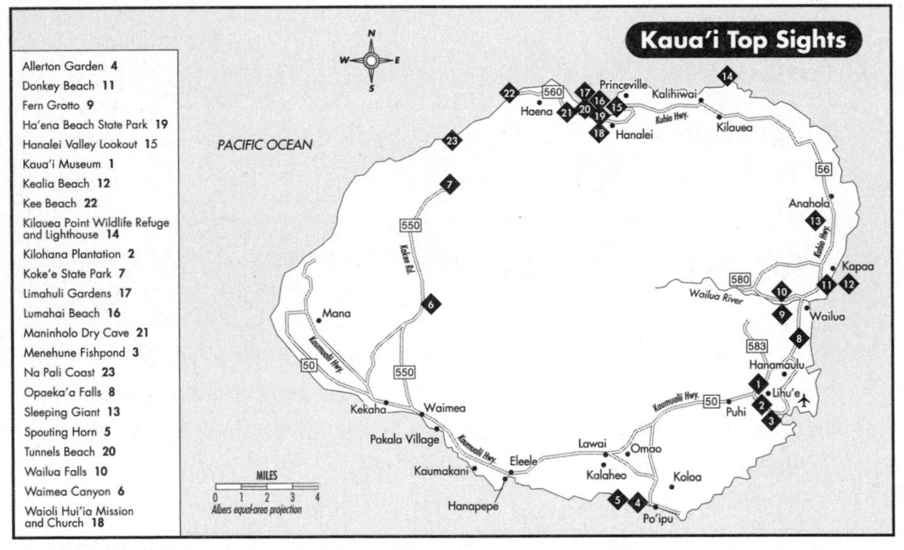

Kauai's top sights.

Plan My Trip: Ultimate Itineraries for Kaua'i

If you can't find something special to do on Kaua'i—whether you're with your family, on your own, or touring around with your special loved one—you just don't know how to have fun. Here are several itineraries designed to fit your particular travel mode, complete with good places to eat and spots to take breaks along the way. Most of these are designed to take about one day, though in several cases we've also included suggestions for stretching the schedule to two days.

ITINERARY #1: FOR YOUNG FAMILIES

Day 1

1. **Breakfast:** After breakfast at the **Tip Top Motel Café & Bakery** in Lihu'e, hop into the car and drive north on Route 56 (the Kuhio Highway, Lihu'e's main drag). Turn left on Route 583, also known as Ma'alo Road. Follow this for 4 miles to **Wailua Falls,** where you can chill out in the shady, misty grotto of one of Hawaii's most renowned cascades.
2. **Lunch:** After the falls, drive a few miles up Route 56 to Kapa'a for a stop at a Kaua'i landmark of sorts, **Bubba Burgers,** where you can not only enjoy the famous charbroiled hamburgers, but also fresh-fish specials, fish burgers, fish and chips, and more. If you're the sort who likes to advertise your vacation trips on your chest, you might want to buy a Bubba Burgers T-shirt, which has a definite cool quotient back on the mainland.
3. Drive another 15 minutes further north of Kapa'a to milepost 20 and lovely kid-friendly **Anini Beach.** Hang out in the golden sand and maybe do some snorkeling in the clear, calm waters.
4. Shower off at Anini, then head a few minutes further up the highway to milepost 23, where you'll come to the **1870s plantation town of Kilauea.** Head down Lighthouse Road to beautiful and scenic Kilauea Point, where you can see a historic lighthouse and watch whales at sea.

continues

continued

The historic Kilauea lighthouse sits on Kaua'i's northernmost point.
(Photo courtesy of HVCB/Robert Coello)

5. **Dinner:** If you're looking for a festive place for dinner before turning around and heading back down the road to your hotel, you might want to drive about 15 minutes further up the road to the laid-back North Shore town of **Hanalei** and stop in at **Zelo's Beach House** restaurant.

Day 2

1. **Breakfast:** After breakfast at **Eggbert's** in **Kapa'a,** visit the Kaua'i **Children's Discovery Museum** in town for some culture, history, and interactive fun that the kids will love.
2. **Lunch:** While you're in Kapa'a, check out the **Olympic Café** right on the main drag at 1-4387 Kuhio Highway (Route 56). This is an open-air place, where you can get a wide variety of both creative local and recognizable American food. The kids *and* you will enjoy it.
3. **Dinner:** In the afternoon, spend some quality time on pretty, family-friendly **Kalipaki Beach,** just off Rice Road at mile marker 0 in Lihu'e. After swimming, get some refreshments and some Pacific Rim cuisine at **Duke's Canoe Club,** which is right by the beach in the Marriott Resort.

Itinerary #2: For Older Families

Day 1

1. **Breakfast:** Grab breakfast at your place of accommodation, then learn a bit about Kau'i's history and culture at the **Kaua'i Museum** in downtown Lihu'e.
2. Head up Route 56 to the town of Wailua and the **Wailua River,** Kaua'i's only navigable waterway, fed by freshwater pouring down from **Mt. Wai'ale'ale.** It is said to be the wettest spot on Earth. Catch a flat-bottom boat to the atmospheric **Fern Grotto.**
3. **Lunch:** Proceed north a few miles to the hip little town of Kapa'a, a good place to stop for lunch as well as browse a few galleries.
4. Head a few minutes further up the highway to milepost 23 and drive down Lighthouse Road for some quality time at beautiful and scenic **Kilauea Point.**
5. Drive another 20 minutes west on Routes 56 and 560 past the **Hanalei Valley Lookout** at **Princeville,** and down the hill into Hanalei. Cruise by the picturesque **Wai'oli Hui'ia Church,** stopping for a short visit if you have time, and on to the end of the road at **Ke'e Beach** in Ha'ena State Park, where you can gaze upon the **Na Pali Coast.**
6. **Drinks and Dinner:** Return to Princeville for some music and refreshments at the Hanalei Bay Resort's **Happy Talk Lounge,** followed by a magnificent dinner with a view at the adjacent **Bali Hai** restaurant.

Day 2

1. **Breakfast:** Get up early, have breakfast at the hotel, and drive west from Lihu'e on Route 50, 45 minutes to the town of Waimea. Turn up Route 550 and drive the 12 miles to spectacular **Waimea Canyon.**
2. Continue to the end of the Waimea Canyon Road through **Koke'e State Park** to **Kalalau Point,** where, weather permitting, you'll drink in the picture postcard sight of the **Na Pali Coast** from an elevation of about 4,000 feet.
3. **Lunch and Shopping:** Descend the Canyon Road, taking the fork onto Koke'e Road, which will lead you down to the small, dusty

continues

continued

town of **Kekaha.** Enjoy the shopping, deli and **Lappert's Ice Cream** at the well-stocked gift shop where Koke'e Road comes into town.

4. Continue back toward the east on Route 50, stopping for some leisurely sightseeing at the atmospheric town of **Hanapepe.**
5. **Drinks and Dinner:** Back on Route 50, drive to Po'ipu for some sunset drinks and delectable Pacific Rim cuisine at **The Beach House.**

ITINERARY #3: IF YOU'RE TRAVELING ALONE

1. **Breakfast:** Grab some breakfast at the scenic **Kaua'i Marriott Resort & Beach Club.** Then spend an hour watching the boats and windsurfers at Lihu'e's lovely **Kalapaki Beach,** which is right there adjacent to the property.
2. Drive 15 minutes north on Route 56 to the hip little town of **Kapa'a,** where you can browse the shops and galleries.
3. **Lunch:** Drive about 20 minutes further up the highway to milepost 23, where you'll come to the **1870s plantation town of Kilauea.** Pick up some gourmet sandwiches at **Starvin' Marvin's Kilauea Deli.**
5. Head down Lighthouse Road to beautiful and scenic **Kilauea Point,** where you can gaze upon miles of ocean and hundreds of sea birds.
6. Drive a few miles further up Route 56 to the Princeville Airport, where you can catch a helicopter for an exciting air tour of the fabulous **Na Pali Coast.**
7. Once you've landed, cap off a near-perfect day with drinks, some pupus, and a stunning view of Bali Hai at **The Living Room Lounge** in the **Princeville Resort.**

Itinerary #4: A Romantic Getaway

1. **Breakfast:** After breakfast at the hotel, head up Route 56 to the town of Wailua and the **Wailua River,** Kaua'i's only navigable waterway. Catch a flat-bottom boat to the atmospheric **Fern Grotto,** where people get married nearly every weekend.
2. Drive north past Kapa'a, looking for a turnoff on the ocean side of the road at mile marker 11. There you'll find a parking area and a well-worn path will take you about a quarter-mile down a hill to secluded **Donkey Beach.**
3. **Lunch:** Enjoy some early afternoon drinks and pupus, along with an unbelievable view, at **The Living Room Lounge** in the Princeville Resort.
4. After refreshments, return to Route 56 and drive down the hill into lovely **Hanalei.** If it was our money we were spending, we would go straight to Captain Sundown boat tours for a memorable three-hour, sunset catamaran cruise down the Na Pali Coast.
5. **Dinner:** After your cruise, check out the delicious fresh food and homegrown live music at the cool and casual **Hanalei Gourmet** restaurant in downtown Hanalei.

Itinerary #5: Easy-Going; Nonstrenuous

1. **Breakfast:** Have breakfast at the place of your choice, then head up Route 56 and to the town of Wailua and the **Wailua River,** Kaua'i's only navigable waterway. Catch a flat-bottom boat to the atmospheric **Fern Grotto.**
2. **Lunch:** Return to the Lihu'e area and proceed to **Kilohana Plantation** for a delightful lunch at **Gaylord's.**
3. Spend the afternoon at **Kilohana Plantation,** where you can shop in the galleries and take a carriage tour of the grounds. In late afternoon, refresh yourself with high tea at **Kilohana.**

continues

continued

4. **Dinner:** Repair to **Duke's Canoe Club** at the **Kaua'i Marriott Resort & Beach Club** in **Lihu'e,** where you can enjoy leisurely drinks and dinner overlooking beautiful **Nawiliwili Bay.**

Day 2 (optional)

1. Drive 15 minutes north of Lihu'e on Route 56 to **Kapa'a** and sign on to a scenic **Hollywood Movie Tour,** including lunch, along Kauai's east and north coasts.
2. **Shopping and Dinner:** After the tour, spend an hour browsing around Kapa'a's many shops and galleries, then enjoy some eclectic and delectable dinner cuisine amid the palms at **Café Coco.**

ITINERARY #6: CULTURE IN PARADISE

Day 1

1. **Breakfast**: Have breakfast at the **Tip Top Motel Café & Bakery,** then soak in the rich history and arts of the island at the **Kaua'i Museum** in downtown Lihu'e.
2. Experience how the ruling classes lived in the day when sugar was king at the **Kilohana Plantation,** where you can shop in the galleries and tour the manicured grounds.
3. **Lunch:** While you're at Kilohana, enjoy a grand lunch at **Gaylord's,** set amid the beautiful gardens.
4. Follow Route 50 west to just past mile marker 2 across the street from **Kauai Community College.** Turn right and proceed to the **Menehune Fishpond** overlook, where you can contemplate how the ancients built the wall for this large reservoir one stone at a time.
5. **Dinner:** Continue on to the Po'ipu area for dinner at the fabulous **The Beach House,** which has had a virtual lock on the title for *Honolulu Magazine*'s "Best Kaua'i Restaurant" for many years.

Day 2

1. **Breakfast:** Have breakfast at your hotel, then drive 15 minutes north of Lihu'e on Route 56 to **Kapa'a,** where you can browse the superb artwork in the **Aloha Gallery** and other art stores.

2. Drive another 20 minutes west on Routes 56 and 560 to the ultra-picturesque **Wai'oli Hui'ia Church and Mission** in Hanalei.
3. **Lunch:** Grab a bite to eat at **Tropical Taco** in downtown Hanalei. Sit on the porch and watch the real culture of Kaua'i as it goes by.
4. Go a little further west on Route 560 and spend a couple of hours at the stunning **Limahuli Gardens** in Kalaheo, selected by the American Horticultural Society as the best natural botanical garden in the United States.
5. **Dinner:** Drive back to Kapa'a for some unusual world fusion cuisine and great music at **Blossoming Lotus** in Kapa'a.

ITINERARY #7: ADVENTURE IN THE GREAT OUTDOORS

Day 1

1. **Breakfast:** Get up early and cruise up Route 56 to the top of the island—to the **Anini Beach Windsurfing School,** and try your hand at looking cool as you glide over the turquoise waters.
2. **Lunch:** Drive a few miles further west to check out a fresh fish taco and homemade lemonade at **Tropical Taco** in downtown Hanalei.
3. Rest your muscles and stimulate your mind with some of the best snorkeling in Hawaii at **Tunnels Beach,** located at milepost 8 on Route 560 west of Hanalei.
4. **Dinner:** You've earned a good meal, so proceed directly to **Hanalei Gourmet** in downtown Hanalei for solid, fresh food and some local entertainment.

Day 2

1. **Breakfast/Lunch:** If you're on the north coast, grab some sturdy shoes, a pack, and something for lunch, then go directly to **Ke'e Beach** and walk the first two scenic miles of the Na Pali Coast's famous **Kalalau Trail.**

continues

2a. **Dinner:** Relax back at **Ke'e Beach** in the afternoon, then reward yourself with a fun dinner at **Zelo's Beach House** back in Hanalei.

2b. If you're staying in Lihu'e or southwest of there, get up early and drive out west past stunning **Waimea Canyon** to **Koke'e State Park.** Hike the 3.5 mile **Alakai Swamp Trail,** which crosses the unique **Alakai Swamp** at over 3,000 feet.

2c. In the afternoon, return to Port Allen for some sailing off the coast, then top off the day with the microbrews and fine food of the **Waimea Brewing Company** in Waimea.

The Top Kaua'i Attractions, A to Z

Allerton Gardens Lawa'i; South Coast

Here's your chance to walk through 100 acres of oceanfront gardens on the historic Allerton Estate, site of the former summer cottage of Queen Emma, wife of King Kamehameha IV. The Queen herself planted the deep purple bougainvillea during the 1870s that is still to be seen along the cliff walls. In 1937 the Allerton family purchased the property, transforming it into a masterpiece of landscape design, with extensive pathways amid beautiful sculptures, pools, fountains, and flowers. Now the National Tropical Botanical Garden conducts guided tours of the estate among acres of exotic and lavish tropical plantings. Bring bug spray and a bottle or two of water for the two-and-a-half-hour tour. *3530 Papalina Road, Kalaheo. Tours run Tuesday–Saturday. Advanced reservations required:* ***808-332-7324.*** *www.ntbg.org/gardens.*

Fern Grotto Wailua; East Coast

This natural amphitheater is formed of solid lava and covered with (you guessed it) large tropical ferns. To get here you catch one of several boat tours in Wailua Harbor. On the way up the river you'll be serenaded by Hawaiian musicians playing traditional songs. You'll also hear a history of the area (lands along the river were the sacred capital of ancient Kaua'i), and you'll probably be treated to a hula demonstration, whether you want one or not. The scenic ride up to the grotto takes about 45 minutes and will set you back about $15 to $20 per person. *Take Route 56 north from Lihu'e toward Wailua. You'll find cruises and boat rentals on the south side of the Wailua River, just before the highway bridge.*

Although worthwhile, seeing Fern Grotto demands a significant commitment of time (allow at least two hours) and usually involves hoards of other tourists, so you may want to plan this diversion for a day of its own if you're driving all the way to the north coast from Lihu'e or points south and west.

Ha'ena State Park Hanalei; North Coast

This north coast gem is the site of several "wet caves" filled with dank, cold water, as well as gorgeous **Ke'e Beach,** literally the end of the road in Kaua'i. Ke'e Beach is more than merely a beautiful reef-protected strand that faces west into the vast Pacific (an awesome place for sunsets). It's also the beginning of the famed **Na Pali Coast,** the only roadless portion of Kaua'i coastline, where 4,000-foot mountains rise dramatically from the crashing sea. Here at Ke'e you'll probably see native Hawaiian monk seals sunning themselves, as well as the occasional sea turtle. *No admission fee. Open 24 hours. 808-274-3444.*

Hanalei Valley Lookout Princeville; North Coast

Here you can drink in a view of jagged emerald-green mountainsides and flooded fields of taro (the plant from which the Hawaiian staple, poi, is made), making the scene look like a postcard from somewhere in Southeast Asia. This marks the beginning of a region that is quite unlike any other in Hawaii, and is more or less Kaua'i as it has always been. *Located where Route 56 turns into Route 560, across the highway from the Princeville Shopping Center.*

Hanapepe South Coast

If you're touring anywhere along the south coast, you should stop for at least a few minutes in this atmospheric town, which you may recognize from the movie *The Thorn Birds.* In 1992 Hurricane Iniki devastated this place, but it has been mostly rebuilt in its original style since, with lots of interesting shops, galleries, and small restaurants housed in funky storefronts. Also check out the picturesque swinging footbridge over the Hanapepe River. *Located on Route 50 at mile marker 17.*

Kapa'a East Coast

This nineteenth-century plantation town was devastated by Hurricane Iniki in 1992, but has been reconstructed to retain its historic and funky feel. This is a good place to stop for lunch at one of the many eateries that cater to surfers and other assorted hipsters. It's also loaded with interesting shops and galleries. *Located on Route 56 about 8 miles north of Lihu'e.*

Kaua'i Children's Discovery Museum Kapa'a; East Coast

Loaded with hands-on exhibits about island history and life on the sea, kids—and their parents—could spend several hours here learning about the island ways of life. As the museum organizers like to say, here you can touch, see, feel, and learn. *4-831 Kuhio Highway in Kapa'a, under the whale tower at the Kaua'i Village (Safeway) Shopping Center. Open Tuesday–Saturday 10 A.M.–5 P.M. Members and children under 1 get in for free, children 1 to 17 yrs. $4, adults $5.* ***808-823-8222.*** *www.kcdm.org.*

Kaua'i Museum Lihu'e; East Coast

This local history and art museum for Kaua'i and the nearby Ni'ihau is a good place to begin your visit on The Garden Isle, especially so if those famous Kaua'i rains are putting a damper on your beach plans. Here you'll enjoy the permanent exhibition of ancient Hawaiian artifacts such as calabashes, poi pounders, pohaku, and tapa. Heck, the gift shop alone is worth a visit, with a fine collection of rare Ni'ihau shell lei (made only by denizens of that island), hand-turned wooden bowls, reference books, and other locally produced arts, crafts, and gifts. The museum also holds community-wide celebrations such as the May Day Lei Day, and the Christmas Craft Fair. *4428 Rice Street, Lihu'e. Open Monday–Friday 9 A.M.–4 P.M., Saturday 10 A.M.–4 P.M. Admission: around $7.* ***808-245-6931.*** *www.kauaimuseum.org.*

Kilauea Point National Wildlife Refuge Kilauea (North Coast)

This dramatic, 203-acre promontory is the northernmost spot on Kaua'i and a place where you'll enjoy breathtaking views of the ocean. From the end of this narrow peninsula, next to the quaint 1913 lighthouse, you'll also be able to observe the largest colony of seabirds in the main Hawaiian Islands, including Laysan albatrosses, red-footed boobies, wedge-tailed shearwaters, great frigate birds (boasting 7-foot wingspans), and Hawaii's state bird, the nene. (Just watch where you step!) Offshore you may spot sea turtles, dolphins, and, between November and April, humpback whales. *Open 7 days a week from 10 A.M.–4 P.M. Admission is about $3 for adults. Take Route 56 north from Lihu'e for about 40 minutes at turn right on Kilauea Road just after mile marker 23. Follow that to the end.* ***808-828-1413.***

Kilohana Plantation Lihu'e

You could spend the day and have a nice dinner to boot at this sprawling 35-acre sugar plantation that dates back to the turn of the last century—the days of high society and royalty on Kaua'i. Amid the rolling tropical gardens is a restored 16,000-square-foot, Tudor-style 1935 manor house, packed with specialty shops, art galleries, and one of the better restaurants on Kaua'i: Gaylord's. You can tour the grounds for free, take rides on a horse-drawn carriage or even a sugarcane wagon pulled by Clydesdales, pause for high tea in the manor house, get a fine dinner, and even take in an evening lu'au on Tuesdays and Thursdays. Here you can imagine plantation life as it was back in the day, reveling in its bygone luxury among the T-shirted fellow tourists around you. *3-2087 Kaumualii Highway, Lihu'e. Open Monday–Saturday 9:30 A.M.–9:30 P.M. and Sunday 9:30 A.M.–5 P.M.* ***808-245-5608.*** *www.kilohanakauai.com.*

Koke'e State Park West Kauai

This is Kaua'i's high country, a sprawling 4,345 acres sitting at an elevation of between 3,000 and 4,000 feet, and adjacent to dramatic **Waimea Canyon** and the **Alakai Swamp,** perched at over 3,000 feet, with acres of scrub native rainforest and shallow bogs. Koke'e is a hiker's paradise, with trails for nearly every level of ambition and stamina. At the end of the park road, a couple of miles past the Koke'e Lodge, **Kalalau Point** gives you a spectacular panoramic view of the Kalalau Valley along the rugged **Na Pali Coast.** The **Pu'u o Kila Lookout** a little further on also provides awesome views but with fewer people. Full facilities. *Take Route 50 west from Hanapepe toward Waimea. Turn right just after mile marker 23 and proceed up on Waimea Canyon Road. No admission fee. Call* ***808-335-6061*** *for lodging information;* ***808-274-3444*** *for information on camping.*

Koke'e State Park can be cool and rainy on almost any day, with the weather most likely to cloud up in the afternoons. Call ***808-245-6001*** for weather conditions before you leave.

Limahuli Gardens Kalaheo; North Shore

This North Shore sister of the superb Allerton Gardens offers 17 acres of verdant tropical greenery covering three ecological zones. In 1997, Limahuli Garden was selected by the American Horticultural Society as the best natural botanical garden in the United States—and no wonder, with its hundreds of native Hawaiian plant species, a fascinating naturalist program, and an incredible backdrop of lush tropical peaks. *3530 Papalina Road, Kalaheo. Open Tuesday–Friday, and Sunday 9:30 A.M.–4 P.M. $25 per person for guided tour. $15 per person for self-guided tour. Guided tours last about two and a half hours by reservation.* ***808-826-1053.*** *www.ntbg.org/gardens.*

Maninholo Dry Cave Hanalei; North Coast

Located beside the road on Route 560 in **Ha'ena State Park** west of **Hanalei,** this is just one of three large sea caves that local legend says was dug by the goddess Pele for a home. You can walk into the cave a couple of hundred feet if you dare, but it's dark and drippy.

Menehune Fishpond Lihu'e

This ancient Hawaiian fish pond, 1,000 to 1,600 years old and about a half-mile inland from **Nawiliwili Harbor** near Lihu'e, was supposedly built one stone at a time by—legend has it—hundreds (maybe thousands) of very small Hawaiian people called the Menehune. However, they might not have actually been that small, as the Tahitian word *manahune* actually means "commoner," or small in social standing. Nevertheless, it was an impressive accomplishment. The pond was used by the ancients to raise fish for eating, and still has a pretty diverse population of local inhabitants with gills. *Follow Route 50 to just past mile marker 2 across the street from Kauai Community College. Turn right on Puhi Road, and then left on Hulemalu Road.*

Na Pali Coast Northwest Kaua'i

Kaua'i's spectacular Na Pali Coast on the remote northwest side of the island can honestly be called one of the most famous and dramatic sights in the world, with emerald green mountains dropping thousands of feet into the blue Pacific. (In Hawaiian, *na pali* means "the cliffs.") This is the Hawaii of postcards and television travelogues. However, there are no roads on this rugged 15-mile stretch of coastline—only a spectacularly scenic but rugged trail. If you're not up for hiking, you can still enjoy the Na Pali experience by boat or helicopter leaving from North and South Shore locales.

Opaeka'a Falls Lookout Wailua; East Coast

Opaeka'a Falls is hundreds of feet high and is named after the thousands of shrimp that used to frolic at its base. Although the falls itself is not accessible by river or trail, you can check it out from the Opaeka'a Falls Lookout. If you get there by midmorning, the sun will be at your back and in the best position for photographing this memorable scene. *Take Route 56 north from Lihu'e to mile marker 6, turning left on Kuamo'o Road.*

If you look closely along the road to Opaeka'a Falls lookout, you may see several ancient heiaus (sacred shrines), including Poliahu Heiau, named for the snow goddess who was said to have lived on The Big Island's Mauna Kea volcano.

Check out this dramatically situated natural pool located on a lava bench beside the ocean near Princeville. The state has closed Queen's Bath to bathers during the winter, and even in the summer some pretty powerful waves come in at times, so be careful. At Princeville turn right off Route 56 onto Ka Haku Road. Turn right again on Punahele Road and again on Kapiolani Road. Park at the end of Kapiolani and follow the dirt trail for about 25 yards. At the end of the trail turn left and walk about 300 yards to the Bath.

Princeville North Coast

This upscale, planned community is surprising for the laid-back North Shore, but it's a nice place. Named after Prince Albert, the son of King Kamehameha IV and Queen Emma, who died in 1862 at the age of four, Princeville is known for its dramatic ocean bluff, low-rise condominiums, manicured golf courses, and views of the rugged "Bali Hai" mountains to the south and west. If you're not already staying here, it's worth a drive through, and perhaps a stop for refreshments at the **Princeville Hotel** or the **Happy Talk Lounge** at the **Hanalei Bay Resort**—both of which overlook lovely **Hanalei Bay** and the mountains beyond.

Russian Fort Elizabeth State Historical Park Waimea; South Coast

Located on the eastern bank of the **Waimea River** where it flows into the sea, this 17-acre park holds the remains of a Hawaiian-design Russian fort that was central to a bit of local history.

In 1815, Dr. Georg Scheffer tried to claim Kaua'i for Russia, even building this fort with the support of Kauai's King Kaumualii. The problem was that he didn't have the support of Russia itself, and ultimately, he was expelled by King Kamehameha after he took over Kaua'i, uniting all of Hawaii. Only the remains of the fort are left, but you can take a self-guided tour around the grounds. Open daily dawn to dusk. *Located on Route 50 near mile marker 22 east of Waimea.*

Sleeping Giant Kapa'a; East Coast

You'll see this long, rounded mountain ridge rising up from the coastline north of Kapa'a. Legend has it that this was an overgrown warrior who ate constantly and was tricked by villagers into consuming a great number of rocks hidden in a mixture of fish and poi (the starchy Hawaiian mash made of taro plants). The giant ate so much that he fell into a deep sleep and has yet to wake up. *Off Route 56 north of Kapa'a.*

Spouting Horn is Kaui's own "Old Faithful."

(Photo courtesy of HCVB/Ron Dahlquist)

Spouting Horn Koloa; South Coast

Children of all ages will love this Hawaiian version of Old Faithful—a hole in a seaside lava shelf that spurts saltwater 50 feet into the air when one of those rolling South Shore waves rushes underneath the rocks. It's especially impressive around sunset, when the spray creates a psychedelic rainbow effect. *Turn toward the ocean on Koloa Road (Route 530) just past mile marker 11 on Route 50. Continue to Po'ipu Road and turn right again, then again at the fork onto Lawa'i Road. Spouting Horn is about one mile down the road on the left.*

Wailua Falls Wailua; East Coast

This is one of the most beautiful cascades in all of Hawaii, and clearly recognizable from the opening sequences of the old *Fantasy Island* television series. Spend a few minutes here (you can even scramble to the base of the falls if you dare, though the trail is muddy and dangerous). Here you can contemplate not only the greenish quality of light surrounding you, and the rainbow effect generated by the fine tropic mist, but also how ancient Hawaiians used to dive from the top of the falls to prove their mettle. *From Lihu'e, find your way to Route 56 (the Kuhio Highway, Lihu'e's "main drag"), and head north. A mile or so from downtown, at the village of Kapai, take a left on Route 583, also known as Ma'alo Road. Follow this for four miles to the falls.*

Wai'oli Hui'ia Mission and Church Hanalei; North Coast

This graceful, green and white building, set amid swaying coconut palms, is one of the most photographed and painted buildings in all of Hawaii. Sunday services here are known for their Hawaiian hymns.

Kaua'i's first non-Polynesian settlers were missionaries Reverend William Anderson and his wife, Mary Ann, who came all the way from Kentucky. They built the **Wai'oli Mission House** in 1837 using coral limestone blocks, and added the **Waioli Church** in 1841 after their congregation grew. Five years after the Andersons arrived, they were joined by missionaries Abner and Lucy Wilcox and their family. Restored in 1921, the house is now listed on the National Register of Historic Places and is one of the finest examples in Hawaii of how builders of the day combined New England architecture with designs used in Hawaiian thatched buildings. A large part of Abner Wilcox's library can still be seen in his study. *Open most days, with tours on Mondays, Wednesdays, and Thursdays from 10 A.M.–1 P.M. Admission: free!* ***808-245-3202.***

Waimea Canyon: "The Grand Canyon of the Pacific" West Kauai

This dramatic "Grand Canyon of the Pacific" is a surprising gash in a broad plateau; the edges of the canyon stand about 3,000 to 4,000 feet above the sea.

Waimea is on a smaller scale than the better-known canyon in Arizona, but it has some beautiful buttes, ruddy red rocks, and precipitous drop-offs. The canyon is as much as 3,567 feet deep, a mile wide, and 12 miles long.

Unlike the mostly dry upper reaches of the real Grand Canyon, there's a lot of water at Waimea with large waterfalls cascading off some of the buttes. You can make it to the rim of the canyon from the town of Waimea, or from Kekaha. The best places to view the Canyon are the **Waimea Canyon Lookout** between mile markers 10 and 11 on Waimea Canyon Road, or the **Puu Hina Hina Lookout** between mile markers 13 and 14. Note that Waimea Canyon State Park is directly adjacent to **Koke'e State Park,** where you can enjoy even miles of great hikes, as well as unique, upcountry flora and fauna.

There are no gas stations located along the Waimea Canyon Road, nor are there any in the town of Kekaha, the alternate western gateway to the park. Therefore, it's best to fill up in Waimea before starting the trip, unless you're planning on coasting down the 12 miles back from the Canyon (not recommended!). However, there is a **Lappert's Ice Cream** shop at the beginning of the Canyon road in Kekaha, a worthy way to provision for the trip up into the canyon or to reward yourself on your way out … or both.

Kaua'i's Top Beaches

Kaua'i offers more beach per mile of coastline than any of the other Hawaiian islands. All of these strands face sparkling turquoise-blue waters, and many of them are backed by dramatic mountain vistas.

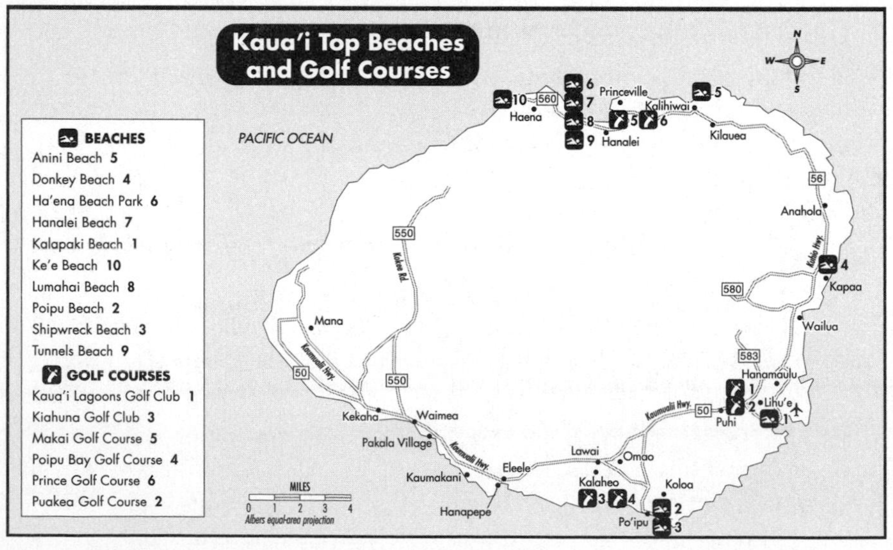

Kauai's top beaches.

Generally, the beaches along the South Shore are the safest for swimming and bodysurfing, with large waves appearing occasionally in the summer. Unless protected by a reef, many of the North Shore beaches have dangerously rough surf, especially in the winter. The beaches on the Eastern Shore tend to be windy, often with chaotic waters and strong rip currents.

Some beaches have facilities such as picnic tables, restrooms, and showers, but many don't. None have information phones, though you can get daily beach reports by calling the Kaua'i Division of Parks and Recreation at **808-241-6660,** or going to www.Kauaiexplorer.com.

Here are a few of our favorite beaches on Kaua'i.

North Shore

Anini: *Follow Route 56 past Kiauea. Cross over the Kalihiwai Bridge and then take a right on another road named "Kalihiwai" (go figure). Then turn left on Anini Road.*

Ha'ena Beach Park: *Route 560 between mileposts 8 and 9 west of Hanalei.*

Hanalei: *Just off Aku Road in Hanalei.*

Lumahai: *Take the path leading from the road between mileposts 4 and 5 west of Hanalei on Route 560.*

Ke'e (North Shore): *Restrooms, changing rooms, and showers. Located at the end of Route 560 west of Hanalei.*

Tunnels (North Shore): *No facilities. At the end of the dirt road at milepost 8 on Route 560 west of Hanalei.*

East Shore

Donkey: *No lifeguards or facilities. Look for a turnoff and parking area at milepost 11 north of Kapa'a on Route 56.*

Kalapaki: *Full facilities, as well as surf lessons, catamaran cruises, beach volleyball, and sailboat rentals. Turn right off Route 56 onto Rice Road at mile marker 0. Access to the beach is from the Anchor Cove Shopping Center or through the Kaua'i Marriott Resort.*

South Shore

Poipu: *Full facilities. On Po'ipu Road.*

Shipwreck: *No facilities, but excellent for hiking nearby. At milepost 11 on Route 50 turn right on Koloa Road (Route 530). Continue to Po'ipu Road and turn right again. The road forks near the ocean; take the left fork. Access is via the public access walkway between the Hyatt and Po'ipu Bay Resort Golf Course.*

Great Dining with Atmosphere: The Best Places to Eat

Ah yes! The only thing on Kaua'i that can possibly compete with the sublime scenery and laid-back ambience is the food, which is both varied and darn good. Here you'll find no shortages of great places to eat in every price range, with choices ranging from sophisticated Pacific Rim cuisine and gourmet vegetarian fare, to tropical tacos and burritos, Hawaiian hamburgers, traditional saimin (noodles with meat or eggs) and *laulau* (morsels of fish or pork wrapped in a taro leaf), and fresh-fruit smoothies and shave ice stands found along the side of the road … and sometimes down jungle paths.

It's not necessary to "dress up" for restaurants in Hawaii, where a casual, laid-back lifestyle reigns. An Aloha shirt and slacks are usually sufficient for even the top-end establishments.

North Shore

The Bali Hai Restaurant Princeville *Pacific Rim* $$$$$

This open-air restaurant in the Hanalei Bay Resort scores big in terms of atmosphere. It's a bit pricey, but worth the splurge, boasting an awesome, sunset-facing view of Hanalei Bay and the Bali Hai mountains, along with savory creative Pacific Rim cuisine. *Located at the Hanalei Bay Resort, 5380 Honoiki Road. (Enter Princeville at the main gate, take the third left onto Liholiho Road, then turn right onto Hono'iki Road.) Reservations recommended: Open daily. Breakfast 7 A.M.–11 A.M., lunch 11:30 A.M.–2 P.M., dinner 5:30 P.M.–9:30 P.M. Children's menu.* ***1-800-826-6522.***

Hanalei Gourmet Hanalei *American* $$$

This friendly, hip room in downtown Hanalei features everything from burgers to delicious fresh fish, with the daily specials written on a large blackboard next to the bar. At night you'll enjoy live music and perhaps be treated to a spontaneous hula demonstration by the musicians—a treat that is worlds apart from the pre-packaged fare that one sees at the typical touristy lu'au. *Located in the Old School Building at Hanalei Center, 5-5161 Kuhio Highway. Open daily from 8 A.M.–10 P.M.* ***808-826-2524.*** *www.hanaleigourmet.net.*

Tropical Taco Hanalei *Mexican*

Serving tasty fresh tacos and burritos out of his truck for many years, Roger Kennedy became something of a Hanalei institution. Now he's moved his operation to a little sit-down place in the heart of town, where you can dine on fresh fish, meat, or veggie burritos—either inside or on the porch. A great place for lunch. *Located in the Halele'a Building on Kuhio Highway. Open daily.* ***808-827-8226.*** *www.tropicaltaco.com.*

Starvin' Marvin's Kilauea Deli Kilauea *American* 

Whether you're visiting the nearby Kilauea Lighthouse or going to the beach, this is a great place to pick up a special picnic lunch, though there is a dining room here. Offerings include oversize sandwiches, fresh grilled fish, curried chicken and basil, grilled veggie and gorgonzola quiches, salads, and desserts, as well as breakfasts featuring macadamia nut pancakes and Hawaiian-style Eggs Benedict. *2430 Oka Street. Open Monday through Friday 7:30 A.M.–6 P.M., Saturday 7:30 A.M.–3 P.M.* ***808-828-0726.***

Lihu'e and the Coconut Coast

Blossoming Lotus Kapa'a *Gourmet Vegetarian* 

This elegant restaurant features a superb "world fusion" gourmet vegan menu, served amid beautiful artwork in a soothing atmosphere. A fine wine list and juice bar complements such offerings such as the Moroccan spiced and seared tofu with gingered adzuki bean couscous, and oyster mushrooms with sautéed greens, with live local music most nights. 4504 Kukui Street. *Open daily with lunch from 11 a.m.–3 p.m. and dinner 5:30 p.m.–9 p.m. Sunday champagne brunch from 11 a.m.–3 p.m.* ***808-822-7678.*** *www.blossominglotus.com.*

Café Coco Kapa'a *Eclectic* 

One of our favorites, this place is located in a restored plantation-era cottage, with additional outdoor seating amid tropical foliage. It's both romantic and unpretentious, with fresh, delicious food. The crepes with wild rice and portobello mushrooms are so good that they should be illegal, as is the Moroccan spiced seared ahi, served with a curried vegetable samosa and banana chutney. *4-369 Kuhio Highway. Open for lunch Tuesday–Friday from 11 A.M.–5 P.M., and dinner Tuesday–Sunday from 5 P.M.–9 P.M. Closed Monday.* ***808-822-7990.***

Eggbert's Kapa'a *American* $$

Steaks, stir-fries, fresh fish, burgers, and Hawaiian specialties make this a fun and satisfying place for lunch, but the breakfast offerings are especially notable. You can design your own omelets from an incredible array of ingredients, or enjoy the famous banana pancakes or many other delectable items! *4-484 Kuhio Highway, Coconut Marketplace. Open daily 7 A.M.–3 P.M.* ***808-822-3787.***

Gaylord's at Kilohana Lihu'e *American* $$$

Located on a 1,700-acre former sugar plantation, Gaylord's is a trip back to a grander age of high society. The main dining room extends in a horseshoe shape around lush gardens and overlooks the mountains beyond. Gaylord's features venison, lamb, seafood, pastas, and desserts, as well as some Hawaiian-accented dishes, and a great breakfast buffet. Fresh herbs and vegetables grown in the Kilohana gardens enhance all dishes. *3-2087 Kaumualii Highway. Open daily at 7:45 A.M. for breakfast, 11 A.M. for lunch, and 5:30 P.M. for dinner.* ***808-245-9593.***

Hamura'a Saimin Stand Lihu'e *Hawaiian* $$$

This classic Kaua'i institution is more than just a good, inexpensive restaurant where you can get real Hawaiian food. It's a cultural experience. Try the saimin, delicious noodle soup with garnishes, and the barbecue sticks. *2956 Kress St. Open Monday–Thursday 10 A.M.–8 P.M., Friday and Saturday 10 A.M.–midnight, and Sunday 10 A.M.–9 P.M. Credit cards not accepted.* ***808-245-3271.***

Tip Top Motel Café & Bakery Lihu'e *American/Hawaiian* $$

This little family-style place in downtown Lihu'e ain't fancy, but it offers excellent breakfasts and baked goods with an authentic Hawaiian flair, as well as decent island lunch food, including good sushi! *3173 Akahi Street. Open daily 6:30 A.M.–2 P.M.* ***808-245-2333.***

Po'ipu

The Beach House Po'ipu *Pacific Rim* $$$$$

Creative and delicious food, fresh local ingredients, and awesome sunset views by the ocean are hallmarks of this Po'ipu establishment, a longtime "Best Kaua'i Restaurant" selection by *Honolulu Magazine.* Try the mahi-mahi lightly crusted with macadamia nuts, or the shiitake-crusted mussels in black bean sauce with ginger lime beurre blanc. Yeah, baby! *5022 Lawai Road, Koloa (Po'ipo area). Open daily; for cocktails and pupus 5 P.M.–10 P.M., dinner 5:30 P.M.–10 P.M. from about October 1–March 31, and 6 P.M.–10 P.M. from about April 1–September 30. Reservations recommended.* ***808-742-1424.*** *www.the-beach-house.com.*

Brennecke's Beach Broiler Po'ipu *American/Seafood* $$

A bit of a local landmark, this seafood and burger place ain't fancy, but it is situated right across the road from Po'ipu Beach Park. That means you can gaze at the body surfers and the deep blue horizon while dining on decent food, including excellent hamburgers, fresh fish sandwiches, and a good salad bar. Look for the early dinner specials each day. *2100 Hoone Road. Open daily 11 A.M.–10 P.M. with a deli open at 8 A.M. for made-to-order beach picnics.* ***808-742-7588.*** *www.brenneckes.com.*

Roy's Po'ipu Bar & Grill Po'ipu *Pacific Rim* $$$

No visit to Kaua'i would be complete without a stop at this lively and crowded place owned by Hawaii's most successful celebrity chef, Roy Yamaguchi. Savory Euro-Pacific fusion cuisine, fresh local ingredients, a good wine list, highly efficient service, and surprisingly reasonable prices will leave you smiling and sated, assuming you don't let the shopping center location dissuade you! *2360 Kiahuna Plantation Drive, Shopping Village, Koloa (Po'ipu area). Open daily beginning at 5:30 P.M.* ***808-742-5000.*** *www.roysrestaurant.com.*

West Kaua'i

Waimea Brewing Company Waimea *Hawaiian* $$$

Stop here *after* you visit Waimea Canyon. Otherwise, you may want to spend the entire afternoon in this breezy and beautiful coconut grove sampling WBC's awesomely delectable fare and selection of microbrews. The Mango Stout barbeque ribs will grab your attention, as will the coconut prawns and orange-glazed mahi-mahi or the Portuguese black bean soup. Daily specials and great sandwiches add to the allure. *9400 Kaumualii Highway (on the Waimea Plantation Cottages property). Open Sunday–Thursday 11 A.M.–9 P.M., Friday–Saturday 11 A.M.–11 P.M. Reservations recommended.* ***808-338-9733.*** *www.waimeabrewing.com.*

Hanapepe Café & Expresso Bar Hanapepe *Vegetarian* $$$

Groove to the Hawaiian slack-key guitar on the sound system while enjoying excellent vegetarian fare in the laid-back ambience of this small café in a bookstore. Try the veggie Caesar salad along with some fresh warm foccaccia bread, or perhaps one of the renowned garden burgers available here. Breakfasts are also great. *3830 Hanapepe Road. Open Tuesday–Saturday 9 A.M.–2 P.M. Coffee and dessert until 3 P.M. and Friday 6 P.M.–9 P.M.* ***808-335-5011.***

Wrangler's Steak House Waimea *American* 

Okay, enough of the exotic food. The kids are whining for something more "normal," and you're seeking a reasonably priced, quality place to take the family. Wrangler's fits the bill, featuring large cuts of beef served in a cowboy museum atmosphere. The secret here is that you can sit on the veranda and also still satisfy your craving for Hawaiian fare, including grilled ahi. *9852 Kaumualii Highway (Route 50). Open daily.* ***808-338-1218.***

Entertainment and Nightlife

Don't let anybody tell you that there's not much nightlife on sleepy, rural Kaua'i. Sure, it's slightly quieter than Waikiki, but what it lacks in shear entertainment volume it makes up for in real Hawaiian quality and spirit.

To find out about top-shelf concerts by internationally recognized performers, contact the Kaua'i Concert Association (**808-245-SING**), which produces many of the top performing arts events on the island, ranging from jazz master Chick Corea and Odetta to the Aspen Santa Fe Ballet.

Another way to find out who or what is playing where is to pick up a copy of the local newspaper, the ***Garden Island Times*** (www.Kauaiworld.com/calendar) or free publications such as ***Kaua'i Gold, This Week on Kaua'i,*** and ***Kaua'i Beach Press.*** You can also listen to local public radio station KKCR, found at 90.9 and 91.9 on the FM dial.

Live Music

Quiet little Kaua'i actually happens to be a hotbed of live music, usually performed by talented local musicians at restaurants and lounges.

One of the best places to catch good home-grown music on the north coast is at **Hanalei Gourmet,** located in the Old School Building at Hanalei Center, 5-5161 Kuhio Highway, Hanalei (**808-826-2524**). Just down the road is the **Happy Talk Lounge** in the Hanalei Bay Resort (5380 Honoiki Road, Princeville; **808-826-6522**), one of those places where you might hear "Puff ...", but overall fine local musicians perform both contemporary Hawaiian music and "blast from the past" hits.

In Lihu'e, a fine place to go for live Hawaiian music every night of the week is **Duke's Canoe Club** in the Kaua'i Marriott Resort & Beach Club at 3610 Rice St. (**808-246-9599**), where the broad selection of tropical drinks and great bay view make the music sound even sweeter.

On the east coast, you can enjoy tasteful live performances each night of the week at **Blossoming Lotus** in downtown Kapa'a at 4504 Kukui Street, just off the Kuhio Highway, Route 56 (**808-822-7678**).

Along the South Shore, drop in on the open-air **Keoki's Paradise,** 2360 Kiahuna Plantation Drive in the Po'ipu Shopping Village, Koloa (**808-742-7534**), where atmospheric tiki torches and tropical vegetation augment live bands playing great contemporary Hawaiian music.

DJs and Dancing

If you've had enough of sensitive songwriters, or maybe just want to shake your bootie and get down with your own bad self after a day on the beach, well ... you can do that, too. There are a few places in Kaua'i where you can gyrate to some good tunes. One of the better joints is **Gilligan's Disco,** 4331 Kaua'i Beach Dr., Lihu'e, located at the **Outrigger Kaua'i Beach Hotel; 808-245-1955,** with country line dancing, Latino, tunes from the '70s and '80s tunes, and even some karaoke. Another good bet is **Rob's Good Time Grill, Rice Shopping Center,** Lihu'e; **808-246-0311,** which has a decent bar, theme nights, and a DJ every evening playing hip hop and the latest danceable pop hits.

Theater and Performing Arts

Entertainment can get a little more highbrow as well. The 560-seat theater at the **Kaua'i Community College Performing Arts Center,** located at 3-1901 Kaumuali'i Highway (Route 50), west of downtown Lihu'e (**808-245 8270**), may be the island's foremost venue for performers from all over the country, as well as an annual music scholarship competition.

If you're in western Kaua'i, you can check the listings for the 200-seat **Waimea Theatre** in Waimea (**808-338-0282**), which offers movies and live performances.

However, the best way to find out about quality live theater in Kaua'i is to contact one of the local theater groups, for example the Lihu'e-based **Kaua'i Community Players (808-245-7700;** www.Kauaicommunityplayers.org), has been presenting between one and three dramatic offerings and Broadway musicals each year since 1978. **The Kaua'i Dance Theatre** (**808-332-9737**) offers dance classes for children through adults, staging two performances each year during the summer and holiday season; and the **Garden Island Arts Council** (**808-245-2733;** www.gardenislandarts.org), which sponsors and produces a wide variety of performing arts events, art exhibitions, workshops, and more.

The Best Lu'aus

Unfortunately, this traditional feast with Polynesian-style entertainment has become very commercial in most places—it's big business, and many lu'aus have become more like Las Vegas floor shows than traditional Hawaiian entertainment. Still, there is a qualitative difference in lu'aus, so here are a few of the best you'll find on Kaua'i. These generally last three or four hours, and charge $50–$75 for adults, half-price for children. All feature an all-you-can-eat Hawaiian feast, an open bar, and lavish entertainment.

Gaylord's at Kilohana Lihu'e

Held on the picturesque Kilohana estate, this lu'au may not be the most authentic on the island, but gets high marks for pure entertainment value. *3-2087 Kaumualii Highway (Route 50). Tuesday–Thursday, 6:15 P.M.–9 P.M.* ***808-245-9595.***

Smith's Tropical Paradise Kapa'a

This is one of the best commercial lu'aus on the island, set amidst 30 acres of tropical flora and fauna. *174 Wailua Road. June–August the lu'au is held Monday–Friday (check-in 5 P.M.). September–May on Monday, Wednesday, and Friday (check-in 4:45 P.M.).* ***808-821-6895.***

Kaua'i Coconut Beach Resort Kapa'a

This is one of the more authentic lu'aus on Kaua'i, located in a beautiful, custom-designed outdoor pavilion amid a coconut grove. 4-484 Kuhio Highway (Route 56). *Tuesday–Sunday, 5:30 P.M.–8:30 P.M.* ***808-822-3455.***

Princeville Resort Princeville

Hanalei Bay and the Bali Hai mountains provide a spectacular backdrop to this somewhat lavish lu'au. This is one of the more pricey lu'aus, at $99 per adult, and the bar drinks are free only until 7:30 P.M. *5520 Ka Haku Road. Thursdays at 6 P.M. (open at 5:30 P.M.).* ***808-826-9644.***

AUTHENTIC KAUA'I: FINDING A REAL LU'AU

If you're up for a true Hawaiian experience that can be more rewarding than any pre-packaged lu'au staged by a hotel or other commercial outfit, check the local radio stations and newspapers—such as KKCR—90.9 and 91.9 on the FM dial and the ***Garden Island Times*** (www.Kauaiworld.com/calendar)—for community fundraisers. At these local events you'll be partying with real island residents rather than hundreds of other tourists, and the food and entertainment will reflect the authentic Hawaiian culture of today.

Shopping on Kaua'i

If it weren't for all of that great scenery, you could spend an endless amount of time shopping in Kaua'i. The towns of **Kapa'a** and **Hanapepe** are especially good places for shopping, as each is loaded with plenty of small funky shops and galleries. If you're looking for more pricey jewelry and gifts, you will find no shortage of the higher-end choices in resorts such as the **Princeville Resort** and the **Kaua'i Marriott Resort & Beach Club,** or among the interesting stores at **Gaylord's at Kilohana,** just outside of Lihu'e. Here's where you can get a few of our favorite things.

Lihu'e and Environs

The Kukai Grove Center at 3-2600 Kaumuali'i Highway in Lihu'e is Kauai's largest shopping center, featuring a wide range of gifts. In fact, the **Kukui Grove Exhibition Hall** mounts superb exhibitions by local artists at least four times a year. However, your time will probably be better spent at **Gaylord's** on the **Kilohana Estate** at 3-2087 Kaumualii Highway outside of Lihu'e (**808-245-5608**), where you'll find a number of interesting shops and high-end art galleries, featuring beautiful jewelry, handcrafted Hawaiian gifts, clothing, artwork, and more—just about everything and anything you might want to bring back from Kaua'i. These stores are located both upstairs and downstairs in the main plantation house.

Kapa'a

This nineteenth-century plantation town has an historic and funky feel, and is loaded with interesting shops, galleries, and restaurants. The **Kinipopo Shopping Village** at 4-356 Kuhio Highway (**808-822-3574**) offers a variety of shops featuring Hawaiian wear, vintage maps, fine art, and jewelry. **The Aloha Gallery** (**808-821-1382**), right on the corner in the center of town, offers some of the best paintings on the island. **The Coconut Marketplace** at 484 Kuhio Highway (**808-822-3641**) features more than 70 shops boasting artwork, antiques, jewelry, craft items, and more.

North Shore

Although shops can be found all over the North Shore, the two centers for the best shopping are the high-end shops of the **Princeville Resort,** and downtown **Hanalei,** where you can find everything from vintage used clothing to handmade jewelry, Oriental rugs, pearl bracelets, and much more.

The town's **Ching Young Village Shopping Center** at 5-5190 Kuhio Highway (**808-826-7222**) is loaded with gift shops and galleries, including the **Artists Gallery of Kaua'i** (**808-826-6441**), which features the work of numerous accomplished island artists.

South Shore

The laid-back Old West–style town of **Hanapepe** boasts numerous stores and galleries—some featuring artisans in the back room making wooden furniture, jewelry, and other authentic Kaua'i gifts. On most Friday nights from 6 P.M.–9 P.M., local artists and local musicians team up to offer a fun and entertaining "open house." **The Beach House** at 5022 Lawai Road in Koloa (**808-742-1424**) is a superb restaurant, but also happens to have a beautiful jewelry gallery. Expensive stuff, but gorgeous.

At **Spouting Horn** a group of outdoor stands and booths sell necklaces, bracelets, watches, and clothing. Feel free to bargain.

Sunshine Markets

Kaua'i's open air and farmers markets (also called sunshine markets) dot the roadsides in various parts of the island Monday through Saturday. These are the best places to get scrumptious fresh produce and handmade crafts at great prices. In addition to the regular markets listed below, you're likely to pass numerous other markets and crafts stands along the highways of Kaua'i. Schedules tend to change, so call **808-241-6390** to confirm times and places.

- **Monday:** Koloa Ball Park, Maluhia Road, noon.
- **Tuesday:** Just west of Hanalei on Route 560 at 2 P.M.; at the Neighborhood Center in Kahaheo (on Papalina Road off Kaumuali'i Highway; Route 50) at 3:30 P.M.
- **Wednesday:** Kapa'a Ball Park behind the armory, near the Kapa'a Bypass Road, 3 P.M.
- **Thursday:** Hanapepe Town Park (behind the fire station), 3:30 P.M.; Kilauea Neighborhood Center Ball Park, off Kilauea Road, 4:30 P.M.
- **Friday:** Vidinha football stadium parking lot, Ho'olako Street in Lihu'e (near the airport), 3 P.M.
- **Saturday:** Christ Memorial Church in Kilauea, 9 A.M.; Kekaha Neighborhood Center, Elepaio Road, at 9 A.M. in Kilauea; Hanalei Community Center, next to Wai'oli Park off Kuhio Highway (Route 560), at 9 A.M.

Enjoying the Very Best Activities on Kaua'i

Kaua'i offers a wide range of activities for every lifestyle. Aside from the many opportunities to frolic in nature's majesty, there is plenty to do in the historical and cultural realm.

Hollywood Movie Locations

Kaua'i has been a favorite movie and television location for years. In fact, all of the films in the *Jurassic Park* series, *South Pacific*, *Blue Hawaii*, the 2005 remake of *King Kong*, *Honeymoon in Vegas*, *George of the Jungle*, the *Fantasy Island* TV series, *Raiders of the Lost Ark*, and many others, had scenes filmed on location here.

Several tour companies can take you by bus or van to a selection of the sites where movies and television shows were made; many show clips of the actual movie scenes play on a television in the vehicle. One of the best tour companies covering these sites is **Hawaii Movie Tours**, 4-885 Kuhio Highway (Route 56) in Kapa'a, **808-822-1192;** www.hawaiimovietour.com), which provides a fun and informative traditional tour of many movie locations. Tours run from 9 A.M. to 2 P.M. daily.

Kaua'i Land Tours, also at 4-885 Kuhio Highway (Route 56), Kapa'a (**1-877-742-7893**) has taken the movie tour concept to new heights—literally, offering not only the standard "coastal" tours of numerous locations (about $112), but also "4 x 4 Off Road Tour" (about $125 for a 6-hour tour) and even a land-air combined tour to some of the more inaccessible sites that includes a helicopter ride (an all-day affair for about $270).

Sightseeing Tours

If you'd prefer to sit back and let others do the planning, driving, flying, or sailing, scores of Kaua'i companies are waiting to take you anywhere you want to go. It's easiest to simply book these tours right at your hotel front desk after you arrive, but in case you like to plan ahead yourself, we'll give you the names of a few of the better and more interesting operators. For example, **Kaua'i Vacation Tours (1-866-897-1637)**, one of the better outfits, offers daily "History and Legends of Kaua'i" land tours (about $95), as well as a huge range of helicopter and air tours, horseback riding, kayak, sailing and scuba/snorkeling tours, ATV off-road excursions, and dinner and sunset cruises.

South Shore Tour and Taxi (808-742-1525), a local Kauai outfit based in the Po'ipu Beach area, offers a great way to see the real Kaua'i from an islander's perspective, with cars and vans driven by local experts who will take you just about anywhere you want to go.

Aloha Kaua'i Tours (1-800-452-1113) specializes in snorkeling in and around the island's reefs, including opportunities to snorkel with sea turtles, which will set you back $80 or so.

Enjoying Outdoor Kaua'i

People go to Hawaii to be outdoors—but that concept is taken to the max in Kaua'i, where most of the island is still in a wild state. Even the relatively built-up areas along the coastline have benefited from development coming only recently, with a commitment to preserving beauty firmly in place. Whether your thing is golf, windsurfing, hiking, sailing, whale-watching, or anything in between, you'll be pleased with what Kaua'i has to offer.

The Best Golf Courses

Kaua'i's lush vegetation and spectacular views have made it a natural locale for great golf. Fortunately, some of the sport's top designers have risen to the occasion, teaming up with resorts and other sources of funding to create a number of world-class courses. Here are the best on the island.

Kaua'i Lagoons Golf Club, Kiele Course, Lihu'e. This Jack Nicklaus course has been awarded a gold medal by *Golf Magazine*, and no wonder: it boasts a challenging layout as well as awesome views of the ocean. *Kaua'i Marriott, 3610 Rice St., Kalapaki Beach. Greens fees start at about $100.* ***808-245-5050.***

Kiahuna Golf Club, Po'ipu area. This South Shore course, designed by Robert Trent Jones Jr., incorporates the ancient remnants of an authentic Hawaiian village into its design, and is surrounded by lush, natural beauty. *2545 Kiahuna Plantation Drive. Rates start at $75 after 2 P.M.* ***808-742-9595.***

Makai Golf Course, Princeville Resort. This 27-hole North Shore course, designed by Robert Trent Jones Jr., is composed of three nines: Ocean, Lakes, and Woods. *5520 Ka Haku Road. Greens fees begin at $47 after 4 P.M.* ***808-826-3580.***

Po'ipu Bay Golf Course, *Koloa. This* 18-hole award-winner on the South Shore property of the Grand Hyatt Kaua'i Resort is another Robert Trent Jones Jr. creation, and is nestled between the Po'ipu coast and lush mountains. *1571 Po'ipu Road. Rates begin at $185.* ***1-800-858-6300.*** *www.poipubaygolf.com.*

Prince Golf Course, Princeville Resort. Spanning acres of rolling tableland, this championship course on the North Shore also incorporates tropical jungles and ravines, and is generally considered to be the best golf course in all of Hawaii. If your game is halfway decent, you owe it to yourself to splurge on this one. *5520 Ka Haku Road. Greens fees begin at $85 after 3:30 P.M.* ***1-800-826-5000.***

Puakea Golf Course, *Lihu'e.* This spectacular 18-hole course was designed by Robin Nelson, Hawaii's most prolific golf course architect, around deep ravines and streams, with great mountain views. Nine-hole fees start at about $55. *4150 Nuhou Road.* ***808-245-8756*** *or* ***1-866-773-5554.*** *www.puakeagolf.com.*

Cruising the Na Pali Coast

If you're not up for hiking Kaua'i's rugged Na Pali Coast, you can still bask in the Na Pali experience by boat—sailboat, catamaran, or a specially designed Zodiac—on one of many tours leaving from Port Allen/Hanapepe in the south or Hanalei on the North Shore.

Here are some of the best Na Pali tour outfits:

- **Kaua'i Sea Tours**, 4310 Waialo Road, Eleele (Port Allen/Hanapepe area); Offers catamarans and rigid-hull Zodiacs. Rates start at $129 for half-day tours. **1-800-733-7997** or **808-826-PALI;** www.kauaiseatours.com.
- **Capt. Andy's Sailing Adventures,** Ele'ele (Port Allen/Hanapepe area). A 55-foot catamaran with tasty food and rates beginning at $95 makes this tour a winner, especially if you opt for the sunset cruise. This same company also runs **Capt. Zodiac** raft tours to the Na Pali coast and elsewhere. The five-and-a-half hour "Snorkel Picnic Cruise" will set you back about $130. **1-800-535-0830** or **808-335-6833;** www.napali.com.

- **Na Pali Catamaran,** Hanalei. This is one of the few Na Pali sailing companies allowed to depart from the north coast due to ecological concerns in Hanalei Bay. The friendly crew will bring you from the mouth of the lush Hanalei River in a large authentic outrigger canoe to their 34-foot catamaran in Hanalei Bay; from there you'll cruise down the coast. From March to May you'll get a three-hour whale-watching cruise for about $120; and from May to October a four-hour snorkel tour for about $140. In the winter months, these guys go out only when conditions allow, so call ahead! **808-826-6853** or **1-866-255-6853;** www.napalicatamaran.com.
- **Captain Sundown,** Hanalei. This is another North Coast outfit that runs motor and sailing cruises every day from May through October, including a sunset sail on Mondays, Tuesdays, Thursdays, and Fridays. Fares are about $140 for adults, $120 for kids 7 and under. **808-826-5585;** www.captainsundown.com.

Hiking Kaua'i

Kaua'i is loaded with winding trails traversing the high country and wilderness areas of the interior. Complete trail maps, recommendations, and necessary permits are available at the Hawaii State Park offices at 3060 Eiwa Street in Lihu'e (**1-877-274-3446**).

The most famous hike in Kaua'i is the 11-mile **Kalalau Trail** along the high sea cliffs and five lush valleys of the **Na Pali Coast.** Originally an ancient footpath, the trail was officially designated in the late 1800s, with portions rebuilt in the 1930s. It starts at Ke'e Beach at the end of the road west of Hanalei. The complete hike can be divided into three segments: Ke'e Beach to Hanakapi'ai Valley (two miles), Hanakapi'ai to Hanakoa Valley (four miles) and Hanakoa to Kalalau Valley (five miles). That first segment—Ke'e Beach to Hanakapi'ai is very scenic and can easily be accomplished as a one-day round-trip, provided you're in halfway decent shape.

The other superlative spot for hiking on Kaua'i is at **Waimea Canyon** and the highlands of **Koke'e State Park.** Both offer a multitude of trails of varying difficulty, with local park offices offering trail maps and helpful guides. Note that the plateau here sits at 3,000 to 4,000 feet above sea level, and the weather can often be cool and damp at the higher elevations. Try to start your hike early in the day, as clouds often obscure the dramatic views during the afternoon.

Top hikes in this Waimea Canyon/Koke'e area include:

- **Alakai Swamp Trail:** This gem of 3.5 miles traverses the unique Alakai Swamp at over 3,000 feet, through scrub native rainforest and shallow bogs. It ends at a vista called Kilohana on the edge of Wainiha Pali, offering stunning views (weather permitting). Note: portions of the trail are boardwalk; the rest is often wet, slippery, and muddy. The trail starts at a parking area a quarter mile north of the Na Pali Kona Forest Reserve entrance sign.
- **Koaie Canyon Trail:** With good scenery and swimming holes, this moderately difficult hike follows a 3-mile route along the south side of Koaie Canyon. It starts about a half mile up the Waimea River from the bottom of Kukui Trail.
- **Kukui Trail:** This fairly difficult but highly scenic 2.5-mile affair drops down the west side of Waimea Canyon 2,000 feet to the canyon floor ending at the Wiliwili Camp site. The trail starts along Route 550, about three quarters of a mile beyond milepost 8. Camping is by permit only.
- **Poomau Canyon Lookout Trail:** Feeling a bit lazy? This short and easy trail starts a mile and a half beyond the Forest Reserve entrance sign on the Mohihi-Camp 10 Road, and will give you a superb view of Poomau and Waimea canyons.
- **Waimea Canyon Trail:** This 11.5-mile hike is moderately difficult, starting at the bottom of the Kukui Trail and going all the way to the town of Waimea, fording the Waimea River several times. (No camping is allowed south of Waiala'e Stream.)

Surfing, Fishing, Kayaking, and More!

Not many people come to Hawaii without the intention of getting wet at least once. Why not go beyond the beach and go out on the water? All of the top Kaua'i tour companies will set you up with a completely guided and supplied adventure on the water. However, assuming you may want to book some select activities yourself, we've included a few of our favorites here.

- **Surfing:** Well, you're in Hawaii, so you've got to do it, right? Well, *be careful*. Although the relatively gentle waves of the Po'ipu area on the South Shore are best for beginner and intermediate surfers, waves in all of Hawaii can be large and dangerous, especially on Kaua'i's North Shore in the winter, where the waters are for experts only.

Stop by **Margo Oberg's School of Surfing in Po'ipu** (**808-332-6100** or **808-639-0708**; www.surfonkauai.com) for 90 minutes of instruction and a half-hour of practice. They provide the surfboard and leash, and before the afternoon is out there's a pretty good chance you'll be hanging 10. Of course, you can rent a board at any number of small shops that line Kaua'i's coasts and just get out there.

- **Windsurfing:** Protected yet breezy Anini Beach on the North Shore is the place to catch the wind in your sail. Lessons and equipment rental, along with expert and friendly instruction, are available at **Anini Beach Windsurfing School** (**808-826-9463**; that's 826-WIND, in case you didn't notice!) On the South Shore, check out **Windsurf Kauai** in Hanalei (**808-828-6838**). A three-hour lesson costs $75, including equipment; rentals are $25 an hour, $50 for a half-day, and $75 for a full day. Serious windsurfers should head to Hanalei Bay or Tunnels Beach on the North Shore.
- **Kayaking:** Kaua'i's amazing coastline, assortment of reef-protected waters, and jungle-fringed rivers makes it an uncommonly good place for kayaking. **Kayak Kauai Outbound** (**808-826-9844** or **1-800-437-3507**; www.kayakkauai.com) offers both river ($85) and coastal tours ($145–$185) from Hanalei and Po'ipu. Meanwhile, **Rainbow Kayak Tours** (**1-866-826-9983** or **1-866-826-2505**; http://www.rainbowkayak.com) provides peaceful and beautiful excursions up the Wailua River for the fantastic price of around $22 for adults, $10 for kids.
- **Fishing:** Kauai's waters are superb for fishing—primarily for marlin, mahi-mahi, ono, and ahi tuna, because the waters off the coast get very deep, very quickly. Nawiliwili harbor in Lihu'e is the principal port, along with Port Allen in the south and Hanalei on the north coast. A few of our favorite charters include **Kai Bear Sportfishing** (**808-652-4556**) which offers a variety of four-, six-, and eight-hour charters, with prices starting at $140 and going up from there. **Anini Fishing Charters** (**808-828-1285**) sails from the North Shore, with rates beginning at $125 per person. **Explore Kauai Sportfishing** (**808-572-3333**) departs from Port Allen, with a $120 per person starting rate.
- **Horseback Riding:** Just picture yourself on a tall steed, majestically making your way across a green hillside with a misty waterfall in the background. You can live this fantasy for about $80 to $135 for

rides ranging from an hour to over four hours. On the North Shore, check out the **Princeville Ranch Stables (808-826-6777;** www.princevilleranch.com), located on Route 56 just after the Princeville Airport. Advance reservations are required and riders must be at least 8 years old. On the South Shore, go to **CJM Country Stables (808-742-6096;** www.cjmstables.com) at 1731 Kelaukia Street in Koloa. Advance reservations are recommended.

For anyone who loves natural beauty and the great outdoors, Kaua'i is one awesome place. On this lush, green island, it's truly "choose your pleasure."

Part 6

Moloka'i and Lana'i

Moloka'i and Lana'i are the classic Hawaii of old, not yet overrun by tourists. In fact, they may be too laid-back for some folks. Still, these smaller islands near Maui offer peace, beauty, and serenity, as well as dramatic scenery and unique histories.

Relaxing in Moloka'i

In This Chapter

- The geography and character of Moloka'i
- Getting to Moloka'i
- Getting around Moloka'i
- Deciding where to stay on the island
- Moloka'i's best lodging choices

Moloka'i is one of the best places to find a taste of the real Hawaii—the islands as they were before waves of tourists crashed upon their shores.

Rising precipitously from the sea between **Maui** and **O'ahu** (you can see its hulk clearly from both islands), this is a land of stunning natural beauty and charm, deserts, rainforests, waterfalls, the longest beach in Hawaii, and—on its spectacular north coast—the highest sea cliffs in the world. If you love the great outdoors, this is the place!

But Moloka'i may be most well known for what it *doesn't* have: not much commercial development, no massive mega-resorts, no fast-food chains, no stoplights, no traffic jams, and no building higher than a palm tree. It's an island almost untouched by time.

Snapshot

Moloka'i:

Size: 260 square miles

Population: 7,400

Number of Visitors Annually: 70,000

Highest Point: Mount Kamakou, 4,961 feet

Miles of Shoreline: 88

Number of Golf Courses: 2

Number of Beaches: 15

For more than a century, Moloka'i was a place for a different kind of refuge. A remote area was the site of a leper's colony.

History, natural beauty, and a quiet, authentic Hawaiian lifestyle are what you get in Moloka'i. In our estimation, it's definitely worth a visit. There are relatively few places to stay here, but in this chapter we'll cover some of the best.

Moloka'i offers a beauty and romance all its own.

(Photo courtesy of HVCB/Ron Dahlquist)

Flying into Moloka'i

Located about 6 miles northwest (and inland) of the main town of **Kaunakakai,** a small, red-roofed ranch-style building with three gates is what passes for the primary commercial air terminal in Moloka'i. (There is one other small airport near the former leper colony at Kalaupapa on the island's north shore.) Generally called "Moloka'i Airport" (MKK), it is also known as Ho'olehua Airport. This little place serves its purpose well, hosting numerous regularly scheduled flights to and from the other islands. Hawaiian

Airlines actually flies jets, though you're most likely to get a propeller plane on the other airlines. Most flights to Moloka'i originate in **Honolulu,** with several flying directly from Maui.

You'll find car rental desks in the terminal, along with a lei stand and humble snack bar. Some hotels, ranches, and resorts provide shuttle service.

For more information on air travel here and elsewhere throughout Hawaii, see Chapter 3.

Airlines That Fly into Moloka'i

Name	*Local*	*Toll-Free*
Aloha Island Air	808-567-6115	1-800-652-6541
Commercial Flyer	808-833-8014	1-800-652-6541
Hawaiian Airlines	808-567-6510	1-800-882-8811
Moloka'i Air Shuttle	808-567-6847	888-266-3597
Pacific Wings	888-575-4546	888-575-4546
Paragon Air	1-800-428-1231	1-800-428-1231

Traveling to Moloka'i by Ship

You can travel to Moloka'i by ship on the 149-passenger **Moloka'i Princess** or **Lahaina Princess** (**808-667-6165** or **1-800-275-6969;** www.mauiprincess.com), which run two round-trips daily from **Maui's Lahaina Harbor.** Cruising at about 20 knots, either ship makes the Lahaina-Kaunakakai trip in about 90 minutes. At press time, one-way fares were $40 for adults and $20 for kids.

You can also book through the Princess offices for day tours, golf outings, overnight lodgings, and even a car for travel around Moloka'i: upon your arrival, a Princess shuttle will take you to your vehicle!

Rental Cars

Even laid-back Moloka'i has some national car rental companies—not many, though. And what you lose in selection you gain in convenience and simplicity. Renting a car at Moloka'i involves just a few minutes at a booth in the small airport, and literally a few steps to the adjacent lot. In addition to the well-known brands **Budget** and **Dollar,** you can also rent from the home-grown **Island Kine Auto Rental & Sales (808-553-5242)**, offering clean and reliable cars, vans, pickup trucks, jeeps, and four-wheelers at reasonable rates. They'll even sell you the car if you find you just can't leave.

Given the lack of public transportation options on Moloka'i, renting a car for the entire stay is really the way to go, giving you the freedom and flexibility to get around to all parts of the island. However, be sure to reserve in advance, as there are a limited number of cars in the small lot, and the agencies generally don't have many to spare!

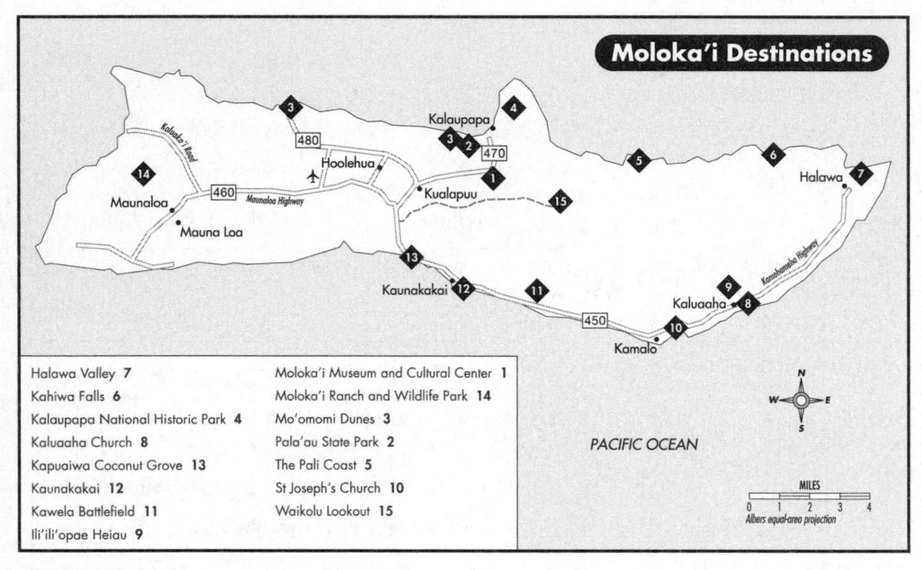

Moloka'i's highways and key destinations.

Taxi and Shuttle Service

There are only a couple of serious taxi-style services in Moloka'i (though enterprising vehicular entrepreneurs pop up now and again). One is **Moloka'i Off-Road Tours and Taxi (808-553-3369;** www.Moloka'i.com/offroad/), which offers shuttle service to the various hotels and lodges around the island for flat fees. They also offer a range of island tours starting at about $32 per person.

The other primary taxi service—one that actually uses a meter—is **Hele Mai Taxi (808-336-0967)**, whose friendly drivers will take you anywhere on the island at good rates, while blessing you with a little authentic Moloka'i tour narration along the way.

Some hotels, ranches, and resorts provide shuttle services for guests, so call your host for details. There is no scheduled public bus service on Moloka'i.

Day Tours to Moloka'i from Maui and O'ahu

Being only 20 miles and a 15-minute flight from both Maui and O'ahu, Moloka'i (or at least its main attractions) can be toured in a day from other islands. The **Maui Princess** ferry company (**808-275-6969** or **808-667-6165;** www.mauiprincess.com) offers numerous day tours from both Maui and O'ahu, starting at about $180. **Moloka'i Tours** (**1-800-410-8176;** www. Moloka'itours.net) will also set you up at competitive rates.

NOTE: As of our publication date, Moloka'i Air Shuttle (808-567-6847) had been shut down because of a technical dispute with the Federal Aviation Administration. We recommend that you check their phone number and the web for news on when and if the company will reopen.

Here's about what you can expect to spend (for a one-way ride) between Moloka'i airport and popular destinations around the island (fares subject to change):

What Transportation Costs in Moloka'i

Destination	*Taxi Fare from Airport*
Halawa Valley	$50
Hotel Moloka'i	$22
Kaunakakai	$18
Kalaupapa	$20
Murphy's Beach	$38
Puko'o	$35

Getting Your Bearings: Island Locales

Moloka'i is not a particularly big place, measuring 38 miles long by only 10 miles wide, but like most Hawaiian islands it is mountainous with great diversity in climate and foliage. The long axis of the island extends east and west, with the eastern portion rising in a mountain range crowned by 4,961-foot Mount Kamakou.

Like all of the other Hawaiian islands, Moloka'i has a windward and leeward side. **East Moloka'i** gets those moist trade winds that blow across the Pacific in these latitudes, making it a lush, tropical paradise. **West Moloka'i,** on the other hand, is (you guessed it) semi-arid, with rolling plains, some fairly bare hills, and dusty ranches. The dividing line between east and west—and the respective climates—is the main town and port of **Kaunakakai,** right in the middle of the southern coastline.

MOLOKA'I VISITORS INFORMATION

Moloka'i Visitor's Association, P.O. Box 960, Kaunakakai, HI 96748; **808-800-6367;** www.Moloka'i-hawaii.com.

Kaunakakai and Central Moloka'i

Most of Moloka'i's commercial services—stores, restaurants, a bakery, and a wharf—are located in dusty, funky Kaunakakai, about equal distance from the west and east ends of the island on the southern coast. This town is about three blocks long, and from certain angles looks like something out of the old American West, complete with a few Hawaiian cowboys. This is where you'll land if you take the ferry over from Maui, and where most people head after landing at the airport about 6 miles away.

Snapshot

Central Moloka'i Destinations:

- Kalaupapa National Historic Park
- Kapuaiwa Coconut Grove
- Kaunakakai
- Malama Cultural Park
- Moloka'i Museum and Cultural Center
- Pala'au State Park

See Chapter 15 for more information and itineraries.

Kaunakakai used to be the royal summer residence of King Kamehameha V, and later was a bustling port for pineapple plantations, but all of that has now gone by the wayside. Still, there are a few things to do here, with a couple of decent restaurants, so it's not a bad base for visiting other parts of the island.

About 12 or so miles straight north from Kaunakakai, on the north shore of central Moloka'i, you'll find one of the island's most famous attractions. **Kalaupapa** is the settlement where Father Damien de Veuster ministered to natives stricken with Hansen's disease (better known as leprosy) beginning around 1866, and which continued as a settlement for leprosy victims until 1969. Today, Kalaupapa is a fascinating National Historical Park still populated by a few aging residents, accessible to visitors by foot or mule.

In the nineteenth century, leprosy was considered an incurable, highly contagious, and very frightening disease. The solution was to isolate sufferers in a remote place—like a less-visited corner of a Hawaiian island—and keep everyone else away. Modern medicine, though, has determined that the disease is bacterial in nature, relatively easily treated, and not very easy to spread. The vast majority of people have a natural immunity to the bacteria.

East Moloka'i

Moloka'i's rugged and lush eastern side has some of the most spectacular scenery in Hawaii, including the world's highest sea cliffs rising majestically into the mist on Moloka'i's **North Coast** (Pali Coast). This area was the location for several scenes in the *Jurassic Park* movies, and you can see why. It encompasses several uninhabited valleys, the largest being **Waikolu, Pelekunu,** and **Wailau,** and includes **Kahiwa Falls,** the highest in all of Hawaii, plunging 1,750 feet into the ocean.

There are no roads east along the northern coast from Kalawao, so this area is wilderness, accessible only by helicopter, by boat, or by foot, making it a true paradise for those of you who may be seeking a wild, almost prehistoric experience.

Snapshot

East Moloka'i Destinations:

- Halawa Valley
- Iliiliopae Heiau
- Kahiwa Falls
- Kaluaaha Church
- Kawela Battlefield
- Moa'ula Falls
- Murphy's Beach
- Pali Coast

See Chapter 15 for more information and itineraries.

The southern coast of East Moloka'i is much more accessible, with Route 450 (The Kamehameha V Highway) extending all the way out to the eastern tip of the island at **Halawa Valley Bay.** In this same area you can enjoy another impressive cascade, **Moa'ula Falls.** The highway to the east end also boasts some excellent beaches, including **Murphy's Beach Park.**

West Moloka'i

West Moloka'i is probably the least touristy part of the island, made up of semi-arid plains, rolling hills, small settlements, and some nice beaches. Oh yeah, there's also a modest condo development near the town of **Maunaloa,** which, strangely enough, developers are working to make into a tourist destination. Western Moloka'i boasts several secluded and pristine beaches, including Papohaku (the largest white-sand beach in Hawaii), **Kaupoa,** and **Kawakiu,** as well as amazing **Mo'omomi Dunes** on the northwest coast—the site of ancient Hawaiian burial sites and the bones of prehistoric birds that have been found nowhere else in the world. West Moloka'i is also home to the **Moloka'i Ranch,** which at 70,000 acres takes up a third of the island, and includes a beach and even a zoo!

Snapshot

West Moloka'i Destinations:

- Moloka'i Ranch
- Mo'omomi Dunes
- Pala'au State Park
- Papohaku Beach
- Waikolu Lookout

See Chapter 15 for more information and itineraries.

Driving Times from Moloka'i Airport

Halawa Valley	2 hours
Kaunakakai	15 minutes
Kepuhi Beach	30 minutes
Mapulehu	25 minutes
Maunaloa	15 minutes
Pala'au Park	15 minutes

Moloka'i Accommodations: Ultimate Places to Stay

Compared to most other islands in Hawaii, Moloka'i is fairly slim pickin's when it comes to accommodations, with a small handful of hotels, a few B&Bs, and a few more condos and private homes.

We've picked out a selection of the best, organized under each lodging category.

Hotels and Resorts

Hotel Moloka'i Kaunakakai $$$

The only real hotel on Moloka'i, this place is nothing too fancy, but it's kind of cool, with several open-air Polynesian-style bungalows, a swimming pool facing the beach, and an atmospheric laid-back vibe. It offers an old-Hawaii experience, with nice views of Lana'i in the distance. There's also a pool and a restaurant. *Kamehameha V Highway (P.O. Box 1020), Kaunakakai, HI 96748.* ***808-553-5347.*** *www.hotelMoloka'i.com.*

The Lodge & Beach Village at Moloka'i Ranch Maunaloa $$$

This little venue of highly civilized living on Moloka'i offers 22 luxury ocean-view rooms with private lanais—all with wet bar with complimentary bottled water, high-speed data ports, irons and ironing boards, and more. There's also a good restaurant here. The resort also offers a "Beach Village," where you can sleep in comfy "luxury" tents right in front of beautiful Kaupoa Beach. *100 Maunaloa Highway (Route 460), Maunaloa, HI 96770.* ***808-660-2824*** *or* ***888-627-8082.*** *www.Moloka'iranch.com.*

Pu'u O Hoku Ranch East Moloka'i

Do you really want to get away from it all? This striking place, frequented in the past by John F. Kennedy, Jimmy Stewart, John Denver, and other celebs, is way out on the eastern tip of the island, set atop a hill with views of the ocean and Maui, and surrounded by two acres of lawn and gardens. Normally rented to large groups—retreats, seminars, workshops, and conferences—it also offers two cottages for individuals. *P.O. Box 1889, Kaunakakai, HI 96748.* ***808-558-8109.*** *www.puuohoku.com.*

More Intimate Lodgings and B&Bs

Ka Hale Mala Kaunakakai

Located about 5 miles west of Kaunakakai, this private, and spacious (900-square-foot) apartment will sleep four very comfortably. It's surrounded by tropical gardens and a small orchard, and is only five minutes from the beach. You'll enjoy the gourmet breakfasts. *P.O. Box 1582, Kaunakakai, HI 96748.* ***808-553-9009.*** *www.Moloka'i-bnb.com.*

Kamalo Plantation East Moloka'i

Located across the highway from Father Damien's historic St. Joseph Church, and at the foot of Moloka'i's highest mountains, these two private guest cottages can sleep up to four people each and are set amid a lovely five-acre tropical landscape. Cottages require a two-night minimum; no credit cards, and no breakfast. *Kamehameha V Highway about 10 miles west of Kaunakakai. P.O. Box 300, Kaunakakai, HI 96748.* ***808-558-8236.*** *www.Moloka'i.com/kamalo.*

Best Condos

Kaluakoi Resort West Moloka'i

These condos near Papohaku Beach opened in 1977 and sit on 6,700 acres. The resort-style setup boasts an 18-hole golf course, a swimming pool overlooking the beach, and a restaurant. The condos themselves are studios and one-bedroom units, decorated with tropical furnishings. Dining and shopping are within walking distance. Most of the condos here are rented by the owners. *Kaluakoi Road, Kaluakoi Resort, P.O. Box 289, Maunaloa, HI 96770.* ***808-552-2721.***

Wavecrest Resort East Moloka'i

East of Kaunakakai along Route 450 (Kamehameha Highway) at mile marker 13 you will come upon this low-rise condominium complex, which includes clean, economically priced units, a beachside swimming pool looking out at Maui in the distance, and lighted tennis courts. A palm-shaded lawn serves as a decent place to watch the lights of Maui blink on after sunset by the sea. *P.O. Box 541, Kaunakakai, HI 96748.* ***808-558-8101.***

Ultimate Private Homes

Aloha Beach House East Moloka'i

This Hawaiian-style, two-bedroom, 1,600-square-foot oceanfront home on Waialua's white-sand beach really rocks—but in a quiet, soothing way. It sleeps up to five guests comfortably and is furnished with a king-size bed, three twin beds, full-size washer/dryer, microwave, gas stove, dishwasher, TV/VCR, masks, snorkels, boogieboards, beach towels, and chairs. *P.O. Box 79, Kilauea, HI 96754.* ***808-828-1100*** *or* ***888-828-1008.***

Hale O Pu Hala East Moloka'i

This new three-bedroom, two-bath home in Waialua with a large master suite fronts a private sandy beach with spectacular views of the sunrise and the islands of Maui and Lana'i. *Owner contact: 5001 E. Birkdale Lane, Spokane, WA 99223.* ***808-558-8150*** or ***509-990-9484.***

Moanui Beach House East Moloka'i

Located 20 miles east of Kaunakakai right at one of Moloka'i's best snorkeling beaches, these two two-bedroom cottages are surrounded by peaceful fields, with a private ocean beach right out front. It features a large screened lanai and an outdoor shower. *P.O. Box 300, Kaunakakai, HI 96748.* ***808-558-8236.***

Visiting Moloka'i is kind of like going back in time, to when Hawaii was truly a world with a slower "stop and smell the hibiscus" pace of life. Now you more or less know your way around and where to stay. For details on restaurants (what there are of them), beaches (awesome!), shopping (a few places, anyway), outdoor sports, and other activities, peruse Chapter 15!

Enjoying Moloka'i

In This Chapter

- The ultimate itineraries for Moloka'i
- The best places to dine in Moloka'i
- The most interesting things to see in Moloka'i
- The best things to do in Moloka'i

Moloka'i, the "Friendly Isle," is relatively untouched compared to tourist-ready **Maui** or bustling **Honolulu**—and that might be just what you're looking for. Famously known for its lack of traffic lights and, well, traffic, Moloka'i is a place where you can really get away from it all.

This isolation was put to particular use in the 1800s, when sufferers of Hansen's disease (leprosy) were settled at the Kalaupapa and Kalawao "colonies," as they were called. The 816 lepers were cared for primarily by the Belgian missionary Father Damien de Veuster, who served not just as priest, but also as doctor and primary caregiver for the settlement. He himself contracted the disease and died in 1889, 16 years after arriving on the island. Modern science now has determined that

Hansen's disease is not as contagious as originally thought, and drugs now make it possible to treat the disease.

Today, Moloka'i is still home to fewer than 40 residents of the Kalaupapa settlement, a National Historic Site, with limited access allowed for tours.

Moloka'i boasts several beautiful and secluded beaches, including this one at Waialua.

(Photo courtesy of HVCB/Ray Mains)

The Top Five Things to Do in Moloka'i

1. Take the mule ride down to **Kalaupapa Historic Park,** followed by a tour of Father Damien's leper colonies.
2. Spend a lazy day on the gorgeous **Papohaku Beach.**
3. Check out the famous Phallic Rock at **Pala'au State Park.**
4. Make the trek to **Kawela Battlefield** and experience the echoes of Hawaii's fierce battles past.
5. Immerse yourself in Moloka'i's isolation in **Halawa Valley,** site of impressive waterfalls and ancient *heiaus* (Hawaiian temples).

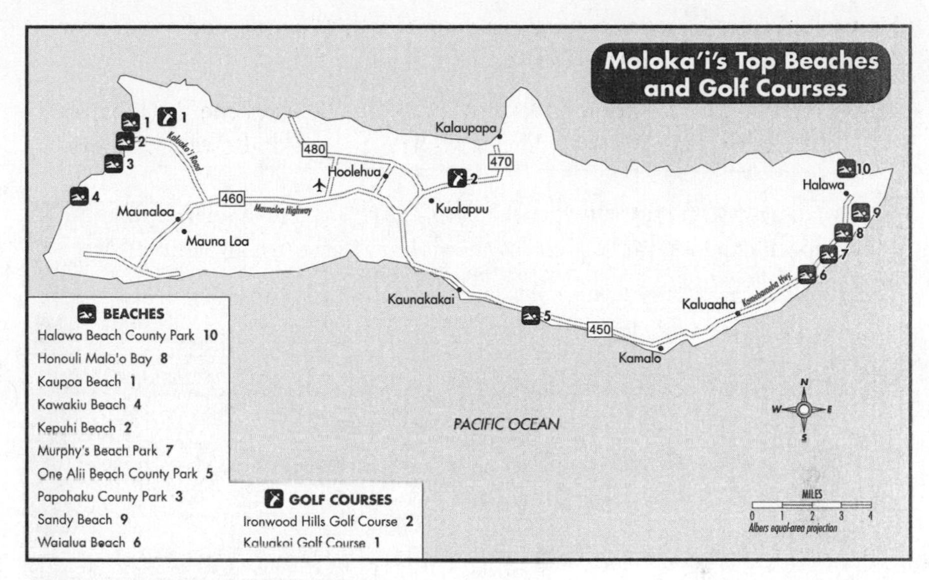

Moloka'i's beaches and golf courses.

Plan My Trip: Ultimate Itineraries for Moloka'i

Moloka'i is a great place to be spontaneous—pick a beach, any beach—but there are a few things you might want to plan ahead for. Following are some suggested itineraries for a typical day on Moloka'i, whatever your lifestyle.

The descriptions of each stop are generally brief, written to give you a feel for each. You'll find more through write-ups of each place later in the chapter. *It's usually worthwhile to make advance reservations for recommended restaurants and tours.*

ITINERARY #1: FOR YOUNG FAMILIES

1. **Breakfast: Kanemitsu Bakery** is a good breakfast choice for everyone, and it's right in **Kaunakakai,** so there's no long wait for grumbling stomachs, tiny or full-grown.

continues

continued

2. **Lunch:** While you're in town, pick up picnic supplies and head to **Sandy Beach,** a great protected and kid-friendly cove for even beginning swimmers and snorkelers.
3. An easy stop after a long beach day is **St. Joseph's Church,** a one-room chapel built by Belgian missionary Father Damien in 1876.
4. **Dinner:** Who wants french fries? Who wants moco loco? **Moloka'i Drive Inn** (back in Kaunakakai) will get it to you, and fast.

ITINERARY #2: FOR OLDER FAMILIES

1. **Breakfast and Lunch:** After breakfast at your place, get those lazybones out of bed (that's you, parental units) and go for a real adventure: a mule ride down from **Pala'au State Park** to **Kalaupapa,** and a tour of the settlements that were at one time populated by more than 800 sufferers of Hansen's disease. Good news: **lunch** is provided on the tour.
2. Take advantage of your free afternoon to relax at the beach in **Kepuhi Bay;** swim, sunbathe, and enjoy another incredible view.
3. **Dinner:** Lunch was hours ago! Fill up with burgers, chicken, and (of course) pizza at the **Moloka'i Pizza Company** back in **Kaunakakai.**

ITINERARY #3: FOR SINGLES

1. Now this is worth waking up early for: ocean kayaking along the North Shore with **Moloka'i Outdoors.** There's no better view of those world-famous, 1,600-foot cliffs than from the water! Oh, and the rest of the coast's not bad either.
2. **Lunch:** You worked off enough calories for a dinner-sized plate lunch at **Oviedo's Lunch Counter,** right? Or maybe just some chicken katsu á la carte.

3. Grab a good beach read and some portable tunes, and enjoy the calm waters and late afternoon sun at **Murphy's Beach,** farther down the eastern coast.
4. Is it getting dark? Spook yourself a little with a quick stroll around **Kawela Battlefield,** the site of two major battles for the conquest of Hawaii by its chiefs.
5. **Dinner:** After a day out in nature, head back to civilization with a couple of good cocktails and pupus for dinner at the **Paniolo Lounge.**

ITINERARY #4: A ROMANTIC GETAWAY

1. **Breakfast:** Just this once on your vacation, try to head out at a reasonable hour—and not just to grab good **breakfast** pastries (and a little something for lunch) at **Kanemitsu Bakery** in Kaunakakai.
2. The real reason you'll want to roll out of bed is simply so you can lie back down on **Panohaku Beach.** It's 3 miles long, so you're sure to find a picture-perfect stretch all to yourself.
3. **Lunch:** Since you're in the neighborhood, treat yourself to a picnic in the gorgeous **Pala'au State Park,** overlooking the Kalaupapa peninsula. And, if the timing's right, why not take the short walk to, ahem, **Phallic Rock?**
4. **Dinner:** Back into town for cocktails and some romantic island music—go ahead, stay for dinner—at the **Hula House** in **Hotel Moloka'i.**

ITINERARY #5: EASY-GOING; NONSTRENUOUS

1. **Breakfast:** Wake up at your leisure, grab some fresh fruit, and bring a book for a long, lovely morning at **Dixi Maru Cove** on the island's west side. In the summer it's a great spot for spectacular snorkeling in calm waters.

continues

continued

2. **Lunch:** Head back toward Kaunakakai, but stop in Kualapu'u for some local-style nosh at **Kamuela's Cookhouse.** Go on, get the plate lunch—that was a pretty exhausting morning, wasn't it?
3. Arrive in Kaunakakai just in time to spend an afternoon doing something really strenuous—shopping. Don't miss **Moloka'i Island Creations** if you're shopping for friends back home.
4. **Dinner:** Back west just in time for sunset (good thing it's a small island!) and stately dinner at the **Maunaloa Dining Room** in Moloka'i Lodge.

ITINERARY #6: CULTURE IN PARADISE

1. **Breakfast:** Fortify yourself for the day with a stop at the local favorite **Kanemitsu Bakery** in Kaunakakai. Grab a loaf of their famous Moloka'i Bread or some of their famous sandwiches for lunch later!
2. Make arrangements in advance in Kaunakakai to spend your morning touring **Ili'ili'opae Heiau,** the second largest heiau in Hawaii and the site of both human sacrifice and great learning for Hawaiian priests.
3. **Lunch:** Did you pack a lunch? Hope so, because you're so near to **Kawela Battlefield** it would be a shame to miss it. The site of two major battles for Hawaiian unification in the eighteenth century. We're told this battlefield is also home to warrior ghosts who walk at night; who are we to doubt such a story?
4. **Dinner:** Head back to Kaunakakai and get an early dinner at the **Moloka'i Drive-Inn.** We highly recommend the teriyaki burger—and the tripe soup!

ITINERARY #7: ADVENTURE IN THE GREAT OUTDOORS

1. **Breakfast:** Get up, grab something at the **Kanemitsu Bakery** in Kaunakakai to go and head out for the **Halawa Falls Hike** (organized by **Moloka'i Fish & Dive**), a 4.2-mile return hike through **Halawa Valley** to **Moaula Falls.** Get your trip's history lesson in as you learn about the many ancient *heiaus* and archaeological sites in Halawa Valley, while taking in your lush surroundings.
2. **Lunch:** As experienced outdoors types, you probably packed snacks—but let's face it, you'll be hungry. For lunch, head back to Kaunakakai and **Oviedo's Lunch Counter.** Their plate lunch will set you right again.
3. Time to head to the west side of the island and **Wailoku Lookout,** for a great view of Moloka'i's impressive sea cliffs. Once you turn off the main highway, park wherever you like and enjoy the hike out to the lookout—you may want to make it longer or shorter depending on how much time you have before sunset.
4. **Dinner:** Okay, adventure fiends! Back to Kaunakakai and a well-deserved splurge for dinner at **Hotel Moloka'i's Oceanfront Restaurant,** which blends Pacific and American cuisine.

The Top Moloka'i Attractions, A to Z

Halawa Valley East Moloka'i

Halawa Valley was once home to a large population of Native Hawaiians and large expanses of taro agriculture in its wetland fields. Today it has returned to the Hawaiian wilderness, and you can pretty much take your pick as to what you're most interested in. The 250-foot Moaula Falls, the 500-foot Hipuapua Falls, a secluded beach park, and many ancient *heiaus* are all nestled in the park's lush foliage. *Located 27 miles east of Kaunakakai at the end of Route 450.*

Moloka'i's awesome Halawa Valley qualifies as a tropical paradise.

(Photo courtesy of HVCB/Ron Dahlquist)

Kahiwa Falls East Moloka'i

Kahiwa Falls, located at the head of a remote valley on Moloka'i's north coast, is the tallest waterfall in Hawaii, towering over 2,000 feet. Unfortunately, it is very isolated and is generally viewable only from an airplane or helicopter tour.

Kalaupapa National Historic Park Central Moloka'i

Once home to Father Damien's famous leper settlements at Kalawao and Kalaupapa, and still home to a few dozen residents, Kalaupapa, set at the base of Moloka'i's famous 1,600-foot sea cliffs, has much to offer the visitor. You can tour the settlements and their historic churches, the Moloka'i Lighthouse, the Pu'u Uau lookout over the Kuahako crater, the lava tubes, the rainforest, and maybe even spot the endangered Hawaiian monk seal on the park's beaches. In other words, it's not to be missed—although due to limited access, you'll need to visit with an authorized tour group (see Sightseeing Tours). *Located on the North Shore of Moloka'i on the Kalaupapa Peninsula. www.nps.gov/kaka.*

Kaluaaha Church East Moloka'i

The remains of the first Christian church on Moloka'i, built on the island in 1844 by Protestant missionaries, look more like an old military fort or some sort of pre-Victorian bunker. With walls 3 feet thick and thin slits for windows, it's both an historical and an architectural curiosity. *East on Route 450, Kaluaaha.*

Kapuaiwa Coconut Grove Central Moloka'i

This coconut grove contains hundreds of swaying palms planted in the 1860s by King Kamehameha V to shade the royal bathing pools. Now it's an excellent spot from which to enjoy a sunset. There were originally 1,000 palms here—one for each warrior in the King's army. *Located about 1.5 miles west of Kaunakakai on Route 450.*

Kaunakakai Central Moloka'i

The main town on Moloka'i is your best bet for restaurants, shops, and information and bookings for tours. It has all the small-town charm that might seem, to some of us, to be an urban legend. *Located 8 miles from Moloka'i Airport on Route 450.*

Kawela Battlefield East Moloka'i

Kawela is the site of two major battles in the wars to conquer and unite the Hawaiian Islands. During the first, in 1736, the Hawaiian and Moloka'i armies successfully fought off invading forces from Oahu. The second major battle, in 1794 against King Kamehameha I, had a different result. Thousands of warriors died here, and according to Hawaiian legend, at night they return as the Night Marchers, warrior ghosts who march to do battle at the coast. You'll probably find this beautiful area a bit eerie, though, any time of day—quiet and watching. *You will find it between mile markers 6–13 on Route 450, east of Kaunakakai.*

Ili'ili'opae Heiau East Moloka'i

The second largest heiau in Hawaii (the first is the Piilanihale heiau on Maui), Iliiliopaie is more than 320 feet long and 120 feet wide. It served as a site of human sacrifice as well as a learning center for kahuna (Hawaiian priests) from other islands to come and be educated. The site is mainly reachable by foot or on horseback, and is on private land, so it is best visited on organized tour. *Located 16 miles east of Kaunakakai on Route 450.*

Moloka'i Museum and Cultural Center Central Moloka'i

Located on lush farmland, this cultural center is also the site of the restored R. W. Meyer Sugar Mill, complete with operational steam engine. The center itself features changing displays as well as information on the German Rudolph Meyer, a sugar planter and supervisor for the Kalawao settlement for over 30 years. *Located near mile marker 4 on Route 270. Open Monday–Saturday 10 A.M.–2 P.M., closed Sunday. Admission: adults $2.50, children $1,* ***808-567-6436.***

Moloka'i Ranch and Wildlife Park West Moloka'i

The *paniolo* (Hawaiian cowboy) has been part of Hawaiian life since the 1800s. This huge ranch, started back in 1897, encompasses about 53,000 acres, or approximately one third of the entire island! It's a working cattle ranch, with real-life cowboys doing their thing on a daily basis. In the 1970s the owners wisely decided to make it into a tourist attraction, with everything from a ranch tour and mule rides, to an actual 350-acre wildlife park, populated by all kinds of exotic animals from Asia, Africa, and beyond. *Located in the town of Maunaloa at the end of Route 460. Tours leave from the nearby Kaluakoi Resort Tuesday–Saturday at 8 A.M., 10 A.M., and 1:30 P.M., and Sunday at 10:30 A.M. Admission: adults $35, kids $18.* ***808-552-2797*** *or* ***1-877-726-4656.***

Mo'omomi Dunes West Moloka'i

Part of Pala'au State Park, amazing Mo'omomi Dunes is the site of ancient Hawaiian burial grounds and the bones of prehistoric birds that have been found nowhere else in the world. *Located at the end of Route 47.*

Pala'au State Park Central Moloka'i

This park is more than 230 acres of forest, sitting atop the beautiful sea cliffs of Moloka'i and overlooking Kalaupapa peninsula. There's also a short hike to the Kauleonanahoa, also known as the Phallic Rock, an ancient fertility statue that women used to journey to if they wanted to become pregnant. Hiking and mule tours of Kalaupapa Park also start from this point. *Located at the end of Route 47.*

The Pali Coast East Moloka'i

The spectacular Pali Coast on Moloka'i's North Shore boasts the highest sea cliffs in the world, rising precipitously 3,300 feet from the ocean. There are no roads to these cliffs, but you can see them from the end of the hiking trail to Waikolu Lookout or from the top of the cliffs at Kalaupapa National Historic Park.

St. Joseph's Church East Moloka'i

This small, one-room church was built by Father Damien in 1876, restored in 1971, and features a statue of the priest in front of the building. *Located on Route 450 just after mile marker 10.*

Waikolu Lookout Central Moloka'i

This dramatic lookout into Waikolu Valley is just before the town of Umipaa on a four-wheel-drive-only dirt road. Nearly as interesting is the "Sandalwood Hole," used by merchant seamen to measure a ship's worth of sandalwood during the height of the sandalwood trade in the nineteenth century. *Take a right on the 4WD road just before Umipaa on Route 460.*

Moloka'i's Top Beaches

It sometimes feels as though there's a beach for every person on Moloka'i. That's how easy it is for you to find peace, quiet, and real seclusion—plus all the postcard views of paradise coastline you could ever desire.

Dixie Maru Cove West Moloka'i
Take Route 450 to Kaluakoi Road; the beach is at end of the road. Facilities.

Halawa Beach Park East Moloka'i
Located at end of Route 450 at Halawa Valley.

Honouli Malo'o Bay East Moloka'i
Take Route 450 east; just past mile marker 21. No facilities.

Kaupoa Beach West Moloka'i
Follow Route 450 to Kaluakoi Road; the beach is at end of the road; from there, follow the clearly marked pedestrian path. Facilities.

Kawakiu Bay West Moloka'i
Take Route 450 to Kaluakoi Road; the beach is near the Paniolo Hale condos. Full facilities.

Kepuhi Bay West Moloka'i
Take Route 450 west; make a right on Kaluakoi Road and follow the signs to the Kaluakoi Resort.

Murphy's Beach East Moloka'i
Located at mile marker 20 on Route 450. Full facilities.

One Ali'i Beach Central Moloka'i
Located on Route 450 just east of Hotel Moloka'i. Full facilities.

Papohaku Beach West Moloka'i
Take Route 450 to Kaluakoi Road; the beach is 2 miles past Kaluakoi Resort. Full facilities.

Sandy Beach East Moloka'i
Located east on Route 450 between mile markers 21 and 22. No facilities.

Great Dining with Atmosphere: The Best Places to Eat

Just in case you weren't sure, you shouldn't go to Moloka'i for the fine dining. However, there are a handful of options—and even a couple of nice restaurants—to keep you fed and satisfied during your stay.

Here are our picks for the best restaurants in Moloka'i.

Hotel Moloka'i Oceanfront Kaunakakai *Pacific Rim* $$$$

With its rustic décor, this restaurant is the popular choice for a Moloka'i fine dining experience. The restaurant's ocean side is open-air. Perfect for an upscale brunch or a romantic dinner; live music is offered daily from 4 P.M.–6 P.M. The Kapakahi stirfry is highly recommended. *Route 450. Open daily 7:30 A.M.–10:30 A.M., 11:30 A.M.–2 P.M., 5 P.M.–9 P.M.* ***808-553-5347.*** *www.hotelMoloka'i.com/hotel.html.*

Kanemitsu Bakery Kaunakakai Hawaiian/American $

This bakery is definitely the local favorite for sandwiches and other lunchtime foods, not to mention their famous Moloka'i Bread, of which there are 19 varieties. This is a good place to stop for pastries on the go and picnic supplies. *79 Ala Malama Street. Open Wednesday–Monday 5:30 A.M.–6:30 P.M.* ***808-553-5855.***

Maunaloa Dining Room Maunaloa Pacific Rim $$$$

Located at the Moloka'i Ranch Lodge, this restaurant really evokes the stately dining rooms of the Old West. This is the place to go for a good rack of lamb or a thick steak—consider this fair warning, vegetarians. *At the Moloka'i Ranch Lodge, 100 Mauna Loa Highway. Open daily 7 A.M.–10 P.M.* ***808-660-2824.***

Moloka'i Drive-Inn Kaunakakai Hawaiian/American 

It's nothing fancy, but sometimes good, filling burgers and sandwiches—or tripe soup, perhaps?—are all you need, especially on this laid-back leg of your trip. If you choose to dine in, enjoy the weather on the outdoor patio. *Corner of Kamehameha V Highway and Kamoi Street. Open Monday–Thursday 5:30 A.M.–10 P.M., Friday–Sunday 6 A.M.–10:30 P.M.* ***808-553-5655.***

Moloka'i Pizza Café Kaunakakai Italian/American $$

Okay, so it's not like there's a lot of competition, but Moloka'i Pizza Café's hand-tossed pizzas won't leave you with any complaints. There are burgers, chicken, and ribs in case you're not in a pizza frame of mind. *15 Kaunakakai Place. Open Monday–Thursday 10 A.M.–10 P.M., Friday–Saturday 10 A.M.–11 P.M., Sunday 11 A.M.–10 P.M.* ***808-553-3288.***

Oviedo's Lunch Counter Kaunakakai Hawaiian/Filipino $

Oviedo's is the place to go for *ono* and filling plate lunches. Be sure to try the sweet and sour ribs—but make sure you're hungry. *145 Puali Street. Open daily 10:30 A.M.–6:30 P.M.* ***808-553-5014.***

Entertainment and Nightlife

For the most part, entertainment on Moloka'i consists of a beach read and a good game of charades. Nightlife doesn't extend much later than an after-dinner cocktail. However, there are a few options for a night out. There's Hula Shores at the **Hotel Moloka'i (808-553-5347)**, for free daily entertainment and a special "Aloha Fridays" show featuring hula, storytelling, and a craft fair. You also can take in a movie at the **Maunaloa Town Cinemas (808-552-2707)**, a three-screen movieplex at 1 Maunaloa Highway. If you're on-island in May, you should most certainly check out the **Moloka'i Ka Hula Piko** at Papohaku Beach, which celebrates hula's roots on Moloka'i (the birthplace of hula, as legend has it). The festival is free and includes dances, chants, live music, games, and food. For more information, call the Moloka'i Visitor's Association at **1-800-800-6367.**

Shopping in Moloka'i

Besides stopping at the random farm for fresh produce, shopping options are pretty much limited to what Kaunakakai has to offer. For surf clothing and accessories, try **Moloka'i Surf (808-553-5093)**, 130 Kamehameha V Highway. For clothing and accessories with more of an island flavor, including hand-painted sarongs, **Moloka'i Island Creations (808-553-5926)**, 62

Ala Malama Street, has what you need. The **Imports Gift Store (808-553-5734)** at 82 Ala Malama Street has various knick-knacks on offer.

You'll find good deals at the weekly farmers and craft market held in town every Saturday on the main street across from the library.

Enjoying the Very Best Activities in Moloka'i

Moloka'i is a choice destination to enjoy the best of what Hawaii has to offer. Following are some of our favorite choices to help you make the most of your remote island getaway.

Sightseeing Tours

You've got a few good bets here—probably the most variety of anything on the island, in fact. **Moloka'i Outdoors (808-553-4477;** www.molokai-outdoors.com**)** offers several land and sea adventures, from kayaking or deep sea fishing to bike and hike tours and, of course, the tour you don't want to miss, of Kalaupapa Park. **Moloka'i Fish & Dive Activities (808-552-0184)** also offers a wide array of tours, including several historical hikes for people with every level of experience. Or try the **Moloka'i Mule Ride (808-567-6088;** www.muleride.com), which provides a truly unique descent from Pala'au State Park, down the sea cliffs to Kalaupapa.

While these tours operate under excursions booked through **Damien Tours (808-567-6171)**, for the tour of the Kalaupapa and Kalawao settlements, you may choose to go through them directly if you're on a tight schedule.

The Best Golf Courses

If you'd like to play a few holes during your stay on the Friendly Isle, you have exactly two choices:

The Kaluakoi Golf Course Maunaloa

This course is situated on the resort of the same name. It's a 160-acre, 18-hole course, 6,564 yards, with a handful of holes right next to the beach. *Located on Kaluakoi Road in Maunaloa; Greens fees are $80 an $35 after 2:30 P.M.* ***808-552-0255.***

Ironwood Hills Golf Course Kualapu'u

Your other option is the nine-hole, an older plantation course at about 1,200 feet elevation with beautiful views of central Moloka'i's lush hills. The course operators recommend reservations for tee times. You may walk the course, although golf carts as well as clubs are available for rent. *Located off the Kala'e Highway (Route 470) in Kualapu'u. Greens fees are only $28.* ***808-567-6000.***

Hiking and Biking on Moloka'i

You've got a few dynamite hiking and biking options on Moloka'i.

The island's relatively quiet roads and plethora of trails make it a good biking locale. You can rent bikes and accessories at $20 to $25 a day ($80 to $100 weekly) from **Moloka'i Bicycle** at 80 Mohala Street in Kaunakakai (**808-553-3931**). All rentals include helmet, lock, map, and a water bottle; and you can also rent car racks, child carriers, and jogging strollers. The friendly proprietors there will also give you the lowdown on all the best spots to go.

The island's trails offer anything and everything from moderate half-day hikes to the real multi-day treks for experienced hikers. Several of these hikes require permits from the **Nature Conservancy of Hawaii** (**808-553-5236**) or **Maui District's Forestry and Wildlife Office** in Wailuku on Maui (**808-984-8100**); call for more information.

Maunahui—Makakupaia Central Moloka'i

This 17.5-mile trail begins in the Maunahui Forest Preserve, climbs to 3,700 feet at the Wailoku Lookout, and descends through the Makakupaia Forest Preserve to One Ali'i Beach Park. The terrain is rugged but rewarding; the lookout alone is arguably worth the effort. *On Maunahui Access Road at Route 46 heading west. Call the Nature Conservancy for permits.*

Pepeopae East Moloka'i

Perhaps Moloka'i's best-known hike, Pepeopae is a 3-mile round-trip trek, but you'd better have four-wheel-drive to get down the 12-mile dirt road to the trailhead. The trail itself winds through clouds, forest, and bog on the Pepeopae Reserve to a pleasant overlook at its end. *Take Highway 460 west from Kaunakakai for 3.5 miles and turn right before the Maunawainui Bridge onto the unmarked Moloka'i Forest Reserve Road. Call the Nature Conservancy for permits.*

Moloka'i Forest Road Central Moloka'i

Quite close to Kaunakakai, this 10-mile hike takes you through pasture, forest, and past the sandalwood measuring pit, and again toward the Wailoku Lookout. *Take Highway 460 northwest from Kaunakakai for about 3.5 miles, to the Mokola'i Forest Access Road.*

Surfing, Snorkeling, Fishing, and More

If you love the great outdoors, and you like to explore it all by yourself, Moloka'i is the place for you.

- **Surfing:** Surfers should visit Moloka'i in the summer, when the west-coast waters are a bit calmer but still offer plenty of big waves (just not life-threatening ones). Try going to Papohaku Beach or Hale O Lono Beach. On the east side of the island, Halawa Valley and Murphy's can get some good waves. **Moloka'i Outdoors (1-877-553-4477;** www.molokai-outdoors.com) offers surfing lessons for beginners or those who just want a little supervision, as well as snorkeling gear.
- **Fishing:** If it's fishing you're after, try **Moloka'ifishing.com (808-567-6789,** www.molokaifishing.com). These guys offer both deep-sea and near-shore fishing. If you want to charter your own boat, the north and east sides of the island are best for fishing.
- **Birding:** The island is a great place for birding, particularly in the winter. Contact the **Nature Conservancy of Hawaii (808-553-5236)** about their monthly tours of the **Kamakou** and **Mo'omomi Preserves,** both great spots for bird-watching. Serious birders might want to contact the **Kakahaia National Wildlife Refuge (808-875-1582)** to schedule an interpretative tour.

It's obvious that a Moloka'i vacation is not for everyone. Some folks would no doubt go a bit stir-crazy in the generally slow, old-timey atmosphere of the place. But if you're into really decompressing—lazing on some pristine beaches, hiking in untamed Hawaiian wilderness, getting to know the locals, and maybe even playing a little golf—a few days here would be time very well spent.

Chapter 16

Relaxing in Lana'i

In This Chapter

- Lana'i's geography and character
- Getting to Lana'i
- Getting around Lana'i
- Lana'i's best lodging choices

If you're looking to get away from it all in a quiet tropical locale—a place where you can easily find seclusion on an abandoned beach or hillside, or settle into a small-town atmosphere—yet still be pampered with a limited but superb choice of fine food, golf, and comfortable accommodations, the small Hawaiian island of Lana'i may be your best prescription.

A generation ago **Lana'i** was not much more than a 140-square-mile pineapple plantation owned by the Dole Pineapple Company. The pineapple fields are largely gone and tourism is now king, but Lana'i is still known as the "Private Island."

Lana'i is no **Waikiki,** although it's only 45 minutes by boat and 10 minutes by air from the island of O'ahu. With a population of just over 3,000, Lana'i is quiet and "down-home," as reflected in its 1920s-era town, **Lana'i City.** Set inland at 1,600 feet above sea level, it is nicely cooled by some altitude. There are no traffic lights on the island, and only two of the main roads are paved.

There's not much nightlife, either, although the island makes up for that with some amazing beaches, beautiful hiking trails, and great snorkeling spots.

Snapshot

Lana'i:

Size: 141 square miles

Population: 3,193

Highest Point: Lanaihale, 3,370 feet

Number of Golf Courses: 2

Number of Beaches: 5

Coastline: 47 miles

Paradoxically, Lana'i is also a bit swanky in spots, thanks to two Four Seasons resorts that opened here in the 1990s. Microsoft kingpin Bill Gates, who seems to know a good thing when he sees it and can afford to go anywhere he wants, got married here.

Overall, Lana'i probably deserves the reputation as Hawaii's sleepiest spot. But that may be just what you need.

Lana'i's Experience at Ko'ele is one of the best golf courses in Hawaii.

(Photo courtesy of HVCB/Ron Dahlquist)

Flying into Lana'i

Lana'i Airport (LNY) is a small, one-runway affair with a modern but small passenger terminal. It is located about 3 miles southwest of Lana'i City, just a five-minute drive. There are no direct flights to LNY from the mainland United States, but you can easily fly here from **Maui** and **Honolulu,** with multiple flights each day. In the small terminal you'll have no trouble picking up your bags and hitting the Kaumalaupa'u Highway into town. The terminal also offers a snack bar and gift shop.

The resorts and car rental company provide shuttles to and from the airport. There is also a limo service available at the airport. If you've booked a car, or need a ride into town, you can use a Lana'i City Service courtesy phone at the airport's baggage claim.

Airlines That Fly into Lana'i

Name	*Local*	*Toll-Free*	*Website*
Aloha Airlines	808-567-6115	1-800-367-5250	www.alohaairlines.com
Hawaiian Airlines	808-565-6977	1-800/882-8811 1-800-367-5320	www.hawaiianairlines.com
Island Air	808-565-6744	1-800-652-6541	www.islandair.com
Pacific Wings	808-873-0877	888-575-4546	www.pacificwings.com

Traveling to Lana'i by Ship

A ferry company called **Expeditions** makes multiple trips each day from Lahaina, Maui, to Manele Harbor on the south coast of Lana'i (**808-661-3756** on Maui, or **1-800-695-2624;** www.go-Lana'i.com). The boat ride is quite scenic, taking in the islands of Maui, Lana'i, Moloka'i, Kaho'olawe, and, if it's clear enough, even The Big Island. Humpback whales also are visible during the voyage in-season from November through March. Tickets cost about $25 each way for adults.

Expeditions also offers daylong guided tours and golf packages.

Rental Cars

Dollar Rent a Car (808-565-7227, 800-533-7808, or **800-800-4000**) is the only national rental car company on Lana'i, offering a limited supply of vehicles ranging from economy to passenger vans. There are only a few paved roads on the island, and plenty of dirt roads leading to interesting places, so you should consider booking an SUV for your stay here.

The rental car agency is in town, and the folks who run it will pick you up at either the airport or the boat dock.

Lana'i City Service (808-667-7721) will also set you up with a rental car at the **Lana'i Plantation Store** in town, though they are affiliated with Dollar (you'll notice that the phone number is the same), so it's six of one, half a dozen of another.

Because cars and SUVs are in high demand here, the daily rates are high, averaging $120 to $130. It's just part of the price you pay for the privilege of enjoying the "Private Island."

Taxi and Shuttle Service

The only real taxi service on Lana'i at this writing is **Lana'i City Service (808-667-7721)**, which will charge you about $5 per person between the airport and town, and about $10 per person between Manele Bay and town. Of course, the **Lana'i Plantation Store** (here's that number again: **808-565-7227**) will provide you with taxi service from the center of town to the beach for about $10.

Taxi service on Lana'i is available and relatively cheap, but, as on Molokai, advance bookings are recommended.

Here's about what you can expect to spend for a one-way ride between Lana'i Airport and popular destinations around the island (fares subject to change):

What Transportation Costs in Lana'i

Destination	*Taxi*	*Shuttle*
Downtown	$10	free
Kaumalapa'u Harbor	$15	free
Manele Bay	$10	free

You also can check out **Rabaca's Limousine Service (808-565-6670)**, which will transport you around the island if you book in advance.

For the most part, unless you want privacy and total control of your schedule, taxis aren't really necessary or recommended on Lana'i, because the Four Seasons runs their own shuttle buses about once every hour between their two properties, the Manele Bay Hotel and the Lodge at Ko'ele. The shuttles are supposed to be for guests only, but we've found that the drivers are often amenable to giving nonguests a lift as well.

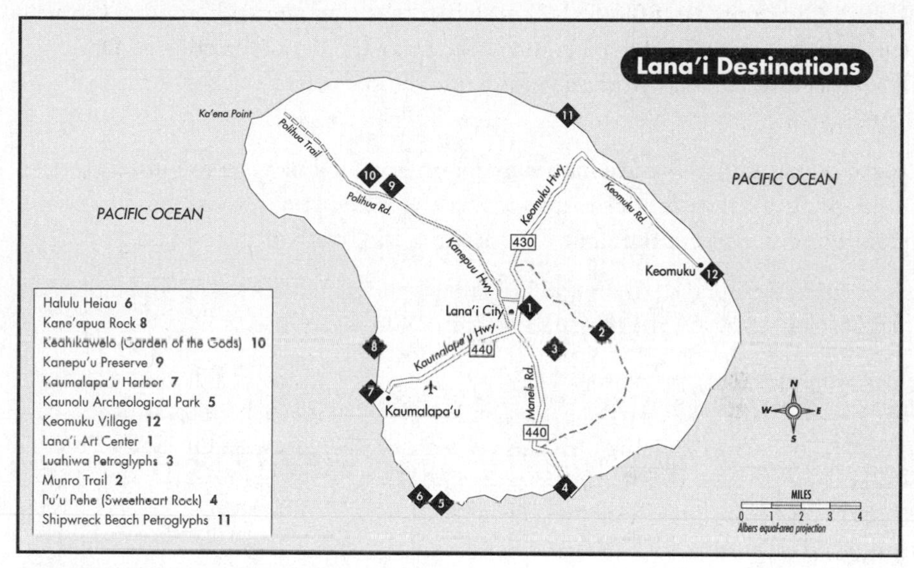

Lana'i's highways and key destinations.

Day Tours Around Lana'i

The **Expeditions** ferry company based in Maui (**808-661-3756** on Maui, or **800-695-2624;** www.go-Lana'i.com) offers daylong guided tours and golf packages for Lana'i. Rabaca's Limousine Service (**808-565-6670**) offers jeep tours around the island, as does **Adventure Lana'i Ecocentre** (**808-565-7373;** www.adventureLana'i.com). **The Lodge at Ko'ele** (**808-565-7300** or **800-321-4666**) offers its own excursions on small buses and on horseback.

Getting Your Bearings: Island Locales

Lana'i is a small, teardrop-shaped island, only 18 miles long from north to south, and 13 miles wide east to west. However, like the larger Hawaiian islands, it boasts an interesting variety of microclimates and natural attractions. A modest mountain ridge runs down the center of the island, roughly northwest to southeast. This includes Lana'i's highest point, **Lanaihale** (3,370 feet), which sits in the middle of the island. The mountain's eastern flanks descend in rugged slopes down to empty beaches. The western side of Lanaihale drops to a central plateau.

The island's only town, Lana'i City, sits on that plateau amid Norfolk Pines at an elevation of 1,600 feet above sea level. Here the days are cooler than along the coast, and in the winter the nighttime temperatures can drop to 50 degrees.

Lana'i's main port, **Kaumalapa'u,** is about 6 miles down the road from Lana'i City on the island's largely empty east coast. A resort development at beautiful **Manele Bay** is about the same distance directly south of Lana'i City.

The northwest end of the island is its most remote, and is a wild and empty area of otherworldly rock formations, grassy hillsides and remote beaches.

LANA'I VISITORS INFORMATION

Hawaii Visitor's Bureau: **808-923-1811;** www.gohawaii.com.

Destination Lana'i: **808-565-7600** or **1-800-974-4774;** www.visitLana'i.net.

Lana'i Weather: **808-565-6033.**

Lana'i City and Central Lana'i

Built as a plantation town by the Dole Pineapple Company in the 1920s, this tidy settlement of quaint and brightly painted homes is set amid Norfolk Pines (planted in the early 1900s by New Zealand naturalist George Munro) on a grid of streets containing a couple of food stores, a few restaurants, a hotel, and the only gas station on the island.

Just a few blocks north of downtown you'll find the elegant **Lodge at Ko'ele,** where you can enjoy world-class golf, horseback riding, fine dining, and more. A few miles to the south is the **Munro Trail,** which climbs from the town's 1,600-foot elevation to the summit of **Lanaihale** (house of Lana'i), where on a clear day you can see Maui, Moloka'i, The Big Island, and even O'ahu.

Snapshot

Lana'i City Destinations

- Lana'i Art Center
- Luahiwa Petroglyphs
- Munro Trail

Also nearby, on a hillside overlooking the Palawai Basin, you can visit a fragile field of ancient rock drawings called the **Luahiwa Petroglyphs.**

South Lana'i

About a 10-minute drive south of Lana'i city you'll find a resort area around scenic **Manele Bay.** Here, the swaying palms, gorgeous turquoise water, and impressive sea cliffs will remind you more of the stereotypical scenes so common in the rest of Hawaii.

The white sands and clear waters of **Hulopo'e Bay** and Manele Bay make up a marine life conservation area. Here, the white expanse of Hulopoe Beach Park is ideal for swimming, snorkeling, or spotting a spinner dolphin or whales breaching offshore. If you have a four-wheel-drive vehicle, you also can check out the ancient Halulu Heiau (shrine) or the Kane'apua Rock, located near Lana'i's southern sea cliffs at its southernmost point.

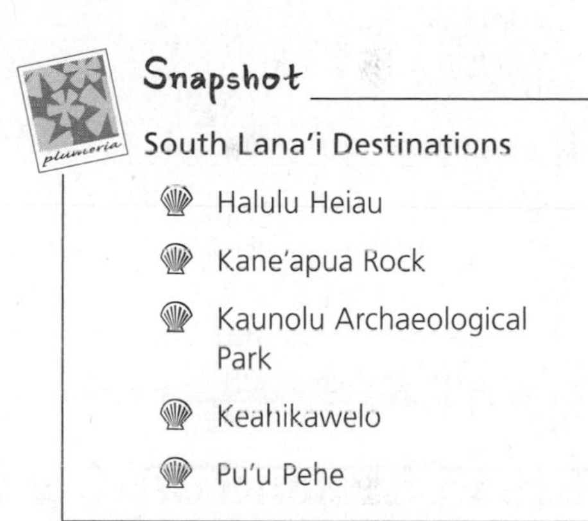

If luxury is your thing, you might want to consider staying at the Four Seasons Manele Bay Resort. It's pricey, but both the views and services are about as good as it gets.

North and East Lana'i

Remote and rather windswept, these regions of Lana'i are still no more than 8 miles from Lana'i City. About 6 miles north is the **Garden of the Gods,** a Martian landscape of rocks and giant boulders. **Ka'ena Point,** at the end of a four-wheel-drive road at the island's western point, is home to Lana'i's largest *heiau* (ancient place of worship). You also can drive down **Maunalei Gulch** to **Shipwreck Beach** on the east coast, the site of a wrecked World War II Liberty Ship, a ruined lighthouse, and the strange "Bird Man of Lana'i" petroglyphs, stick figures with birdlike heads.

North and East Lana'i Destinations

- Garden of the Gods (Keahikawelo)
- Keomuku Village
- Shipwreck Beach

West Lana'i

Lana'i's west coast is generally an empty area as far as tourists are concerned. It's main features are **Kaumalapa'u Harbor,** which was once a bustling port when Lana'i was still an epicenter of pineapple exports, and still a departure point for fishing boats; as well as the **Kanepu'u Preserve,** the last remaining remnant of the island's original dryland forests.

Snapshot

West Lana'i Destinations

- Kanepu'u Preserve
- Kaumalapa'u Harbor

Lana'i Driving Times from Lana'i Airport

Lana'i City	5 minutes
Munro Trail	15 minutes
Hulapo'e Bay	25 minutes
Manele Bay	25 minutes
Kaiolohi'a	35 minutes
Keahikawelo	45 minutes

Lana'i Accommodations: Ultimate Places to Stay

It's generally more expensive to stay on Lana'i than the other islands due to limited accommodations. There are three hotels on Lana'i, several bed-and-breakfast retreats, and a campground.

The accommodation descriptions that follow are organized alphabetically under each lodging category, though we've also included a handy chart that lists them by locale.

Hotels and Resorts

Hotel Lana'i Lana'i City 

Set amidst Lana'i City's tall Norfolk Pines at over 1,600 feet above sea level, this 75-year-old plantation is an atmospheric bit of old Hawaii. Built in 1923 by Jim Dole to house muckity-mucks visiting the Dole Pineapple Company, it's now a homey and highly comfortable 11-guest-room retreat featuring natural wood floors, old-style fixtures, and even a veranda where you can enjoy morning coffee and afternoon drinks. And there's one of Lana'i's best restaurants right on the premises. (Not that there is much competition on the island.) *828 Lana'i Avenue, Lana'i City, HI 96763.* ***808-565-7211*** *or* ***877-665-2624.*** *www.hotelLana'i.com.*

The Lodge at Ko'ele Lana'i City

Located just west of Lana'i City at the cooler, refreshing elevation of 1,500 feet, this quiet and awesomely relaxing lodge is a Four Seasons property that will remind you of a Victorian English manor with tropical accents. It offers huge stone fireplaces in the common rooms, beautiful and comfortable rooms, long porches with wicker chairs, a swimming pool, three tennis courts, and one of the best championship golf courses in Hawaii. This is elegant, upcountry living, and Lana'i City is a short walk down the road. Want to go to the beach? A shuttle run by the Lodge's sister property at Manele Bay will take you there. *1 Keomoku Highway, Lana'i City, HI 96763.* ***808-565-7300*** *or* ***800-321-4666.*** *www.fourseasons.com/Lana'i.*

Manele Bay Hotel South Lana'i

This 250-room Four Seasons hotel is Lana'i's only beach resort, and the priciest, most luxurious place to stay on the island. Located on the bluffs above the island's Hulopo'e Beach, it offers spectacular ocean views, beautiful grounds, one of the most stunningly placed swimming pools in the islands, the requisite spa, and the Challenge at Manele golf course, designed by Jack Nicklaus. *One Manele Bay Road, Lana'i City, HI 96763.* ***808-565-2000*** *or* ***800-321-4666.*** *www.fourseasons.com/manelebay.*

More Intimate Lodgings and B&Bs

Dreams Come True Lana'i City

Yes, this four-bedroom, four-bath plantation home is a B&B, and a nice one at that. Furnished with antiques and surrounded by a tropical orchard, it offers private attached bathrooms outfitted in Italian marble and whirlpool tubs, as well as Internet access and a full breakfast each day. The owners will help you with bookings and activities and also offer the home as a vacation rental. It's within walking distance of town. *1168 Lana'i Avenue, Lana'i City, HI 96763.* ***808-565-6961*** *or* ***800-566-6961.*** *www.circumvista.com/dreamscometrue.html.*

Hale Moe Bed and Breakfast Lana'i City

You can reserve a portion or all of this well-kept house, which sports a newly remodeled kitchen. Fresh fruit and pineapple are offered at breakfast. *502 Akolu Place, Lana'i City, HI 96763.* ***808-565-9520*** *or* ***808-565-6656****. www. stayLana'i.com.*

Camping

Castle & Cooke Resorts Campground South Lana'i

Yes, you can camp on Lana'i. Castle & Cooke runs six tent campsites just inland from Hulopoe Bay on Lana'i's south coast, about 6 miles south of Lana'i City. The facility includes restrooms, outdoor showers, grills, picnic tables, and drinking water. Rates run at about $5 per night, with a maximum stay of 3 nights. *P.O. Box 630310, Lana'i City, HI. Permits required.* ***808-565-2970.***

The best place to rent camping gear on Lana'i is the **Adventure Lana'i Ecocentre (808-565-7373)**.

Ultimate Private Home

Captain's Retreat

Want your own place in Lana'i? This four-bedroom, 3,000-square-foot cedar home is just a couple of minutes' walk from downtown Lana'i City. It features a wraparound redwood deck and a lovely landscaped lawn. An upstairs master suite offers a king-size bed, walk-in closet, full bath, and private patio. Downstairs, there are three bedrooms and two full baths. It also includes a fireplace for those cool central Lana'i nights. ***808-268-1834*** *or* ***949-673-0540.***

Compared to other Hawaiian islands, Lana'i is incredibly compact, with limited options for tourism. Still, what it *does* have is ready-made for visitors—almost as if the entire island was a single resort. For details on great restaurants, beaches, shopping, outdoor sports, and other activities, see Chapter 17!

Chapter 17

Enjoying Lana'i

In This Chapter

- The ultimate itineraries for Lana'i
- The best places to dine on Lana'i
- The most interesting things to see on Lana'i
- The best things to do on Lana'i

Once known as "Pineapple Island," today **Lana'i** might be better called "Luxury Secluded Vacation Island."

Of course, this tiny piece of paradise (only 140 square miles) has plenty to offer the vacationer, from Hawaiian history to quality beach time. The island is home to two resorts owned and operated by **Four Seasons,** one additional independent hotel, some B&Bs, and a few eateries.

Tourism is a more recent phenomenon as the pineapple industry's moment has passed, but there's still lots to do—and lots more to see than the requisite idyllic beaches. You've got an arid desert rock garden, a lush rainforest, as well as Cook Island pine forests brought over from New Zealand.

There's nothing like a sunset among Lana'i's upcountry Norfolk Pines.

(Photo courtesy of HVCB/Ron Dahlquist)

The Top Five Things to Do on Lana'i

Lana'i has a surprising diversity of sights for such a small place—and the upside is it shouldn't be hard to see them all!

1. It's not called the Garden of the Gods for nothing—set aside an early morning or late afternoon to take in the mystery of **Keahikawelo's rock formations,** otherwise known as the **Garden of the Gods.**
2. Visit a historic fishing village, the vacation spot of a warrior king, and a respected place of refuge all at the **Kaunolu Archaeological Park.**
3. Marvel at the island's ecological diversity by taking a drive (or if you have a few days, a hike) along the **Munro Trail**—the view alone of six other islands from Mt. Lanaihale is worth the trip!
4. Immerse yourself in history with an afternoon inspecting the hundreds of **Luahiwa Petroglyphs,** right in central Lana'i.
5. Gorgeous seaside views and Hawaiian legend combine at **Pu'u Pehe,** or **Sweetheart Rock,** in south Lana'i.

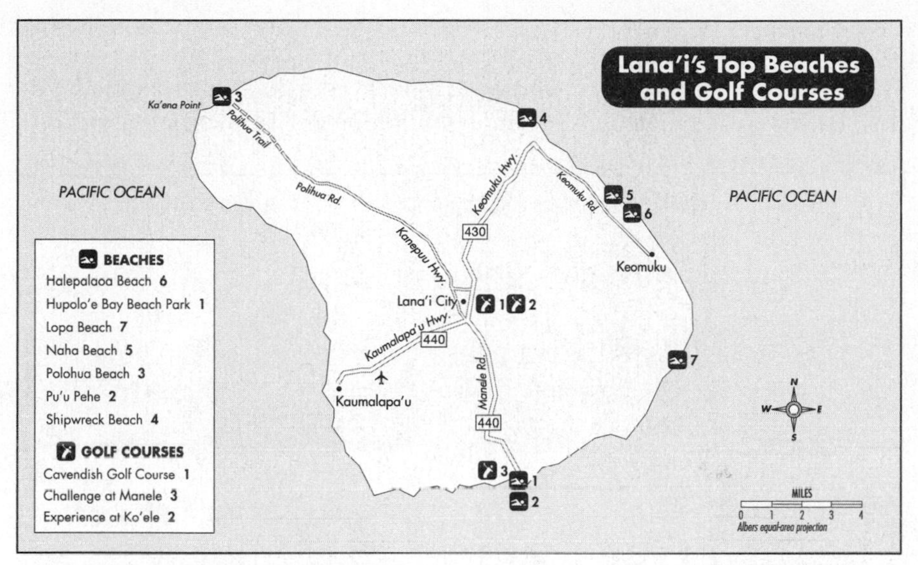

Lana'i's beaches and golf courses.

Plan My Trip: Ultimate Itineraries for Lana'i

Lana'i is small, and most of the roads are four-wheel-drive (4WD) only. Those rugged roads take a big chunk of time to traverse, even in a big ol' SUV. So you might not have as much extra time as you think for seeing all of the sights.

The descriptions of each stop are generally brief, written to give you a feel for each. You'll find more thorough write-ups of each place later in the chapter.

It's usually worthwhile to make advance reservations for recommended restaurants and tours.

ITINERARY #1: FOR YOUNG FAMILIES

1. **Breakfast:** Enjoy the breakfast spread at the hotel, then head out for a beach day at **Hulopo'e Beach** at the southern end of the island. There's fantastic snorkeling and calm swimming for even beginner swimmers, particularly in the tide pool.

continues

continued

2. **Lunch:** If you didn't pack a picnic, make your way back to Lana'i City and grab something simple and filling at **Pele's Other Garden.**
3. If the kids aren't tuckered out, it's worth a short visit before dinner to the **Kaunolu Archaeological Park**—you might not be up for the whole hike, but you can check out the remains of the fishing village and enjoy the forgotten feel of the place.
4. **Dinner:** Get the kids psyched for a "dress-up" dinner at the **Lodge at Ko'ele.** The food is delicious, and don't worry, there's always something for the *keikis* to enjoy.

ITINERARY #2: FOR OLDER FAMILIES

1. **Breakfast:** Grab a bite to eat at the hotel, and then spend the morning out on the water! Enjoy a snorkeling or sailing adventure—meal included!—on the family-owned **Trilogy.**
2. Once you're back on dry land, take an afternoon stroll around the **Kanepu'u Preserve** and enjoy the nearly 50 plant species unique to the area.
3. **Dinner:** Chill out with something easy at the **Blue Ginger Café** back in Lana'i City.

ITINERARY #3: FOR SINGLES

1. **Breakfast:** You're on vacation, so make it an easy morning. Enjoy a leisurely breakfast and scope out Lana'i City at **Coffee Works.** Go ahead and have ice cream for breakfast—we won't tell.
2. **Lunch:** Try some swimming, snorkeling, or even a scuba dive at **Pu'u Pehe.** Don't forget to check out the bird heiau at Sweetheart Rock while you're there. Then, enjoy a delicious lunch and view cliffside at the **Challenge at Manele Bay.**
3. While there's still daylight, head east and spook yourself at the ghost town of **Keomuku Village.**

4. **Dinner:** Hawaiian meets Cajun? See for yourself at **Henry's Rotisserie.** The relaxed atmosphere makes it a great spot for cross-table chatting.

ITINERARY #4: A ROMANTIC GETAWAY

1. **Breakfast:** Are you getting a late start? Don't worry, grab a bite to eat at **Coffee Works** on your way out of town, then head straight to **Haleopaola Beach** on the northern coast is a lovely place for an intimate stroll any time of morning … er, afternoon.
2. **Lunch:** On your way back south, stop in Lana'i City and split a pizza at **Pele's Other Garden**. Don't pig out too much—you want to save your appetite for your romantic dinner tonight!
3. Everyone knows there's something desperately romantic about a shipwreck—and at **Shipwreck Beach,** you've got two visible wrecks to gaze on from afar. Make sure you don't miss the mysterious **"Bird Man" petroglyphs** nearby.
4. Head down south on Route 440 to **Pu'u Pehe Beach,** home of the **Sweetheart Rock.** Tell each other the tale of the jealous husband and promise to never doubt each other. Then, make sure nobody's listening and laughing hysterically.
5. **Dinner:** As the daylight fades, head back towards civilization and a cozy, elegant dinner at the Four Seasons' **Manele Bay Hotel.** Because nothing's more romantic than luxury, after all.

ITINERARY #5: EASY-GOING; NONSTRENUOUS

1. **Breakfast:** Get started on your beach read over a good home-cooked breakfast at the locally owned **Blue Ginger Café.** While you're there, pick up some picnic supplies.

continues

continued

2. **Lunch:** Just because you're taking it easy doesn't mean you don't deserve the best—spend your day swimming, lounging, and picnicking with a classic Hawaii view at **Lopa Beach** on the northeast part of the island.
3. Head back down to Lana'i City and see what's on offer at the **Lana'i Arts Center** for the evening, whether it's a performance or film screening, or even just a stroll around the gallery.
4. **Dinner:** Take your time and savor cocktails (umbrella optional) and excellent dining at the **Lodge at Ko'ele.**

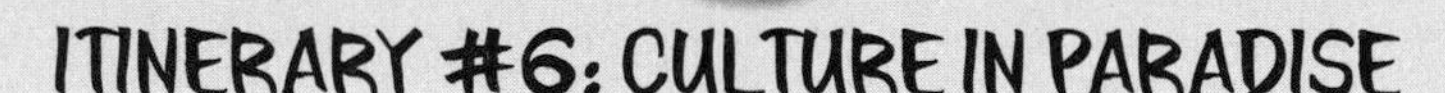

ITINERARY #6: CULTURE IN PARADISE

1. **Breakfast:** Grab a bite at the hotel, then head south to the **Halulu Heiau,** a favorite fishing spot for King Kamehameha the Great and very well kept. Feel the peace of this ancient place of refuge.
2. On your way back north for lunch, stop and explore the Luahiwa Petroglyphs, some of the most fascinating and best-preserved petroglyphs in Hawaii.
3. **Lunch:** As you head north on today's trajectory, make time for a bite at the Blue Ginger Café—good sandwiches should tide you over through the afternoon.
4. Continue north on Route 440 to Keahikawelo (a.k.a. **Garden of the Gods**), the most awe-inspiring site on Lana'i and definitely a front-runner for one of Hawaii's top sites to see. As the sun begins its downward descent, watch the shadows elongate and take in the wonder of this desolate place.
5. **Dinner:** Make your way back to Lana'i for a first-class dinner at the **Manele Bay Hotel.**

Itinerary #7: Adventure in the Great Outdoors

1. **Breakfast:** You don't want to waste your morning, so get up early, grab a good breakfast at Lana'i City's **Coffee Works,** and try sea kayaking or even, yes, a surfing safari with **Adventure Lana'i Ecocentre.** They really are experts and your best bet for some high-impact outdoor action.
2. **Lunch:** Hungry? Never fear, the massive servings at **Pele's Other Garden** back in Lana'i City will energize you for the afternoon's exploring.
3. It might be only 2 miles, but the **Hulopo'e-Huawai Fishing Trail** on Lana'i's southern coast packs a wallop—as well as some really breathtaking ocean views and a surprising diversity of foliage.
4. **Dinner:** Tired? You? Never! So why not try one last adventure. Dine at **Henry's Rotisserie.** Hawaiian and Cajun sound like unlikely plate-fellows, but you're in for a pleasant and truly original surprise.

The Top Lana'i Attractions, A to Z

Garden of the Gods North and East Lana'i

See "Keahikawelo" section.

Halulu Heiau South Lana'i

This well-preserved hilltop heiau in the ancient fishing village of Kaunolu was one of the last built, and used as a place of refuge for criminals, as well as a safe haven for women and children in times of war into the nineteenth century. It was also the favorite vacation fishing spot for King Kamehameha the Great. *Take Route 440 (Manele Road) south from Lana'i City, turn right on Kaupili Road and take the fourth dirt road. 4WD recommended.*

Kane'apua Rock South Lana'i

This natural jetty of lava rock, located near Lana'i's southern sea cliffs at the island's southernmost point, is an excellent fishing spot and a striking scenic lookout. Take Route 440 (Manele Road) south from Lana'i City, continue on Kaupili Road, and take the fourth dirt road. *To the right of Kaunolu Village. 4WD recommended.*

Kanepu'u Preserve West Lana'i

The Hawaiian islands were once covered with dryland forests; today, the Kanepu'u is the largest remnant of these, and contains 49 unique plant species. This 590-acre preserve is a beautiful setting for a contemplative hike—or if you'd prefer a guided hike for larger groups, contact the Nature Conservancy of Hawaii. *Located at the end of Polihua Road, northwest of Lana'i City. Open for self-guided tours 9 A.M.–4 P.M. 4WD recommended.* ***808-572-7849.***

Kaumalapa'u Harbor West Lana'i

This quiet harbor was once a bustling port when Lana'i was still an epicenter of pineapple exports. Today, it serves as the departure point for most fishing expeditions and offers the sightseer an idyllic view of lush hills and deep blue water. *On Route 440 (Kaumalapa'u Road) about 7.5 miles west of Lana'i City.*

Kaunolu Archeological Park South Lana'i

Probably first established in the fifteenth century, today the Kaunolu fishing village is a National Historic Landmark, housing the Halulu heiau, the vacation home of Kamehameha the Great, and the foundations of more than 100 Hawaiian homes, storerooms, and burial sites. Honolulu's Bishop Museum has constructed a self-guided interpretative hike for you to better enjoy this ancient and culturally significant site. *Take Route 440 (Manele Road) south from Lana'i City, continue on Kaupili Road, and take the fourth dirt road. 4WD recommended.*

Keahikawelo (Garden of the Gods) North Lana'i

Only 7 miles northwest of Lana'i City, the Garden of the Gods is a desolate, haunting area scattered with awe-inspiring rock formations and no vegetation whatsoever. This eerie rock garden is best viewed at dawn or dusk, when slanting shadows and dramatic light best highlight Keahikawelo's striking colors and mysterious shapes. *Located on Polihua Road at the far edge of the Kanepu'u Preserve, northwest of Lana'i City. 4WD recommended.*

Keomuku Village East Lana'i

When Keomuku's water supply was contaminated in the late nineteenth century, this bustling town became a ghost town. Today, only a few structures remain, including the Malamalama Church, built during plantation days in the 1800s and recently renovated. Today, you can attend church services in Hawaiian here. *Take Route 430 northeast and turn right on the dirt road.*

Lana'i Art Center Lana'i City and Central Lana'i

Open since 1991, the Lana'i Art Center provides classes and workshops, along with theater productions, a free film series, and changing exhibitions of local art in the gallery. There are frequent open-house events, so check the website before your visit! *339 7th Street.* ***808-565-7503.*** *www.Lana'iart.org.*

Luahiwa Petroglyphs Lana'i City and Central Lana'i

These rock drawings by early Hawaiian settlers on Lana'i convey a powerful sense of the island's important place in Hawaii's cultural history. Although difficult to get to (double-check your directions in town), the Luahiwa Petroglyphs are richly rewarding—there are hundreds of them, depicting men, women, animals, and canoes. *Take Route 440 (Manele Road) south of Lana'i City, turn left on the first gravel/dirt road after the guardrail ends. Pass the water tower and gulch to find the petroglyphs.*

Munro Trail Lana'i City and Central Lana'i

This dirt road drive is only 7 miles long, but takes anywhere from two to three hours to drive (or nearly 16 hours to hike!), winding through the rainforest and Cook Island pines, planted by New Zealand naturalist George Munro. Its summit, about 3 miles in at Mt. Lanaihale, is 3,370 feet above sea level and offers views of six islands on a clear day. *Take Route 440 north from Lana'i City until it becomes Keomoku Road. Turn right at Cemetery Road and follow the signs to Munro Trail.*

Pu'u Pehe (Sweetheart Rock) South Lana'i

Follow the shoreline trail to the left of Hulopo'e Beach and you will soon overlook Pu'u Pehe, a former bird heiau (according to archaeologists) or the tomb where a grieving husband buried his wife before plunging to his death (according to Hawaiian legend). Either way, the rock itself, triangular in shape and red in color, is gorgeous, and the walk to the overlook is quite romantic. *Take Route 440 (Manele Road) south to Manele Road and follow that to the end.*

Lana'i's Munro Trail is challenging, but yields spectacular views.

(Photo courtesy of HVCB/Ron Dahlquist)

Shipwreck Beach Petroglyphs East Lana'i

This beach, the site of a wrecked World War II Liberty Ship and ruined lighthouse, is still perilous for fishermen—but offers a special pleasure to the sightseer. The strange "Bird Man of Lana'i" petroglyphs, stick figures with birdlike heads, are symbols whose meaning has been lost, although they still fill the viewer with wonder. *Take Route 430 (Keomoku Road) north and west for 8.5 miles. As you near the sea, take the dirt road to the left for another 3 miles past old fishing cabins.*

Lana'i's Top Beaches

Lana'i boasts a number of beautiful beaches, and on about three quarters of them you'll have the sand to yourself, with primitive or nonexistent facilities. And some of the island's most beautiful beaches are remote, requiring an SUV for access, with often treacherous waters. It's just the price you pay for that natural, pristine experience. Be sure to exercise extreme caution before entering the water!

Halepalaoa Beach North and East Lana'i

No facilities. Take Route 430 (Keomoku Road) northeast and turn right on the dirt road. Next to Keomoku Village.

Hulopo'e Beach South Lana'i

Restrooms and picnic tables, but no lifeguard. Take Route 440 (Manele Road) south and follow the road to the end. Full facilities.

Lopa Beach North and East Lana'i

No facilities. Take Route 430 northeast (Keomoku Road) and pick one of several 4WD roads.

Naha Beach North and East Lana'i

No facilities. Follow Route 430 (Keomoku Road) and pick one of several 4WD roads.

Polihua Beach West Lana'i

No facilities. Follow Route 440 north to Polihua Road. Located at the far edge of the Kanepu'u Preserve. 4WD recommended.

Pu'u Pehe South Lana'i

No facilities. Take Route 440 (Manele Road) south of Lana'i City about 13 miles; follow the signs to Hulopo'e Beach.

Shipwreck Beach East Lana'i

No facilities. Drive along Route 430 (Keomoku Road) north for 8.5 miles. As you near the sea, take the dirt road to the left for another 3 miles past old fishing cabins.

Great Dining with Atmosphere: The Best Places to Eat

As the tiny, isolated island that Lana'i is, the restaurants and cafés are few and far between compared to Honolulu or other parts of Hawaii. But the greatest part of Lana'i is how quaint it is and how easy it is to find locally owned businesses.

With that said, here are our picks for the best restaurants on Lana'i.

The Lodge at Ko'ele

The Lodge offers several dining options, from the casual ambience of The Experience at Koele golf course clubhouse, overlooking the pond at the first hole (light American) for lunch; to the formal Dining Room, offering local estate-grown ingredients, creative Pacific Rim cuisine, and a superb wine selection. *One Keomoku Highway, Lana'i City. Clubhouse open 10:30 A.M.–4:30 P.M. Dining room open daily 6–9:30 P.M.* ***1-800-536-3866.***

The Manele Bay Hotel

Take your pick of one of several restaurants at this luxurious hotel known for its Hawaiian fare. The Challenge at Manele Bay Clubhouse and Huele Court are great for breakfast and lunch, while the Ihilani Restaurant offers a high-class option for evening dining. *One Manele Bay Road, South Lana'i. Open daily.* ***808-565-7700*** *or* ***1-800-321-4666.*** *www.fourseasons.com/manelebay/dining.html.*

Blue Ginger Café

Locally owned, this café serves breakfast, lunch, and dinner. They have a small menu, with only a few offerings for each meal. *On the corner of 7th Street and Illima Avenue in Lana'i City. Open daily from 6 A.M.–9 P.M.* ***808-565-6363.***

Coffee Works

This espresso bar and ice cream shop also offers coffee and small gift baskets for sale. *604 Illima Avenue (on the corner of 6th and Illima). Open Monday–Friday 7 A.M.–6 P.M., Saturday from 7 A.M.–2 P.M.* ***808-565-6962.*** *www.coffeeworkshawaii.com.*

Henry Clay's Rotisserie

This historic landmark dates back to the 1920s. The chef blends traditional Hawaiian foods with his Cajun roots to create interesting and unique fare. *828 Lana'i Avenue. Dinner served 5:30–9 P.M.* ***1-877-ONLANA'I*** *or* ***1-877-665-2624.*** *www.hotelLana'i.com/rest.html.*

Pele's Other Garden

This place calls itself Lana'i's New York–style Deli and Bistro, so if you're missing a taste of home, this is the place to go. They're really only open for lunch so enjoy their overstuffed sandwiches, pasta salads, and pizzas midday. *On the corner of 8th and Houston in Lana'i City. Open daily from 10 A.M.–5 P.M.* ***808-565-9628*** *or* ***1-888-POG-DELI.***

Entertainment and Nightlife

Enjoying the sun, surf, and stores of Lana'i is certainly a great way to spend your vacation. But you may also want to check out what's going on at night, from music to movies.

Music

If you enjoy music on the piano or want to get a taste of some traditional Hawaiian tunes, you should check out the **Hale Ahe Ahe Lounge at the Resort at Manele Bay (808-565-2000)** located on the southern coast of Lana'i near Hulopo'e Beach. Catch a relaxing show and drink after a long day. **The Lodge at Ko'ele (808-565-7300** or **808-565-4000)** offers the same material and a similar venue but in central Lana'i.

Theater and Performing Arts

For a unique theater experience you should visit the **Lana'i Theater** at 465 7th Street (**808-565-7500**). This historic 1930s landmark can accommodate up to 150 people and offers live performances and movies. If you'd rather stay in to catch a flick, you can rent a movie just down the street at the **Lana'i Family Store** at 443 7th Street (**808-565-6485**).

Art Galleries

The Lana'i Woodworkers at 1028 Illima Avenue (**808-565-9897**) create and sell handmade pieces of furniture. For more traditional art, **Mike Carroll** has a gallery at 443 Seventh Street (**808-565-7122;** www.mikecarrollgallery.com) that showcases his paintings that blend his passions for nature and art. Another art gallery worth checking out is the **Heart of Lana'i Art Gallery** at 758 Queens Street (**808-565-7815**), which features art of all types including paintings, pottery, and woodworking.

The Lana'i Art Center's (808-565-7503; www.Lana'iart.org, 339 7th Street) gallery is open Monday through Saturday from noon to 4 P.M. and features work from over 30 local artists. The Center has a gift shop in addition to the gallery that sells cards, jewelry, and other handmade goodies.

Shopping on Lana'i: Clothing, Jewelry, Markets, and More!

Shopping on Lana'i will not be the adventure or experience that Honolulu can provide, but Lana'i does have its own character. While you won't find a large shopping mall, the smaller, local stores will meet your needs. For groceries or other necessities, you can head to the **Pine Isle Market,** 356 8th Street (**808-565-6488**), that offers dry goods, meats, photo supplies, and more. **The International Food and Clothing Center** at 833 Illima Avenue (**808-565-6433**) offers the same items in addition to hardware supplies, beer, and liquor. They are closed on Saturday, however. The oldest retail grocery store in Lana'i is **Richard's Shopping Center** at 434 8th Street (**808-565-6047**). They also have a small section of gifts and souvenirs.

If you're looking for something other than groceries, though, there are plenty of other places to explore. **Gifts with Aloha** at 363 7th Street (**808-565-6589**) features work from local Lana'i and Hawaii Artists. For clothing and accessories, you have a few options, like **The Personal Shopper** on Illima Street (**808-565-7334**), which offers clothing, accessories, home decorations, and Filipino food products. In **The Local Gentry** at 363 7th Street (**808-565-9130**), you can find any clothing item that you or a family member forgot to pack. Finally, **Dis 'N Dat Shop** (**866-347-6328**) at 418 8th Street, boasts unique Hawaiian jewelry and trinkets.

Enjoying the Best Activities and Outdoor Lana'i

You're missing out on a great part of Hawaii if you don't get out into the pristine nature that it offers. Scenes like those pictured in the TV hit *Lost* are a reality, so get out and see what's there.

Water Sports and Sightseeing

What's Hawaii without a great ocean experience? Most would say it's not a truly Hawaiian adventure. Here's a look at a few companies that offer tours for you and your family to enjoy while on Lana'i.

- **Adventure Lana'i Ecocentre** offers ATV and Land Rover rentals, guided 4x4 treks, sea kayaking, and diving tours, instructional clinics and surfboarding safaris. They also rent camping equipment and mountain bikes, so if you have a need for adventure, this should be your first stop. ***808-565-7373.*** *www.adventureLana'i.com.*

- **Lana'i Surf School and Safari** provides surfing lessons, private or groups, for beginners to advanced practitioners. They also rent out boards for day use. They don't have a shop, but will meet you at your hotel with all of the gear you need. ***808-306-9837.*** *www.Lana'isurfsafari.com.*

- **Spinning Dolphin Charters** of Lana'i offers private sportfishing charters, whale-watching, and snorkeling tours. With a CPR-certified captain and fully-outfitted boat, you're in safe hands. *Price: $100/hour, four-hour minimum (three hours for whale-watching) and six-person maximum. Refreshments provided.* ***808-565-6613.***

- **Trilogy** is a family-owned and -operated ocean sport company. They offer snorkeling, scuba diving, rafting, and sailing opportunities. Many of their tours are pre-set and often include a meal. Some tours also only take place on certain days of the week or certain seasons, so plan ahead if you use Trilogy. ***1-800-MAUI-800.*** *www.visitLana'i.com.*

Golf Courses on Lana'i

If you plan to go to Hawaii to spend a lot of time golfing, Lana'i is not the place for you as far as the variety of courses is concerned. The island does lay claim, however, to two of the best courses in the country, but there is only one other municipal course beyond that.

Cavendish Golf Course. Located near Lana'i City, this nine-hole, par-36 course is set amid the area's famous Norfolk Pines. It's a one-of-a-kind place, with no clubhouse, no tee times, no score cards, and no club rentals. To play, just show up and slip a donation into the wooden box next to the first tee ($5–$10 recommended). *9 holes. Par 36, 3,071 yards. Keomoku Road near Lodge at Ko'ele, Lana'i City.*

The Challenge at Manele. This leeward course was designed by Jack Nicklaus and has some of the most astounding views on any course in Hawaii. *18 holes. Par 72, 7,039 yards. Greens fees are $225. One Manele Bay Road, Lana'i City.* ***808-565-2222.***

The Experience at Ko'ele. Designed by Greg Norman and Ted Robinson, this course has been named one of the top ten resort courses by *Golf Magazine. 18 holes. Par 72, 7,014 yards. Greens fees $225. One Keomoku Highway, Lana'i City, HI, 96763.* ***808-565-4000*** *or* ***808-565-4653.***

Hiking the Island

Getting into the tropical vegetation and spotting native Hawaiian birds is part of the thrill and draw of these lush islands. Here are a few snippets of what Lana'i's natural wonderland has to offer:

- **Hulopo'e-Huawai Fishing Trail** is a short trail near Hulopo'e Beach. It is aptly named since the trail travels along the coast and provides easy access to various fishing areas. Don't be fooled, though, this trail is difficult and not for the weak of heart. **Distance: 2 miles.** *Take Route 440 south out of Lana'i City for about 5 miles. When the highway makes a left turn, continue straight on Kaupili Road and take the first left on New Manele Road. Follow this road down to the ocean.*
- **Ko'ele Nature Hike** starts at the Lodge at Ko'ele and travels a loop onto Koloiki Ridge, passing through upland forests of Norfolk Pines along the way. From the ridge you'll be able to see Maui and Moloka'i in the distance. **Distance: 5 miles.** *Trail starts at the Lodge at Ko'ele Reflecting Pool. Ask the Lodge concierge for a map.*
- **Munro Trail** is a four-wheel-drive and hiking trail just north of Lana'i City. It winds through lush forest up to Lanaihale, the highest point on the island at 3,370 feet. On a clear day, you'll be able to see all of the Hawaiian islands from this point. **Distance: 8 miles.** *Take Route 440 north from Lana'i City until it becomes Keomoku Road. Turn right at Cemetery Road and follow the signs to Munro Trail.*
- **Shipwreck Beach Trail** got its name because the body of water it follows is actually the channel that separates Lana'i from Moloka'i. This channel has caused several ships to run aground. The World War II Liberty Ship was purposely abandoned just off Lana'i's northeast coast and has remained on the reef for over 50 years. What a sight to see while on a walk! **Distance: Up to 7 miles down the beach.** *Take Route 430 (Keomoku Road) north and west for 8.5 miles.*

Lana'i is like a private reserve for those who want a manageable resort experience combined with plenty of opportunities for beauty and seclusion. It's at once manicured and wild—just the place to pamper yourself while enjoying the sun and sea.

Hawaii A to Z: Facts at Your Fingertips

Here's a select listing of useful agencies and services throughout Hawaii, organized by type of service and island.

AAA Offices

AAA, 1130 Nimitz Highway, Honolulu, HI 96817, Suite A-170; 808-593-2221 (O'ahu); 1-800-736-2886 (other islands); Open Monday through Friday 9 A.M.–5 P.M.; Saturday 9 A.M.–2 P.M.; www.aaa.com

Airlines

- Air Canada: 1-888-247-2262; aircanada.com
- Air Pacific: 1-800-227-4446; www.airpacific.com
- Aloha Airlines: 1-800-367-5250; www.alohaairlines.com
- American Airlines: 1-800-433-7300; www.aa.com

- American Trans Air: 1-800-435-9282; www.ata.com
- Continental Airlines: 1-800-525-0280; www.continental.com
- Delta Airlines: 1-800-221-1212; www.delta.com
- China Airlines: 1-800-227-5118; www.china-airlines.com
- go! Airlines: 1-888-IFLYGO2; www.iflygo.com
- Hawaiian Airlines: 1-800-367-5320; www.hawaiianairlines.com
- Island Air: 1-800-652-6541; www.islandair.com
- Japan Airlines: 1-800-525-3663; www.jal.com
- Korean Air: 1-800-438-5000; www.koreanair.com
- Molokai Air Shuttle: 808-567-6847; 888-266-3597
- Pacific Wings: 1-888-575-4546; www.pacificwings.com
- Paragon Airlines: 808-244 3356; www.paragon-air.com
- Philippine Airlines: 1-800-435-9725; www.philippineairlines.com
- Quantas Airways: 1-800-227-4500; www.quantas.com
- United Airlines: 1-800-241-6522; www.ual.com

Airports

General Airport Information: www.state.hi.us/dot/airports/index.htm

Big Island:

- Hilo International Airport (ITO): 808-934-5838; Lost and Found: 808-934-5863; 808-934-5898
- Kona International Airport (KOA): 808-329-3423; Lost and Found: 808-329-5073

Kaua'i:

- Lihue Airport (LIH): 808-246-1448; Lost and Found: 808-246-1410

Lana'i:

- Lana'i Airport (LNY): 808-872-3830

Maui:

- Kahului Airport (OGG): 808-872-3893; Lost and Found: 808-872-3421

Moloka'i:

- Kaunakakai (Moloka'i) Airport (MKK): 808-567-6361

O'ahu:

- Honolulu International Airport (HNL): 808-836-6413; Lost and Found: 808-836-6547

Accessibility and Disability Resources

- Accessible Journeys: 808-846-4537; www.disabilitytravel.com
- Flying Wheels Travel: 507-451-5005; www.flyingwheelstravel.com
- Hawaii Center for Independent Living: 414 Kauwili Street, Suite 102, Honolulu, HI 96817; 808-522-5400; www.search.volunteerhawaii.org

ATM Locators

- Cirrus: 1-800-424-7787; www.mastercard.com/cardholderservices/atm
- Plus: 1-800-843-7587; www.visa.com/atms

Bed and Breakfast Agencies

- www.bestbnb.com
- www.bbonline.com/hi
- www.bnbfinder.com
- www.bedandbreakfast.com

Better Business Bureau

The Better Business Bureau: 1132 Bishop Street, Suite 1507, Honolulu, HI 96813-2813; www.hawaii.bbb.org

Bicycle Rental

Big Island:

- Hilo Bike Hub: 318 E. Kawili Street, Hilo; 808-961-4452
- Mid-Pacific Wheels: 1133-C Manono Street, Hilo; 808-935-6211
- Hale Hana Centre: 74-5583 Luhia Street, Kailua-Kona; 808-326-2453

Kaua'i:

- Outfitters Kaua'i: Po'ipu Plaza, 2827A Po'ipu Road, Po'ipu Beach; 808-742-9667 or 808-742-7421
- Kauai Cycle and Tour: 1379 Kuhio Highway, Kapa'a; 808-821-2115
- North Shore Bike Doktor: 5-5052 Kuhio Highway, Hanalei; 808-826-7799

Lana'i:

- The Lodge at Ko'ele: Lana'i City; 808-565-7300 or 1-800-321-4666; www.fourseasons.com/koele

Maui:

- Maui Downhill: 199 Dairy Road, Kahului; 808-871-2155 or 1-800-535-BIKE; www.mauidownhill.com
- Haleakala Bike Company: Hana Highway, Haiku; 808-575-9575 or 1-888-922-2453; www.bikemaui.com
- Maui Mountain Cruisers: 1-800-232-6284; www.mauimountaincruisers.com

Moloka'i:

- Moloka'i Bicycle: 80 Mohala Street, Kaunakakai; 808-553-3931

O'ahu:

- Barnfield's Raging Isle Surf & Cycle: 66-250 Kamehameha Highway, Hale'iwa; 808-637-7707
- The Bike Shop: 270 Ku'ulei Road, Kailua; 808-261-1553
- Hale Nalu Surf & Bike: 85-876 Farrington Highway, Wai'anae; 808-696-5897; www.halenalu.com
- Planet Surf: 159 Kailulani Avenue in Waikiki; 808-924-9050

Bus Services

Big Island:

- Alii Shuttle: 808-775-7171
- Hele-On Bus: 808-961-8744; www.hawaiicounty.com

O'ahu:

- TheBus: 808-848-5555; www.thebus.org
- Handi-Van: 808-523-4083; www.honolulu.gov/dts/index.htm
- Waikiki Trolley: 808-591-2561 or 1-800-824-8804; www.waikikitrolley.com

Kaua'i:

- Kaua'i Bus Company: 808-241-6410

Maui:

- Holo Ka'a Public Transit: 808-879-2828
- Maui Bus: 808-871-4838

Camping

See National Parks and State Park Locator.

Car Rental Companies

National Companies:

- Alamo: 1-800-327-9633; www.alamo.com
- Avis: 1-800-321-3712; www.avis.com
- Budget: 1-800-527-7000; www.budget.com
- Dollar: 1-800-800-4000; www.dollar.com
- Enterprise: 1-800-736-8222; www.enterprise.com
- Hertz: 1-800-654-3011; www.hertz.com
- National: 1-800-227-7368; www.nationalcar.com
- Tradewinds: 1-888-388-7368; www.tradewindsudrive.com

Big Island:

- Harper Car & Truck Rental: 808-969-1478 or 1-800-852-9993; www.harpershawaii.com

Maui:

- Maui Car Rentals: 1-800-567-4659; www.mauicarrentals.net
- Word of Mouth Car Rentals: 808-877-2436; www.mauirentacar.com

Moloka'i:

- Island Kine Auto Rental & Sales: 808-553-5242
- Lana'i City Service: 808-565-7227

O'ahu:

- Tradewinds: 808-834-1465 or 1-888-388-7368; www.tradewindsudrive.com

Chamber of Commerce

Chamber of Commerce of Hawaii: 1132 Bishop Street, Suite 402, Honolulu, HI 96813; 808-545-4300

Convention Bureaus

Hawaii Visitors and Convention Bureau (HVCB): Suite 801, Waikiki Business Plaza, 2270 Kalakaua Avenue, Honolulu, HI 96815; 1-800-923-1811; www.gohawaii.com

Cruise Lines and Ferries

- Celebrity Cruises: 1-800-647-2251; www.celebritycruises.com
- Expeditions (Maui-Lana'i): 808-661-3756; www.go-lanai.com
- Hawaii Super Ferry: 808-543-3519; www.hawaiisuperferry.com
- Lahaina Cruise Company (Maui-Moloka'i): 808-275-6969 or 1-808-667-6165; www.mauiprincess.com
- Norwegian Cruise Lines: 1-866-234-0292; www.ncl.com

- Princess Cruises: 1-800-PRINCESS; www.princess.com
- Royal Caribbean: 1-866-562-7625; www.royalcaribbean.com

Customs Offices

- Office of the Chief Counsel, Immigration and Customs Enforcement, U.S. Department of Homeland Security, 595 Ala Moana Boulevard, Honolulu, HI 96813; 808-522-8252

Gay and Lesbian Resources

- The Center: 2424 South Beretania Street, Honolulu, HI 96823. Open Monday–Friday 10 A.M.–6 P.M., Saturday from 12 P.M.–4 P.M. 808-951-7000; www.thecenterhawaii.org
- International Gay & Lesbian Travel Association: 1-800-448-8550; www.iglta.org
- Out in Hawaii: www.outinhawaii.com
- Gay/Lesbian/Bisexual/Transgender Audio Bulletin Board: 808-823-6248

Helicopter Tours

Big Island:

- Blue Hawaiian: 808-961-5600
- Tropical Helicopters: 808-961-6810
- Mauna Loa Helicopters: 808-334-0191

Kaua'i:

- Air Kaua'i: 808-246-4666
- Helicopter Tour in Paradise: 1-877-742-7983
- Jack Harter Helicopters: 1-888-245-2001

Maui:

- Air Maui: 808-238-4942; www.airmaui.com
- Blue Hawaiian Helicopters: 808-871-8844; www.bluehawaiian.com
- Sunshine Helicopters: 808-871-0722; www.sunshinehelicopters.com

O'ahu:

- HeliUSA: 808-826-6591 or 1-866-936-1234; www.heliusahawaii.com
- Makani Kai: 808-834-5813; www.makanikai.com
- Paradise Helicopters: 808-329-6601; www.paradisehelecopters.com

Horseback Tours

Big Island:

- Dahana Ranch: 808-885-0057
- Kings' Trail Rides: 808-323-2388
- Parker Ranch: 808-885-5006
- Waipi'o Na'alapa Trail Rides: 808-775-0419
- Waipi'o Ridge Stables: 808-775-1007

Kaua'i:

- Princeville Ranch Stables: 808-826-6777

Lana'i:

- The Lodge at Ko'ele: 808-565-7300 or 1-800-321-4666; www.fourseasons.com/koele

Maui:

- Ironwood Ranch: 808-669-4991; www.ironwoodranch.com
- Lahaina Stables: 808-667-2222; www.mauihorse.com
- Makena Stables: 808-879-0244; www.makenastables.com
- Mendes Ranch: 808-871.5222; www.mendesranch.com
- Pony Express Tours: 808-667-2200; ponyexpresstours.com

Moloka'i:

- Moloka'i Mule Ride: 808-567-6088
- Pu'u O Hoku Ranch: 808-558-8109; www. puuohoku.com

O'ahu:

- Gunstock Ranch: 808-341-3995 or 808-293-2026; www.gunstockranch.com
- Happy Trails Hawaii: 808-638-7433; www.happytrailshawaii.com
- Kualoa Ranch: 1-800-237-8515; www.kualoa.com

Hospitals and Emergency Care Centers

Big Island:

- Hilo Medical Center: 1190 Waianuenue Avenue, Hilo; 808-974-4700
- Kona Community Hospital: 79-1019 Haukapila Street, Kealakekua; 808-322-9311
- North Hawaii Community Hospital: 67-1125 Mamalahoa Highway, Waimea; 808-885-4444

Lana'i:

- Lana'i Community Hospital: 628 7th Street, Lana'i City; 808-565-6411
- Lana'i Family Health Center: 628-B Seventh Street, Lana'i City; 808-565-6423

Maui:

- Hana Medical Center: Hana Highway, Hana; 808-248-8924
- Maui Memorial Hospital: 221 Mahalani Street, Wailuku; 808-244-9056
- Urgent Care Maui: 1325 South Kihei Road, Suite 103, Kihei; 808-879-7781
- West Maui Healthcare Center: Whaler's Village, 2435 Ka'anapali Parkway, Suite H-7, Ka'anapali; 808-667-9721

Moloka'i:

- Moloka'i General Hospital: Kaunakakai; 808-553-5331

Kaua'i:

- Kaua'i Medical Clinic: 3420 Kuhio Highway; 808-822-3431

O'ahu/Honolulu:

- Kapiolani Medical Center: 98-1079 Moanalua Road, Honolulu; 808-486-6000
- Kuakini Medical Center: 347 Kuakini Street, Honolulu; 808-536-2236
- Queens Medical Center: 1301 Punchbowl Street, Honolulu; 808-538-9011
- Straub Clinic and Hospital: 888 South King Street, Honolulu; 808-522-4000

O'ahu/Elsewhere

- Castle Medical Center: 640 Ulukahiki Street, Kailua; 808-263-5500
- Wahiawa General Hospital: 128 Lehua Street, Wahiawa; 808-621-8411

Hostel Locators

- www.hawaiihostels.com
- www.hiayh.com
- www.hostel.com
- www.hostelworld.com
- www.hostelz.com

House Rental Locators

- www.beachhouse.com
- www.cyberrentals.com
- www.eliteprop.com
- www.hawaiianbeachrentals.com
- www.rentalsillustrated.com
- www.triphomes.com

Limo Services

General:

- Carey Limo: 1-888-563-2888

Big Island:

- Gold Coast Town Car Service: 808-325-5530
- Principle Limousine Service: 808-325-5466

Kaua'i:

- Any Time Shuttle: 808-927-1120
- Custom Limousine: 808-246-6318
- Kaua'i Limousine: 808-245-4855

Lana'i:

- Rabaca's Limousine Service: 808-565-6670

Maui:

- Aloha Maui Limousine Service: 808-873-2034 or 877-877-2034
- Star Maui Limousine: 808-875-6900 or 1-877-875-6900

O'ahu:

- Airport Limo Service: 808-946-1001
- Alpha Limousines: 808-955-8898
- Blue Hawaii Limousine: 808-366-2222
- Duke's Limousine: 808-738-1878
- Royal Pacific Limousine: 808-223-7822

Movie Theaters

Big Island:

- Honoka'a Peoples Theaters: Mamane Street, Honoka'a; 808-775-0000
- Keauho'u Cinemas: Keauho'u Shopping Center, 78-5725 Alii Drive, Keauhou; 808-324-7200

- Kress Cinemas: 174 Kamehameha Avenue, Hilo; 808-961-3456 (Recording)
- Makalapua Stadium Cinemas: 74-5469 Kamakaeha, Kailua-Kona; 808-327-0444
- Na'alehu Theater: Mamalahoa Highway, Naalehu; 808-929-9133
- Palace Theater: 38 Haili Street Hilo; 808-969-3626
- Prince Kuhio Theaters: Prince Kuhio Shopping Plaza, 111 East Puainako Street, Hilo; 808-961-3456

Kaua'i:

- Coconut Marketplace Cinemas: Coconut Marketplace, 4-484 Kuhio Highway, Kapa'a; 808-821-2324
- Kukui Grove Marketplace: 4368 Kukui Grove, Lihu'e; 808-245-5055

Maui:

- Maui Mall Megaplex Cinemas: 70 E Ka'ahumanu Avenue, Kahului; 808-871-6684
- Maunaloa Town Cinemas: 1 Mahaolu Street, Kahului; 808-552-2616
- Ka'ahumanu Theaters: 275 West Ka'ahumanu Avenue, Kahului; 808-875-4910

Moloka'i:

- Maunaloa Town Cinemas: One Maunaloa Highway, Maunaloa; 808-552-2707

O'ahu:

- Consolidated Theatres Aikahi: 25 Kane'ohe Bay Drive, Kailua; 808-593-3000
- Consolidated Theatres Kahala 8: Kahala Mall, 4211 Waialae Avenue, Kahala; 808-593-3000
- Consolidated Theatres Kapolei 16: 890 Kamokila Boulevard, Kapolei; 808-593-3000
- Consolidated Theatres Ko'Olau Stadium 10: 47-260 Hui Iwa Street, Kane'ohe; 808-593-3000
- Consolidated Theatres Mililani Stadium 14: 95-1249 Meheula Parkway, Mililani; 808-593-3000

- Consolidated Theatres Pearlridge West 16: 98-1005 Moanalua Road, Aiea; 808-593-3000
- Regal Cinemas Pearl Highlands Stadium 12: 1000 Kamehameha Highway, Pearl City; 808-455-8890
- Regal Cinemas Windward Stadium 10: 46-056 Kamehameha Highway, Kaneohe; 808-234-4006
- Wallace Theatres Keolu Center Cinemas: 1090 Keolu Drive, Kailua; 808-263-4171
- Wallace Theatres La'ie Cinemas: 55-510 Kamehameha Highway, La'ie; 808-293-7516

National Parks

Big Island:

- Ala Kahakai National Historic Trail: 73-4786 Kanalani Street, #14, Kailua-Kona, HI 96740; 808-326-6012; http://www.nps.gov/alka
- Hawaii Volcanoes National Park: P.O. Box 52, Hawaii National Park, HI 96718; 808-985-6000; www.nps.gov/havo
- Kaloko-Honokohau National Historical Park: 73-4786 Kailua-Kona, HI 96740; 808-326-9057; www.nps.gov/kaho
- Pu'uhonua o Honaunau National Historical Park: P.O. Box 129, Honaunau, HI 96726; 808-328-2326; www.nps.gov/puho

Maui:

- Haleakala National Park: P.O. Box 369, Makawao, HI 96768; 808-572-9306; www.nps.gov/hale

Moloka'i:

- Kalaupapa National Historical Park: P.O. Box 2222, Kalaupapa, HI 96742; 808-567-6802; www.nps.gov/kala

O'ahu:

- Pu'ukohola Heiau National Historic Site: 62-3601 Kawaihae Road, Kawaihae, HI 96743; 808-882-7218; www.nps.gov/puhe
- USS *Arizona* Memorial: 1 Arizona Memorial Place, Honolulu, HI 96818-3145; 808-422-0561

Police

- Big Island: 808-326-4646 in Kona; 808-961-2213 in Hilo
- Kaua'i: 808-245-9711
- Lana'i: 808-565-6428
- Maui: 808-244-6300
- Moloka'i: 808-553-5355
- O'ahu: 808-529-3111

Post Offices

There are numerous post offices all over Hawaii. To find the nearest location, call 1-800-275-8777. Here are the main offices for each island:

- Big Island: 154 Waianuenue Avenue Suite 1, Hilo; 74-5577 Palani Road, Kailua-Kona
- Kaua'i: 4441 Rice Street, Lihue
- Lana'i: 731 Lana'i Avenue, Lana'i City
- Maui: 1760 Honoapiilani Highway, Lahaina; 138 South Pu'unene, Kahului
- Moloka'i: 120 Ala Malama Avenue, Kaunakakai
- O'ahu: 1170 Nu'uanu Avenue #105, Honolulu

Shuttles

Big Island:

- Arnott's Lodge: 808-969-7097
- Hawaii Naniloa Hotel: 808-969-3333
- Kohala Coast Resort Association: 808-886-4915 or 1-800-318-3637
- SpeediShuttle: 808-329-5433 or 1-877-521-2085

O'ahu:

- Island Express Transport: 808-944-1879
- Waikiki Airport Express: 808-954-8652

Kaua'i:

- Kaua'i Marriott Resort and Beach Club: 808-245-5050
- Radisson Kaua'i Beach Resort: 808-245-1955

Maui:

- Airporter Shuttle: 808-877-7308 or 1-800-231-6984
- Kapalua Executive Transportation Services: 808-669-2300
- SpeediShuttle: 808-242-7777 or 1-877-521-2085

State Park Locator

Most of the beaches with facilities in Hawaii are state parks, and there are state parks in other locales as well. For a complete rundown of state parks, call 808-587-0300 or go to www.hawaii.gov/dlnr/dsp.

Surf and Water Sports Rental and Lessons

Big Island:

- Big Island Watersports: Kailua-Kona, HI 96745; 808-324-1650; www.bigislandwatersports.com
- Kona Honu Divers: 74-5583 Luhia Street, Kailua Kona, HI 96740; 808-324-4668; www.konahonudivers.com
- Ocean Sports: 808-885-5555

Kaua'i:

- Anini Beach Windsurfing School: Hanalei, HI; 808-826-9463
- Kayak Kauai Outbound: 5070 Kuhio Highway #A Hanalei; 808-826-9844 or 1-800-437-3507; www.kayakkauai.com
- Margo Oberg's School of Surfing: Kapilli Road, Po'ipu; 808-332-6100 or 808-639-0708; www.surfonkauai.com
- Windsurf Kauai: Kilauea; 808-828-6838

Lana'i:

- Adventure Lana'i Ecocentre: 338 8th Street, Lana'i City; 808-565-7373; www.adventureianai.com
- Lana'i Surf School and Safari: Lana'i City; 808-306-9837; www.lanaisurfsafari.com

Maui:

- Maui Waveriders: 3353 Keha Drive, Kihei; 808-875-4761
- Maui Windsurf Company: 22 Hana Highway, Kahului; 808-877-4816 or 1-800-872-0999; www.maui-windsurf.com
- Rivers to the Sea: North Shore, Maui; 808-280-8795 or 808-280-6236; www.riverstothesea.com
- Sailboards Maui: 22 Baldwin Avenue, Pa'ia; 808-871-7954; www.sailboardsmaui.com

Moloka'i:

- Bill Kapuni's Snorkel & Dive: Kaunakakai; 808-553-9867
- Moloka'i Outdoors: Kaunakakai; 1-877-553-4477; www.molokai-outdoors.com
- Moloka'i Action Adventures: Kaunakakai; 808-558-8184

O'ahu:

- Barnfield's Raging Isle Surf & Cycle: 66-250 Kamehameha Highway, Building B, Haleiwa; 808-637-7707; www.ragingisle.com
- Hale Nalu Surf & Bike: 85-876 Farrington Highway, Wai'anae; 808-696-5897; www.halenalu.com
- Hans Hedemann Surf School: Park Shore Waikiki. 2586 Kalakaua Avenue, Honolulu; 808-924-7778. 5000 Kahala Avenue Honolulu; 808-739-8888. 57-091 Kamehameha Highway Kahuku; 808-293-6000; www.hhsurf.com
- Hawaiian Watersports: 354 Hahani Street Kailua; 808-262-5483; www.hawaiianwatersports.com
- Kailua Sailboards and Kayaks: 130 Kailua Road, Kailua; 808-262-2555; www.kailuasailboards.com

Taxi Services

Big Island:

- A-1 Bob's Taxi: 808-959-4800
- Aloha Taxi: 808-325-5448
- Elsa Taxi: 808-887-6446
- Hilo Harry's Taxi: 808-935-7091
- Kona Airport Taxi: 808-329-7779
- Paradise Taxi: 808-329-1234

Lana'i:

- Lana'i City Service: 808-565-7227
- Rabaca's Limousine Service: 808-565-6670

Kaua'i:

- Kaua'i Taxi Company: 808-246-9554

Maui:

- Alii Cab Company: 808-661-3688
- Maui Airport Taxi: 808-877-0907

Moloka'i:

- Hele Mai Taxi: 808-336-0967
- Moloka'i Off-Road Tours and Taxi: 808-553-3369; www.molokai.com/offroad

O'ahu:

- AMPCO Express: 808-861-8294
- Coast Taxi: 808-261-3755
- Hawaii Kai Hui/Koko Head Taxi: 808-396-6633
- Star Taxi Hawaii: 808-942-7827

Tour Operators

General:

- Polynesia Adventure Tours: 808-877-4242; www.polyad.com
- Roberts Hawaii: 800-954-8652 or 1-866-898-2519; www.robertshawaii.com

Big Island:

- Polynesian Adventure Tours: 808-356-1900 or 1-888-349-7888; www.hawaiitours.org
- Tom Barefoot's Tours: 808-661-8889; www.tombarefoot.com

Kaua'i:

- Aloha Kaua'i Tours: 1-800-452-1113
- Hawaii Movie Tours: 808-822-1192; www.hawaiimovietour.com
Kaua'i Land Tours: 1-877-742-7893; www.trykauai.com
- Kaua'i Island Tours: 808-245-4777; www.kauaidiscovery.com
- Kaua'i Vacation Tours: 1-866-897-1637; kauaivacationtours.com
- South Shore Tour and Taxi: 808-742-1525

Lana'i:

- Expeditions: 1-800-695-2624; www.go-lanai.com
- Lana'i Ecocentre Centre: 808-565-7373 www.adventurelanai.com
- The Lodge at Ko'ele: 808-565-7300 or 1-800-321-4666; www.fourseasons.com/koele
- Rabaca's Limousine Service: 808-565-6670

Maui:

- Akina Aloha Tours: 808-879-2828; www.akinatours.com
- Barefoot Cashback Tours: 808-661-8889; www.tombarefoot.com
- Ekahi Tours: 808-877-9775 or 1-888-292-2422; www.ekahi.com
- Fantasy Island Activities and Tours: 808-667-9740
- Temptation Tours: 808-877-8888; www.temptationtours.com

Moloka'i:

- Damien Tours: 808-567-6171
- Moloka'i Fish & Dive Activities: 808-552-0184
- Moloka'i Outdoors: 808-553-4477
- Moloka'i Tours: 1-800-410-8176; www.paragon-air.com/molokai.htm

O'ahu:

- E Noa Tours: 808-591-2561; www.enoa.com
- O'ahu Nature Tours: 808-924-2473: www.oahunaturetours.com

Visitor Information

General:

- www.gohawaii.com
- www.hawaii.com
- www.hawaii.gov
- www.50states.com/hawaii.htm

Big Island:

- Big Island Visitors Bureau: 250 Keawe Street, Hilo; 808-961-2126; and 250 Waikoloa Beach Drive, Waikoloa; 808-886-1652; www.bigisland.org
- Kona-Kohala Resort Association: 69-275 Waikoloa Beach Drive, Kamucla; 808-318-3637; www.kohalacoastresorts.com
- Mauna Kea Summit Adventures: 1-800-322-2366; www.maunakea.com

Kaua'i

- Kaua'i Visitors Bureau: 4334 Rice Avenue, Suite 101; 808-245-3971 or 1-800-262-1400; www.Kauaivisitorsbureau.org or www.Kauaidiscovery.com
- Kaua'i Historical Society: 4396 Rice Avenue; 808-245-3373; www.lauaihistoricalsociety.org

Moloka'i:

- Moloka'i Visitor's Association: P.O. Box 960, Kaunakakai, HI 96748; 808-800-6367; www.molokai-hawaii.com.

O'ahu:

- Hawaii Visitor's Bureau, 2270 Kalakaua Avenue, Suite 801, Honolulu; 808-923-1811; www.gohawaii.com.
- Hawaii Visitors Bureau Information Office, Royal Hawaiian Shopping Center, Hibiscus Court, 4th Floor, Waikiki; 2201 Kalakaua Avenue (fronting the Sheraton Waikiki and Royal Hawaiian Hotels); 808-924-0266; Open 10 A.M.–10 P.M. daily.
- O'ahu Visitor's Bureau, 735 Bishop Street, Suite 1872, Honolulu; 808-524-0722; www.visit-oahu.com

Maui:

- Maui Historical Society, 2375-A Main Street, Wailuku; 808-244-3326; www.mauimuseum.org
- Maui Visitors Bureau, 1727 Wili Pa Loop, Wailuku; 808-244-3530; www.visitmaui.com; open 8 A.M.–4:30 P.M.

Weather Information

- Big Island: 808-935-8555 in Hilo; 808-961-5582 elsewhere; Marine forecast: 808-935-9883
- Kaua'i: 808-245-6001; Marine forecast: 808-245-3564
- Maui: 808-871-5054; Marine forecast: 808-877-3477
- O'ahu: 808-973-4380 in Honolulu; 808-973-4381; Marine forecast: 808-973-4382

Appendix B

Create Your Own Itinerary

Throughout this book we've tried to make visiting Hawaii so simple that you could do it with one hand tied behind your back and the other hand holding a preparatory mai tai. To that end, we've organized this wonderful tome in the most logical, user-friendly manner possible. And, we've even gone further—providing scores of ready-made Ultimate Itineraries that you can use in your day-by-day travels. We've spared no effort in trying to help you, dear reader.

But maybe you're the independent sort, and you just don't feel right doing so little advance work on your own. Everybody has slightly different preferences, so it's only human nature, we guess, to want to customize your trip to one extent or another.

Maybe you want to create your own itinerary, using the information we've provided in these pages. No problem—we won't take offense! In fact, being the swell guys that we are, we'll even help you with that!

Using our super-cool, patent-pending Itinerary Planning System (IPS), you can use the information supplied elsewhere in the book and create your own.

It's really quite simple.

1. Determine How Much Time You Are Taking

The first question you've got to ask yourself is how many days you're going to spend in Hawaii. That's critical to everything else. Calculate the number of full days you will have in Hawaii, not counting traveling time from your home.

- Less than a week
- About a week
- About 2 weeks
- About 3 weeks

2. Decide on Your Vacationing Style

Next you've got to think about your vacationing style.

- Mostly relaxing by the beach or pool (recommended for young families and those looking for an easy-going, nonstrenuous vacation
- A mix of beach time and seeing the sights (recommended for families of all ages, those taking a romantic getaway)
- Forget the beach—see as much as possible (recommended for older families, singles, and those seeking culture in paradise)
- Golf, golf, golf (recommended for older families and singles)
- Like hiking and other active sports (recommended for singles and those seeking adventure)

Begin your planning by using the following to determine how many islands you should visit, based on your vacationing style.

The Number of Islands You Should Visit

Weeks	<1	1	2	3
Style				
Relax	1	2	3	4
Mix	1	3	4	5
Go!	2	3	4	5
Golf	2	2	3	3
Active	1	1	2	3

3. Identify Your Sightseeing Priority

Now you have an idea of the recommended number of islands to visit, based on your style. It's time to choose which specific islands to see, depending on how their unique attributes match up to the types of things you want to see and do.

- Awesome beaches
- Scenery
- Golf
- Other outdoor sports
- Nightlife
- Culture and history

Use our the handy table below to select the best islands for your ideal vacation.

Which Islands to Visit

PRIORITY	1	2	3	4	5
Beaches	Maui	+ Big Island	+ Kaua'i	+ O'ahu	+ Lana'i
Scenery	Big Island	+ Maui	+ Kaua'i	+ Moloka'i	+ O'ahu

continues

continued

Which Islands to Visit

PRIORITY	1	2	3	4	5
Golf	Maui	+ Big Island	+ Kaua'i	+ O'ahu	+ Lana'i
Sports	Big Island	+ Kaua'i	+ Maui	+ O'ahu	+ Moloka'i
Night-life*	O'ahu	+ Maui	+ Kaua'i	+ Big Island	+ O'ahu
Culture/ History	O'ahu	+ Big Island	+ Maui	+ Kaua'i	+ Moloka'i

NOTE: If you're going to Hawaii for three weeks and want a full slate of nightlife, you may want to spend time on only four islands max, focusing on O'ahu and Maui.

Now you have your islands and number of days on each.

4. Choose the Most Appealing Attractions

Using the following form (or something like it that you create yourself), choose the most appealing attractions for each island you're visiting from the book's "Enjoying" chapters:

- Mostly relax by the beach or pool: 1–2 attractions
- A mix of beach time and seeing the sights: 3 attractions
- Forget the beach—see as much as possible: 4 attractions
- Like to golf: 1–2 attractions
- Like hiking and other active sports: 1–2 attractions

Also decide where you want may to eat lunch and dinner, based on our recommendations in the "Enjoying" chapters, and add those names to the list.

Daily Schedule

Day: ________ Island: ______________________________

Attraction 1: ______________________________ Page #____

Attraction 2: ______________________________ Page #____

Attraction 3: ______________________________ Page #____

Attraction 4: ______________________________ Page #____

Lunch: ______________________________

Dinner: ______________________________

Extras: ______________________________

Evening: ______________________________

Complete one of these forms for each day of your vacation, based on the specific islands and number of days calculated in Steps 1–3.

5. Add "Extras" to the Daily Form

"Extras" as we define them here are the optional things you may choose to do or see on the way to or from your major destinations. These include stores, markets, galleries, scenic overlooks, or snack stops.

6. Add Evening Entertainment

Finally, add to the bottom of each form what you might want to do in the evening, based on our recommendations or something else you've heard after you've arrived on the island.

7. Collate and Combine All the Daily Sheets

Decide in which order you plan to visit the islands. Then put all of the daily sheets together and, voilà!, you have a custom itinerary.

8. Book Air, Car, and Hotels

Now that you know exactly where you're going, and for how long, book your accommodations based on your budget and preferred lodging style, whether that be a resort or a campground. Also book your air and ground transportation.

If you're using award miles for your flights, book those before you book your hotel, as seat availability may be limited!

Enjoy your trip!

Index

Numbers

A

B

C

D

E

F

G

H

I

J

K

L

M

N

O

P–Q

R

S

T

U

V

W

X–Y–Z